ENGINES OF EMPIRE

ENGINES OF EMPIRE
Steamships and the Victorian Imagination

DOUGLAS R. BURGESS JR.

Stanford University Press
Stanford, California

Stanford University Press
Stanford, California

©2016 by the Board of Trustees of the Leland Stanford Junior University. All rights reserved.

No part of this book may be reproduced or transmitted in any form or by any means, electronic or mechanical, including photocopying and recording, or in any information storage or retrieval system without the prior written permission of Stanford University Press.

Printed in the United States of America on acid-free, archival-quality paper

Library of Congress Cataloging-in-Publication Data

Names: Burgess, Douglas R., Jr., author.
Title: Engines of empire : steamships and the Victorian imagination / Douglas R. Burgess, Jr.
Description: Stanford, California : Stanford University Press, 2016. | Includes bibliographical references and index.
Identifiers: LCCN 2015045652 (print) | LCCN 2015047877 (ebook) | ISBN 9780804798068 (cloth : alk. paper) | ISBN 9780804798983 (e-book)
Subjects: LCSH: Steamboats--Great Britain--History--19th century. | Steamboats--United States--History--19th century. | Steam-navigation--History--19th century. | Passenger ships--History--19th century. | Imperialism--History--19th century. | Tourism--History--19th century.
Classification: LCC VM657 .B87 2016 (print) | LCC VM657 (ebook) | DDC 387.2/044--dc23
LC record available at http://lccn.loc.gov/2015045652

Typeset by Bruce Lundquist in 10/15 Minion

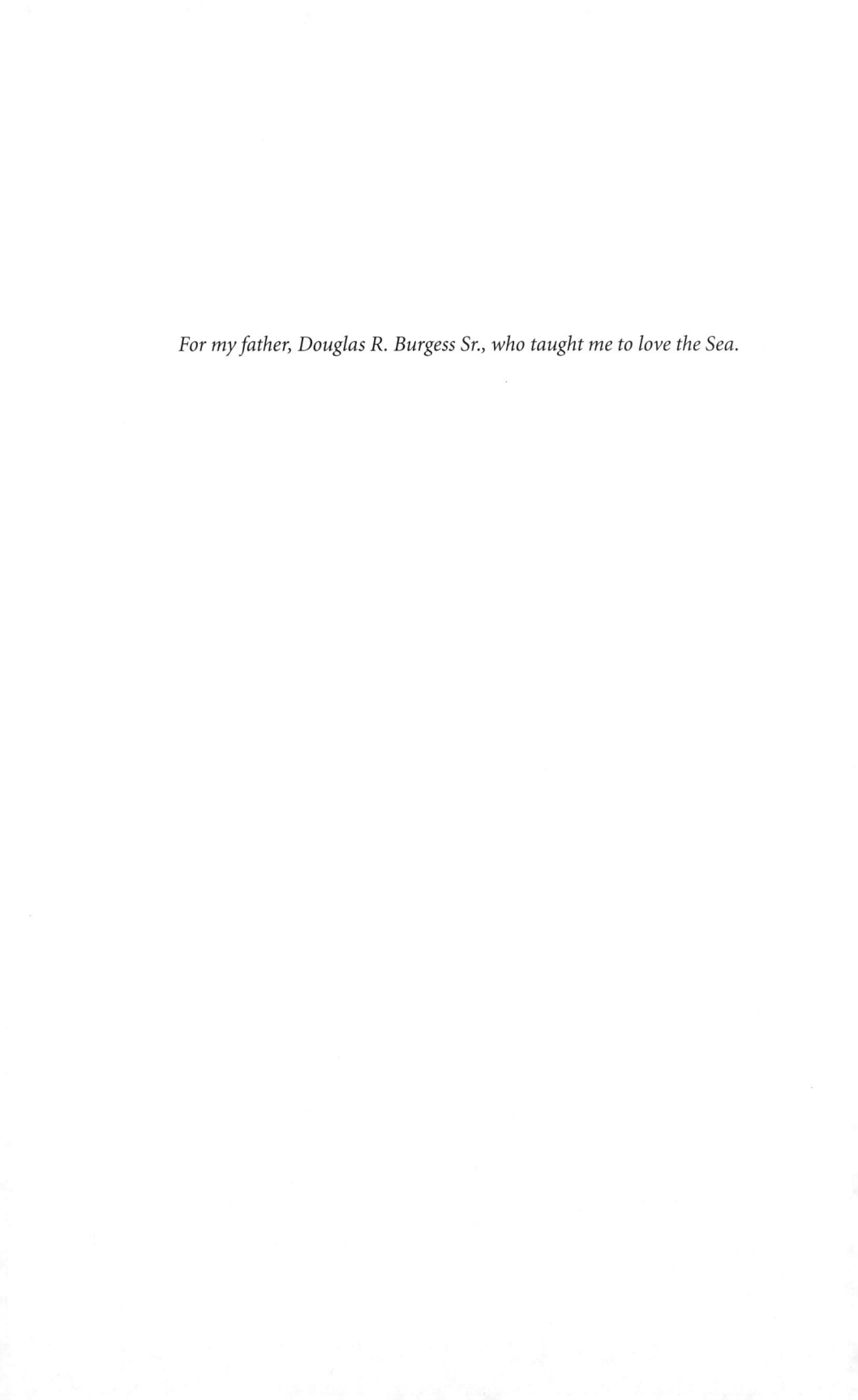

For my father, Douglas R. Burgess Sr., who taught me to love the Sea.

TABLE OF CONTENTS

		Prologue: The Bristol Crowd, 1843	1
		Introduction: Annihilating Space	7
PART I.	SPECTATORS		
	1.	Phantasmagoria: Steam and Spectacle in the Public Sphere	21
	2.	Selling the *Mammoth*: The Commodification of Wonder	43
	3.	Leviathans: Ships as Fantasy	67
	4.	Honor and Glory Crowning Time: Disaster Sermons and the Cult of Technology	92
PART II.	TOURISTS		
	5.	Ordinary Escapes: American Steamboats and the Masquerade of Class	123
	6.	One Small Iron Country: Social Hierarchies on the North Atlantic	147
	7.	Vandals Abroad: Travelogues and the Pleasure Cruise	165
	8.	The Dollars Are Coming: Steam Tourism and the Transformation of Space	192
PART III.	IMPERIALS		
	9.	Tiffin for Griffins: Educating Imperial Administrators on the Long Voyage	223
	10.	The Floating Kaiser: Steamships and National Identity	249
	11.	Sitting in Darkness: Critiquing Imperialism from the Top Deck	270

Conclusion: Transportation Is Civilization	287
Notes	295
Bibliography	327
Index	339

ENGINES OF EMPIRE

PROLOGUE
The Bristol Crowd, 1843

I SAW THE S.S. *GREAT BRITAIN* at Bristol in the fall of 2013. Set in a Plexiglass firmament with an inch of chlorinated water sloshing about to resemble waves, she is certainly a spectacle. Her engine churns slow revolutions under a glass skylight, with a recorded tape of huffing and chuffing to add verisimilitude. Steamer trunks pile up convincingly in the passageways; waxwork children play on the floor of a reconstructed cabin. In the gilt-edged dining room, a trick of audio technology filters ghostly conversation through hidden speakers: "A trifle more gammon, Lady Weatherall?" "Oh, oh, I feel I may be ill!" "What say you to a game of whist later, doctor?" At the far end a string quartet plays Mendelssohn from empty chairs.[1]

There is irony in the fact that this ship—derided as a freak and shunted off the Atlantic run for a hardscrabble life in the Antipodes—should be the sole surviving 19th-century example of that quintessential Victorian innovation: the steam ocean liner. All the others are gone. A ship is a mortal structure that begins to corrode the moment it touches water; like ourselves, it is born, lives, and dies in the span of a few decades.

Yet the *Great Britain* achieved immortality, of a kind. Her persistence owes less to preservation than neglect: Abandoned and forgotten in her own time, she was allowed to rust away on a sandbar in a remote corner of the globe for nearly a hundred years. Had she been the success her creator envisioned, it is almost certain she would have been retired and scrapped long hence. Still, I cannot help but feel that Isambard Kingdom Brunel would be pleased to see her as she is today. She rests in the city he called home, which is still accessed through a system of railway lines and trestles he laid down. The elegant neo-Gothic terminus, only a few short blocks from the *Great Britain*'s berth, was designed by him as well. On the one hand, the ship's presence in our century is testament to the innovations she (and he) pioneered: iron hull, screw propeller, and dimensions that dwarfed all other craft. Whatever the *Great Britain*'s failings as a commercial liner, these advances are incontrovertible; it is right that they should be preserved and honored. On the other hand, like her ill-fated successor the *Great Eastern*,

FIGURE 1. The *Great Britain* today. Permanently resting in the same Bristol cradle where she was built, the ship looks much as she did at the time of her launch in 1843. SOURCE: Author's collection.

the *Great Britain* was more show than ship. Both vessels were at their best tied to the pier, massive and puissant. On the open seas they were miserable failures. Indeed, the only profit either ever turned was in harbor, welcoming crowds of gawkers for tuppence a head.

Hence her afterlife is doubly appropriate: stuffed and mounted, a spectacle of 19th-century engineering for multitudes of day-trippers in shorts and baseball caps. If the experience onboard seems a trifle unreal, well, that too is as it should be. The ship herself is unreal, a phantasmagoria of science and showmanship. She exists between the tangible realm of technology and the monstrous imaginings of Jules Verne; in other words, at the limit of imagination. This was heady stuff for designers, engineers, owners, and the public at large. They loved the implied challenge, the ever-moving horizon between the possible and the absurd. Like most mirages it shimmers at the corners, always just beyond reach. But that does not discredit its lure. Some of the greatest minds of the century sought it with the same fervor as any intrepid explorer would an unknown continent—and built ships like the *Great Britain* to carry them there.

To visit her now is to experience a moment of awe that is profoundly Victorian. Not in the sense of the "eminent" Victorians that Lytton Strachey famously lampooned, but rather the common herd. In an instant we become part of the crowd in 1843, gazing upon this technological wonder for the first time. Our consciousness and theirs are joined in approbation. This democratic leveling was the very object of a spectacle, whether it was a ship's launch or a World's Fair: Every participant, regardless of race or sex or status, enjoyed the same experience and thus felt kinship with one another. But now, having joined the throng at Bristol, let us take a moment to consider our neighbors. The Victorian crowd is all too often rendered as a faceless, sepia-toned multitude, but we know a great deal about this one. It is heterogeneous. Special excursion trains have been running from London since dawn, and the prohibitive price of a ticket plus the availability of a day's leisure suggest that many of those around us possess at least middle-class means. The presence of the Prince Consort (arriving on a locomotive driven by Isambard Brunel himself) is surely as much a draw as the *Great Britain*. Ladies wear their best bonnets. It is a Wednesday morning in July, freshened with a bout of English summer rain, so umbrellas and parasols are held aloft. The crowd is genteel and—given the hour and the closure of the public houses—relatively sober.[2]

Despite the presence of the London interlopers, the majority of these freshly scrubbed faces are locals. First and foremost are the shipyard workers, the men who built the *Great Britain*, whose presence at the launch is not only traditional but essential. A canny public relations campaign swells their numbers; a holiday has been declared in Bristol. Shopkeepers, snuff mill workers, and schoolchildren line the parade route as the prince and his entourage pass by. Local charities wait to present him with honors, and clergymen clasp prepared remarks. The formal welcome will be given by the town clerk, whose name is recorded in the *Bristol Times and Mirror* as "D. Burgess."[3]

Thus, by accident and design, by train and public holiday, a great panoply of the British public is gathered: lords, gentry, engineers, clergy, fishmongers and their wives, maidservants, fitters, mill workers from W. D. and H. O. Wills, stevedores, Mary Carpenter's "ragged" girls, George Muller's orphaned boys, day-tripping Londoners. What are they thinking about? What does this ship represent to them? We see their faces upturned towards the looming hull, and impute wonder and pride. Without doubt those were prominent emotions. But was that all?

With pride comes proprietorship, a sense that this is "our" vessel. Yet the one thing that this crowd shares in common is that almost none of them will actually sail on the *Great Britain*. They have not come to dedicate some public convenience, not even a monument, but rather a pleasure craft for the very wealthy. Politicians and journalists will speak grandly of joining two continents, of amicable exchanges among people, but the audience might be skeptical of such claims. The number of American visitors carried by the *Great Britain* and her confreres is miniscule; the number of Britons even smaller. Properly considered, the *Great Britain* symbolizes nothing so much as the growing disparity between those who might actually afford a steamship ticket and the rest, the multitudes, who will only much later come to be known as the working class. Moreover, contained within its iron walls is a machine—the largest of its kind yet manufactured—that is already wreaking radical transformations on many of their lives. Even in maritime Bristol, tobacco mills have begun to supplant the more traditional industries of sail making, cooperage, and carpentry.[4]

It is a process that the iron-hulled, steam-driven *Great Britain* will accelerate. Do many in the crowd know that the technology enshrined by this ship will render their livelihoods obsolete? If they did, we might expect them to do something about it. Bristol is no stranger to political agitation. Just eleven years before, after a reform bill to increase local representation failed at Parliament, Bristolians rioted for three days. Local estates were looted and destroyed, the chief magistrate chased through town, and the cavalry was called out. Isambard Brunel reluctantly suspended construction of his Clifton suspension bridge to act as a temporary special constable.[5]

Yet there is no hint of outrage in the crowd gathered today. Are they swept up by patriotic puffery, by the "mass of color" of the uniforms and martial music played by the Life Guards Band? Are they bewitched by the pageantry of royalty arriving in its own private locomotive with a cadre of lords and ladies following behind? Or are they simply overawed by the ship herself? If indeed this crowd can be persuaded to feel some pride of ownership in a vessel they do not own, whose wonders are beyond their means, and whose technology may yet mean the ruin of many of their lives, what does this connote for the Victorian public's fascination with steam?

These are familiar questions. It has been over seventy years since Walter Benjamin blamed the postponement *sine die* of the socialist revolution on the "phantasmagoria" of the shopping arcade.[6] The launching of the *S.S. Great Britain* shares much with the Paris arcades: Here is the machine commodified, put on display, made into spectacle. It delights merely by its size and potency; one does not have to book passage in order to be impressed (indeed, as passengers would attest, there was no swifter disillusionment than actually traveling on one of these ships). Yet the fact that such a gigantic object could move added even greater mystique. The phantasmagoria of steam was thus a combination of *ipsum*, the thing itself, and *de potentia rei*, the potential of the thing. Like a great cathedral or work of art, there was inherent wonder in the fact that this shapely mass was created by human hand. Can we say, then, that the Bristol crowd exerts some proprietary claim over the ship because it is a work of human innovation and they, too, are human? Or British? Or even Bristolian? Perhaps, but that can hardly account for the enthusiasm that these great machines engendered even in those with the least to benefit from them.

Something more complex and interesting is going on here. To maintain that the crowd has been bamboozled gives them too little agency, and others too much. There is no deception: The designers, engineers, and owners are genuinely proud of their ship, as is the Prince of Wales. The emotion of the crowd is likewise genuine, if contradictory. Even to refer to "the crowd" as an entity is questionable; E. P. Thompson's warning about condescension to the "working classes" seems particularly relevant in this context.[7] The crowd is not a crowd, but a collection of women and men with differing backgrounds and perspectives, opinions, and ambitions. They will not all respond to the phantasmagoria of steam in the same way, yet their response will have consequences. Just as steam travel transformed the landscape of the modern world, it remapped the landscape of the modern mind by creating new communities: spectators at a launch, bettors on a race, tourists encountering one another on the Atlantic, empire builders en route to their posts, and many others. These communities fostered a shared identity among their members, and between each member and the machine. Each community was tailored to the class and rank of its participants, but membership was open to all. That was the critical point: Whoever you were, whatever your sex or race or social status, there was a club for you. The cult of technology, the allegory of a ship as national symbol, the rise of leisure tourism, even the all-pervasive and all-destructive imperialism contained in Kipling's remark, "transportation is civilization"[8]—invariably trace themselves back to these imagined communities.[9]

It all began with spectacles like this one on the wharfs at Bristol. Yet if we are to try and understand what motivated these men and women, we cannot look down at them as though from the prince's dais.

We must get down amongst the crowd, and look around.

INTRODUCTION
Annihilating Space

IN THE MAIN SALOON OF THE *GREAT WESTERN*, the side of beef had been consumed. It was time for toasts. Alderman Hoxie Talmadge, representing the city of New York, led off. "Victoria Regina!" he cried, "The dominion of youth and beauty extends throughout the world!"[1]

It was the spring of 1838. Victoria had reigned for exactly eleven months, so the alderman's toast was not ironic. The whole company, Americans and British, stood and raised their glasses. Then it was Captain James Hosken's turn. Speaking as the master of the steamship *Great Western*, and for its backers in London, he saluted: "The Navy of the United States! May we never be brought into other than friendly collision!" What exactly a friendly collision might look like Captain Hosken did not say, but everyone was well lubricated and full of beef, so they joined his toast with enthusiasm.

Then a hush fell. The next speaker was a small, rotund man of middle years with a shock of black hair and hooded, piercing eyes. His speeches were so famous, even then, that he would one day be given the fictional task of defending a man in the Devil's own court. But Daniel Webster had a terrible head cold. Snuffling, flourishing a handkerchief, he lumbered to his feet and gave one of the shortest speeches of his career.

"It is our fortune to live at a new epoch," he began, hoarsely. "We behold two continents approaching each other. The skill of your countrymen, sir, and my countrymen, is annihilating space." Then he raised his glass and sat down.[2]

Tremendous applause. The *Great Western* had crossed from Bristol, England, to New York in just over two weeks at an average speed of 16 knots. She was the largest, fastest ship in the world, and the first steamship expressly designed for the North Atlantic run. Her architect wanted to come along for the ride, but on the day of her maiden voyage Mr. Brunel had fallen over 20 feet into the engine room and had to be carried off at Canvey Island. Toasts were raised to his convalescence.

The great cabin where these men sat was 75 feet long and 21 feet wide, roughly the same size as the whole of Christopher Columbus's flagship, the *Santa Maria*.

In the bloated hyperbole of the age it was described as "wadded in a most luxuriant style . . . only dreamed of in the descriptions of the Arabian Nights, and the tales of faery."[3] Trompe l'oeil paintings lined the walls, obligatory cherubim sported around rural landscapes that might have been Cornwall or the Hudson Valley, depending on one's point of view. At the *Great Western*'s bowsprit an immodest Neptune pointed his golden trident at lower Manhattan.

By rights Senator Webster's toast should have been last, but in the ensuing commotion Alderman Talmadge called upon another guest to speak. His pedestrian name, John Ridge, belied his lineage: John Ridge spoke for the only nation in the room as yet unmentioned, the Cherokee. Why he was there and what he was supposed to say can only be imagined; in all likelihood Ridge had been included to give a certain exoticism to the party. Europeans and Englishmen persisted in the belief that America was still primarily an Indian nation, and Americans themselves often manifested an odd pride in this distinctiveness. But Mr. Ridge was determined to disappoint. Picking up on Webster's image of the steam engine annihilating space, Ridge pointedly reminded the assemblage of what that space contained. If it was the Indians' destiny to be driven from their homes and hounded across the wilderness, then so be it. The Cherokee warrior "would retreat to the highest peaks of the Rocky Mountains, there to breathe a long, lingering farewell to the land of his fathers, and to die in defense of his life and liberty." John Ridge raised his glass, alone.[4]

Can the whole history of an era be read in a single exchange of words? Alderman Talmadge and, most especially, Captain Hosken were articulating a new and lasting rapprochement that would become central to world politics. Sixty years after the Revolution, and only twenty-five after that brief, odd skirmish known as the War of 1812, Britain and the United States were finally coming together. Two nations that had almost everything in common ("Except their language," Oscar Wilde would famously amend) recognized the fact, and celebrated it.

The steamship was the metaphorical bridge to bring these two brothers back together. Now for the first time one could embark on a vessel and confidently expect to arrive on the other side of the Atlantic in two weeks, rather than months. The steam engine was indifferent to prevailing winds, its twin paddles churning through the water with regular, measured, reassuring speed. Just as Talmadge's mention of a youthful queen was meant to suggest a new era of friendliness, Captain Hosken's clumsier talk of friendly collisions was a reminder of all that had gone before: decades of enmity and mutual distrust, punctuated by an almost constant war at sea. A new queen, a new era, and now a new device: the steamship, which would replace wooden walls and 20-pound guns with tourists, emissaries, and deep holds filled with mutually profitable goods.

Daniel Webster had spun that metaphor out yet further. The new epoch he invoked was not merely one of renewed friendliness, but empire. Just as the steam engine closed the gaps between like-minded nations, it would stretch their purview and open up new worlds as yet unknown. Isambard Brunel, architect of the *Great Western*, was already turning over in his mind a vastly larger steamship capable of making the voyage from Liverpool to India without refueling, a distance of over 10,000 miles by sea.[5] Webster could not have known this, but he had nevertheless unerringly identified—in three sentences—the birth of imperialism. Annihilating space meant bringing every corner of the world closer to its center, a contraction and consolidation of myriad different peoples, languages, cultures. Where that center would be located was, of course, a matter of dispute.

But John Ridge, of the Cherokee Nation, saw something different. From his perspective, annihilating space was a profoundly violent concept. Daniel Webster had perhaps envisioned empty tracts of sea and wilderness; Ridge filled them in, and inserted himself. His words were a *cri du coeur* from a survivor of Andrew Jackson's infamous Indian Removal Act of 1830, a policy still underway as the dinner party ended. Alexis de Tocqueville, the most celebrated visitor to the United States after the Marquis de Lafayette, watched in horror as Choctaws were expelled from Memphis, Tennessee: "There was one who could speak English and of whom I asked why the Chactas were leaving their country. 'To be free,' he answered, [and I] could never get another reason out of him."[6] Liberty and open space, the qualities that defined American identity, were meeting their cruel inverse—in Tennessee and in the cabin of the *Great Western*. John Ridge was reminding the group of a principle that would bring suffering to millions throughout the next century: One society cannot expand without displacing another.

Sitting in the splendid ocean liner's saloon, the Cherokee emissary recognized a new and disturbing development. Distance had always been the one impenetrable obstacle to imperial dominance. It kept the traffic between Europe and Asia to a mere trickle, enough to transfer goods but not maintain an army. Pashas, emperors, and chieftains maintained cordial relations with the Europeans, secure in the knowledge that their isolation protected them. The exigencies of distance and communication bedeviled even those colonies that had been attempted: the most famous, of course, being the Americas. For decades

American colonists created their own laws and flouted those of England, certain that there was little England could do in response. When it finally tried, the colonies revolted. And won.[7]

Now a new and dangerous change was on the horizon: a device that, by "annihilating space," could bring the western world up to and into those places where it had never been before. If a man could leave London and arrive in New York two weeks later, how long would it be before he could circle the globe with equal impunity? Just what sort of power did that confer, and how would he use it? John Ridge dreaded the answer, and would live to see it borne out.

The concept of annihilating space was hardly unique to that moment.[8] In fact, it seemed to lend itself especially to maiden arrivals: Just two years later, with the coming of Samuel Cunard's *Britannia* to Boston, local Brahmin Josiah Quincy raised his glass to "the Memory of Time and Space—famous in their day and generation, they have been annihilated by Steam."[9] So, too, were John Ridge's fears shared by other chroniclers. Not long after the *Great Western*'s arrival, a New York merchant would confide in his diary anxiety over this new era:

> This powerful agent, which regulates just now the affairs of the world; this new element, which like the other four, is all-potent for good and for evil, has almost *annihilated distance*, and overcome the obstacles which nature seems to have interposed to locomotion ... [10]

Indeed, so ubiquitous was the expression that one historian, in his own recent account of steam imperialism, dismissed it as "cliché" not once but twice.[11] Familiarity may breed contempt, but this response seems reductive: recognizing the popularity of the phrase without acknowledging the real significance behind it. Indeed, a similar dismissive attitude extends to the subject of maritime steam history.

In recent decades, the role of the railroad in societal change has undergone a necessary and welcome reappraisal. Beginning with Wolfgang Schivelbusch's seminal study *The Railway Journey: The Industrialization of Time and Space in the Nineteenth Century*, a cadre of scholars have devoted themselves to examining the transformative impact of mechanized speed on the landscape, social relations, tourism, perception of distance, even the concept of time itself.[12] Railway travel, we are told, detached passengers from their surroundings, bound them (and their colonized peoples) to a unified system of time embodied by the station clock, and created an artificial sense of place by hurtling persons in an enclosed car over a rapidly changing and almost indistinguishable landscape.

Yet the fact that steamships carried these effects even further—divorcing passengers from the landscape altogether, creating self-contained artificial communities onboard for weeks rather than hours, becoming worlds unto themselves whereby passengers would descend (quite literally) into brief and transient contact with foreign ports—has never been fully considered. True, in most studies of technological imperialism, a single chapter is often devoted to the steamboat, but always for its role in maintaining military order along rivers or displacing indigenous communities.[13] The cognate impact of steam *tourism*, specifically the way in which steamship travel altered passengers' understanding of foreign locales (and their own place within them), has never been explored.

This is odd, since tourism itself has, like railway travel, provided considerable material for research.[14] "Recent scholars," wrote one, "tend to stress the dichotomy between travel and tourism, viewing it as an integral part of modern tourism itself."[15] Yet studies of Victorian tourism, which focus heavily on the railway excursion and Thomas Cook's package tours, rarely give the steamships more than a mention.[16] One commented in her introduction on the emergence of critical analysis for rail travel "and to a lesser extent steamships"; on examining the footnote, however, only railroad works were cited.[17] Hemmed in on every side by studies on railways, tourism, technological imperialism, and so on, the steamships exist like a blank void at the center of all this scholarship. Indeed, it seems as though there is a curious reluctance among scholars to—if I might make a bad pun—get their feet wet.

A quick glance at the maritime stacks might provide one clue for this hesitation. Ocean liner history has been the traditional province of amateur enthusiasts; nearly every title is a panegyric to the liners, or the way of life they represented.[18] There is little if any critical analysis in these works. The field, moreover, is severely limited. Perennial fascination with the *Titanic* has spawned an endless stream of titles resurrecting every facet of the lost ship from hull density to Second Class dinner menus;[19] beyond that, other histories cater to a relatively small community of self-described "liner buffs." Again, the authorship is primarily amateur, and the circulation extremely narrow. It is possible that the sheer enthusiasm of these authors and readers has unwittingly deterred more serious consideration. In addition, maritime history has always seemed to exist rather apart from other disciplines, almost as if the ocean itself were a kind of metaphorical barrier.[20] My purpose with this book is thus twofold: first, to extend the same methods of analysis employed by Schivelbusch and others to the as-yet unexplored subject of steamship travel; second, to reach beyond that analysis to a broader consideration of the impact of the steam vessel, in all its maritime forms, on the Victorian mind.

The parameters for such a study were suggested nearly thirty years before, in Michel Foucault's comment that the ship was essentially a "heterotopia . . . a floating piece of space, a place without a place, that exists by itself, that is closed in on itself and at the same time is given over to the sea and . . . [is] the greatest reserve of the imagination."[21] A ship is thus artificial in every sense: a created vessel for a created community, isolated from all other creations and communities, transient, yet bound by the same symbiotic rhythms that define all such places and communities ashore. Chroniclers of the 19th century intuited this, even if they lacked the psychological lingo to describe it. Many wrote of the ship as a world unto itself; when the shore disappeared on the horizon, it was as if the vessel and her passengers had passed into a solipsistic void where the only reality was themselves. Such freedom encouraged flights of imagination, as Foucault understood. Passengers bonded with the vessel in a more direct way than any other man-made object or building: Freudians could get a great deal of mileage from the dozens of diarists that described themselves ensconced in the "womb" of the ship. Moreover, long voyages compelled passengers to create new communities, and it was inevitable that these created spaces would both mirror and contrast with those on shore.[22] Left to themselves, passengers drew from the social norms they left behind in constructing new shipboard societies, yet reveled in the comparative freedom to redefine social barriers and interact with others beyond their usual circle of acquaintance—"heterotopia," as Foucault describes it. Interestingly, we find the same phenomenon even on overnight passages: Mississippi steamboats, for example, were a constantly morphing kaleidoscope of humanity that altered its pattern with each new arrival and departure, yet preserved an essential unity throughout.

As artificial communities, created in part by shipowners and in part by passengers themselves, these vessels are an invaluable lens through which to consider (or reconsider) Victorian society. The project is thus not unlike Marcus Rediker's examination of pirate "libertalias" in the 1720s: A self-created community divorced from ordinary society can often be the most effective tool by which to understand that society.[23] Yet Victorians' relationship with steam was more than self-reflexive. The engine worked a profound change on those that encountered it, from ordinary spectators to tourists to imperial administrators bound for the colonies. Much of this transformation was unreservedly positive.

The potential of the machine, conveyed through repeated spectacles, fired the boilers of human imagination: Suddenly, everything seemed possible. It is no exaggeration to claim that the image of a steamship's hull waiting to be launched became the most recognizable symbol of both technological and societal progress in the 19th century. Yet on the obverse side, this same optimism led to overconfidence, an almost religious veneration of technology, and ultimately an equating of steam with "civilization" that had catastrophic consequences for subjugated peoples around the world.

If that sounds harsh, it is also a necessary corrective for decades of hagiography for men like Robert Fulton, Isambard Brunel, and Samuel Cunard, not to mention the ships themselves.[24] Every national history has a special chapter set aside for its technological progress: the first transcontinental railroad, the first steamboats on its rivers, and so on. These are depicted as triumphs. Railway tracks across the wilderness, or the wake of a steamship, are tangible icons of progress and civilization. How many of us, for example, can call to mind the famous Golden Spike photograph of 1869: two men shaking hands for the camera with their respective crews and twin railway engines facing each other in the dry scrub and desert of Promontory, Utah? To subject this halcyon moment to cold historical analysis seems almost unkind. Yet it has already been done: in Ben Marsden and Crosbie Smith's reconsideration of the "hero" engineer, in Richard White's masterful study of the transcontinental railroads, in Walter Johnson's examination of the "steamboat sublime" and its impact on race relations in the antebellum South.[25] Traditional narratives, as Marsden and Smith write, "populated by the 'gung ho' imperialist, the simple untutored craftsman, the evermore gargantuan steamship . . . might well be visually pleasing and stylistically straightforward, adorning coffee tables and within easy reach on the bedside cabinet. But they comfort rather than challenge."[26]

I propose to extend this critical reappraisal to the steamships specifically—as distinct from railroads, telegraphs, and other 19th-century technology—and there can be no better starting point than Rudyard Kipling's famous dicta in 1905, "transportation is civilization." Kipling was giving voice—almost seventy years later—to the same concept of annihilating space that captivated Daniel Webster. Now the comment was more valedictory than anticipatory. The steam engine had conquered. But what did this mean, and how did it happen? One thing is certain: The transformation was not only on the landscape of the world, but within the landscape of the Victorian mind.

Subjecting the wonder of steam travel to critical reappraisal is not intended to be a condemnation of the invention, the people, or the era. To be sure, they were wondrous times. My purpose here is not to denigrate Victorian achievements, or the awe with which they were regarded, but to understand both. In order to do so, we must take a step back and examine the phenomenon with a dispassionate eye. This breaks down into two related inquiries. First: What impact did the steamship have on Victorian and Edwardian society? Clearly a profound one, yet its actual dimensions have never been explored. Second: How did they themselves conceive of this impact? In other words, how was it incorporated into their imagination, their worldview, their sense of self and others?[27] That is a more fascinating and much harder question. Consequently, this book is not primarily a history of ships or empire, but rather how both were understood and reflected by society itself. Such an insight can only be gleaned from examining a broad range of sources—from the fantastical imaginings of Jules Verne to the travelogues of Charles Dickens and William Makepeace Thackeray and (most importantly) to the recorded observations of hundreds of ordinary men and women who found themselves confronted in one way or another with steam.

This study is divided into three sections, corresponding with the three distinct vantages by which 19th- and early 20th-century Anglo-American society regarded steamship travel.[28] Part I, "Spectators," examines the rise of steam from the perspective of the general public. From the very beginning, inventors and promoters marketed their vessels as mechanical wonders, self-consciously linking the "miracle" of steam with Victorians' love of spectacle. Exhibitions and races were choreographed pageants designed to foster in the public mind sympathy for and identification with individual ships. Ordinary persons who might never cross the Atlantic were nevertheless encouraged to feel vicarious pride in their nation's technological accomplishments and enjoy the thrill of the race when those vessels were tested against another's. Thus steamships quickly became avatars of statehood, embodying not only the technological aspirations of their people but their patriotism as well.

Those early promoters were successful beyond their wildest imaginings. As the largest moving objects in the world, steamships were perfectly suited to carry within themselves the wonder and awe of a World's Fair. Beginning with the Great Exhibition of 1851, which had a direct role in the conception and creation of the *Great Eastern*, ships became inextricably linked to the fair's technological, patriotic, and even moral aspirations. Yet the need to produce such spectacles—

to build vessels that were not only efficient and functional but "wondrous" as well—ultimately had devastating consequences. The general public came to expect each new ship to be a technological marvel, placing unrealistic and impossible expectations upon designers. Engineers overreached, creating ships that were more fantasy than fact. Thus by the end of the century the phantasmagoria of steam overtook the reality. Victorian imaginations, fired with possibility yet heedless to limitations, came to regard the steamship as an object of secular veneration, an embodiment of all the certainties of the age. Carrying the heavy weight of such symbolism, the ships inevitably fell short. When they did, it was an indictment not only of their designers but of society itself.

Part II, "Tourists," shifts perspective to consider the impact of the steamships on the imaginations of those who sailed aboard them. On the one hand, what they found on board was very much like what they left: Socio-economic classes were rigidly segregated, and each class of accommodation was tailored perfectly to its clientele. Hence First Class passengers were received into a luxurious enclave set high above the other decks, reinforcing their sense of exclusion and superiority; Second Class were the literal and metaphorical middle, close enough to First to share its aura of respectability yet still very much apart; Third were the laboring classes, housed in utilitarian dormitories that hinted at the darkest of their possible destinies: the workhouse or prison. Nevertheless, on smaller vessels, steam travel often became the means of escaping the strictures of class. A *mélange* of passengers assured anonymity: No one knew anything of his confrères except what they themselves revealed. Mississippi steamboats and side-wheelers on Long Island Sound became the setting for escapist fantasies, as their humble clientele reveled in the illusion of "fine living" for a night. In an era with few opportunities to escape the drudgery of daily life, where people were constantly reminded to keep to their place, steamboat journeys were rare and treasured transgressions.

As the notion of a pleasure cruise came into being midcentury, along with package tours and cut-rate railway excursions, Victorians discovered a new means of regarding the world and their place within it, as tourists. The cruise experience was unique, for it allowed the tourist to remain ensconced in familiar, comfortable surroundings while the world was brought quite literally to one's door. Instead of being immersed in the wilds of foreign locales, passengers regarded their ship as a fixed point in a kaleidoscopic universe where cities simply passed by like slide images in a projector. With limited time in each port, one learned the novel art of experiencing all of Venice or Barcelona or even the Holy Land in a single day: Travel, with all its myriad inconveniences, gave way to brisk and efficient tourism. Forays ashore were limited to just enough time to see the major sights (often from the brisk trot of a hired carriage); interactions with locals were reduced to haggling for a souvenir on the pier. The effect on Victorians' view of the world was profound. Instead of dispelling preconceived ideas and prejudices, cruising helped confirm them.

In Part III, "Imperials," we examine the ways in which spectacle and steamship tourism combined to create a new kind of traveler: the imperial tourist. Steam imperialism began with the exportation of wonder: bringing the spectacle of steam to those still "sitting in darkness." Aligned with this metaphorical conceit of steam as civilization was the actual impact the vessels had on the maintenance of empire. The vast fleets of the P&O (Peninsular & Oriental), British India, and other firms not only became Britain's lifeline to empire, but for most passengers they were their first exposure to the "mysterious East." Boasting names like *Mooltan* and *Tanganyika*, these ships nevertheless were bastions of Britishness within: combining mock-Tudor fantasies with the exigencies of a tropical climate. More significantly, such vessels served as training grounds for neophyte imperial administrators on their way to take up their posts: It was onboard that "griffins" (as they were called) first learned the language, customs, expectations, and privileges of their new station. Thus the liners had a crucial and yet largely ignored role not only in the preservation of the empire, but in the creation of the imperial mind.

This aspect took on even broader dimensions late in the century, when ships became more expressly patriotic. Following the example set by the German firms, steamships embodied within themselves the culture and form of their respective nations. On the most basic level this translated into choice of architectural styles, or the judicious placing (on German ships) of an imperial bust. By the end of the 19th century, however, steamships had become so intrinsic to notions of empire that even their nomenclature reflected the connection. At the same time as Admiral Mahan published his famous thesis linking sea power to a nation's success,[29] P&O vessels were given the names of the colonies owned by Britain, with the flagship *Kaisar-i-Hind* ("Empress of India") holding dominion over all. Germans proudly titled their ships after the imperial family, as if they were avatars of the Kaiser himself. Cunard, more subtly, raised imperial echoes by naming its ships after Roman provinces. The implication was obvious: Ships were not merely agents of their respective nations, but floating embodiments of empire themselves. And so they would remain, until the final conflagration of the First World War.

It did not take long for the results of steamship imperialism to manifest, and we close this study by considering the later accounts by some of the same chroniclers that had once proclaimed the "wonder" of the steam age. By the turn of the century that fervor cooled, and those who were able to see the imperial world take shape were often horrified by the role of the steamship therein. "Steam as civilization" became the mantra for outright exploitation, subjugation, even genocide. From the Mississippi to the Ganges, steamboats displaced native populations and allowed for dictatorial control of local communities. Even the concept of steam tourism came under critical reappraisal: first as a means of bearing witness (as Mark Twain did) and second as an agent of imperial domination itself. The lofty vantage by which westerners viewed the outside world, from the top deck of a visiting steamer, became the perspective of the colonizer—detached, superior, ignorant, indifferent.

But let us begin as the Victorians did, with a burst of fireworks. They arced over the city of Port Said on the evening of November 17, as Khedive Ismail of Egypt turned a lever and the cataracts of the Suez released. "The barrier is down!" an observer cried ecstatically. It was 1869, *annus mirabilis*—the same year that the Golden Spike was driven in Utah, the White Star Line introduced the modern ocean liner, the Theodore Roosevelts set out to tour Europe, and Mark Twain published *The Innocents Abroad*. The first vessel to pass through the gates was the royal yacht *Aigle*, with Empress Eugenie, wife of Napoleon III, aboard. Following her was the steamship *Delta* of Britain's P&O Lines. It was a moment of consummate technological and imperial theater, leading an overwrought correspondent to declare: "One of the most formidable enemies of mankind and civilization, which is distance, loses in a moment two thousand leagues of his empire.... The history of the world has reached one of its most glorious stages."[30]

That remained to be seen.

PART I
Spectators

1

PHANTASMAGORIA
Steam and Spectacle in the Public Sphere

THINK BACK FOR A MOMENT to the *S.S. Great Britain,* the sea of upturned faces. What if, in that moment, the ship had *not* moved?[1] A launching is a pageant designed to elicit a specific emotional response. There are prayers, songs, speeches, flags. The crowd's job is to be awed, and, if everything works as it should, they will be. Ten thousand tons of moving steel can hardly fail to impress. In March of 1895, for example, over 25,000 spectators gathered at the William Cramp Shipyards of Philadelphia to watch the launching of the largest American liner built, the *St. Paul*. Samuel Clemens, alias Mark Twain, was invited to speak. In typical rambling style, his address praised the ship, its builders and owners, and the crowd that came to view the spectacle. His comments ranged from the absurd ("I do not mean that I care nothing at all for a whale's opinion. . . . Of course it is better to have the good opinion of a whale than his disapproval") to the disquieting ("When the *Paris* was half torn to pieces some years ago, enough of the Atlantic ebbed and flowed through one end of her, during her long agony, to sink the fleets of the world . . ."). But his conclusion was patriotic, symbolic, and (for him) only mildly silly:

> I am glad, with you and the nation, to welcome the new ship. She is another pride, another consolation for a great country whose mighty fleets have all vanished, and which has almost forgotten what it is to fly its flag at sea. I am not sure as to which St. Paul she is named for. Some think it is the one that is on the Upper Mississippi, but the head quartermaster told me that it was the one that killed Goliath. But it is not important. No matter which it is, let us give her hearty welcome and godspeed.[2]

Twain never gave the speech. He stood on the dais on March 25, while out in the harbor the entire Pennsylvania General Assembly were gathered on an iceboat serving as a floating grandstand. Frances Griscom, the shipowner's teen-aged daughter, held a jeroboam of champagne at the ready. But the *St. Paul* did not move. Tugs strained against the hawsers, metal bit against wood, yet the hull remained stubbornly in place. After two hours in the cold, the crowd began to disperse.[3] Mark Twain was due to leave for Europe the next day, appropriately enough on another ship of the American Line. His prepared remarks were shelved forever.

Spectacles are fragile things, all the more so for the symbolism invested in them. Isambard Brunel would learn that for himself at the launch of the giant *Great Eastern*, so disastrous it foreshortened his life. Indeed, launchings often invite a demon of perversity, perhaps because they are so minutely choreographed. There was a long, nasty pause before the *Mauretania* began to slide down her ways in 1906; a few years later, Hannah von Bismarck swung the jeroboam at the *Bismarck*'s bow and missed (Kaiser Wilhelm II caught it on the backswing and finished the job).[4] In 1935, Queen Mary launched the vessel that bore her name and then turned to an aide and said loudly into the microphones, "Should I press the button now?" The launching of the *Imperator* in 1913 was perhaps the most ill-omened of all: A piece of planking fell from the bow and nearly decapitated the royal guests, the anchor chains fell into the river Elbe, and the hull was sent careening towards an opposite quay crowded with spectators.[5] Of more recent memory, Camilla, Duchess of Cornwall, was tasked to christen the *Queen Victoria* in 2008—after well over an hour of *Te Deum* and a prayer from the Archbishop of Canterbury—only to have the bottle hit the bow with a dull clunk and rebound, intact. The confetti cannons went off anyway.[6] In those moments the allegorical pageant failed, and along with it the symbolism of triumphal progress, nationalism, international amity, and so on. They were a reminder of the fragility that lay behind the enterprise.

That fragility, that ephemeral allegory that the launching represents, is what we might call the phantasmagoria of steam. Phantasmagoria were image slides passed through a projector called a magic lantern. The image was projected either onto a flat screen or sometimes steam clouds, creating a kind of hologram. These phantasms were the closest thing in the mid-19th century to moving pictures and often could seem very real indeed. Their purpose was to excite wonder, to convince the observer that the fantastical could indeed be possible. The term dates from the same era as the first steamships. I am borrowing it to describe the amorphous line where technology overlaps with fantasy, which contemporary observers usually termed a "spectacle."

In the early years of steam innovation, spectacles helped introduce the public to a new and seemingly magical form of transit: the carriage without a horse, the ship without sails. They also helped ameliorate fears, rational or imagined, that darkened the public's response. Further, they encouraged investment. It was not a hard sell. The steam engine *was* rather magical, especially when put to some useful trade. It was the promoter's task to persuade Mr. and Mrs. John Bull (and their cousins across the Atlantic, and on the Continent) that its magic was white and not black. "Like an elephant that picks up a needle and tears down a tree, there is no task too small, no work too great for the giant, Steam," wrote one.[7] A friendly giant, or a helpful genie; these were the most common depictions. And how better to illustrate that helpfulness—and power—than by public display?

The point of a spectacle was not to instruct the public on the workings of a steam vessel but to dazzle them with it. Demonstration, display, and spectacle were often presented as synonymous in this era; one need only picture the carnival barker outside the Bearded Lady's tent: "Don't let your children miss this once-in-a-lifetime educational opportunity!" Yet though they often overlap, there is a crucial distinction. Demonstrations are meant to educate; however thrilling, their purpose is to communicate knowledge. Spectacles are meant to astound. The difference is between vivisection and a magic show. As one historian describes it:

> Engineers had a particular problem, more so, perhaps, than men of science, when it came to releasing, at the right moment and to the right audience, sanitised accounts of finished technological products. It was by no means easy to conceal the mess of technological process when the product was an innovative steam-powered mill, an "experimental" railway or a great steamship ready to be launched.... Part of the "representation" of technologies involved cultures of *display* in which marketing and carefully staged demonstration, often in public, went hand in hand.[8]

Promoters of steam power knew better than to bore their spectators with engineering lessons. The best way to appreciate the power and utility of the engine was to watch it work. Steamships and locomotives naturally leant themselves to this sort of performance; stationary engines did not. There is nothing lovely about an engine by itself. At rest it is grotesque, but when working it is a simulacrum of rage, hissing and sputtering, pistons beating the air. It produces a sound unlike anything in nature, a cacophony of shudders, bangs, and flatulence. The true enchantment of the machine—that it can repeat the same motion again and again without ever tiring—also makes it very boring to watch. The pistons moved "monotonously up and down," Charles Dickens declared, "like the head of an elephant in melancholy madness."[9]

But ships and locomotives were another matter. Now the machine was sheathed by an iron exoskeleton that concealed its workings, not unlike the voluminous robes of von Kempelen's chess-playing Turk. When the great wheel turned, it seemed to do so by a kind of witchcraft. Even today there is something wondrous about watching a cruise ship leave dock: The stationary building suddenly breaks away from the pier, screws churning silently beneath the hull, and in that moment becomes a living object. This hints at the second distinction of these machines: They *moved*. Judging their success was as simple as measuring their speed; the faster they went, the better they were. Third and finally, there was the awesomeness of their size. Here the machine disappears altogether: The wonder exerted by the *Great Britain* had nothing to do with her engines but by the simple fact of her scale.

As there were two measures of preeminence—size and speed—there were two forms of spectacle: the exhibition and the race. Exhibitions were public fêtes designed to promote the vessel. The exact nature varied with the intended audience. Launchings, goodwill tours, and open houses amassed large crowds (and, as often as not, made a tidy sum on entrance fees). Like a village fête or a parade, all classes of society were encouraged to attend. Special events, on the contrary, catered to a much smaller and more elite collection of visiting dignitaries, reporters, and the like. Visitors were to be amazed by the ship's massiveness and the luxury of its quarters. While the former was undeniable, the latter could be fudged a bit. Day-trippers to the new Collins liners in the 1850s were greeted by a plethora of Oriental rugs, potted palms, and fine furniture; reporters duly referred to them as "floating palaces." But once the ship left New York, the realities of the rolling Atlantic took precedence: the carpets were rolled up, the fine furnishings stored until the next port day.

There is an echo of Walter Benjamin's Paris arcades here. The sight of those plush steamship lounges surely inspired many day-trippers to strive even harder in the capitalist marketplace to earn enough to gain access to them. But exhibition was more than ginning up potential customers. It was about creating a shared experience (just as was the Great Exhibition of 1851, as we shall see) and also a shared sense of pride. Spectators were encouraged to believe that this marvel of technology owed itself in some small part to them. It is what one might call the celebrity effect. Just as meeting a famous person establishes a connection between yourself and the celebrity, fleeting though it may be, spectators became part of the *community* of the ship simply by having seen it.

Races were a means of establishing precedence among competitors. Sound commercial thinking was at work; the fastest boat or train earned the most passengers or freight. But in a *sportif* era, such races were also public events that attracted as much attention and comment as Ascot or the Derby. They were announced in the newspapers. Punters wagered on the results.[10] Similar to exhibitions, races were a means for persons who had no actual stake in the ship or locomotive to feel vicariously attached to it. There is no more proprietary feeling than placing a fiver on a favored horse. Even if no actual money was involved, spectators along the banks or following the race in their newspapers could hardly help getting caught up in the excitement of it all. Once again, this time through the mechanism of a race, an artificial community is created.

The phantasmagoria of steam was much more than images flashing against a translucent cloud. Pomp and pageantry aside, it worked a profound transformation in the Victorian mind. To chart this transformation, we must consider both the spectacle itself and the intended audience. As interested spectators, the public was conditioned by repeated spectacles to regard steam as a human miracle—a very loaded concept. Steam, as something magical and miraculous, had unlimited power for good—*only* good, for how could a miracle ever be bad? As a work of humankind, it was not subject to divine whim but earthly regulation. In other words, steam locomotion was a servant of man, not some barely tamed natural phenomenon like wind or water or lightning. Its subservience was another mark of its beneficence, and that of its creators, the engineers. The veneration of steam power thus became tantamount to cult worship of human ingenuity. Allegorical imagery was everywhere: in stations, universities, within the ships themselves. Contrary to traditional religious norms, pride became a virtue, and human perfectibility through technological progress replaced old Adam's sin. This was not without consequences, as we shall explore.

. . .

On August 22, 1787, an impoverished inventor named John Fitch invited members of the Constitutional Convention down to the Philadelphia docks to witness a spectacle, the first demonstration of steam on water. In fact, he had been trying to lure them for months. "Sir," he wrote in one such pleading letter to Benjamin Franklin, "In a conference that I had the honor of with your Excellency, I heard you mention that the Philosophical Society ought to be furnished with a Model of a Steam Engine, and having completed one on a small scale, would be exceedingly happy should it meet your Patronage . . ."[11] Fitch was also looking over his shoulder. Millwright James Rumsey was currently working on a similar device and had already—as a Virginian and a gentleman—earned the patronage of General Washington.[12] Smooth-talking and plausible, Rumsey co-opted Thomas Jefferson and, eventually, Franklin as well.[13]

The spectacle on the Delaware was John Fitch's only chance. Dr. Franklin did not come, but others did. It was a warm, clear day, not as muggy as it had been: perfect weather conditions. Three months in, one can imagine the debates in the Hall becoming tedious and contentious; the members were eager for a distraction. Just four days earlier, James Madison suggested that the new legislature "encourage knowledge and discoveries," while Charles Pinckney added that, beyond encouragement, it should also "grant patents for useful inventions."[14] Fitch's boat, appropriately and allegorically named *Perseverance*, was outfitted with a curious set of interlocking oars that, if everything worked as it should, moved the boat at a sluggish but steady 2 knots per hour. It looked like an ugly canoe. Fitch had explored paddle wheels but was forced to abandon the idea: Dr. Franklin thought them impractical. The *Perseverance* set off from the pier with several convention members aboard, did a few lazy turns in the river, got briefly stuck in the mud, and came back. Regrettably, few of the members present recorded their impressions. Edmund Randolph wrote Fitch that the Virginia delegation was "pleased to give it every countenance they could," and Oliver Ellsworth was delighted to learn it had been invented by a fellow Connecticut man. Dr. Samuel Johnson—no relation to Bosworth's idol—wrote to Fitch presenting his compliments and saying that the demonstration "gave the gentlemen present much satisfaction."[15]

The most detailed account comes from another supplicant, Rembrandt Peale, a portrait artist that hung about the Convention hoping some of the members might need his services. "Hearing that there was something curious to be seen at the floating bridge on the Schuylkill at Market Street," he hurried down to the water's edge. There, he writes:

I found a few persons collected, all eagerly gazing at the shallop at anchor below the bridge, with about twenty persons on board. On the deck was a small furnace, and machinery connected with coupling crank projecting over the stern to give motion to the three or four paddles, resembling snow shovels, which hung into the water. When all was ready . . . the paddles began to work, pressing against the water backward as they rose, and the boat to my great delight moved against the tide, without wind or hand . . ."[16]

The demonstration led to a brief lift in John Fitch's fortunes: He departed Philadelphia convinced of the Convention's support. Yet when the ultimate authority, Benjamin Franklin, finally spoke, it was not in his favor. Franklin and a few other members commissioned James Rumsey to go to England and apply for a steam patent. In the end, neither Fitch nor Rumsey would gain the laurels or introducing steam to America's rivers. That honor belonged to Robert Fulton, who knew less about inventing steamboats than he did about marketing them.

Fitch's reasoning was sound, however. Despite the ultimate failure of the spectacle on the Delaware, he had happened upon exactly the right means of introducing steam to the public. In England some years later, in 1829, the first mobile land-based steam engines—eventually termed "locomotives"—began with a competition posted in the *Liverpool Mercury*. The prize was £500, or more than $500,000 today, a princely sum that, as one historian writes, "brought the crackpots out in force."[17] The successful entrant had to move 20 tons of simulated freight back and forth across a 1? mile track forty times, equivalent to the distance from Liverpool to Manchester and back. The fastest locomotive would win. After a series of failed starts (which brings to mind a movie montage of clunkers bursting their boilers, rolling over, catching fire, and so on), two entrants remained: *Novelty*, designed by Swedish engineer John Ericsson, and *Rocket*, by Englishman George Stephenson. On the test track, *Novelty* took an early lead, but *Rocket* proved to be the steadier and won.[18]

Both inventors would go on to colorful careers. Ericsson, after frittering away a few years trying to perfect a perpetual motion machine, ultimately introduced the two most important innovations to marine architecture since the steam engine itself: iron and the screw propeller. He would forever be remembered for his greatest creation, the Union ironclad *Monitor*. Stephenson focused on railroads, with much success. Both men would ultimately collide with a third prominent inventor, Isambard Kingdom Brunel, whose works feature heavily in this account.

Stephenson and Brunel quarreled over steam locomotive versus vacuum-powered railways; Brunel favored the latter, and lost. In 1843, Brunel pitted his paddle wheeler *Great Western* against Ericsson's screw-propelled *U.S.S. Princeton* and lost again (Brunel, a true engineer, promptly transferred his allegiance to locomotives and screw propellers after both trials). But Ericsson would get his comeuppance: Just one year later, with President John Tyler, his cabinet, former First Lady Dolly Madison, and 400 others on board, the *Princeton*'s revolutionary gun exploded in harbor. Two cabinet members and seven others were killed instantly, including the president's valet. It was widely considered to be the end of Ericsson's career.[19]

The history of steam and spectacle is littered with such disasters. Racing drove ships faster than the untested technology allowed, while public demonstrations, displays, and launchings placed untenable schedules on half-finished and finicky machines. But some kind of display was still considered essential to convey the wonder of the device. Even at the end of the 19th century, the average person remained mystified as to how the steam engine actually worked. A new language had been created to describe the sensation of moving at impossible velocities by unknown means. It was a violent lexicon, comprised of such implosive verbs as *injecting, compressing, compounding, firing, stoking, throttling,* and *boiling*. Some terms were so descriptive as to bring a flush to Victorian cheeks: "the steam reverses direction at each stroke, entering and exhausting from the cylinder, driving the injector rod within the output shaft."[20] Others—*thermodynamic, isentropic, adibiatic expansion*—were simply obscure. But a ship moving smoothly and rapidly through the water, or a great mass of iron hull thundering down the ways—those were images anyone could understand.

Robert Fulton himself grasped intuitively that the steamboat was an idea that, if it would work anywhere, had to work everywhere at once. Even as his first ship, the *Clermont*, was still chugging along the Hudson River, he was considering the future. In August 1816, the *Adams Sentinel* newspaper reported that Fulton was making plans to take a new steamer across the Atlantic and put her into service in the Baltic. "This grand undertaking we understand is in fulfillment, or acceptance, of a contract offered to Mr. Fulton by the Emperor of Russia, allowing him exclusive navigation of Steam-Boats in the Russian empire for 25 years."[21] The project never materialized, but Fulton was unperturbed. The richest market was closer to home. "Whatever may be the fate of steamboats for the Hudson," he wrote, "everything is completely proved for the Mississippi, and the object is immense."[22]

The opening of the Ohio Valley and the purchase of the Louisiana Territory in 1803 created, in effect, a second nation. The territory was vast, greater in size than the thirteen original colonies, and bisected by a river that ran from Missouri to the mouth of the Gulf of Mexico.[23] Actually it was not one river but hundreds, each tributary crisscrossing the landscape, all feeding the great effluvial swell southward. Until the introduction of the steamboat, the Mississippi was more nuisance than opportunity. It cut erratically across property lines, bedeviled roads, and demanded an intricate system of bridges that tested the prowess of Victorian engineers. Until that time (the first bridge was completed in 1855), travelers relied on bumboats piloted by rascally locals to reach the opposite bank. Moving goods on the river meant purchasing space on a raft. In New Orleans these were called "*bateaux*," the French word for boat, but in truth they were little more than barges relying on currents for steerage. In the North they were "Kentucky boats," in the South "New Orleans boats." Smaller boats could be as simple as a single deck resting on log pontoons; others, reaching up to 100 feet in length, had bedrooms, dining rooms, and galleys.[24]

Rafts like these moved everything from cotton to livestock to people. Not only were they the mainstay of river commerce, they were also the most efficient way to transport migrating families. Keelboats could reach speeds of 5 knots downstream, with dozens of passengers camping on deck. In contrast, the first decades of the 19th century saw the river choked with makeshift craft that floated along like so much driftwood. Anyone with an axe, cordwood, and hemp could build himself a craft. In 1831, Abraham Lincoln and his partners fashioned just such a barge to carry corn, live hogs, and, *de mortuis*, pickled pork. On arriving they sold the cargo and then the barge itself, for firewood.[25]

Despite the multiplicity of craft, one thing united them: They could only follow the river. Lincoln's disposal of his barge was typical. Until steamboats became common, the approaches of the Mississippi were filled with all manner of abandoned skiffs, barges, and boats. Only on rare instances did entrepreneurs attempt to go against the current, and it was a cumbersome business. A team of dray horses on the riverbank was harnessed with long poles to the deck of the barge. With the pilot shouting orders to the driver, the driver shouting to the tiller man, and the tiller man straining to hear them both, they made slow progress. If the river widened or narrowed, the horses had to follow suit, walking over uneven terrain. In contrast, when they reached a boulder or some other obstacle, the entire harness was dismantled and oars employed.[26] The whole system of barges and rafts was hopelessly arcane, even by Mark Twain's childhood. But its obsolescence had a fascination for him, and to reinforce the idyll of a lost era he would later set his eponymous Huckleberry Finn upon a raft meandering southward. Twain also had a kind word for the "rude, uneducated, brave, jolly, profane, prodigious braggarts" of raftsmen, whose trade was rapidly lost to steam. "By and by the steamboats intruded," he wrote, "and then keelboating died a permanent death."[27]

Mark Twain received his pilot's certificate in the spring of 1859. He had been an apprentice pilot for almost two years. The reward was substantial: Twain now earned a princely $250 a month, nearly as much as the vice president of the United States.[28] Twain arrived on the Mississippi when the steamboat trade was at its zenith—and nadir. Never again would dozens of boats jostle for wharfage along the St. Louis docks, not after 1861. Twain also came on the scene when steam engineering had reached its own pinnacle, allowing for larger and much faster boats. Thus he witnessed a phenomenon that would soon be as distant as chariots in the Circus Maximus: the steamboat race.

"A race between two notoriously fleet steamers," Twain later wrote, "was an event of vast importance.... Politics and the weather were dropped, and people talked only of the coming race."[29] Racing symbolized much more than ordinary competition. In an age of technological marvels, speed meant civilization: rushing headlong into the future, as it were. The fastest vessels hastened that future all the more. Consequently, the steamboat race was a symbolic pageant of technology triumphant over barbarism. The future, in other words, over the past. Both vessels stripped down like wrestlers about to enter the ring. Anything heavy or cumbersome was removed. Spars and derricks, furniture from the lounges, even valuable cargo—all went over the side. Twain joked about captains shaving their heads and removing their kid gloves, but all other measures were doubtless taken.[30]

A whistle from both ships signaled their readiness, and slowly their wheels began to churn backwards. A great cheer went up from the crowd on the quay and the decks of the steamers. Captains took great pains to balance the weight in their boats; strict orders were given for passengers to keep away from the rails to prevent yawing. Then the two ships turned on their rudders, in unison, like pirouetting ballerinas, and with flags streaming out behind them and a second blast of their whistles, they set off down the Mississippi.

"Brag boats" had reputations to uphold, and so raced each other on measured courses regularly. These were often compared to horseraces, but there was a crucial difference. A horse's speed can only be determined by luck and breeding, but steamships benefited from new technology. Thus the most hotly contested races were those between the new upstart and the reigning champion. On one occasion in 1851, the 2-year-old *Dr. Franklin* was challenged by the brand-new *Dr. Franklin No. 2* (or "Old Doctor" and "New Doctor"). The two ships ran apace with each other until New Doctor's captain cut directly across the bows of Old Doctor, forcing the latter to change course. When Old Doctor caught up again, Captain Harris of the New Doctor drew a rifle and threatened to shoot the opposing captain. It made all the newspapers.[31]

FIGURE 2. Two crack steamers race along the Mississippi. A common sight until the Civil War, such races pushed engines beyond their limits and often resulted in explosions and casualties. But nothing mattered except gaining the record.
SOURCE: Library of Congress LC-DIG-pga-00764.

The biggest contests were all-out steeplechases between St. Louis and New Orleans. These were planned months in advance, requiring special arrangements for fueling, clearing of any obstacles on the Mississippi, and notice in all the local papers. By the time of the event, both banks were lined with spectators for hundreds of miles. Mark Twain was lucky enough to observe one such great race between the *Eclipse* and the *A.L. Shotwell*:

Presently tall columns of steam burst from the 'scape pipes of both steamers, two guns boom a good-by, two red shirted heroes mounted on capstans wave their small flags above the massed crews on the forecastles, two plaintive solos linger on their a few waiting seconds, two mighty choruses burst forth—and here they come![32]

With extra fuel and fewer passengers, racing was an expensive proposition. But captains reasoned that a reputation for speed would be profitable in the long run and went to extraordinary lengths to attain it. In the race between the *Die*

Vernon and the *West Newton*, the former's captain achieved an extra knot of precious speed by clamping down on the safety valves from St. Louis to Dubuque.[33]

This sort of recklessness carried terrible costs. Even by the 1850s, the apex of Mississippi steamboats, their technology was still barely understood. Few engineers had more than a basic apprenticeship; technical schools were still largely unknown. The most experienced could not have had much more than a decade of practice at his trade. The steamboats themselves were swiftly and often shoddily built, serving a seemingly inexhaustible demand for more and more ships to keep apace with river commerce.[34] Antebellum photographs of New Orleans and Cincinnati show harbors clogged with dozens of steamers, docked nose-to-tail out into the channel. Worst of all, practically everyone involved with the ships—the owners, engineers, captains, crew, and passengers—seemed woefully ignorant of the dangers. Charles Dickens, who had never seen anything like them, described an evening encounter on the Mississippi, which was more perceptive for coming from an outsider's point of view:

Passing one of these boats at night, and seeing the great body of fire . . . that rages and roars beneath the frail pile of painted wood: the machinery not warded off or guarded in any way, but doing its work in the midst of a crowd of idlers and emigrants and children who throng the lower deck: under the management, too, of reckless men whose acquaintance with its mysteries may have been of six months' standing: one feels directly that the wonder is not that there should be so many fatal accidents, but that any journey should be safely made.[35]

Even when not racing, captains had schedules to maintain, and nothing was more disastrous for business than a reputation as a "slow boat." Speed meant more goods moved more quickly and thus less time between farm and market—or factory and shop. Yet the strain this placed on unreliable engines was immense. Even with the development of safety valves and other measures, the 19th-century steam engine was still profoundly unstable. In April 1852, the Cincinnati packet *Redstone* had just landed her passengers in Kentucky and was warping out into the stream when her engines exploded, "tearing the boat to atoms." Her chimneys were blown like rockets halfway across the river, and nearly all of her passengers died instantly. The captain and first mate were shot clear but were horribly injured. The *Carrollton Mirror Extra* ended its column with this short, grave epitaph: "The *Redstone* had been recently placed in the Madison trade in opposition to the regular packets. At the time of her explosion she was racing against time."[36]

Engineers discovered that the public's demand for speed could not be met by the technology of the age. They overreached, with horrific result. Accidents were common, yet most could have been avoided.[37] Speed was contagion and disease in itself. Mark Twain describes visiting the bedside of a deranged captain whose vessel had exploded under him. "His disordered imagination would suddenly transform the great apartment into a forecastle, and the hurrying throng of nurses into the crew, and he would come to a sitting posture and shout, 'Hump yourselves, *hump* yourselves, you petrifactions, snail-bellies, pall-bearers! Going to be all *day* getting that hatful of freight out?'"[38] The pageantry implied by a steamboat race was made real, but twisted: It was not a battle between technology and the river but technology and itself.

The Mississippi had its dangers, but it was the perfect thoroughfare: wide, flat, and calm. There was no rational argument against steam power on a river: It allowed goods to flow up-current, regularized schedules and subsidized new communities all along its route. The Atlantic Ocean was quite another proposition. Here was the prospect of weeks at sea tendering a white-hot furnace topped by a tank of compressed steam inside a very flammable wooden hull. And what about Atlantic storms? Would they rupture the boiler, break the crankshaft, smash the paddles? If some misfortune occurred, there was no convenient riverbank to swim to, no assistance from any quarter. The ship was a tiny speck in a vast emptiness. There was also the very real problem of fuel: How could a steamship possibly stoke enough coal to keep the monstrous machine going for such a long duration? The prospect, in short, was rather like going to sea atop a giant floating bomb.

Many wondered if steamships were even necessary. Donald McKay's sailing packets were considered the ultimate consummation of marine architecture; long, sleek and beautiful, they were also very fast. Some were surprisingly comfortable as well. The packet *Liverpool*, for example, was considered the height of ship design:

The main deck is 176 feet long, and upon it are built the cabins, bathing houses, apartments for the cuisine, houses for cows, sheep, swine and poultry. The main saloon is constructed upon the most improved idea. It is large enough for forty cabin passengers and is high enough for any man under eight feet in his boots. The staterooms are fitted up somewhat like those of the Ashburton and Stephen Whitney [prominent hotels ashore], and connect so that families can have a suite of rooms as at the Astor House.[39]

Convincing the British and American publics to accept steam on the Atlantic would not be easy. Even in the second decade of the 19th century there were plenty of skeptics who said, from varying positions of authority, that it was impossible and absurd. The "eminent oceanographer" Dr. Lardner ridiculed the whole project: "Steam on the North Atlantic is merely a dream: and as to any idiotic project of making a voyage direct from Liverpool to New York under steam, I have no hesitation in saying that one might as well talk of making such a voyage from here to the Moon!"[40] Little wonder that when, years later, Jules Verne plotted out *From the Earth to the Moon*, the pioneers of steam navigation were his inspiration for the go-getting Impey Barbicane.

To counter Dr. Lardner and his kind (and of more interest to freight shippers than to passengers and oceanographers), the only salient argument for steam on the Atlantic was that sailing ships—however fast, however beautiful—could not keep regular schedules. Relying on the wind often meant spending days becalmed or being blown hundreds of miles off course. With a fair wind and a flat sea, nothing could beat them. McKay's *Champion of the Seas* clocked 465 miles in one day on her maiden voyage between Liverpool and Melbourne, a sailing record that stood until 1984. But that same vessel could, in midwinter, take over two months to sail from Liverpool to New York. The steamship—ugly, stubby, smelly, and loud—knew no such limitations.

It should not be surprising, then, that some of the earliest promoters of Atlantic steam were the men who set the timetables for the British railways. By 1835 the Great Western Railway had already laid over 400 miles of track, and was contemplating an extension that would bring passengers all the way from Paddington Station to the wharfs at Bristol. This proposal, offered by one of the most junior of the company's directors, was met with skepticism by the most senior. The company was already overreaching, the old man argued. Nonsense, his colleague riposted, half in jest: With a steamship they could extend the line all the way to America.[41]

The junior director was Isambard Kingdom Brunel. At 29, he had already developed a reputation for lobbing bombshells of this kind. Not many years before, he confidently proposed digging a tunnel from Dover to Calais, patenting a digging device whose descendant would actually be employed for that task over a century later (but why would we want to join the *French?* his colleagues asked him). In 1825 he drafted plans for a canal through the Panama isthmus. Among his most whimsical inventions was the Atmospheric Railway, whereby vacuum pumps literally sucked passengers from Devon to Dartmoor.[42] Initially, Brunel saw little future in locomotives; he would later change his mind. On the queen's first journey by rail, undertaken with great trepidation in 1842 at speeds approaching 40 miles per hour, Brunel drove the engine. Isambard Brunel was a short man with a very tall hat, rather like the Mad Hatter's, in which he kept memoranda and cigars. He is often credited for bringing the Industrial Age to Britain, and his record was unexcelled: 25 railroads, 8 piers, 3 ocean liners, 5 suspension bridges, and 125 railway bridges that forever altered the English landscape.[43]

It will never be known whether Brunel's offhand comment about transatlantic steam was facetious, but one of the other directors took him at his word. The result was the *Great Western*, the first purpose-built steam liner. Brunel's influence on the design was actually minimal. He knew little about ships, and left most of the work to the experienced Bristol shipbuilding firm of Patterson & Mercer. His most noticeable addition seemed surprisingly retrograde: pointed Gothic arches and quatrefoils on the ceiling of the main saloon. This was done to remind passengers of the neo-Gothic terminals at Paddington and Bristol (both of which Brunel designed).[44]

As construction on the *Great Western* proceeded, company directors became aware that they had unwittingly entered themselves into a race. Several hundred miles to the north, at the Scottish firm of Macgregor Laird, work was underway on the *Royal Victoria*. At 1,890 tons she was already being lauded—unfinished—as the "St. Paul's of naval architecture."[45] The comparison was apt. Like any great cathedral, construction was slow. The newness of the enterprise meant that nearly every established principle of ship construction had to be tested and reevaluated. How would the engines hold up to being set at a 40-degree angle during a storm? Would the boilers pour hot coals onto the deck and set the ship afire? Could her wooden beams withstand the strain of the constant rattle of machinery in open sea? Throughout 1836 and 1837, the *Royal Victoria* took shape with agonizing deliberation, worrying her owners.

How much the *Great Western* benefited from *Royal Victoria*'s growing pangs is impossible to know. Industrial espionage was common enough even then, and there can be no question that both firms watched each other closely. By 1838 the *Royal Victoria* had fallen behind, and it was clear the *Great Western* would sail first. This was unacceptable to *Victoria*'s owner, Junius Smith. Smith considered himself a visionary. He wanted above all things to be credited as the father of transatlantic steam, just as Robert Fulton and George Stephenson had been in their respective fields.[46] What Junius Smith lacked in engineering knowledge he made up for in capital and connections. He financed the *Royal Victoria* and turned all his attention to raising awareness for steam power throughout the country and in Parliament.[47] He had succeeded, brilliantly. Now the *Great Western* was poised to capitalize on that success, and Smith wasn't having any of it. He responded to news of his rival's upcoming maiden voyage by hiring a small, rather dumpy coastal steamer called the *Sirius* and hurriedly provisioning her for a transatlantic crossing.

The idea could only have been born of desperation. The *Sirius* was designed for the passage from Cork, Ireland, to London, and at 178 feet long and 25 feet wide, she was just barely large enough for that task. To send her across the Atlantic would mean turning her into a floating coal barge, which would render the ship dangerously heavy at the start of the voyage and dangerously light at the end. But none of that mattered to Smith, as long as *Sirius* arrived in New York first.

The little ship departed on April 4, 1838, with forty passengers and 450 tons of coal in her bunkers. Four days later, the *Great Western* followed. The London and Bristol newspapers, which had followed the construction race avidly, now fired the metaphorical starting gun. "The *Great Western* is roused at length," one reported:

One may see her excited almost like a living thing. She heaves her huge whale-like sides with impatience. Her paddles instinctively dash into the water, as a war-horse, when he hears a trumpet, paws the ground. And see how the fierce breath of a giant defiance pours out of her eager nostrils! Look to it, *Sirius*![48]

The equestrian language was revealing. Just as the first locomotives had been dubbed "iron horses" and set at once to race against one another, so too had transoceanic steam navigation co-opted the same racing parlance. But if the *Sirius* was an old nag, the *Great Western* was an Arabian thoroughbred. Her engines were nearly double the size, power, and pressure of *Sirius*'s, and her interior appointments exceeded anything that had ever gone to sea. The main saloon was 75 feet long, decorated with 50 murals displaying the usual 19th-century pastiche of pastoral scenes, sporting parties, allegories of art and industry, and cherubim. At the bow a bronzed Neptune parted the waves with dolphins attendant on either side.[49]

Impressive as she seemed, the *Great Western*'s flaws soon became apparent. Only seven passengers had booked cabins for the maiden voyage, which didn't say much for the ship's commercial prospects. En route to the English Channel the insulation around the boilers caught fire, engulfing the *Great Western* in smoke and nearly killing Brunel, who fell on a ladder while on his way to help fight the flames. At sea, the ship's stokers discovered for the first time the backbreaking work that would be their lot on the Atlantic for nearly a century and rebelled. One of their number tried to throw the captain overboard, and the others dropped their shovels in protest until the man was released from confinement.[50]

This brought home a grim reality: Steamships might not rely on a favorable breeze, as the sailing packets had, but they were desperately dependent on coal and manpower. A few hundred miles away, the crew of the *Sirius* was learning the same lesson. Her boilers had already consumed nearly all the fuel in the ship, and by voyage's end the stokers were reduced to throwing in furniture, bedding, hatch covers, barrels of resin—anything that would burn. The scene was so memorable that the American and British newspapers picked it up; many years later, Jules Verne would recall and add it to the climactic voyage in *Around the World in Eighty Days*.

Sirius arrived in New York first, giving Junius Smith the right to claim the first successful commercial transatlantic crossing entirely under steam.[51] This victory was undercut by the appearance of the *Great Western* just twelve hours later. Abruptly the spectacle of the race transformed into one of exhibition. The *Great Western* stole the show. "If the public mind was stimulated by the arrival of the *Sirius*," one newspaper reported, "it became intoxicated with delight upon view of the superb *Great Western*."[52] All the hyperbole and accolades abruptly and almost comically shifted from one vessel to the other, as this description in the New York *Evening Post* makes clear:

At three o'clock p.m. on Sunday, the 22nd of April, *Sirius* first descried the land, and early on Monday morning, the 23rd, anchored in the North river immediately off the Battery. The moment this intelligence was made known hundreds and thousands of people rushed toward the waterfront. Nothing could equal their excitement. . . . While these people were yet wondering how *Sirius* so successfully made out to cross the rude North Atlantic it was announced about 11 a.m. on Monday, the 23rd, from the telegraph that a huge steamship was in the offing. "*Great Western, Great Western!*" was the cry on everybody's lips, and about two o'clock p.m. the first curl of her ascending smoke fell on the eyes of the thousands of spectators, and a shout of enthusiasm split the air.[53]

With little else of interest to report, every newspaper in New York seized on the spectacle of the race, and the even more momentous arrival, and described the scene. Each depiction was more overwrought than the last, as editors struggled to find new angles. "The approach of the *Great Western* to the harbor, and in front of the Battery, was most magnificent," one wrote:

> The Battery was filled with the human multitude, one half of whom were females, their faces covered with smiles, and their delicate persons with the gayest attire. Below, on the broad blue water, appeared this huge thing of life, with four masts and emitting volumes of smoke. She looked black and blackguard, rakish, cool, reckless, fierce and forbidding in somber colors to the extreme.[54]

In actual fact the *Great Western*, aside from the novelty of her funnel and paddle boxes, looked no different from any of the other sailing packets that passed through New York for decades. The wonder was not in her physical appearance but in her timing: She had crossed the Atlantic in fourteen days, making up three and a half days against the *Sirius* en route, clearly demonstrating the superiority of her engines. In every real sense, she had won the race. This was certainly true as far as the public was concerned. Like paparazzi at an airport, the crowds and newspapers promptly abandoned the *Sirius* and hurried to congratulate Captain Hosken of the *Great Western*: "With that strenuous abandon attainable only in the Empire City," *The Enquirer* enthused, New York celebrated "that most irrefragable testimony of the practicability of steam navigation between the Old and New Worlds."[55] Steam was spectacle, as the editors of *The Sun* immediately grasped: "We thought of the artificial seas poured into the Roman theatres of the gratification of the emperors; and we thought that Rome in all her glory never witnessed a scene like this."[56]

Beyond spectacle, the race of the *Sirius* and *Great Western* seemed to hold the promise of an undefined yet glorious age to come. "Visions of future advantage to science, to commerce, to moral philosophy, began to float before the mind's eye," the *Morning Herald* reported. If readers were left wondering how a 200-foot steamboat might improve their "moral philosophy," irrepressible editor James Gordon Bennett spelled it out in detail:

> The advantages [of steam navigation] will be incalculable: no more petty rivalries, or national antipathies; no odious misconstructions and paltry jealousies, but a mutual love and respect growing out of an accurate knowledge of one another's good qualities, and a general emulation in the onward march of mind, genius, enterprise and energy, towards the perfectibility of man.... In the popular style of encouragement, and in one very appropriate to the subject, we most emphatically say, Go ahead![57]

There is a great deal to unpack in this statement. Herein, the pageant of the steamship's arrival in harbor becomes an allegory for the march of human progress. Steamships would banish ignorance, for what surer way to understand another culture than to visit it oneself? They would foster amity between nations through constant contact and communication. In sum, they would "annihilate space," as Daniel Webster remarked, and in doing so would transgress and ultimately dissolve the old, artificial boundaries between state and state, culture and culture.

The utopian future depicted here was both ancient in origin and shockingly new. Philosophers had dreamed for millennia of a unified world built on shared humanity. The perennial question was how it would be achieved. Prior to the 19th century, the most common answer was through religion: hence centuries of crusades and attempts at forced conversion. The other possibility, born of the 18th-century *philosophes*, was enlightened government. Yet here James Gordon Bennett was introducing a third: technology. It would not be through worship or political systems that humankind finally achieved utopia, but "the march of mind . . . towards the perfectibility of man." This was revolutionary indeed, for it entrusted humanity's future to an unlikely custodian: the engineer. Bennett might have been indulging himself in hyperbole, but he had accurately caught the zeitgeist of the age. Engineers would indeed become the heroes of a new Victorian cult of technology, and steamships would become symbols of the triumph of mankind over its "barbarous," pre-Industrial past. But that was yet to come.

More concretely, the *Great Western* was also a source of news from abroad. For the first time such news could be expected on a regular basis, as Philip Hone, a prominent New Yorker, noted in his diary:

Arrival of noon to-day this fortunate steam-packet [the *Great Western*] made her appearance, after a voyage of sixteen days, having sailed on the 20th of February. None of her competitors have made their trips with equal despatch and regularity. Owing to an unprecedented delay in the arrival of the regular packets, we have been without accounts from England for forty-one days, which gap has now been filled up by the arrival of the "Great Western." There does not appear to have been much doing the other side of the water during this long period. The most important event was the marriage of the Queen.[58]

There were other practical matters to consider. The novelty of a steam crossing was all very well, but the *Great Western* could not have a maiden voyage twice, and sooner or later the spectacle would subside and all that would be left was the machine itself. The *Evening Post* asked the question on everyone's mind: "Can steam packets be made to pay?"[59]

Yes, they could. The *Great Western* soon settled into a workaday routine, ferrying back and forth across the Atlantic, and panegyrics about her arrival were replaced by a more mature appreciation of her reliability.[60] Passenger lists steadily increased until the ship regularly sailed fully booked. After a few years of service, some travelers even allowed themselves to be nostalgic about the lost, halcyon days of sail: "There is no conversation [on board]," one lamented. "The progress of the ship . . . machinery, and the price of cotton and tobacco are the only topics. . . . I return not by steamer. I shall go to Halifax and take passage in a Falmouth packet, where there is more of society and less of a mob."[61] Nothing could have more clearly rung the death knell on sail than such condescension.

In the meantime, poor Junius Smith never received the acclaim he wanted, and deserved. The *Royal Victoria* was finally completed in 1838 as the *British Queen* and was set at once in competition with the *Great Western*. But Brunel's vessel proved to be the faster and had the advantage of having arrived first— a fact that never ceased to enrage his rival Smith. After the foundering of his second liner, the *President*, in 1841, Smith retired from the steamship trade. The *Great Western* sailed on, to the delight and profit of her owners. Even as new competitors arose—most prominently a mild-mannered Halifax entrepreneur named Samuel Cunard—the *Great Western* still set the bar.

By 1841 steam had arrived in the public consciousness. The manner of its arrival would frame Victorians' perception of it for decades to come: the race and the exhibition. Spectacles such as the contest between the *Rocket* and the *Novelty*, the *Sirius* and the *Great Western*, even old and new *Dr. Franklin* raised fascination for the wonder of steam travel and its seemingly limitless potential. James Gordon Bennett spoke of it bringing peoples together, and so it did— but not in the way he envisioned. Instead of bridging the gap between existing communities, the race created new ones and pitted them against one another. Choosing which group to join was as simple as choosing which ship to favor.

In the coming decades, as England, America, and others began to compete on the Atlantic run, these small groups of enthusiasts would grow until they encompassed the public as a whole, and steamships would become the floating embodiments of their respective nations. The contests, too, would become increasingly fevered as the stakes rose. Ultimately, instead of fostering amity between nations, steamship races drove a wedge between them. But the dominant narrative of steam as unifier left no room for dissent. Even those whom the steamboats displaced—the native populations along the Mississippi, for example—were expected to goggle in awe at the sight of them and express gratitude for their arrival. Hence while some communities were created by steam, others were destroyed, as we shall see.

As it was being introduced to steam travel through racing, the public was also conditioned to expect some sort of match whenever a new vessel appeared. In practical terms such contests were meaningless: The difference of a few hours between Liverpool and New York would not incommode even the tightest schedules. Yet it could ruin a competitor. By the end of the century, beautiful ships like the *City of Rome* and the *Kaiser Friedrich* were rejected by their owners simply because they were not the fastest on the Atlantic. Moreover, despite bland expressions of mutual goodwill, steamship races pitted one nation against another in contests that grew increasingly acrimonious over time. In the early 1850s, Philip Hone exulted in his diary of the Collins liner *Atlantic*, an American vessel:

The great steamer "Atlantic" went to sea to-day. She went off in fine style; but the fog compelled her to stop three or four hours at Staten Island. She will create a sensation in England. If John Bull does not open his eyes in wonder, and scratch his head in jealousy, he will have lost his usual characteristics. Let him beat her if he can; if he does, we will try again.[62]

But with great speed came greater risks. Mississippi boats regularly exploded their boilers, and steamship captains plowed their ships through treacherous fogs, icebergs, and other ships.[63] There was no good reason for such recklessness, but the public demanded it all the same. That was the nature of a spectacle: It must never fail to amaze, whatever the cost.

Finally, the race also became an allegory for the advance of civilization. Charging toward the unknown, steam vessels annihilated space and brought with them a mechanized vision of human progress. They gave the public new heroes: the engineer and the captain. Both were seen as doing daily battle with the retrograde forces of nature, and their ultimate triumph was measured in miles per hour. This was an easy, tangible, and self-explanatory means of rating human progress, and as the century wore on it seemed to some observers as if society was hurtling toward perfection. Only a relative few wondered if something else might lie beyond the horizon.

So much for the race. But what of the exhibition? The arrival of the *Great Western* in 1838 was a poor herald for what was to come. Despite all the hoopla in the press, she was visually unremarkable and seemed hardly worth all the bother. But that would soon change. Emboldened by success, Isambard Brunel returned to the directors of the Great Western Line with plans for a second ship. Exponentially larger and more revolutionary, he gave her a name that seemed to ensure the public spectacle that would follow. He planned to call her the *Mammoth*.

2 SELLING THE *MAMMOTH*
The Commodification of Wonder

IN AN 1839 EXHIBITION at the Royal Academy in London, J. M. W. Turner unveiled his masterwork: *The Fighting Temeraire*. In the soft amber wash of a darkening sky, the old ship of the line is towed to her graveyard by a steam tug. The *Temeraire* is skeletal, white and lovely; the tug is dark, stubby and belching smoke over the doomed vessel's pristine decks. It was an essay on mortality. Turner, at the height of his prowess and fame, was 64 years old. Critics praised his works but lamented their "indistinctness." In another generation he would be called the father of impressionism. But the world he depicted with his quivering hand was ephemeral, passing away under his brush and all around him.[1]

The steam age, which had arrived so abruptly in Britain and the United States, seemed to promise a future that was infinitely smokier, dirtier, noisier, and more dangerous than the past.[2] Victorian diarists often wrote of the spoiled landscape viewed from their train carriage windows—coal pits and trenches dug into the earth, sooty smokestacks belching over factories—seemingly without realizing it was the very machine beneath their feet that drove this transformation. Others were more perceptive. William Wordsworth, 74 years old and living in semiretirement, viewed with alarm the ever-increasing number of day-trippers invading his beloved Lake District. News of a proposed railway line from Kendal to Windermere moved him to protest in verse:

Is there no nook of English ground secure
From rash assault? Schemes of retirement sown
In youth, and 'mid the busy world kept pure
As when their earliest flowers of hope were blown,
Must perish;—how can they this blight endure?[3]

The idea that both nature and society were under mechanized attack became a common theme amongst the dissenters. "A railroad train in motion was a snorting, smoking, roaring thing," one historian has written, "for all the beauty of its movement, it was an assault on the human senses."[4] So was the steamship: The *Great Western*'s passengers often complained of greasy smells, sooty clothes, and the never-ending clatter of the engines.[5] Yet the ships' menace had less to do with blight on the landscape than what they were perceived to bring with them. In the United States, the maiden 1840 arrival of Samuel Cunard's *Britannia* brought forth the customary paeans but also a measure of concern. At Boston's Federal Street Unitarian Church, Reverend Ezra Gannett preached that the *Britannia* was the most important event in the city since the turn of the century and one that would "strengthen the bonds of kind and just consideration between the Eastern and Western continents." But, unlike James Gordon Bennett, the prospect of unfettered transatlantic communication frightened him:

The arrival of a steam ship every fortnight at our doors, freighted with the influence of the Old World is no less eager to send than we are to receive, must increase the danger of us losing our independence, as well as our neglecting to cultivate originality of character.[6]

The ambiguity in Gannett's sermon was echoed elsewhere. In Victor Hugo's *The Toilers of the Sea*, first published in 1866, the steamship is an accepted fact of life—but not necessarily a welcome one. The little Guernsey community where the novel is set relies on the steam launch *Durande*: "It was the sole source of his fortune," Hugo writes of the ship's owner, M. Lethierry, and "it also made the fortune of the district." When the ship is wrecked, the town is thrown into turmoil; the plot turns, in fact, on the protagonist's attempt to "rescue" the ship's engine, an obvious allegory for civilization's struggle with the forces of nature. Yet despite their indebtedness to steam, there is distrust and fear among the populace as well:

The weak point in the *Durande*'s success was that people had no confidence in it. . . . New ideas suffer from the disadvantage that everyone is against them, and the slightest thing that goes wrong discredits them. One of the commercial oracles of the Norman archipelago, a banker named Iauge who came from Paris, was once consulted about investing money in steamships. He is said to have replied, turning his back on the enquirer: "The proposition you have in mind is a conversion—the conversion of money into smoke."[7]

What was most surprising about these dissenting voices was their rarity. Stanchions of the Old Guard like Wordsworth and the Duke of Wellington might bemoan changes in the landscape, but the public overall embraced steam transport with a fervor that surprised even its promoters. Part of this was simple convenience, yet there was also an indefinable sense that the world was becoming smaller, more intimate, more democratic. Steam not only annihilated space, but—seemingly—class barriers as well. As one historian has written, "the nineteenth century is the only period in human history when the richest and most powerful traveled by the same transport system as the common people."[8]

How one viewed the prospect of greater communication told much about the person. Reverend Gannett might be appalled at the potential loss of American distinctiveness; others, of a more cosmopolitan stripe, were thrilled. James Gordon Bennett, for one, and Mark Twain for another, welcomed the decline of provincialism and prejudice that the steam age appeared to herald. There was also a third group, a loose coalition of missionaries and imperialists (or some combination thereof) that correctly perceived a smaller world would be easier to control. In 1869, to commemorate the twin arrivals of the American transcontinental railroad and the Atlantic cable, author Margaret Carrington (whose husband Henry was a noted Indian killer during Red Cloud's War) wrote ecstatically that

the Christian world and all civilized people [may] rejoice that the islands of the sea and the barbarism of Asia have been brought so near to our homes that with only a single wire to underlie the Pacific, the whole earth will become as a whispering gallery, wherein all nations, by one electric pulsation, may throb in unison, and the continent shall tremble with the rumbling of wheels that swiftly . . . transport its gospel and commerce.[9]

She might have added the steamships as well, which carried gospel, commerce, ammunition, soldiers, and western culture far greater distances than the railways or cables ever could.

As the largest steam-powered machines in the world, passenger ships gradually assumed an allegorical mantle combining these distinct but related themes of democracy, civilization, and empire. It was hard going at first: The *Great Western* and Cunard's *Britannia*, though perfectly serviceable, lacked what today might be called the "wow factor." One was not awestruck by them. They did not summon up visions of grandeur or imperial might. But this would change in 1844, with the introduction of Brunel's second ship, the *Mammoth*.

A promotional pamphlet written in 1845, on the eve of the new ship's introduction to service, briefly memorialized the trials and tribulations that went into creating the largest vessel on earth. It is a wonderful example of Whig history, decades before that term came into vogue. Here all the pettifogging naysayers are put in their place, company directors and engineers take on a heroic caste, and the steamship becomes an allegory for civilization triumphant:

> No sooner had the *Great Western*, in contempt of the elaborate and confident assertions of philosophers ... that it would be impossible for her to succeed in crossing the Atlantic—performed her voyage with the greatest ease to New York and back, than the Directors found that steamships of larger dimensions would offer better chances of remuneration. Guided again by the suggestions of that superior man [Isambard Brunel], who had before emboldened them to build the *Great Western*, they now determined that their second ship should be built of iron instead of wood, and subsequently propelled by the screw instead of the paddle wheel; and the *Great Britain* steam-ship as she now is, is the stupendous progeny of the genius of Mr. Brunel, and of their faith in it.[10]

The truth was rather more complex. Begun in 1839, the *Mammoth* underwent four complete revisions in design and emerged five years later unrecognizable from the initial proposal. Brunel's first draft contemplated a wooden-hulled liner of some 1,500 tons displacement, with reciprocating engines driving a pair of cycloidal paddles at 11 knots, making her both the largest and fastest ship on the Atlantic run. In appearance she looked like a slightly beefier *Great Western*.

But between the signing of the draft agreement and the start of construction, Brunel's vision of the ship altered dramatically. The *Archimedes*, the first-ever screw-driven vessel, arrived in Bristol in 1840. Brunel was intrigued enough to order a screw for the *Mammoth*. This meant that the ship's proposed engines, already well under construction, were rendered useless. Completely new (and untried) machinery would be needed to turn a screw at the stern rather than paddles at the sides. The paddle boxes themselves, hanging "like dromedary humps"[11] on either side of the ship, were dismantled. Investors had learned to expect delays when dealing with Brunel's erratic genius and were indulgent—up to a point. "Your Directors," the Great Western Steamship Company wrote its stockholders, "have warmly to acknowledge the aid afforded them by the science of Mr. BRUNEL; nothing indeed can exceed the obligation under which the company is indebted to that gentleman."[12] Nothing, that is, except their obligation to the stockholders themselves. That was the problem.

Fortunately for Brunel, the logic of the screw seemed to be borne out in a public demonstration in 1843. With the *Mammoth*'s screw-propulsion system already in its final stages, the paddles of her older sister, the *Great Western*, were pitted against a screw-propelled vessel designed by John Ericsson. Ericsson's ship, the *U.S.S. Princeton*, won handily. Emboldened by his rightness on screw propulsion, Brunel adopted a second and even more radical change. Another Bristol visitor in the late 1830s was the *Rainbow*, John Laird's iron ship. Iron had several advantages over wood: It was more resilient, did not corrode as quickly, and allowed for the construction of much larger vessels (wood hulls had the tendency to flex at the bow and stern, or "hog," at lengths over 300 feet).[13] But it had never been contemplated on such a scale, and no single foundry in Britain could accommodate the massive order. The *Mammoth* was hammered together piecemeal, and construction slowed down to a crawl. Costs rose to a staggering £100,000, with the ship still unfinished. "We are sick of the continued demands, and want of money," a group of stockholders complained, "Judging from past experience . . . the more we spend the more we shall be required to supply."[14] No longer impressed by "the science of Mr. Brunel," some advocated selling the hulk to another unwary sucker.[15]

Brunel believed that science must never bow to mammon and remained sanguine that the ship would earn back her reputation (and her investment) once complete. The *Mammoth* was already the most famous engineering project, according to *Punch*, since the Pyramids. The completed hull would be 322 feet long and displace 3,674 tons, twice as big as the *Great Western* or any other ship on the Atlantic. The company directors might be weary of Brunel's demands and wary of the ungainly result, but they understood perfectly the marketing potential of the largest ship ever built. It was they, not he, who suggested the name *Mammoth*; Brunel thought it cheapened the enterprise. Eventually a majority of the directors agreed and settled for the more modest *Great Britain* instead. To a superstitious public, giving a ship so prideful a cognomen and setting her loose on the Atlantic seemed to invite divine wrath—a lesson the White Star Line pointedly ignored when it decided, in 1908, to name its trio of ocean liners *Olympic*, *Titanic*, and *Gigantic* (they learned later—when the *Gigantic* finally appeared in the wake of the *Titanic* disaster, her name was changed to *Britannic*).[16]

The publicity machine cranked out a near-constant stream of promotional literature, while endorsements were sought from everyone from prominent engineers to peers of the realm. "Mr. Creuze's opinion is clear and distinct, that iron should supersede wood in Her Majesty's ships of the largest size," one read; "Mr. Grantham is of the same opinion, and his reasoning is sound on all points."[17] The campaign seemed to be working. *Mechanic's Magazine* gave an entire issue to detailing the ship's innovations, and the *Times* said grandly, "It must be granted the experiment is of vast importance in a national point of view." Captain Claxton, the *Great Britain*'s future commander and a director of the line, reminded readers that similar doubts had plagued the last enterprise:

Yet still fresh in the memory [are] the nautical and philosophical prophets who concerned themselves in 1836 and 1837 with the then future fortunes of that great pilot of Atlantic steaming, the *Great Western*, [who] predicted, with undoubting assurance, "that from her extreme length *she would break her back*—that it would be impossible for her to steam so much as 2,000 miles;" and they denounced the gross temerity and ignorance of her builders. In obstinate defiance of the foreknowledge of these gentlemen, and notwithstanding the ignorance and rashness of her builders, she has now steamed for seven years.[18]

By the time of her launch, the propaganda campaign surrounding her was so successful that the *Great Britain* bore a near-intolerable load of expectations. At first, it looked like she might meet them. As we saw in the Prologue, her launch in 1844 was an allegorical triumph for innovation over adversity. Compounding the allegory was the mystical symbolism of the *Great Britain*'s figurehead: a heraldic crest flanked by cog wheels, a dove, a carpenter's square, and a caduceus, capped by a beehive that looked extraordinarily like one of Mr. Brunel's hats.[19]

After that moment of triumph, however, everything went wrong. Through sheer ignorance, the ship had actually been built wider than the lock through which she had to pass; Brunel removed the masonry on both sides, but it was not enough. After months of joggling and delays, the ship squeezed through. Brunel brushed the incident off: "She stuck in the lock; we *did* get her back."[20] It was an embarrassing affair, and the recklessness and ignorance it hinted at were a warning of things to come.

The *Great Britain* arrived in London in January 1845 and at once attracted 1,500 visitors per day, including the young queen. A thousand yards of Brussels carpeting was laid down on the decks—gleefully reported by the press as more extravagance of the Great Western Line, but actually done to protect the ship from thousands of shuffling feet. The number of potential passengers amongst this throng was small, but that hardly mattered: Having not yet broken any speed records, nor even crossed the Atlantic, the ship needed all the favorable publicity she could get. Her most novel innovations—the screw propeller, the iron hull—had not been tested. All that remained was her size, and that was what they were selling. Despite the directors' claim that "a large sum of money has not been uselessly squandered in gaudy decoration," the pamphlets issued to visitors suggested the reverse:

> From this promenade you descend into the main or dining saloon, which is 98 feet 6 inches long, by 30 feet wide. This is really a beautiful room. . . . Down the centre are twelve principle columns of white and gold, with ornamental capitals of great beauty. Twelve similar columns also range down the walls on either side. Between these latter and the entrances to the sleeping berths are eight pilasters, in the Arabesque style, beautifully painted with ornamental birds and flowers. . . . The walls of this apartment are of a delicate lemon-tinted drab hue, relieved with blue, white and gold.[21]

For all the publicity, only forty-five passengers booked the *Great Britain*'s maiden voyage in July 1845. The ship company was not unduly concerned; only seven had crossed on the *Great Western*'s debut. The voyage didn't break any records, either: fourteen days, twenty-one hours, at an average speed of 9.25 knots. This was a full day longer than the current record held by the Cunard ship *Cambria*. Again, the directors were not worried, at least in public. It often took time to break in the machines. The important thing, they reminded themselves, was that the *Great Britain* had made it: Her screw propeller worked, and her iron hull seemed to hold its own (despite some serious rolling issues). Brunel could plausibly claim vindication.

New York gave its customary tumultuous welcome, and the newspapers once again lauded the new ship as a combiner of nations and annihilator of space. But privately they revealed some trepidation. One local diary entry is revealing:

> The great iron steamer *Great Britain*, the leviathan of steam, the monster of the ocean, and unquestionably the largest and most magnificent specimen of naval architecture that ever floated, arrived here yesterday, at three o'clock, in fifteen days from Liverpool, under the command of that fine fellow and successful navigator, Captain Hosken, who has made the *Great Western* proverbial for safety and despatch, and the ocean a macadamized road for her traveling. The *Great Britain* has been looked for with some anxiety. A deep interest, accompanied with some doubt, awaited her arrival, arising from her prodigious size, the novelty of her construction . . . and the material of which she is constructed.[22]

As it had been for the *Great Western*, the real test would be how the *Great Britain* settled into her routine. On her second eastbound voyage, something went seriously wrong with the ship's compass, depositing her in Nantucket instead of Sandy Hook. The problem was later determined to be her iron hull, which skewed magnetic readings. In September she faced her first Atlantic storm and lost her foremast and three blades of her propeller. Hastily repaired in New York, the propeller again disintegrated on the return trip, and the *Great Britain* made the crossing under sail in twenty days. The company, horrified, pulled her out of service for the entire winter. *Mechanic's Magazine*—the same journal that had lauded her size and innovation at her launch—now scoffed at "a leviathanism which was wholly uncalled for."[23]

In truth, such teething pains were hardly exceptional, given the newness of the ship's technology, her great size, and the multiple revisions made during construction. Indeed it was very likely these delays that brought her to grief; after waiting so long, the ship company rushed her into service unprepared. They not only needed the ship, they needed the headlines.[24]

The spectacle surrounding the *Great Britain* was also fatal for another reason. Any ordinary vessel, even a steam ocean liner, might endure such startup difficulties and still go on to enjoy a long and profitable life. Over a century later, the *Queen Elizabeth 2*'s engines gave so much trouble on delivery that she, too, was pulled from service, and all her inaugural voyages canceled. But after months of puffery in the press, with all the hopes of the British nation symbolized in her name and hull, the *Great Britain* could not afford to be anything less than astounding. The problem resolved itself into a paradox worthy of Lewis Carroll or W. S. Gilbert: If the ship was *expected* to astound, how could she ever astound? In any event, the *Great Britain* not only failed to astound, she failed to impress. By midyear her owners were already placed in the invidious position of defending a white elephant. While admitting that "the untoward delays that . . . arose in getting the vessel ready for sea are already before the public," they added hopefully (and inaccurately), "every difficulty has happily been overcome."[25]

With little choice, the Great Western Steamship Company sank yet more money into recasting the propeller and strengthening the hull. By the summer of 1846, a full year after her debut, she seemed ready. The *Great Britain* made two round-trips, each bedeviled by minor disasters like the failure of an air pump and the wearing out of a chain drum, but things seemed to be looking up. The passenger lists grew steadily. Then in September—one year exactly since the first propeller catastrophe—the ship grounded herself again, this time off the Irish coast. The newspapers were full of it:

Oh! I cannot tell you of the anguish of that night! The sea broke over the ship, the waves struck her like thunder claps, the gravel grated below. There was the throwing overboard of coal, the cries of children, the groans of women, the blue lights, the signal guns, even the tears of men, and amidst all, the Voice of Prayer.[26]

The fact that everyone was safely rescued, and the ship herself in no immediate danger hardly dampened these accounts.

Despite the successful evacuation, the *Great Britain* held fast to the shoals. In the eyes of the British public, she became a pariah. There was the sense that they had been deceived, even betrayed. All the technological promise of the ship seemed a sham. Worse still, her undoing reflected poorly on the nation that created her. Just as the public had come to believe it shared some part in the making of the *Great Britain*, they now felt that their property—in the national sense—was made worthless. The spectacle, in short, had failed. The fact that the *Great Britain* could never have justified the expectations demanded of her hardly mattered: The exhibition, which had proved so useful in the past for introducing steam to a reluctant public, now became the ship's undoing. Other vessels from other lines—Cunard, Guion, P&O—appeared on the Atlantic with comparatively little fanfare and pursued unspectacular careers to the profit of their owners. Sometimes they sank, or rammed one another, or disappeared without a trace, but these were not affronts to the national consciousness as *Great Britain*'s grounding had been. They even borrowed her innovations (by the 1870s every major Atlantic liner had a steel hull and a propeller) yet gave neither her nor her creator an ounce of credit. The *Great Britain* overreached—technologically, but more importantly, socially—and reaped the consequences.

Six months of insurance wrangling followed the disaster, as the Great Western Steamship Company tried to offload the moribund ship on her underwriters. The *Great Britain* remained in sight of land, and Brunel went to inspect her. On the one hand he was cheered; the iron hull had withstood. But the same could not be said for her investors. Brunel raged at them: "I was grieved to see this fine ship lying unprotected, deserted and abandoned by all those who ought to know her value, and ought to have protected her, instead of being humbugged by schemers and underwriters."[27] Yet the fault was partly his. The ship's size attracted and repelled and brought all her other shortcomings into glaring relief. She looked big and flashy, but she was not ready for transatlantic service and perhaps never would be. Victorians had a word for this: the *Great Britain* was a "curiosity." It was significant that the only profit she ever turned was as a London sideshow, drawing crowds to gawk at her freakishness. The ship was eventually pried off the sandbar and towed to the Bramley-Moore Dock. In 1847, after two years in service and only a handful of voyages, the *Great Britain* was sold, "like a huge mass of iron suffering from premature rust,"[28] to a dubious firm that wanted to use her for Liverpool to Australia migration. The sale marked the end of the Great Western Steamship Company: Financially exhausted and hounded in the press, it sold off the *Great Western* a few weeks later and folded.

There was a lesson in the *Great Britain*, but Isambard Brunel refused to see it. Her disastrous career was a precursor of what would follow with the even larger *Great Eastern*: delays, revisions, insolvency, and giantism coupled with brilliant innovation decades ahead of its time. For all her faults, the latter cannot be doubted. Time and testing would prove the worth of iron hulls over wood and screw propellers over paddles. Even her sheer size was eventually eclipsed—first by the *Great Eastern* and eventually by all liners. But the visionary aspects of the ship did not alter the fact that she was a dud. Tied to the pier, glistening with fresh paint, and towering over the multitudes, she seemed to fulfill the promise of her original name, *Mammoth*. Under way, her failures became apparent.

Brunel saw the opposite. He regarded the ship's difficulties as nothing more than the usual startup glitches for untested technology and was confident the *Great Britain* would repay her creditors, given time. When the creditors refused, Brunel deemed it a betrayal of the ship and himself. "The finest ship in the world," he declared, with no false modesty, was tossed aside "like a useless saucepan."[29] Reluctantly, he too abandoned the *Great Britain* and returned to designing railway trestles. His conspicuous success allowed him to recoup his reputation and gave credence to the claim that he had been undone by the pusillanimity of the company men. Nevertheless the *Great Britain* remained his one great failure. Cold comfort came from the very professional men who had derided his attempts from the start. The ship was, one wrote, "one of the greatest triumphs of modern genius, one of the most surprising and gratifying results of scientific skill the world has ever witnessed." But, the gentleman added in the same breath, "may [it] no longer be an injury and a loss to those who achieved it."[30]

Another lesson could be gleaned from the spectacle of the *Great Britain*, one of more immediate interest to Victorian entrepreneurs. The brouhaha of her introduction, from Bristol to London to New York, proved conclusively that mechanical exhibitions could pay, so long as they provided a sufficient show. Prior to her, no single invention seemed likely to draw such a crowd. Yet she had the disadvantage of being a moving, functioning vessel—in short, a spectacle that must someday be replaced by workaday routine. But what if such inventions were gathered together, placed within a great hall, and displayed for all to see? They needn't even necessarily work, so long as their size or potency impressed.

Thus was the Great Exhibition born from the germination of the *Great Britain*. It was no accident that many of the same men responsible for the ship, Brunel included, became early and ardent proponents of the exhibition. The Great Exhibition of 1851, where the nations of the world came to London's Hyde Park to display masterworks of technological prowess, revolutionized the relationship between Victorian society and their machines.[31] Arriving conveniently at the halfway mark of the century, it ushered in a new era of technology as phantasmagoria. On the one hand, it gave engineers a perfect showcase to display the fruits of their genius; on the other, it cemented the link between steam and showmanship that the *Great Britain* introduced. Most importantly, it brought together the greatest engineering minds of the age and challenged them to test the boundaries of the possible, to create machines that were not only practical and serviceable but magical as well, satisfying the public hunger for spectacle that the exhibition itself engendered. The unlikely but ultimate result of these combined factors was the *Great Eastern*.

To understand the enormity of the exhibition's impact, we must consider what came before. Resistance among the Old Guard to newfangled devices is perennial, as it reflects the anxiety of one generation confronting the next. But in the 19th century, antediluvian attitudes were interwoven with greater fears for the social order. As E. P. Thompson famously illustrated, the Industrial Era gave the working class its voice.[32] Though derided by Marx as a means for enslaving the masses through the monstrous vision of the sweatshop, technology offered them greater freedoms as well.[33] The "labor-saving device," a term coined early in the century, represented a radical new kind of thinking. It meant that the laboring poor need not always be laboring—indeed should be entitled to some free time. But how would they occupy that time?

Drunkenness, debauchery, and revolt, said the Duke of Wellington. The hero of Waterloo, whose Apsley House occupied the enviable address of Number One, London, was the Old Guard personified. His military and political careers were devoted to the preservation of the status quo. As such, he was one of the first to recognize the transformative power of steam, and it appalled him. Railroads, he said, would do nothing but "encourage the lower classes to move about."[34] When an early pioneer of Atlantic steamships sought an interview with the Iron Duke, his card was brusquely returned at the door with a note scrawled on the obverse:

His Grace had "no leisure to receive the visits of gentlemen who have schemes in contemplation of the alteration of public establishments."[35]

Attitudes like his did not ultimately hamper development, but they did restrict its audience. Though the railway lived up to the duke's worst fears, steamships remained playthings of the rich. Only the wealthiest could afford passage on a Cunard or Collins liner, and the majority of orders for new steam vessels were, until well into the 1850s, private yachts. Likewise, if the greater British public wanted to view wonders of the decorative or industrial arts, they had to do so through shop windows, for they would not be allowed inside. Such objects were hid from view, shielded behind the blank whitewashed walls of Kensington and Knightsbridge.

In the late 1840s, a number of prominent reform-minded businessmen and engineers resolved to open technology to the masses. Their model was the Paris Industrial Exhibition of 1849 that, while limited in scope, nevertheless proved the working class could view such marvels without being whipped into a jealous frenzy.[36] In fact the opposite sentiment prevailed: Encountering these objects, even through glass, gave the public a shared experience with the elites and a vision of what they could strive towards—the very essence of capitalism. Promoters reinforced this idea, as they would at the 1851 exhibition, by stressing that none of the objects on view were currently for sale. The rich would not be allowed to cart away the fair one piece at a time; it was there for all.

The driving force behind the Great Exhibition was an inventor and industrialist named John Scott Russell. In an era of polyglots, Russell was preeminent: Besides inventing "wave-line" principles that revolutionized naval architecture,[37] he taught physics, mapped railroads, opened a shipyard to construct vessels according to his own theories (whose projects included a personal yacht for none other than George Stephenson, inventor of the *Rocket*), and became an expert on contemporary art. It was in this capacity that he served as president of the Royal Society of Arts, where his vice president was Isambard Kingdom Brunel.

Russell conceived the Great Exhibition as an opportunity to display the supremacy of English art and engineering. He and a coterie of interested men approached Prince Albert, the Prince Consort, to see if he would join them. Albert was delighted, and from then on the exhibition would bear his name. Ironically, having inspired the idea and encouraged backers, Russell's prickly personality so alienated the other directors that he was ultimately removed from the project; the official catalogue of the exhibition, which offers an exhaustive history of its planning and development, does not mention him once. Russell, hurt and humiliated, plotted revenge.[38]

Nevertheless, his grandiose vision (and, by extension, Brunel's) was evident throughout. The Crystal Palace, housing over 100,000 exhibits, was the largest structure built to that time: 1,848 feet long, 456 feet wide, laid out as an elongated cross with a central concourse devoted to British manufacture and transepts given to other nations' pavilions. While size conveyed prestige, it also raised fears of instability and ungainliness. An early design, just barely larger at 2,200 feet, was "condemned, not less for its extraordinary ugliness, than that it would have been unnecessarily large, cumbrous and costly."[39] Architect Joseph Paxton avoided the problem by constructing the hall as a giant greenhouse of wrought iron and glass. Though it could get stiflingly hot in summer, the Palace was relatively light and very durable; commentators could laud its dimensions ("four times the size of St. Peter's, and six times that of St. Paul's"[40]) without incurring the wrath of hubris. Isambard Brunel contributed two ornamental towers, each 282 feet high, placed at either end of the structure and holding water for the fountains.[41]

The Crystal Palace succeeded because it struck a balance between the colossal and the practical, adapting new materials in an innovative way. Massive it was, but also restrained. No such restraint, however, applied to its contents. Eager to display a cornucopia of imagination's fruits, planners elected for a hodgepodge approach. "On entering the building for the first time," the guidebook notes, "the eye is completely dazzled by the rich variety of hues which burst upon it on every side."[42] Piously attempting to depict these wonders led to moments of unintended hilarity and insight into how Britons viewed the world:

Crossing the Transept, we have paper and stationary; Jersey, Ceylon and Malta, with the Fine Arts Court behind them; railway and steam machinery in motion, building contrivances, printing, and the French machinery, Persia, Greece, Egypt, Turkey, Portugal, musical instruments and chemicals.[43]

Opening the exhibition, Prince Albert called it "a living picture of the point of development at which the whole of mankind has arrived in the great task, and a new starting point from which all nations will be able to direct their further exertions."[44] The editors of the official guide were so inspired by this passage that they quoted it twice.

By any standard, the Great Exhibition was a triumph. Over 6 million visitors passed through the Cast Court, took turns on the mechanical camel, drank iced lemonade, and relieved their bladders in Mr. Jennings's "halting stations." Thomas Cook, pioneer of the package tour, sold 150,000 tickets for guided excursions. Queen Victoria spent over fifty hours touring the fair, partly in pride of her beloved Albert and partly to mingle with her people.[45] Even the Duke of Wellington came. "Whether the Show will be of any use to anyone may be questioned," he groused, "but of this I am certain: nothing could be more successful."[46] Benjamin Disraeli, a realist of the first caliber, called it "a godsend to the Government . . . diverting public attention from their blunders."[47]

In fact, Prince Albert was correct. The Great Exhibition revealed a composite image of Victorian society, its aspirations, imperialism, and fetish for technology. It reinforced the potential of imagination applied to science: printing presses, stenographic machines, folding pianos, a giant steam hammer that could bend whole sections of ships or crack an egg—all housed within a structure that was itself perhaps the greatest wonder of all. Yet this was a selective reading. Amongst

FIGURE 3. London's Great Exhibition of 1851, which wedded technology, patriotism, and wonder in the public imagination. Three of its strongest proponents would go on to produce the *Great Eastern*. SOURCE: Library of Congress LC-DIG-pga-01028.

the miracles on display were some devices that even contemporaries recognized as quackery, like the infamous 30-pound Swiss army knife (with 80 blades) or Colonel Lloyd's patented storm indicator "in which leeches crawling out of the water, as is their habit when there is much free electricity, are made to ring bells."[48] Moving briskly past such monstrosities, most of the visiting public chose to ignore their lesson. The path of technological advance was not a straight road, nor unhampered by failure. When the inventor's client was the public itself, the risk of disaster multiplied.

Thus the Great Exhibition introduced two additional elements that would have great consequences for steam technology: veneration for the colossal as an expression of engineering prowess (*vide* the Crystal Palace itself) and the melding of science and spectacle that comes when advancements are displayed before the crowd. These were not unalloyed gains. With the colossal comes overextension, with spectacle the risk to disappoint. Engineering now not only had to fulfill basic needs, it had to *astonish*. Even Colonel Lloyd's electrified leeches, in their own way, put on a show. The need to excite wonder and Victorians' love for the grandiose were symbiotic, mandating devices that were not just larger or faster than their predecessors, but astonishingly so. An element of the fantastical crept into Victorian technology at the Great Exhibition, and it did not go unnoticed. Couched amongst the hyperbole of the exhibition's catalogue was a stern, unheeded warning: "The pseudo-magician, destroyed by the spirits he has evoked but knows not how to control, is a picture of the inventor who builds his invention on a system of blind guesses."[49]

There would be a time for such warnings; it was not then. Judging by the plethora of bizarre curiosities on display, blind guesswork buttressed the Great Exhibition just as much as Paxton's iron beams. The problem was how to discern revolutionary innovation from crackpot fantasy, and—although the authors of the catalogue would be loathe to admit it—an exhibition hall was not the best forum for distinguishing the two. The only true criterion was not utility but wonderment, and few objects were better placed to inspire wonder than the giant steamships. Many of the prominent firms contributed ship models, deck plans, or even—in the case of Cunard Line—a giant bisected segment of the *Scotia*'s hull. In part this was a recognition of their intertwined relationship; just as Thomas Cook is credited for launching the cheap package tour by commandeering special railroads to bring tourists to the Crystal Palace, steamships played a vital role in promoting the exhibition overseas to encourage transatlantic tourism to England.

But it was more than that. If the Great Exhibition based its technological spectacle in part on the *Great Britain*, future exhibitions would build from this example, and steamship lines would be even more aware of the shared phantasmagoria of arriving in one technological wonder in order to view another. In 1873, Hamburg–American Lines published a special pamphlet encouraging Americans to visit the upcoming World's Fair at Vienna, "a rare opportunity to the observing traveler and the thinking man of business, as well as to the mere sight-seer." Those "mere sight-seers" would get quite a show, and the line subtly reminded readers of the importance of steam in putting it on:

Austria's . . . fleet has been sent to the most distant ports, on the peaceful mission to encourage commerce and industry, and at home, the entire intellect of the nation has been summoned to make this exposition what all its predecessors only partly achieved—an *International Exhibition* and a *World's Fair*. . . . The main building will be three thousand feet long and two hundred and fifty feet wide . . . double the size of St. Peter's in Rome.[50]

Dazzled by such statistics, potential passengers were encouraged to believe that the technological spectacle—the World's Fair—began the moment they stepped on board. Having listed all the statistics of the main pavilion, the pamphlet almost immediately followed with those of the ships themselves:

Their length over deck averages 350 feet, their extreme width 42 feet. They have a straight stem and round stern and a flush deck running the entire length, thus affording passengers all the facilities and pleasures of a promenade. . . . The Upper Saloons are fitted up in magnificent style—the walls are tastefully ornamented, seats and lounges are made in whatever upholsterers' and cabinet-makers handicraft can provide.[51]

A couple years later, at the 1876 Centennial Exhibition in Philadelphia, the American Steamship Company supplied a giant Corliss engine for the Machinery Hall. President Ulysses S. Grant officially opened the exhibition by turning on a valve, engaging the engine, and thus supplying the motive power for the 800 other machines in the hall.[52] The symbolism was heavy: At one hundred years of age, the heart of America was undeniably steam-powered.

The most ambitious exhibition of the century, the 1893 Columbian Exhibition at Chicago, served as a showcase of every kind of mechanical engineering. This time, instead of a steam valve, the president turned an electric switch that ignited the lights of the White City and turned on its fountains. Within the Louis

Sullivan-designed Transportation Building, nearly every major steamship line contributed something. Cunard offered nine ship models, ranging from the *Britannia* of 1840 to the brand-new *Campania*;[53] Inman one-upped them with an entire cross section of the *City of Paris*. "The marine exhibit of Great Britain is exceptionally fine," Rand McNally's official guidebook noted, "nearly all of her ship-building firms being represented by models."[54]

Interestingly, however, it was the humbler Fall River Line—steamboats servicing New York and New England—that most compellingly articulated the link between steam and spectacle—and the allegory of technology as civilization (before going overboard and taking preeminence within that pantheon of carriers):

> In the World's Columbian Exhibition no more interesting exhibit is to be found, perhaps, than that contained in the Transportation Building, whereby the evolution and development of the carrying systems of the world, operating by land and water, is illustrated. The exhibit contains, among many other exceedingly attractive specialities, a working model of the steamboat *Puritan*, a representative steamboat of the Fall River Line—a vessel that has become widely famous in connection with a transportation enterprise widely known upon the face of the earth as an agency unrivaled, and as an epitome of the *progressive* and the *possible* in this *department of world's affairs*.[55]

The Fall River Line might have aggrandized its own role somewhat, but its characterization of steamships as "the epitome of the progressive and the possible" was spot on. No larger machines existed on earth, and none so obviously embodied the technological, social, and even spiritual aspirations of the age. Likewise, the centrality of steam travel within the "department of world affairs" was undeniable. Steamships brought visitors from all over the world to the Columbia Exhibition, to an even greater degree than the Great Exhibition of 1851.

This time, the steamship lines were fully prepared. Cunard Line published a special guide for British passengers visiting the fair, offering helpful advice on railway travel between the company's terminus in New York and the fairgrounds in Chicago. At the back were "useful hints to passengers," including: "A supply of rugs and shawls should be taken for while sitting on deck, and in the matter of dress, plain, useful garments are all that are required on board. It is not usual to dress in the evening for dinner, and dresses made of serge will be quite serviceable." In case the lure of Chicago in February was not enough on its own, passengers were also encouraged that a winter passage on the *Campania* or

Lucania could be "very enjoyable," and in fact "a gale of wind forms a pleasant incident in an Atlantic voyage, and few travelers would like to cross the Atlantic without seeing one of the grandest and most beautiful sights of ocean travel, an Atlantic storm." Indeed. For slugabeds who weren't moved by bracing winds or lashing spray, Cunard thoughtfully catered to them as well:

> A new feature aboard Campania & Lucania . . . is the addition of large and well-ventilated entertaining rooms, drawing room, library and smoking room en suite, so that a passage can be made under the pleasantest conditions without ever going on deck.[56]

By this time, few would have remembered or cared about the *Great Britain*, which after thirty years' hard labor had ground herself again, this time off the Falkland Islands. The spectacles at Bristol, London, and New York were as far removed from the Victorian consciousness as crinolines and stovepipe hats. But the debt owed to her by the exhibitions, and the steamship firms themselves, went on. Steam was spectacle, and from her advent until well into the next century, no liner could be launched without pomp and ceremony, nor assume preeminence among its peers unless it was proclaimed the largest, fastest, grandest— "astounding" or "a floating palace." Exhibitions and World's Fairs were periodic reminders of the ships' centrality within western society, their combined allegorical roles as unifier of peoples and embodiments of human ingenuity. The strain this placed on engineers, however, was increased manifold even from that of Brunel and the *Great Britain*. Now with technology enshrined, as it were, at the very heart of the western world, steamships had to impress on an even vaster scale. And thus the *Great Eastern* was conceived.

. . .

One of the most discussed pieces amongst the collection on display at the Great Exhibition was an allegorical vase crafted by Messrs. Elkington of Birmingham. Representing the triumph of science and industrial arts, Prince Albert stands at the summit, rewarding prizewinners, as Newton, Bacon, Shakespeare, and James Watt look on. At the base, writhing in anguish, are Rebellion, Hatred, and Revenge.[57] The allegory was apt. John Scott Russell, frozen out of the Great Exhibition and denied his true share of credit, was desperate for the chance to regain prestige. Russell returned to what he knew best: ships. He also solicited the help of the century's greatest engineering mind, his colleague Isambard Brunel, and together in the fall of 1851 they began to draft the plans for a kind of floating Great Exhibition that would revive Russell's reputation and solidify Brunel's. With the debacle of the *Great Britain* still in the public mind, it could be truly said that both men felt they had something to prove.

Luckily, Russell found a co-conspirator with the same brilliance and disregard for shibboleths as himself. "The wisest and safest plan in striking out a new path," Brunel wrote Russell in an early letter, "is to go straight in the direction that we believe to be right . . . without yielding in the least to any prejudices now existing."[58] Brunel was no stranger to Old Guard obstructionism. His projected Great Western Railway provoked furious opposition amongst the peerage who asserted, among other things, that it would encourage pederasts to travel to Eton and prey on little boys.[59] When Brunel offered plans for an iron ship, the *Great Britain*, the Duke of Wellington opined that it would sink like a stone.[60]

Their visions of the *Great Eastern*, however, were different. Still embittered from the Great Exhibition snub, yet fired by its promise, Russell conceived the new vessel as his own Crystal Palace, built by his shipyard as if in response to a dare. This was very much in the spirit of the age. The gentlemen's wager that sent Verne's Phileas Fogg around the world was no more fantastic that the case of publisher James Gordon Bennett who, blackballed from Newport's most exclusive club, purchased the land across the street and built his own. Building the *Great Eastern* would be a similar act of defiance, on a commensurately vaster scale.[61]

Whatever his private motivations, Brunel's conception arose from a logistical and imperial conundrum. The Governor-General of India governed a territory larger than the Roman empire under Augustus. Yet the problem of maintaining such a far-flung dominion was endemic; as early as 1847 the viceroy was predicting its demise: "The administration of all the departments of a great country by a small number of foreign visitors, in a state of isolation . . . can never be contemplated as a permanent state of things."[62] Even as he wrote, imperial management in India was fraying. The first stirrings of rebellion that would eventually bring on the Indian Mutiny of 1857 were already apparent.

The problem was distance. Until the Suez Canal was completed in 1869, it took over a month for a ship to travel from London to Bombay, and another three weeks to reach British possessions in the Pacific. Moreover, ships tasked with maintaining this link were comparatively small and required constant re-coaling throughout the journey. All that coal had to be brought out to colonial resupply ports on other small, slow ships. The British empire was much like the old *Great Britain*: vast, but underpowered.

The depth of this dilemma is to be found in a parliamentary report dated June 5, 1851, one month after the opening of the Great Exhibition. Ponderously titled *First Report from the Select Committee on Steam Communications with India*, it is an extraordinary document. Four separate firms had placed bids for opening steam navigation to India, China, and Australia. Like Penelope's suitors, they appeared before the committee and made the best case they could. Eastern Steam offered a fleet of paddle liners; the Pacific Steam Packet Company promised screw-powered steamers of 1,000 tons and 200-horsepower; the unlovely-named Screw Steam Navigation Company upped the ante with screw-driven ships "1,400 or 1,700" tons; P&O smugly offered its bid "but without mentioning the class of vessel they propose to employ."[63]

The committee, composed mostly of amateur engineers and professional politicians, was rather boggled. Six hundred pages of testimony from sea captains, colonists, tea traders, and so on seemed designed to elicit basic facts: How long did it take to reach India? Would a paddle steamer take less time? Was a screw steamer faster than paddles? How much coal would be needed for the crossing? How many emigrants could each ship take? "Do you find," the committee asked one colonist, "that when emigration is going steadily, there is a great increase of emigrants to those colonies?" Well, yes, said the bemused Australian. More ships could certainly take more people. Another member ventured on trickier ground. "Are you aware that the tender for this line has been proposed by screw steamers?" Yes, the man answered. "And are you aware that those vessels are said to be better adapted for conveying goods and emigrants than paddle steamers?" Yes, the answer came. "It appears probable that that will be the case."[64]

It was clear what kind of answers the committee was hoping for. Mr. Frederick J. Moore, a former sea captain in the Antipodes, gave them just what they wanted, and in so doing provided a fascinating glimpse at the rapidity with which steam had spread around the world:

[Sir John Hogg] Do you think the trade and commerce of Australia and New Zealand, with the mother country, and with India, are now of such an extent, and increasing to such a degree, as to render both communications practicable?

[Mr. F. J. Moore] Yes I do; quite necessary to their welfare, and I think also that we should not have a regular communication by steam established there for three years before the traffic would be nearly doubled; such is the advantage to be derived from steam communication to those colonies. I remember, 12 years ago in Sydney there was scarcely a steamer to be seen; but when I returned to it, after considerable absence, I found that every hour, almost, there were steamers running out of Sydney harbor along the coast . . . and towns are springing up along the whole coast of Australia in consequence that would never have been formed but for the facility of steam intercourse.[65]

The imaginations of the committeemen were fired. They envisioned a fleet of screw-driven iron-hulled steamers scything through the waves, connecting India and Australia ever closer to the mother country. An unlikely witness poured cold water on these fantasies: none other than Captain Christopher Claxton, former master and shareholder of the *Great Britain*. His testimony was invaluable, for no one—with the exception of Isambard Brunel—knew more about screws and iron than he. But, as it turned out, he knew too much. "The *Great Britain* was a steamer which was propelled by a screw, was it not?" the Committee asked him. "What was her primary motive power?" In other words, what was her top horsepower? "We never worked up to that," Claxton answered grimly. "The boilers were deficient. . . . I believe she was worked very nearly up to [full] power when she ran ashore on Dundrum Bay."[66]

One can imagine a heavy silence following this exchange. When asked about her iron hull, Claxton was more enthusiastic, yet his answers still carried the weight of failed dreams: "She [the *Great Britain*] lay for 12 months with large holes in her bottom, one of which you might drive a wheelbarrow through. . . . She was perfectly capable of being repaired; her upper works were not injured in the slightest degree, and the iron . . . not at all the worse for it."[67]

The most damaging testimony came, however, when the committee shared with Claxton the various proposals for inaugurating steam transport to India. Claxton unequivocally scoffed at them. The *Great Britain*, twice as large as any other vessel (including those proposed), had been put on the Liverpool–Australia run. Yet even she was too small to maintain regular service and needed frequent re-coaling en route. A ship of 1,200 tons—in other words, half her size—would require almost twice as many stops. But "with regard to the *Great Britain*," a committee member protested, "should you argue conclusively that what you have not been able to do in her you would not be able to do in other ships? Have there been no improvements introduced since she was built?" Certainly there had, Claxton confirmed. Ferryboats and naval destroyers were zipping along on screws; "but I am speaking of a very heavy screw with a large ship of 1,800 tons."[68]

In other words, the oversized, underpowered *Great Britain* proved that technology simply did not exist in 1851 to facilitate such transport.

In the end, the committee recommended dividing the route between multiple carriers and allowing the free market to determine the best:

The Committee also stated their conviction that any arrangement which might tend to promote an exclusive traffic on the Indian lines, in the hands of one company, was open to serious objection, and in the recommendation which they suggested for the Government they wished to lay down the principle that the only security to the public for the full advantage by these communications must be open and fair competition.[69]

Had this been done, the directors of the Great Eastern Steam Navigation Company later claimed, "the public would, years ago, have had the advantage of a far superior class of vessels to any hitherto constructed, the value of which, in the case of the Indian mutiny, would have been incalculable."[70] Instead, despite the committee's recommendation, the British government chose to grant its mail commission exclusively to Peninsular & Orient Lines—which hadn't even submitted a completed bid. It was not entirely unexpected: P&O was the only firm to have any ships already extant and had pioneered steam travel to the Mediterranean and elsewhere. Nevertheless, other companies cried favoritism, including the director of Eastern Steam, Mr. Henry Thomas Hope. Despite having no actual ships, Hope had submitted the lowest bid, and understandably felt that the entire commission of inquiry had been nothing but a sham. "The natural result," Hope and his fellow company directors claimed later, was inevitable: "The [P&O] service has continued to be very inefficiently performed, although the growing requirements of the public have forced on the Peninsular and Orient Company a weekly, instead of semi-monthly, communication."[71]

It was at this point that Mr. Hope, a member of the Great Exhibition directorial board, came into contact with two other members: John Scott Russell and Isambard Brunel. The engineers presented Hope with a unique proposal. Together they would build a ship—one single ship, not a fleet—that would wrest the mail contract back from P&O and establish Eastern Steam's preeminence on the Indian run. Hope accepted with alacrity. For him, as for Russell and Brunel, the *Great Eastern* was an instrument of vengeance.[72] "It was therefore agreed," a memoriam for the company declared later, "in conjunction with several enterprising and influential parties, to reorganize that Company for the express purpose of carrying out the scheme, and the *Great Eastern* steamship was accordingly commenced."[73]

To Christopher Claxton, the lesson of the *Great Britain* was that she was too big; to Isambard Brunel, she was too small. Her failure on the Liverpool–Australia line had nothing to do with her screw, which (he maintained) worked perfectly well. It was simply that she did not carry enough passengers or freight to make such a giant expenditure on coal practicable. This was precisely the problem that Brunel tackled, and his solution had an elegant simplicity. Instead of a fleet of little steamers that needed to stop and refuel constantly, he proposed a single vessel large enough to carry its own coal for the entire journey. Bunkers of such colossal scale meant building a ship of proportional size around them, and hence the final result was a steamship over 700 feet long displacing 22,000 tons and carrying 4,000 passengers; one vessel doing the work of an entire fleet. Fully loaded, she would accommodate enough emigrants and freight to more than pay for the fuel expenditure; indeed, given the figures Brunel presented to investors, she was the cheapest solution possible:

The problem being, as it was, of the highest importance to the interests of *commerce* and the *progress of the human race*, naturally attracted the attention of the scientific and commercial world, and it was at last solved by the projection of a *leviathan ship*, large enough to carry coals for the longest voyage which could be undertaken, and yet with sufficient space to accommodate an enormous number of passengers and cargo. It was found on examination that as the larger the vessel the greater would be the proportionate carrying power, so the cost per ton of a vessel of the size projected would be cheaper than that of an ordinary steamer. This theory has been tested by the construction of the *Great Eastern*.[74]

In a later era such reasoning would be considered perfectly sound: The 85,000-ton *Queen Mary* and *Queen Elizabeth*, which entered service in the 1930s, replaced no less than eight smaller Cunarders. As company chairman Sir Percy Bates explained it to his shareholders in 1930:

The speed is dictated by the time necessary to perform the journey at all seasons of the year. . . . The size is dictated by the necessity to make money providing sufficient saleable passenger accommodation to pay for the speed. In the opinion of its technical advisors . . . the Cunard Company is projecting a pair of steamers which, though they will be very large and fast, are, in fact, the smallest and slowest which can fulfill properly all the essential economic conditions.[75]

That was very well, but in 1851 the idea of combining 4,000 souls into one hull had an almost biblical ring to it: Cunard's flagship, the *Scotia*, displaced a mere

3,871 tons and carried fewer than 800 passengers. Brunel professed himself indifferent to the disparity; for him the mathematics had a beauty of its own:

> As to size, if we are to go around the world, I do not think we can do less than—length, 730; beam, 85; draught deep, 34. . . . The same amount of capital and the same expenditure in money for fuel now required for a line of ships of the present dimensions would build and work ships to carry double the number of passengers, with far superior accommodation, in about half the time, simply by making the vessel *large enough to carry its own coal.*[76]

This was undeniable, yet numbers like these also had an element of the absurd. The cool logic in which they were offered—and the complacency with which Brunel, Russell, and Hope contemplated bringing such a creation into being—have few parallels in human ambition. They were products of the heady, heedless optimism of the Great Exhibition, and they belong to the same genre of fantasy as Jules Verne's Baltimore Gun Club, calmly calculating the gunpowder and initial velocity needed to fire a projectile from the earth to the moon.

3

LEVIATHANS
Ships as Fantasy

IT WAS THE YOUNG FRENCHMAN's first visit to Britain—his first trip anywhere, really—and it had not been a success. Since childhood, his imagination had been fired by the land of Sir Walter Scott's dashing knights errant; now he would see it for himself. He arrived in the summer of 1859 carrying a satchel filled with the great works of English literature and an impossible load of expectations.[1]

England was quick to disappoint. Industrialized and imperial, it had little time for foreigners or their whims. Pub dwellers stared at him with bovine indifference; the gentry were patronizing. His own ignorance did not help. He did not know the difference between England and Scotland. "Ah, the land of Fergus and MacGregor!" he cried, as they passed through the Lake District. His gaze sought ramparts and towers, but the English seemed to have replaced them all with factories. Upon being asked to display the local curiosity to an eager tourist, his hosts brought him to a worked-out coal pit. Steam dredges and rock crushers were scattered around the maw, abandoned, rusting. Jules Verne stared down into the inky darkness and felt as if he was looking into his own soul.

At journey's end, he found himself on the Isle of Dogs. It was not an island at all, but a peninsula jutting out into the Thames a few miles outside London where the East India Company kept its ships. Gray and cheerless, a few scattered sheds crisscrossed by railway ties and littered with maritime detritus, it seemed the very image of all that Verne despised. Then he saw something that captivated him.

Rising over the scrum of the yards, monstrous in scale, was the unfinished hulk of Isambard Brunel's flagship *Great Eastern*. There was nothing else like her anywhere on earth. Conceived in midcentury, she would be unsurpassed in size for almost sixty years. When launched (a process which itself took over a year) she was six times larger than any other vessel afloat: nearly 700 feet long, over 100 feet wide, with 22,500 tons displacement, and designed to carry 4,000 passengers from London to Bombay without stopping once.

But mere recitation of her dimensions cannot convey the full wonder of seeing the *Great Eastern* for the first time. The ship was so vast, so utterly unlike any known form, that she could have dropped down into the mud of Millwall from another world. The fleet of ocean liners she was groomed to supplant all looked alike: wooden hulls, three stubby masts, a single funnel, and paddle boxes slung over their sides. The *Great Eastern* had five funnels, six masts, a screw propeller, *and* a pair of giant paddle wheels large enough to rival the Ferris wheels of half a century later.[2] Most astonishing of all, she was built of iron. The hull rose up in its stocks like a medieval fortress, a solid black wall pocked with hundreds of tiny apertures and joined with over 3 million rivets, each soldered by hand. Her spars would carry 6,500 cubic feet of sail, more than the biggest clipper ever launched.[3] Just as her older sister had originally borne the name *Mammoth* before cooler heads prevailed, the public and the builders dubbed the new ship *Leviathan* after the sea monster described in the Book of Job.[4] The comparison was apt. Gazing at the giant ship testing her engines, Verne might easily have called to mind the biblical allusion:

His back has rows of shields tightly sealed together;
each is so close to the next that no air can pass between.
They are joined fast to one another; they cling together and cannot be parted.

His snorting throws out flashes of light; his eyes are like the rays of dawn.
Firebrands stream from his mouth; sparks of fire shoot out.
Smoke pours from his nostrils as from a boiling pot over a fire of reeds.
His breath sets coals ablaze, and flames dart from his mouth.[5]

Observers would struggle for decades to find the right words to convey the awesomeness of the spectacle. Most failed. *The Shipbuilder* devoted an entire series to cataloguing the *Great Eastern*'s innovations, everything from her steam-powered tiller to the patented lifeboat davits, and ended up floundering in minutiae. Only poets, apparently, could do her justice. Henry Wadsworth Longfellow contributed: "Sublime in its enormous bulk/ Loomed aloft the shadowy hulk."[6] But the pithiest and most accurate description came from Herman Melville, who visited the *Great Eastern* in 1857 and knew something about ships. "Vast toy," he wrote in his diary. "No substance. Durable materials but perishable structure. Won't exist a hundred years hence."[7]

To Jules Verne, however, it seemed as though the giant ship would last forever. Gazing at her through the plate glass of the railway carriage, he made two resolutions: first, to write a novel that conveyed the wonder of the technological marvel he had just witnessed; second, to travel aboard the *Great Eastern* himself.[8]

Both would take almost a decade, but both would come to pass.

. . .

Throughout the planning and construction of the *Great Eastern*, Isambard Brunel's attitude remained that of a disinterested engineer devising logical solutions to a perceived problem. Since that problem was the possible demise of the British empire, the solutions were correspondingly dramatic. Brunel never intended his ship to be singular; if successful as he envisioned, she would inspire a fleet of similar vessels. Such ships could become the lifelines of empire, maintaining regular contact between Britain and her possessions around the world. "Vessels much larger than have been previously built could be navigated with great advantage from the mere effect of size,"[9] he wrote in one of the many circulars sent out to drum up investment.

It would take a year and a half to raise sufficient funds, and another year of planning. Construction began in the fall of 1854 and almost immediately stopped, as Brunel submitted revisions. Nor were his the only ones. From the outset Brunel tried to share the burden of designing the great ship and called upon all the prominent engineers of the age. The James Watt Company contributed the steam engines, and Professor Piazzi Smith, Queen Victoria's Astronomer Royal, designed the gyroscope. This brain trust also helped assuage the fears of would-be investors (especially those with long memories of the *Great Britain*) as one of Brunel's early letters attests:

Practical men concur with me, not merely in the practicability of constructing the vessel, but in the great advantage as regards speed, seaworthiness and safety resulting merely from increased size. . . . On the mechanical part I offer my own opinion, and may quote those of the first practical men of the day—Messrs. Maudslay, Watt, and J. Scott Russell, all of whom have assisted me in the project.[10]

This suggested harmony among the "practical men," yet none prevailed. Just as he had watched the directors of the Great Exhibition edge him out of the way, Russell now saw the *Great Eastern* become a creature of Isambard Brunel. Having already laid the keel plates and begun framing, the whole project ground to a halt when Brunel suddenly recommended a double bottom. It was a sensible innovation—a sort of ship-within-a-ship that was well ahead of its time—but it meant more delays, more money.[11] Then another delay, when Brunel experimented with the cellular construction he had patented for box girders. The engineer fired off these revisions by courier from London, where he was planning another rail line. Russell, looking out his soot-stained window at the iron hulk, gave way to despair: "I have *slaved* to get these specifications ready..."[12]

Construction went on, haltingly, sometimes pausing for months at a time as Brunel and Russell quarreled. At one point Brunel accused the contractor with stealing 900 tons of iron from the project, a very serious charge. Russell was incensed, yet it might well have been true. Members of the Great Exhibition had accused him of lying and falsifying documents; there was always something rather dodgy about John Scott Russell. For his part, Brunel resented the contractor taking credit for innovations that were rightly Brunel's, especially when everyone knew where the blame would lie if the project failed: "Everybody understands the proposed large steamer to be 'Brunel's absurd big ship.'"[13]

And still the memoranda kept coming. Some were unwittingly funny, giving insight into a very preoccupied mind: "August 7. Memoranda for engines. There can be no reason why a sensitive governor should not act in less than one revolution of a crank, or two such governors, one to each end ... to give elasticity. Query hydraulic governors?"[14]

Meanwhile—as it had been for the *Mammoth*, and as if they had learned nothing from past experiences—the promotion campaign for the *Great Eastern* was hard at work. The great question seemed to be what to do with the ship once she was built. It was all very well to stretch technology to its limits, and gratifying no doubt for "the progress of the human race" (as one of its promoters termed it), but, to paraphrase the New York papers on the *Great Western*, could the *Great Eastern* be made to pay?

Her owners assured the public she could. A showy and very expensive pamphlet, *All About the* Great Eastern, complete with illustrations, appeared in W. H. Smith booksellers throughout England and in every railroad station and depot. In a section entitled "The Commercial Prospects of the *Great Eastern*," it purported to offer hard evidence of future profits. "Now, should the great ship fulfill only the most moderate of the anticipations as to her rate of speed," it declared, "it is safe to predict that a total revolution will be effected in the commerce of the world." What would this look like exactly? At the risk of boring its readers, the pamphlet offered a few speculative figures:

On each voyage outward, if the steamer took 10,000 tons of cargo at £5 per ton, the returns in one year would be £600,000; and on each homeward voyage, if she carried the same quantity at £10 per ton (the back freights being more costly in proportion), the annual returns would be £1,200,000. On her carriage of goods alone, therefore, we have £1,800,000 as the gross annual receipts. From first class passengers, reckoning five hundred a month, outward and homeward, paying an average of £90 each, the proceeds would be £1,080,000 . . .[15]

If the modern eye tends to glaze over reading passages like these, it is likely the contemporary one did as well. But even if one did not read it word for word, the numbers—and the multiplicity of zeroes attached to them—were eloquent enough. Yet even more significant than her commercial prospects were her political ones. In the wake of the Indian Mutiny (which Henry Hope and the directors of the Great Eastern Steamship Company maintained never would have happened, had their initial proposal to government been successful), it was imperative that the British raj be constantly resupplied, rearmed, and manned. The *Great Eastern* could do all that, and more. In effect she could become the lifeline of empire:

Why, here is a vessel which can carry a whole *corps d'armee*—infantry, cavalry, and artillery, with all their horses and material. Ten thousand men could be landed in perfect efficiency at any point of danger, ready to step from the deck to the field. Young recruits could be drilled on the voyage, and even taught to march, with tolerable steadiness. Raw militiamen, possessed only of the goose-step at sailing, would arrive perfect warriors at their destination. Here, then, we have a floating fortress, camp, and parade ground all in one. . . . Here we have the means to bind together our too-much scattered dominion—to make one and indivisible our worldwide empire.[16]

There is an audible swagger to these words. The great ship that arrives like a monster from the deep and disgorges her seasoned troops into the fray is a vision of almost Vernian fantasy, yet later decades would prove the efficacy of the author's claims. In the Second World War, giant steamers like the *Queen Mary* and *Queen Elizabeth* carried up to 15,000 troops per crossing and drilled them on deck just as they might have done on the *Great Eastern*. Winston Churchill claimed the *Queens* shortened the war in Europe by a year.[17] But for Victorian readers, the military purpose of the *Great Eastern* could only be solidifying Britain's grasp on her empire, and "the old cliché" of annihilating space took on a new and darker twist:

Our isolated possessions, instead of being sources of weakness, will be elements of strength to the general centre. Our insularity will in effect be annihilated, and we shall acquire a military position corresponding to the extent of our dominion and the numbers and greatness of our race.[18]

The cumulative effect of these claims was a hundredfold that of the old *Great Britain*. Now the spectacle of the ship not only incorporated mankind's progress but Britain's absolute technological, moral, and political superiority, and visions of international amity were replaced with those of imperial domination. The *Great Eastern*, in short, came to symbolize the British empire itself.

Finally, on November 3, 1857, the ship was ready for launch. Her length precluded a conventional tail-first slide into the Thames, so Brunel rigged a curious sideways drop that would immerse the whole vessel at once. It might have worked, had he not also directed—unaccountably—to launch the iron ship on iron rails. Greased wood had minimum friction and maximum give, allowing it to bend as the mass of the ship slid over. Iron had none of these advantages. "We are going to move 11,000 tons, a far greater weight than was ever moved before," Brunel wrote. "There are great strains we have to deal with, but they must be had, and therefore we must meet them boldly."[19] John Scott Russell was unconvinced. Regarding the imminent launch, he predicted, "I don't think there will be any *spectacle*."[20]

Russell was wrong. The company directors decided that the ship, long delayed, had to reintroduce herself to an indifferent public. Thousands of invitations were sent out, reaching everyone from the Prince Consort to the ambassador of Siam. The press machine churned out commemorative leaflets, programs, and a piece of patriotic puffery called "The Leviathan March."[21] Over 20,000 observers came for the ceremony, from day-trippers to the Comte de Paris. As one observer wrote:

A vast concourse of people assembled on land and river to witness the launch. Crowds of naval and scientific men from all parts of the world were there, and, in spite of the inclement season of the year, numerous members of the aristocracy came to see this marvelous feat; nor indeed was royalty, itself, unrepresented. Probably no such multitude had on any previous occasion congregated on the banks of the Thames. It was a magnificent sight, but one, also, the practiced eye could not survey without apprehension of danger.[22]

Brunel was shocked and aghast. No one told him of these plans until the last possible moment, probably to forestall the explosion that occurred. "In the midst of all this anxiety, I learned that all the world had been invited to 'The Launch.' It was not right, it was cruel; and nothing but a sense of necessity of calming all feelings that could disturb my mind enabled me to bear it."[23]

Hydraulic rams were positioned on the ship's side, and steam tugs with heavy chains waited in the river. Timber cradles supported iron rails, upon which were

120 iron rollers greased with lard. At a signal from Brunel the daughter of the company director smashed the obligatory bottle of champagne, and with a blast of a steam whistle the hydraulic rams began to push. "A tremendous cheer then burst from the excited multitude," as all over the yard there arose an uncanny shriek, the sound of metal grinding against metal. The hull bit into the rails, and the ground shook as they grappled. First the stern swung out, then the bow followed. The *Great Eastern* traveled about 100 feet, a third of the distance, before grinding to a halt. "A whisper passed amongst the dense crowd," a witness reported. "Every eye was now directed towards the cradles, but this time they did not stir an inch, and, as the chains tightened, it became too apparent that if the vessel was not forced toward the water they must break."[24] After a few hours, disappointed spectators began to drift away.[25] "Great mortification," wrote the editors of *Scientific American*, "was experienced."[26]

The ship remained there, heeled over and ludicrous, for an excruciating year. The company directors had got their publicity, and the ship was indeed a spectacle—but not the kind desired. People began to crack jokes. "Shrewd practical men, while envying the superabundant wealth of the shareholders, and admiring their boldness in investing in her as a commercial undertaking with so questionable a chance of profit, quietly sneered at the futile attempts to launch the leviathan."[27] Even the *Times,* not known for its levity, poked a little gentle fun at their expense:

> The shareholders stand round in solemn silence, witnessing the awful silent contest for the visible effects of the invisible struggle, as the hours and days roll on and on, and small indeed and gradual is their fruit. There she lies on the very bank of the noble river which is to convey her to the ocean, but she will not wet her lips.[28]

Finally the exhausted company could withstand no more. Investors fled, and the *Great Eastern* went up for auction. The Great Eastern Steam Navigation Company gave way to the Great Ship Company, a transition in nomenclature laden with meaning. The new owners promptly abandoned any thought of India, for which the ship had been designed, and determined instead that she should become the largest liner on the transatlantic trade. Now the focal point was not the maintenance of empire but the "spectacle" of the ship herself. The abortive launch had already proven her to be an even bigger curiosity than the *Great Britain*, and her owners decided to capitalize on that fact.

But as a venture it was doomed from the start. Samuel Cunard had already shown that what determined success on the Atlantic was neither size nor speed, but ubiquity and reliability. Cunard ships might be dumpy, but there were lots of them and they didn't sink. Moreover, as Brunel himself had written, "The full advantage of the great coal capacity for long voyages would not be felt in short voyages, for example, to New York."[29] This was ironically echoed in a promotional pamphlet written for the now-defunct Great Eastern Steam Navigation Company, which unaccountably appeared after the sale to the Great Ship Company and predicted a glowing future for the *Great Eastern* on the Indian route, which was no longer contemplated:

At first sight it may appear that a vessel of 22,000 tons, carrying 8,000 tons of cargo, is too large for any existing line of traffic; that she will be unable to procure the necessary amount of freight out and home to ensure a profit; and that no markets are to be found large enough to supply her demands and consume her importations. It may be admitted that there are not many paths of commerce in which the great ship could possibly travel; yet there is one line and one traffic, at least, which offer the most favorable prospects even to a vessel the size of the *Great Eastern*. That traffic is trade to the East.[30]

By 1859 a tone of desperation crept into the memoranda of the Great Ship Company. The vessel was finally launched, reluctantly, and Brunel canceled all his other projects to see it through to completion. His irascibility and perfectionism were never more debilitating. Also, he was dying. In 1858 he contracted Bright's disease and was forced to leave England for a long sojourn in Egypt, searching for a cure. He returned no better. The day before her sea trials, Brunel came for a last inspection, posed for a photograph from the London Stereoscope Company, and fell over with a stroke. Many said the ship had killed him, including his son and biographer, Isambard Brunel Jr.: "The difficulties which he had to encounter certainly were neither fewer nor less vexatious than those which had arisen at earlier periods in her history; but they were the last with which he had to contend."[31]

England mourned, and in that spirit the *Great Eastern* made ready for her first transatlantic voyage. Finally moving on her own accord, she seemed momentarily to live up to the awesomeness her designers and promoters had promised:

When, therefore, the chains were cast off, their weight caused them to quit the ship with surprising velocity, and to emit not so much a shower of sparks as a perfect blaze of flame, accompanied by a roar that must have been heard almost as far as the tolling of the great Westminster bell. It is hardly an exaggeration to say that they announced, as with a salvo of artillery, that the *Great Eastern* was free.... The spectacle appeared to afford the multitude, who lined both banks of the river, the liveliest gratification, for they cheered with a lustiness and a perseverance that have seldom been exceeded.[32]

Nevertheless, a series of freak accidents and fatalities, some of which might otherwise have been blamed on the unwieldiness of the ship, were added to Brunel's funeral cortège. Off Hastings, her first time in open sea with a handful of reporters and company men on hand, an explosion shook the fo'c'sle and sent the forward funnel rocketing into the air. Three crewmen died, including one who had thrown himself overboard to escape the blaze and was consumed horribly by the paddle wheel. A few weeks later the ship's master, Captain Harrison, drowned along with the coxswain and ship's surgeon when their gig overturned in a harbor squall. Fires, drownings, mechanical accidents, and other calamities dogged the *Great Eastern*; one author put the final death tally at twenty-two. There was even a rumor making the rounds of two joiners, father and son, who had been sealed in the ship's double bottom and whose ghostly hammering could be heard throughout her career.[33]

Nothing could be less propitious for a maiden voyage than a rumor that the ship was cursed. Company directors did all they could to counterbalance the bad publicity, sending her up to London and then to Holyhead to be exhibited to the multitudes like a three-headed calf. The maiden voyage was delayed, then delayed again. People began to wonder whether the *Great Eastern* would sail at all, especially after it was discovered that the Great Ship Company had fired the majority of the ship's crew but kept the brass band and photographer.[34]

Disenchantment had not yet reached America, where preparations for the "big ship" were ongoing. Eight cities bid to become the *Great Eastern*'s terminus, but the unlikely winner was Portland, Maine. The little town was ecstatic and built the $125,000 Victoria Pier to accommodate her. Then at the last moment the Great Ship Company changed its mind and opted for New York instead. The next piece of news was that the maiden voyage, rescheduled for June 2, was delayed again until June 23, 1860. The *New York Times* concluded grimly, "It is quite doubtful whether she will come at all. The whole career of this gigantic ship seems to have been one gigantic blunder."[35] The *Great Eastern* hadn't even sailed, and editors were already writing of her in the past tense.

She finally did sail, with a handful of curious passengers, and some doubts were laid to rest. The ship crossed in respectable if not remarkable time, taking advantage of calm summer seas. Her reception in New York was everything the promoters hoped it would be and helped recoup some of the financial losses incurred by the maiden voyage. New Yorkers came aboard and were amazed. Yet there was a

FIGURE 4. The *Great Eastern* at speed. Notice the diminutive size of the craft around her. SOURCE: Library of Congress LC-DIG-pga-00795.

sideshow quality to this amazement, which even such an august press as *Scientific American* could not help but perceive. In opening their description of the vessel, they began, "The 'leviathan' steamship arrived at this port on the 28th of June, and her appearance in our waters has created a much greater national excitement than the pow-wow got up for the recent reception of 'John Japan' and his boy 'Tommy.'" What followed was an extended disquisition on the mechanics of the ship, such as one might expect from an engineering journal, yet it closed with a kind of *cri du coeur* that was as accurate and poignant as it was, in its way, prescient:

Although we cannot but regard the *Great Eastern* as a failure in *payability,* yet she is not so in a scientific sense. She is a grand experiment; and the knowledge which has been acquired in her construction, we do not doubt, will enable Scott Russell now to build a superior vessel of like dimensions at nearly one-half the cost. Some persons have said that she would be the last big ship that would be built, and that vessels from two to three thousands tons are most suitable, all things considered. We entertain, however, different opinions.[36]

The editors of *Scientific American* seemed ready to write the ship off as a failed, albeit fascinating, prototype. But for her owners she still had to turn a profit, and that meant propagating the fiction that her "maiden voyage" was but the beginning of a long and successful career. Accordingly, on the Fourth of July, 1860, the whole vessel was thrown open as a giant carnival. It was an anxious hilarity: Secession of the southern states seemed imminent, and the Old South's commercial and cultural ties to Britain were causing concern. The *Great Eastern*—bedecked in red, white, and blue bunting—was a reassuring sight. George Templeton Strong was among the thousands that came on that day, and wrote in his diary "the huge cylinders and piston rods are awful to behold." He meant full of awe. Strong also mentioned, in passing, that the ship was much dirtier than he expected.[37]

This was not to be wondered at. Buried in the files of the New York Historical Society is a tiny survivor of that occasion, titled the "Visitor's Hand Book, or How to See the *Great Eastern*." It is a grimy little booklet, smaller and thinner than a passport, printed on cheap paper with smudged ink. Spelling and syntax errors abound ("Herr is the Wheel..."). On the back cover is a rather dismal advertisement: "CLOTHING: at Greatly Reduced Prices.... This immense summer stock, the last we shall offer in this stand, will be closed out at a great reduction of prices as we have concluded to clear out our entire stock before removal." The bargain-basement aura carries on within the pamphlet itself. It brings guests on a walking tour of the ship, anticipating their route and explaining each room and implement along the way.

Some are of more obvious interest than others. "You have purchased your ticket," the pamphlet begins, "and, by means of a wide and commodious gangway, enter THE CARGO SPACES."[38] Moving rapidly on, the tourist passes by the main deck, funnels, steering apparatus, cable deck, officer's quarters, and main mast, all before finally arriving at the purpose of the trip: the ship's public areas. Rather oddly, they begin with the "SECOND CLASS BATHROOMS," which the booklet assures its readers offer "hot and cold water, salt or fresh, as the bather may choose." But the rest of Second Class is left to their imaginations: "The second class saloon was entirely destroyed at the time of the explosion, and it has not yet been refitted in its former style."[39] Passing on from this rather shocking display of honesty (a far cry from the "pardon our dust" placards of today), the tourist finally encounters the grand saloon. The guide, which had heretofore displayed surprising restraint in describing the ship's appointments, completely let itself go:

Mirrors are placed at the side of the saloon, and on each of them are Arabesque paintings, with children personifying the arts and sciences connected with the building and navigation of the ship. There are portieres of rich crimson silk to all the doorways, and the carpet adds to the general effect. The sofas are covered with rich Utrecht velvet, and the buffets are of walnut wood, richly carved, the tops being made of green marble. This saloon is lighted and ventilated at the sides by large openings, railed off with gilt balustrades, and reaching to the upper deck where there are skylights which can be let up or down as required.[40]

This sounded very grand, but it had been copied word for word from the earlier *All About the* Great Eastern guide, published in London. In fact, the room was already rather threadbare, much of its furniture tattered or lost. The juxtaposition between the noble aspirations of the space as described and the commercial realties that the pamphlet represents was nothing less than heartbreaking. More indicative of the current state of things was a song making the music hall rounds in New York, sung by a minstrel in blackface:

> I went down to the dock, and walk'd on board de steamer—
> It's de greatest one I eber saw—I golly, she's a screamer;
> They took me in de engine room, and I set the works in motion,
> De wheels flew round, de biler bust, I landed in de ocean.
> Chorus—O, my, O de great big steamer all de go,
> O dear, O, the captain he's some pumpkins too,
> Nip up, skid a ma dink, boop de do den do.[41]

For as long as the *Great Eastern* remained in New York, she was a sensation, drawing crowds and revenue. She even attracted satellites: Hawkers and prostitutes roamed the piers, a giant barracks known as the Great Eastern Hotel rose with horrifying speed nearby, sideshow barkers displayed such kindred freaks as Old Adams's Dancing Grizzlies and the 500-pound woman. This highlighted an essential truth. The lure of the *Great Eastern,* like that of the Great Exhibition—indeed, of any spectacle—was ephemeral. Once the initial awe of the crowds was sated, it was time to move on. The *Times* unerringly put the arrival of the ship in the category it belonged:

This summer we have already had the Japanese, are now in ecstasies over the *Great Eastern,* have the arrival of the Benecia Boy to look forward to next week, and are promised the Prince of Wales and Prince Napoleon. We must not and cannot get into hysterics over them all.[42]

Sensing their moment had passed, the Great Ship Company prepared to leave. But no thought was given to a return transatlantic voyage; instead, the company sold excursion tickets for an overnight trip to Old Point Comfort, Virginia. It was a fiasco, with overbooked cabins, shortages of drinking water and food, and gangs of toughs that roused people out of their beds and demanded, with the ruthless gaiety of deranged cruise directors, whether they had "had their ten dollars' worth of fun."[43] If not, they were dragged up on deck to find it. When the ship arrived in Virginia the crew treated southern visitors to a rousing selection of songs from *Uncle Tom's Cabin*, which had been recast as a musical and was all the rage in London.

Down in de cornfield
Heah dat mournful sound:
All de dark-eyes am a-weeping,
    Massa's in de cold, cold ground.

The South had likely not been so rocked since nullification. The *Great Eastern* left hurriedly and returned to New York, where she again tried to play off her status as the Eighth Wonder. But New Yorkers, true to their nature, were becoming jaded. It was the height of the summer season, and other amusements had come to town. Plus there was the general sense that even as a sideshow, the ship failed. "We do not part with her with very much regret," *Harper's Weekly* commented. Her management was "grossly inefficient, the ship dirty, the officers and crew discourteous and rude, and Americans who made helpful suggestions were ignored and insulted." So much for transatlantic brotherhood. The *Times* was even colder: "The *Great Eastern* has returned to the city and is advertised to start immediately for Annapolis Roads. Don't go."[44]

With no other option, the company finally tried to run the *Great Eastern* as a transatlantic liner. But the Civil War reduced passenger loads to a trickle, and the ship was ruinously expensive to keep up. Mechanical failures arose on every voyage—some trivial, others catastrophic—and the only man who really understood them was buried in Kensal Green. A wild storm in September 1861 ripped off the paddle boxes, funnels, rigging, and lifeboats and disabled the rudder. The ship rolled to an angle of 45 degrees, throwing passengers and furniture around for hours.[45] The *Great Eastern* drifted for an entire week until temporary repairs allowed her to reach Queenstown.

Not long after, the Great Ship Company folded. The liner was passed around for years afterward, sometimes engaged in charter work—trooping voyages, laying the transatlantic cable in 1866—other times languishing for years in whatever backwater was large enough to hold her. John Scott Russell, who lived to 1882, refused to visit. But as if determined to remind him of other failures, the planning committee for the Great Exhibition in 1852 moved the Crystal Palace to its permanent home in Sydenham, right down the road from his house.

By 1866 the ship had reached nadir. One observer saw her in the River Mersey, "transformed as a speculation by a syndicate into a floating palace, concert hall and gymnasium ... a deplorable exhibition which would have broken the heart of Mr. Brunel."[46] Then came a reprieve, of sorts. That "syndicate" offered her for lease to the Emperor Napoleon III, to ferry Americans to his forthcoming Paris exhibition. Allegedly they obtained Napoleon's cooperation by circulating the rumor that Sultan Abdul-Aziz intended to turn the ship into his own personal harem. With 4,000 beds (plus crew) it would have been a formidable one. Napoleon chartered her instead, and spent several million francs restoring the ship. Among other disappointments, the contractors discovered that despite her much-vaunted claims, passenger accommodation had only been completed for 1,500 persons. The rest, the whole of Second and Third Class, was nothing but empty space.[47]

In the spring of 1867 the *Great Eastern* was ready, spotless in fresh paint and looking like a simulacrum of a successful ocean liner. Her first voyage from Liverpool to New York under the Société des Affréteurs du *Great Eastern* attracted a surprising number of prominent passengers. Most of them were Americans; few had any idea of the ship's speckled career. The Société encouraged this ignorance, borrowing Captain Sir James Anderson from Cunard and assembling a patchwork collection of crew filched from other ships, all under strict injunction not to reveal that they were, in fact, cast members. The ruse held, and amongst the throng embarking on board the *Great Eastern* on March 23, 1867, was one man fulfilling a promise made nearly a decade before: Jules Verne. Like the magic lantern, Jules Verne's novels described a world that was almost, but not quite, real. Their success lay in their plausibility, cultivated through the same wearisome catalogue of statistics and dimensions that accompanied any genuine scientific endeavor.

Verne's voyage on the *Great Eastern* rightly belongs to this category. Though actual, it was conveyed as a novel set aboard a mechanical marvel filled with unlikely coincidences and star-crossed lovers. Later readers would arbitrarily divide the story in twain, separating Verne's description of his own experience on the ship (fact) from the love triangle involving Ellen Drake, her villainous husband Harry, and her former love Fabian (fantasy).[48] But this does the author an injustice. While it is certain no duel ever took place between the third and fourth funnels, the fantastical element to *A Floating City* is not its characters but its setting. However actual Verne's experience, the ship herself was never quite "real." She had been called back into being at the whim of an emperor and would return to desuetude not long after. Hence she was a fitting backdrop for the *Floating City*'s improbable plot: a moving city at sea that was no less phantasmagoria in its own way than Impey Barbicane's moon cannon.

The voyage marks a watershed in the history of science as spectacle, halfway between reality and fantasy, aboard a vessel that contained within herself equal parts of both. Verne's depiction of the *Great Eastern* was accurate, down to the pounds psi of torque produced by each of her three engines, yet the overall impression strained credibility. Was it really possible that the ship was "longer than the Pont des Arts," with masts rising "to the height of 207 French feet, which is taller than the spires of Notre Dame"? Was Verne right in describing the upper promenade decks as "two wide streets, or rather boulevards" where passengers "bowed and spoke to each other in passing as formally as if they were walking in Hyde Park"?[49] Jules Verne's task was to convey the colossal scale and technological marvels of the ship without sounding like (as he was) a fabulist. It was precisely this skill he would later employ to depict the *Nautilus* and dozens of other fictional craft.

Verne had not seen the *Great Eastern* since her fitting out in 1859, and his first glimpse was impressive. Most passengers arriving at the pier never saw the whole of the vessel; tied alongside the wharf, she resembled a long black wall with spars. But Verne approached the ship by tender, catching sight of her at anchor in the Mersey. "One would have taken her for a small island," he wrote. "She appeared with her bows toward us, having swung round with the tide; but soon the tender altered course and the whole length of the steamship was presented to our view; she seemed what in fact she was—enormous!"[50]

For all the many thousands of visitors that passed through the *Great Eastern*, surprisingly little account is left of the areas where passengers spent most of their time. Chroniclers wrote of her "awful" engines, the broad open areas on deck, the monstrous paddles, and all the technological gimcracks Brunel had installed. To some extent this reflects their audience, a very masculine one of technical enthusiasts more likely to be enraptured by the ship's gyroscope than the pattern of its damask wallpaper. Consequently few bothered to report that she was beautiful. Thirty years before, Charles Dickens derided the main saloon of Cunard's *Britannia* as "a hearse with windows," and relatively little had changed in the manner of interior decoration since then. Yet with an enormous space to work with, interior designers on the *Great Eastern* created the very first luxury liner. Cabins were twice the size of any other ship, large enough to contain two beds, a rocking chair, washbasin, and a settee that concealed a bathtub with hot and cold running water. (It is impossible to resist mentioning that the next ship to offer a bath in every cabin was the *Caronia* of 1948.)

Public spaces were even more extraordinary. The main lounge featured decorative skylights, golden pillars, velvet couches, and a plethora of mirrors so that loungers could see themselves reflected no less than eight times from a variety of angles. Pen-and-ink renderings depict a vaulted space larger in perspective than the Hall of Mirrors at Versailles, and photographic evidence bears out some of this claim. One image shows a crinolined matron standing in the ship's main saloon; the ceiling rises three times her height. A second depicts the drawing room, much smaller, yet encrusted with gilt on every surface and featuring tufted settees wrapped around decorative pillars.

Verne was no less conscious of his audience's predominant gender (though its median age dropped considerably) and thus spent the majority of his time describing mechanical wonders. One brief sojourn inside was to the smoking room, a male preserve, which he described as "a magnificent apartment with fourteen windows; the ceiling white and gold, and wainscoted with lemon-colored panels."[51] Interestingly, he also noted that carpenters were still at work on the decoration, suggesting that the restoration work (or, more accurately, set designing) was unfinished. Throughout the novel there are oblique hints, often unconscious, that the *Great Eastern* was an unfinished prop with wet paint and paper-mâché trompe l'oeil curling at the edges.

Still, it is Verne's catalogue of engineering marvels that was meant to excite the greatest wonder. First and foremost were the engines, driven like Nemo's *Nautilus* "by some gigantic and mysterious power," yet perfectly tuned: "The engines of the *Great Eastern* are justly considered masterpieces—I was going to say of clockwork, for there is nothing more astonishing than to see this enormous machine working with the ease of a clock."[52] Yet this observation was made while the ship was still mid-river, making its way sedately towards open sea. Verne could only imagine what they would look like then:

With what force must these wooden paddles strike the waves which are now gently breaking over them! What a boiling of water when this powerful engine strikes it blow after blow! What a thundering noise engulfed in this paddle-box cavern, when the *Great Eastern* goes at full speed![53]

Verne would soon discover what so many had before him: that the *Great Eastern* always appeared most puissant when standing still. The giant paddles *looked* impressive, with "wheels measuring fifty-three feet in diameter and 166 in circumference, weighing ninety tons, and making eleven revolutions a minute." That they worked at all was something of a wonder in itself, given their size, and Verne was not above poking a little fun at his own readers and their obsession with technical trivialities:

At this point Cockburn, the statistician, who had not spoken to me the entire voyage, came up and said—

"Do you know, sir, how many turns the wheels have made during our passage?"

"I do not, sir."

"One thousand, seven hundred and thirty-three."

"Ah! Really sir, and the screw?"

"Six hundred and eight thousand, one hundred and thirty."

"I am obliged to you, sir, for the information."

And he left without any farewell whatsoever.[54]

In fact the ship was underpowered, which became clear as they made laborious progress across the Atlantic. A doctor acquaintance described her at dinner as "a giant whose strength is not in proportion to her size; her engines are too feeble for her." Nor was she any more stable than other ships. Brunel believed that she would never roll, her length being greater than the largest recorded wave. That was immediately proven false; few ships ever tossed their passengers about like the *Great Eastern*, due to her great metacentric height. Earlier Verne pictured "her boldness before the powerless sea, her indifference to the billows, her stability in the midst of that element which tosses [other liners] like ship's boats."[55] But once in mid-ocean, in a scene that could have been drawn directly from Charles Dickens's first storm on the *Britannia*, Verne described ascending the saloon stairs on his knees "like a Roman peasant devoutly climbing the steps of the *Scala santa*." The all-knowing doctor claimed to be aboard during the famous 1861 storm when the *Great Eastern* was left adrift, but this is a doubtful coincidence, and so we must wonder whether "Dr. Pitferge" is in fact an invention of Verne's: a sort of Cassandra predicting demise at every turn.

The strength and speed of the *Great Eastern* ultimately failing to impress, the narrator turned his focus to the last undisputed aspect of wonder. "If the *Great Eastern* is not merely a nautical engine, but rather a microcosm, and carries a small world in it, an observer will not be astonished to find . . . all the instincts, follies and passions of human nature."[56] For this analogy to work, there must be many intervening layers between top and bottom, each teeming with graduating scales of humanity.

Jules Verne had identified the *Great Eastern*'s most crucial innovation—not her size or machinery alone, but the fact that she was large enough to contain an entire society. She did not merely contain it, but shaped its collective experience, a perfect meld of science and spectacle wherein the observer is not just viewing the machine but a functioning part of it. In a rare moment of hyperbole, Verne claims the ship "capable of receiving 10,000 passengers, so that out of the 373 principal districts in France, 274 are less populated than this floating sub-prefecture with its average number of passengers."[57] Tragically, the average number of *Great Eastern*'s paying passengers was around 150, not even enough for a hamlet.

Verne took great delight in describing his fellow passengers, creating broad caricatures of the American tourist that would have delighted his readers no less than Mark Twain's ruthless depiction of the "furriners" encountered on his travels, undertaken the same year. Twain found disgust with his shipmates' psalm-singing puritanical fervor, but Verne was amused by the endless religious services offered on the Sabbath, where even the ship's bell seemed to have a religious tone. Americans, it appeared, were both pious and gluttonous. "The Californians certainly distinguished themselves by their proclivity for champagne," Verne wrote primly. "Nearby her husband sat an old laundress, who had found gold in the San Francisco washing tubs, emptying a bottle of champagne in no time; two or three pale, delicate looking young ladies were eagerly devouring slices of red beef." After dinner, as energetic continentals burned off calories by walking the deck, "a few corpulent Americans swung themselves backwards and forwards in their rocking chairs."[58]

A Floating City is sometimes described as a novella, running a short 169 pages. Verne dashed it off while working on another, much larger project, tentatively titled *Voyage Beneath the Waters*. Later revised to *20,000 Leagues Under the Sea*, the novel is redolent with echoes of Verne's earlier journey. Some are explicit: Captain Anderson of the *Great Eastern* is briefly mentioned as a Cunard skipper whose vessel is rammed by the mysterious "monster," and later in the novel M. Aronnax spies a strange object lying on the sea floor:

It was on the 17th of May, about 500 miles from Heart's Content, at a depth of more than 1,400 fathoms, that I saw an electric cable lying on the bottom . . . measuring 2,000 miles in length, and weighing 4,500 tons, which was embarked on the *Great Eastern*.[59]

Other references are subtler. The use of scientific jargon and the endless recitation of dimensions in *20,000 Leagues* intend to convince the reader of the submarine's plausibility. It is a new element in Verne's novels and almost certainly modeled on the dry yet dazzling statistics of the *Great Eastern*. Consider these two passages, side by side. First from *A Floating City*:

[T]his steamship measures 673 feet at the load waterline, between the perpendiculars; the upper deck is 680 feet from stem to stern; that is to say, its length is double that of the largest transatlantic steamers; its width amidships is about 71 feet, and behind the paddles 107 feet.

The hull of the *Great Eastern* is . . . double, and is composed of a number of cells placed between the deck and hold; besides these, thirteen compartments, separated by watertight partitions, increase the security against fire or the inlet of water.[60]

Now Captain Nemo explaining the *Nautilus*:

The length of this cylinder, from stem to stern, is exactly 232 feet, and its maximum breadth is twenty-six feet. . . . Its area measures 6,032 feet; and its contents about 1,500 cubic yards; that is to say, when completely immersed it displaces 50,000 feet of water and weighs 1,500 tons.

. . .

The *Nautilus* is composed of two hulls, one inside, the other outside, joined by T-shaped irons, which render it very strong. Indeed, owing to this cellular arrangement it resists like a block, as if it were solid.[61]

Thus launched, so to speak, Verne's novels came to reflect an endless fascination with the spectacle of steam technology, its limits, and the sheer wonder of observing a machine in motion. His Frenchman's pride in Ferdinand de Lesseps and the opening of the Suez Canal inspired him to speculate on just how swiftly one could circumnavigate the globe. A hint of his next project was contained in the last: Aronnax calls the canal a feat "the ancients dared not undertake," and the misanthropic Captain Nemo agrees: "Yes, M. Aronnax, you have the right to be proud of your fellow countryman. Such a man brings more honor to a nation than great captains."[62]

The result was *Around the World in Eighty Days*, a panegyric to the power of steam. After a brief excursion in a balloon, Phileas Fogg completes the remainder of the journey by rail and steamship, the "wonder" in this case being the ease with which a traveler can make connections even in far-flung ports. Unlike the *Nautilus,* here most of the steamers are factual; as the novel was serialized in the Paris *Temps,* steamship lines offered to "sponsor" Fogg's continuing travels if Verne made mention of them in later chapters. He refused, but the idea reinforced the overlap between fiction and reality.[63] Among the many marvels Fogg experiences en route is the American transcontinental railway, completed in 1869: "New York and San Francisco are thus united by an uninterrupted metal ribbon, which measures no less than three thousand seven hundred and eighty-six miles."[64]

Around the World in Eighty Days captivated the public imagination as no previous work of Verne's had done. This was due in part to the approachability of its conceit: Unlike cannons to the moon or submarines beneath the sea, a transit of the globe in eighty days was theoretically possible to complete in the present, not the distant (or mythic) future. Verne would later attest that the idea came to him from a newspaper, just as it did in Phileas Fogg's Reform Club:

I took up a copy of *Le Siécle* one morning, and found in it a discussion and some calculations showing that the journey around the world might be done in eighty days. The idea pleased me, and while thinking it over it struck me that in their calculations they had not called into account the difference in the meridians and I thought what a denouement such a thing would make in a novel, so I went to work to write one.[65]

Given the practicability of the enterprise, it was inevitable that someone would eventually try to emulate Fogg; given the growing prominence of so-called yellow journalism in the 1880s, it was probably also inevitable it would be a reporter. What was perhaps more unusual was that the reporter was a woman, Nellie Bly. An early proponent of exposé journalism, she had already been thrown out of Mexico for inciting revolution and thrown into a mental asylum at the behest of her boss, Joseph Pulitzer, who wanted to uncover the truth about the living conditions therein. Compared to such horrors, a trip around the world seemed relatively benign. Pulitzer marketed it like a steeplechase, with eager readers tracking her progress from week to week. Yet it was not enough for Ms. Bly to race against the clock. Arriving in Hong Kong, she was curtly informed by the local steamship agent, "You will lose." Asked for further particulars, the man went on, "Aren't you having a race around the world?" Yes, Nellie replied, a race against time. "Time?" the agent answered, befuddled, "I don't think *that* was her name."[66]

In a final inevitability, rival *Cosmopolitan* magazine had dispatched another female journalist, Elizabeth Bisland, to beat Nellie Bly and complete the race in under seventy-five days. Amid a fury of speculation, Bisland narrowly lost.

This race around the world symbolized the combination of steam, wonderment and competitiveness as few other events could. What was most surprising, especially in comparison to Fogg's fraught adventures, was the relative ease with which these women traveled. "I was a young woman, quite alone," Elizabeth Bisland later wrote, "and doing a somewhat conspicuous and eccentric thing, yet throughout the entire journey I never met with other than the most

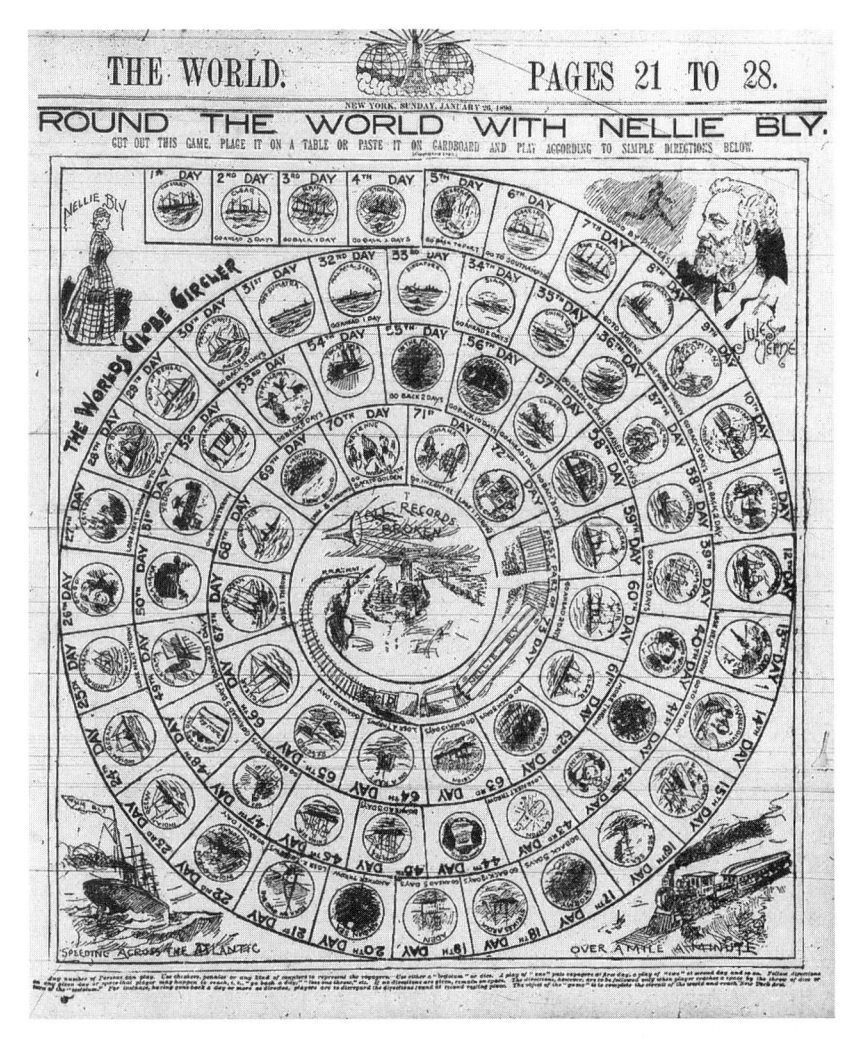

FIGURE 5. Joseph Pulitzer's *World* newspaper avidly followed Nellie Bly's tour around the globe. Here readers are invited to play a dice board game mimicking her adventures. The game is flanked by four crucial figures (*clockwise*): Bly, Jules Verne, a steam train, and a steamship. SOURCE: Library of Congress LC-DIG-ppmsca-02918.

exquisite and unfailing courtesy and consideration; and if I had been a princess with a suite of half a hundred people I could have felt no safer or happier."[67] It was clear she referred as much to the people onboard as those she encountered ashore—indeed, given the speed at which she traveled, she spent hardly any time ashore whatsoever.

Nellie Bly was even more explicit. Travel, which suggested rush and hassle, had been reduced by steam to a kind of gentle, passive indolence:

After dressing I wandered up on the next deck and was told that breakfast was over long ago. I went out on deck, and the very first glimpse of the lazy looking passengers in their summer garments, lounging about in comfortable positions, or slowly promenading the deck, which was sheltered from the heat of the sun by a long stretch of awnings, and the smooth, velvety looking water, the bluest I had ever seen, softly gurgling against the side of the ship as it almost imperceptibly steamed on its course, and the balmy air, soft as a rose leaf, and just as sweet, air such as one dreams about but seldom finds; standing there alone among strange people, on strange waters, I thought how sweet life is![68]

By the time Nellie Bly's account appeared, the *Great Eastern* was already in the process of demolition. Yet the fantastical world that Jules Verne built from the skeleton of the *Great Eastern* was, in a way, inevitable. The ship had always been slightly unreal. In 1858, as the *Great Eastern* lay near completion, Isambard Brunel brought his friend and fellow engineer W. S. Lindsay down for a tour. George Stephenson, inventor of the *Rocket*, joined them. Lindsay looked over the ship, then turned to Brunel and told him he was premature; the world wasn't ready:

Turn her into a show, something to attract the masses . . . she will never pay as a ship. Send her to Brighton, dig a hole in the beach and bed her stern in it, and if well set she would make a substantial pier and her deck a splendid promenade; her hold would make magnificent saltwater baths and her tween decks a superb hotel. . . . She would be a fine attraction for Londoners, who would flock to her in their thousands.[69]

Stephenson laughed, but Brunel never spoke to Lindsay again.

Yet Lindsay was prophetic. After Jules Verne traveled home to France, the *Great Eastern* returned to Liverpool and her former career as a showboat. As late as 1886 visitors could still find her tied to the pier, masts shorn, with "LEWIS'S BON MARCHE . . . LEWIS'S ARE THE FRIENDS OF THE PEOPLE" written in giant white capitals along her sides. To maritime architects she was a pariah. Even as they copied many of Brunel's innovations—the double hull, watertight compartments, placing the public rooms amidships—they gave him scant credit. Only W. S. Lindsay, in his seminal text on the history of merchant shipping, was generous enough to offer a comment for posterity:

But it will hardly be gainsaid that the building, launching, and navigating of such a ship are events in the history of merchant shipping . . . and should my imperfect record survive for the next hundred or fifty years, there may be found in these pages a collection of facts relating to a ship more marvelous than that of Hiero, King of Syracuse, or of the Penteconter of Ptolemy Philopater. . . . For it may be that, a hundred or fifty years hence, the maritime community of the world may have grown to such an extent to justify, with reasonable prospects of profit, another ship of the dimensions of the *Great Eastern*. . . . and perhaps, all that posterity will be able to say against the enterprising promoters of the *Great Eastern* may hereafter be condensed in the flattering eulogium: "their ideas in regard to dimensions were in advance of their age—they were only before their time."[70]

So it was. It would take over fifty years for another ship to exceed the *Great Eastern*'s size, yet that moment came and went unremarked. One early visitor prophesized that she would be "exhibited to our grandchildren as one of the most monstrous crazes of the nineteenth century."[71] Worse than that, she was a warning.

But in another way, the *Great Eastern* fulfilled her destiny. Conceived in the spirit of the Great Exhibition, she was first and foremost a spectacle: a vast, improbable feat of engineering, tangible but not quite real. Underpowered, unbalanced, and ungainly, subject to constant breakdowns, the *Great Eastern* could not have survived repeated transatlantic voyages, much less the long haul to India. Absent that purpose only one remained. Her owners understood and chose to profit by turning her into a "curiosity." Brunel would certainly have blamed them, as he did those who abandoned the *Great Britain*, but they were not wrong. Even her image seemed to convey the magic of 19th-century travel: William Francis Ainsworth's record of his perambulations around the world, published in 1869, featured the *Great Eastern* on its frontispiece, despite the fact that he had never traveled aboard her, and she had never gone farther than New York.[72]

The *Great Eastern* was brought into being to satisfy the Victorian public's relentless desire for wonderment. They wanted to gawk, open-mouthed, at the miracles their society could manifest. This sort of admiration is self-reflexive, as the object becomes merely the mirror through which the viewer regards himself. Pushing the limits of technology reinforced the qualities Victorians most esteemed in themselves: perseverance, genius, and service to the common good. Moreover, it underscored the Whig narrative of human progress towards a utopian end. Looking out at a concourse filled with mechanical wonders, Prince Albert spoke for the age: "Nobody . . . will doubt for a moment that we are living at a period of most wonderful transition, which tends rapidly to accomplish that great era to which, indeed, all history points—the realization of the unity of mankind."[73] What could be a greater harbinger of this unity than a giant steamship, a wonder in its own right, that joined one continent to another?

It was not enough to build the ship. She had to be demonstrated, boasted of, celebrated, but most of all *viewed*. Just as the Great Exhibition helped instill technological utopianism, so did it provide the framework: a public spectacle. In a society so steeped with symbolism that even chamber pots had allegorical scenes painted on them, the particular allegory of the steamship launch was critical. The hull, vast and hollow on the stocks, was seen to hold all the hopes and aspirations of its nation. Conceived for the peaceful task of bringing one culture and people to another, it was the ultimate expression of that nation's goodwill. The launching was a shared, egalitarian experience. In advance of the *Great Eastern* debacle, one London newspaper wrote, "[M]en and women of all classes were joined together in one amicable pilgrimage to the East [of London, an inside joke] for the *Leviathan* was to be launched at Millwall."[74]

Considering this weighty symbolism, it is little wonder the *Great Eastern* never recovered from her disastrous launch, either economically or in reputation. The spectacle had failed. Later attempts to peddle the ship as a marvel of midcentury engineering always fell short: huge she was, and remarkable, but still never much more than a floating, occasionally moving, prop. Visitors might not have realized it, but passengers did. One of those, Jules Verne, exhausted his store of paeans while the ship was still in harbor. The remainder of his voyage was spent alternately seasick, terrified, or underwhelmed (at one point, as the *Great Eastern* flailed helplessly about in a storm, Verne alleges Captain Anderson to have cried "My ship is disgraced!"). Of the return trip he said only: "Twelve days later we reached Brest."[75]

As the *Great Eastern* was part fantasy herself, it does her no disservice to compare the ship with even more fantastical products of the Victorian imagination. They were all born of the same zeitgeist, which no one understood better than Jules Verne. His novels freed technology from the fetters of reality, allowing readers to revel in the mythic possible rather than face disappointment in the actual present. Likewise, his characters served as paradigms for actual men like Brunel and Russell, but without their failures: Impey Barbicane reaches the moon despite Captain Nicholl's naysaying, Phileas Fogg wins his wager at the Reform Club, Captain Nemo constructs his vessel in defiance of the world. Most important, Verne allowed his readers to bypass the disappointments and blind alleys of experimentation and arrive at the final result: the world of tomorrow.

Nevertheless, even if the technological, political, and social realities underpinning the age continued to disappoint, the flights of wonderment inspired by the *Great Britain*, the *Great Eastern,* and the Great Exhibition knew no bounds. Taking a leaf from Jules Verne's book, literally, Mark Twain published a lighthearted advertisement for "A Curious Pleasure Excursion" in 1874. It summed up the boundless optimism of the era, even as it hinted at the absurdity and hucksterism just beneath the surface:

ADVERTISEMENT

This is to inform the public that in connection with Mr. Barnum I have leased the COMET for a term of years; and I desire also to solicit the public patronage in favor of a beneficial enterprise which we have in view.

We propose to fit up comfortable, and even luxurious, accommodation in the comet for as many persons as will honor us with their patronage, and make an extended excursion among the heavenly bodies. We shall prepare 1,000,000 state-rooms in the tail of the comet with hot and cold water, gas, looking-glass, parachute, umbrella, etc . . .[76]

4

HONOR AND GLORY CROWNING TIME
Disaster Sermons and the Cult of Technology

THE CLOCK. Two Grecian figures stand on either side: one holding a palm branch, a symbol of praise, the other resting her foot on a polished sphere, a symbol of domination. The plinth is supported by griffins, guardians of treasure. Vines and clusters of fruit, traditionally signifying sex and fecundity, are more likely just filler for the unadorned frame. Honor holds a tablet and appears to be writing something upon it, perhaps the ship's name. A laurel wreath rests at the feet of Glory, ready to be placed upon the timekeeper's brow.[1]

The *Titanic*'s clock is one of the most familiar secular allegorical images in modern times. Its likeness is reproduced almost as frequently as those of the ship herself, and in some very unlikely venues. On nearly every cruise ship, for example, passengers may choose it as a backdrop for their Formal Night photos—an act of combined bad taste and folly that would have left previous generations speechless. Appearing in countless books on the lost liner, it always carries the same caption: "Honor and Glory Crowning Time." The irony was enough to work itself into movie dialogue, as in this fictitious sailing day exchange between J. Bruce Ismay, much-reviled director of the White Star Line, Ismay's wife, and doomed millionaire John Jacob Astor:

Mrs. Ismay: Such a beautiful clock!

J. B. Ismay: Thank you, darling. I chose it myself. It's meant to be "Honor and Glory crowning Time."

J. J. Astor: They ought to be crowning you, Ismay! Never mind, every sort of honor and glory ought to be coming your way after today.[2]

The meaning of the allegory, absent its darker connotations *ex post facto*, is less clear. Why should Honor and Glory pay homage to Time? And why should this occupy such a central position aboard the ship—its most visible symbol, in fact? The builders' notes are curiously silent. One of the few contemporary

FIGURE 6. The *Titanic*'s grand staircase, with her famous clock representing Honor and Glory crowning Time. SOURCE: Library of Congress LC-USZ62-26812.

authors to comment on it, English journalist Filson Young, seemed to think it referred to the passengers:

> The Channel air is keen, and the bugles are sounding for lunch; and our traveler goes down the staircase, noticing perhaps, as he passes, the great clock with its figures which symbolize Honour and Glory crowning Time. Honour and Glory must have felt just a little restive as, having crowned one o'clock, they looked down from Time upon the throng of people descending the staircase to lunch. There were a few there who had earned, and many who had received, the honour and glory represented by extreme wealth; but the two figures stooping over the clock may have felt that Success crowning Opportunity would have been a symbol more befitting the first-class passengers of the *Titanic*.[3]

Young's interpretation, though evocative, is unlikely. Compared to other steamship lines, White Star's use of allegorical imagery and statuary was restrained. The French filled their ships with gamboling gods and cherubim, while the Germans weighted theirs with so much pomp and allegory that, in the words of one historian, they "became temples of high baroque, grand galleries of an aspiration so Valkeyrian that only megalomaniacs might dally there in comfort or good conscience."[4] Even Cunard ran heavily to heraldic imagery, as the giant coat of arms over the *Lusitania*'s smoking room fireplace attests.[5] But on the *Titanic*, which had two main staircases, only the forward one was deemed worthy of symbolism. The aft merely displayed a nautical scene by Norman Wilkinson.

Clearly, White Star was trying to communicate something of importance. As the most traversed part of the ship, grand staircases were traditionally where the definitive statement of the ship was made. On board the *Imperator*, which debuted just a few months after *Titanic*, the space was given over to a massive portrait of Kaiser Wilhelm II;[6] on the *France* of 1912, it was a statue of *La Belle France* holding a scepter and a laurel crown above her head. The *Titanic*'s staircase, in fact, was a near-copy of that aboard the Hamburg–American liner *Kaiserin Auguste Victoria* of 1905. The *Victoria*'s clock was capped with the line's motto "*Mein Feld Ist Die Welt*" ("The World Is in My Scope") and flanked by German port scenes.[7]

So what did it mean? The passage of time usually signified perseverance or patience; hence, the act of crowning Time by Honor and Glory could be the reward given to those who struggle long and hard before achieving ultimate success. By this reading, the trials of those who conceived the *Titanic*, and all the previous engineers from Fulton to Brunel who pioneered the various components of her form and design, were crowned by the ultimate realization of the ship herself. If so, the allegory was significant indeed. *France* and *Imperator* chose to honor their respective nations, while the *Victoria* (rather conceitedly) honored her owners. But the *Titanic* appears to be paying homage to her designers and—by extension—all maritime engineers. She was thus not merely an exemplar of her nation but of the engineering community as a whole— appropriately so, since she was the largest and most luxurious vessel built to that time. The ship was a floating symbol of technological triumph in the face of adversity, of the absolute mastery of science over nature. Instead of celebrating their nations or their employers, the *Titanic*'s designers were celebrating themselves.

This hubris had a distinguished pedigree. The phantasmagoria of steam solidified in the latter half of the 19th century into a dangerous, arrogant overconfidence in the machines: What was once ephemeral—the fleeting symbolism of a ship's launch, for example—became permanently embodied by the ship itself. In other words, having told the public for decades that steamships were the wonder of the age, engineers and owners began to believe it. They took risks, ignored dangers, overreached technological limits, and put an intolerable burden of expectation on the ships they created. Steam technology, which had once been advertised as a servant of humankind, now became a metaphor for the inevitable triumph of Victorian society over all adversity. Allegorical imagery aboard ships—in railway stations and maritime terminuses and even along the friezes of the steamship companies' New York offices—combined to create a landscape of infallibility.[8] Ships could not sink, for they were freighted with the certainties of the age.

Many threads interwove to produce this narrative of technological triumphalism. First was the conception of scientific progress as a struggle against the destructive and retrogressive forces of nature. Nothing could convey success more tellingly than a mighty ship plowing through the waves, moving always forward, indifferent to wind or weather. Second, the struggle against nature could be recast as the triumph of civilization over barbarism. This image brings to mind a common travel poster of P&O: The ocean liner, gigantically overscale, drops anchor in some lush harbor and is gazed at wonderingly by shadowy natives at the corner of the frame.[9] They are astonished and reverential; they are greeting a god. Third, technological triumphalism fit perfectly within a larger progressive narrative that viewed all human endeavor as evolving towards a perfect utopian goal. This was Whig history, in which the struggle itself becomes its own guarantor of ultimate success—to try, in other words, was to succeed.

Naturally, these were bigger ideas than could fit within a ship's hull. Taken together, they circumscribed the age. Yet steamships were the largest, most famous, and most visible vehicles for this optimistic, deluded philosophy, culminating with the *Titanic* of 1912. The symbolism of her demise, however, is commonly misunderstood. The parable most often told is one of a universal flaw in human nature that transcends time or context. "The loss of the *Titanic*," one historian has written, "was surely a classic case of that overweening pride and arrogance which provokes the wrath of the gods, known to the Greeks of old as *hubris*."[10] Hubris may be as old as the Greeks, but the precise form that sank the *Titanic* was not; in fact, it dates only as far back as 1859 and the advent of the *Great Eastern*. Ships before her produced spectacles and inspired wonder, but with the *Great Eastern* the spectacle eclipsed the reality, the allegory of technological prowess overshadowed her profound flaws, and the result was pure fantasy. Engineers might have regarded her as an object lesson, but the larger folly—allowing allegory to replace the genuine article, the unreal for the real—was compounded in nearly every future endeavor, up to and including White Star's ill-omened trio of liners. Like the *Great Eastern*, they were conceived and presented to the public as what they were *hoped* to be, rather than what they actually were. There could be no other explanation for equipping a vessel with half the needed number of lifeboats and sending it hurtling full speed into an ice field. This sort of wishful thinking could only end in disaster; the wonder was not that it happened, but that it didn't happen sooner.

. . .

When the *Titanic* went down, some religious figures in England and America were quick to ascribe it to God's wrath. The Reverend Dr. Ernest Stires of Southampton worked himself into such a lather that his histrionics in the pulpit were drawn in a variety of athletic poses and distributed as a kind of promotional literature for St. Thomas's Church.[11] "Man proposes, but God disposes" became a common refrain.[12] This missed the point, but at least it had the virtue of tradition: Long before ships were advertised as "unsinkable," accidents at sea were regularly ascribed to the will of a vengeful Old Testament deity. The very inverse of the secular optimism that launched the *Titanic*, mankind was commonly depicted as hapless before natural forces beyond its control. The sea disaster was a reminder of human frailty until—by the 1880s—Victorians convinced themselves they had overcome such old-fashioned notions.

On Thanksgiving Day, 1846, the steamer *Atlantic* foundered during a fierce storm off Fisher's Island in Long Island Sound. Over 300 feet long and nearly 500 tons, she had just entered service a few months earlier for Cornelius Vanderbilt's New York–Boston line and was considered the finest coastal ferry of her day. Nevertheless, the motion of the storm ruptured her boilers, and they exploded. The burning vessel was thrown on the rocks and splintered apart. Although not the first steamship disaster on record, the loss of the *Atlantic* within sight of land and the harrowing accounts of the survivors made the event something of a *cause célèbre*. Currier & Ives produced a lithograph of the ferry heeled over and breaking up; Daniel Webster wrote to his cousin Fletcher,

You will be glad that we did not venture on the Sound today, after the terrible loss of the *Atlantic*. . . . It is supposed that about fifty lives were lost. Twenty-two bodies were brought up here this p.m. by the *Mohegan*, which got to the wreck this morning. . . . Captain Duston was drowned. Julia will recollect seeing him.[13]

Public reactions to the disaster ranged from horror to grief to a kind of ghoulish fascination, but there was no surprise. Ships sank, and if there was any lesson to be gained it was a reminder of humankind's fragility before the elements. Or, as Miss E. H. Thatcher of New London rendered in a few rather excruciating lines of verse:

And high above its wave wash'd deck,
    A'swinging to and fro—
The solemn bell with mournful knell,
    Sends forth its notes of woe.
No fitter dirge for *him* or *them,*
Than that sad, solemn requiem.
"Roll on, thou deep, dark ocean, roll!"
Vain is the boast of man's control.[14]

Others saw a more spiritual message arising from the wreckage. "Yes, the noble steamer ATLANTIC, one of the proudest monuments of the triumph of art in modern times . . . with all her costly appendages and lavish appointments, lies piecemeal, in promiscuous ruin, on the shores of our Harbor,"[15] Reverend T. J. Greenwood apostrophized from the pulpit. And whose fault was it? Mankind's, of course. To a good hard-shell Baptist like Reverend Greenwood, there was nothing more edifying than to see humanity's best work decimated by a power greater than its own. "Oh! Weak indeed is poor humanity! Powerless are its resources, and puerile its reason, to contend against the strong arm that comes down in the wrath of the tornado . . ."[16] If some of his parishioners might not have seen the mortal sin of pride in the purchase of a one-dollar ferry ticket, the reverend made it plain for them:

An agent more powerful in the work of desolation than is in the ingenuity or skill of man to resist, has stretched forth its mighty arm; and before it, the huge fabric, in all its surpassing grandeur of strength and beauty of man's device, has trembled, and become prostrate, and lies shattered upon our rock-girdled shore, the mighty ruin of the storm wind's wrath. *And man in his pride of strength, has felt his utter impotency, in the midst of a wild war of elements; and he too lies hushed and silent as the now motionless remnants of the wreck that line our shore!*[17]

Reverend Greenwood's was very much a vengeful god, meting out punishment rather than mercy. Yet beyond reminding humankind of its essential weakness, the storm also served as an opportunity for displays of fortitude, heroism, and Christian piety in the face of death: "There, too, in the midst of that fearful scene, was manifested, in all the devoted strength which God has imparted, the *deep*, DEEP love which binds the human heart to heart!" Nor was the reverend alone in perceiving the disaster thus. According to one of the survivors, a Captain Cullum, this same reverential spirit infused the passengers even at the moment of their demise:

> All hope from human aid now vanished, and our only trust was in God, and to him went up devout prayers for our deliverance. All the passengers, numbering about One Hundred souls, were assembled in the cabin. A portion of scripture was read by the Rev. Dr. Armstrong, followed by a prayer that we might be delivered from the perils of the mighty deep and the pangs of death.[18]

Thus the *Atlantic* disaster became the means, after the fact, of reinforcing social mores. Pridefulness was punished, but the original sin of the passengers in embarking on the ferry was mitigated, in their final hour, by a rediscovery and/or reassertion of their faith. This was all very satisfactory. The passengers obliged by conforming to the standard of behavior expected of them, even under dire circumstances. But when, less than a decade later, the *S.S. Arctic* went down, it was a different matter.

It had only been eight years since the *Atlantic*, but they were eventful ones for the development of steam travel. In 1850 the United States made its long-delayed entry onto the transatlantic scene. The Collins Line, with a generous subsidy from Congress, introduced a fleet of vessels with such unheard-of luxuries as steam heat, Brussels carpets, stained glass windows overlooking the stern, an ice room for cold storage, and a barbershop. The *Atlantic, Pacific, Baltic,* and *Arctic* quickly overtook the more staid vessels of the Cunard Line, and for a brief moment it looked as though American supremacy on the Atlantic was assured.

The *Arctic* departed Liverpool on September 20, 1854, carrying the usual collection of wealthy American tourists at the end of their summer sojourn. Seven days out, as the ship nosed her way into the Grand Banks of Newfoundland, a heavy fog descended. Captain James Luce posted an extra watch in the rigging and rang the ship's bell at regular intervals but retained full speed. On the morning of September 27, the *Arctic* collided with the French steamer *Vesta*. Holed on the starboard side, she took on water and began to list. The captain made a desperate decision to try for shore, which proved fatal. With seawater pouring into her engine room, the *Arctic* settled at the stern and began to go down.[19] The crew, completely abandoning their duties, made a mad rush for the few lifeboats and shoved the passengers—men, women, children—out of the way. Boats were launched half full; some overturned as they hit the water, others were shredded by the ship's still-churning paddle wheels.[20] When it was all over, the vast majority of passengers were left standing on the *Arctic*'s sloping deck.[21]

News of the wreck took some time to reach New York, but when it did it had the effect of a bombshell. This was no ferryboat, but the largest, fastest, most luxurious and—supposedly—safest liner in the world. "I was waked this morning by the voices of newsboys," George Templeton Strong records in his diary, "something about the *Arctic* and four hundred lives."[22] The many New Yorkers among the passenger list left a funeral pall over the city as "no common disaster" had befallen it. "For the Collins steamships are the pride and glory of New York," James Gordon Bennett eulogized, "and our citizens regard their triumphs or their defeats—their safety or their dangers—as those of the city itself."[23]

The news, already bad, became worse. As a few straggling lifeboats reached shore, the full horror of the anarchic scene on the *Arctic*'s deck made itself known. "Oh, what a manly spectacle that must have been!" scoffed one newspaper editor. "It is enough to make us all ashamed of humanity, and envy the better nature of beasts in the field."[24] Such disgraceful behavior in the face of death challenged Victorian self-perceptions; it was the very opposite of the pious affirmation that the *Atlantic* disaster had afforded. Worse yet, the loss of the *Arctic* shattered burgeoning confidence in steam travel and, by extension, an even grander concept of human advancement. "What becomes of the whole theory of progress," one editor demanded, "when men approaching or leaving or resting in this metropolitan city of the United States have little more security than among the nomadic tribes of the desert?"[25]

Even as newspaper editors keened, the most strident denunciations came from the pulpit. A few sermons sounded familiar themes: "Only when [fate] deals a blow do we reflect upon our helplessness in the midst of God's invisible angels," Unitarian pastor John Weiss preached, "and upon the vanity of loading ourselves so deeply with the treasures of the earth while there is one element which all our wit and science can never control—the will of God!"[26] It was all very well to remind parishioners of God's mighty will and the frailties of man, but this was no storm-tossed ship left at the mercy of the elements. The *Arctic*—strong, fast, secure—had hurtled willfully to her own destruction. "Is it an inexorable necessity, fixed as the laws which rule the spheres, that consigns so many mortals to an ocean grave?" Dr. Orren Perkins of the Universalist Church in Shirley, Massachusetts, wondered. "Or are men responsible, to some extent, for such disasters as has recently transpired in the destruction of the *Arctic*?"[27]

This was a new departure. In the *Atlantic*, humankind's culpability seemed to reside in Old Adam's sin and was scarcely more specific; God, who willed all things, had willed the *Atlantic* to sink, and that was that. Even with the *Arctic* there were still those, like Henry Ward Beecher, who chose to take the Calvinist view of predestination: "Death was the pilot that steered the craft. He neither revealed his presence nor whispered his errand."[28] But this was no longer the majority opinion. In the case of the *Arctic*, the true culprit seemed all too clear. "Speed!" Senator James Bayard of Delaware had bellowed on the Senate floor in 1850. "Speed against which the British can never hope to compete. Speed of such magnitude as the Government of Britain and its chosen instrument, this man Cunard, ever visualized or could ever hope to achieve against America!"[29]

The Collins liners were conceived as a blatant challenge to Cunard's supremacy, and—as Senator Bayard's words indicated—their congressional subsidy was contingent on that fact. The *Arctic* carried in her grand saloon a painting of Liberty trampling a European prince underfoot. She and her sisters regularly raced the Cunard steamers and other ships, and usually won. But speed was the antithesis of Christian virtue, as Rev. Weiss told his listeners:

The virtue of moderation is at the very antipodes of popular life—the Christian obligation of resigning speed in all things for safety. See what a special argument for the application of that principle the laws of God have just been obliged to frame for us. It is vain that you make the equipment of the stately ship complete in all respects, and provide against accidents from her speed by multiplying the articles which are fictitiously denominated life-preservers.... It is our nature which needs to be modified if the hour of danger is to be also the hour of wisdom.[30]

By this novel logic, assigning to God the blame for such disasters as the *Arctic* was not only impious but cowardly. It was one thing to accept the omnipotence of God, yet that could not excuse human recklessness. "We call such evils Providential Dispensations," said Reverend Perkins,

but be they so or not, they rarely occur when proper human care and forethought are observed. They are very generally the result of rashness: of such risks and recklessness as are so very blamable where so many lives are hazarded.... How is it with the Collins steamers and their rivals of the Cunard line? What is every trip they make across the ocean but a long race, where all on board is risked, that a rival might be distanced by a day, an hour, a few moments even?[31]

It was a reasonable question. In an era when ships were still made of wood and had nothing more than a bell to announce their presence to one another, the decisions leading to the *Arctic* disaster were unconscionable. And for what? Did it really matter if the *Arctic* or the *Persia* arrived a few minutes ahead of the other? The steamship race, conceived as a means for arousing public interest in steam, had quite literally raced out of control. The need to establish supremacy had trumped all other considerations, even the safety of those they transported.[32]

Who, then, would bear the blame? Captain Luce, for running his ship at full speed? Or the Collins Line, for driving him to do so? Both, certainly, yet they were not the only—or even the primary—culprits. "Behind both the commander and proprietor, there is a wrong state of public sentiment—a reckless haste for speed o'er land and sea—which not only does not condemn and protest against

FIGURE 7. The sinking of the Collins liner *Arctic* in 1854 occasioned numerous sermons on the dangers of speed but no change in policy among the Atlantic carriers. The race went on. SOURCE: Library of Congress LC-USZ62-137402.

this sin; but approves, encourages and pays the price," said Reverend Perkins. He summed up the problem succinctly: "Here then the evil lies; in a morbid state of public feeling, which is ever ready to hazard all, for the sake of gaining almost nothing."[33] This was quite true, but it was against human nature to acknowledge its own collective guilt. Far easier to fix the blame on individuals. So it was that the Collins Line retired in disgrace, but ships went right on racing, driven by their respective nations and "the morbid state of public feeling."

The *Arctic* was a salutary shock, but not a lasting one. Even as she went down, another vessel was taking shape that would eclipse—literally and figuratively— all the frail vessels that had come before. This, of course, was the *Great Eastern*. Built of iron and infused with every safety mechanism known or imagined, from a double bottom to watertight cells, her construction seemed a mute challenge to the old, dusty notion of omnipotent nature. Her hull was taller than the tallest wave ever recorded, and longer than the longest. Anything she collided against would be smashed to atoms. How, then, could she sink?

Brunel was prudently reticent, yet the ship's publicity department was not. The *Great Eastern*'s gigantic dimensions and myriad innovations were a source of ceaseless public fascination; for the first time, dry technical data became the stuff of advertising copy. In touting the ship's many wonders, particular attention was given to her cellular construction, an idea Brunel borrowed from his bridges. He also pioneered the double hull, a crucial innovation that the promoters were quick to advertise:

Up to the water-mark the hull is constructed with an inner and outer skin. . . . In fact, the construction consists of two ships—a larger one and a still larger. . . . By this mode of construction it is calculated that danger of a collision is very much lessened, for, though the outer skin may be pierced, the inner one remaining intact . . . the safety of the vessel would be in no wise endangered.[34]

Famous personages were encouraged to visit the building site at Millwall and record their impressions. "The intellect expands," one dutifully wrote, "and takes such exulting flights that we can rationally regard that huge vessel as the latest wonder of the world." The company also churned out reams of specifications, stultifying but deeply reassuring in its calm, precise certainty:

The weight of one of the cylinders, including piston and piston-rod, is thirty-eight tons, or more than seven times the weight of the great bell of St. Paul's. . . . The engines are provided with expansion valves, throttle valves, and governors, all constructed on the most improved principles, and arranged for working in the most efficient manner. The combined paddle-engines will work 11 strokes per minute, with steam in the boiler at 15lb. on the inch, and the expansion valve cutting off at one third of the stroke . . .[35]

On the advent of her entry into commercial service, the Great Ship Company summed her up, warts and all:

Notwithstanding all the trials and difficulties which she has had to encounter, there is no longer any room for doubt but that the *Great Eastern* steam-ship has become one of the greatest of *facts,* and is destined to commence a new era in ocean navigation, to be new proof of the genius of Englishmen, and another and the most striking of their contributions to the civilization of the world.[36]

In truth she was more fantasy than "fact," but the latter half of their claim is indisputable. Despite her abortive career, the *Great Eastern* did indeed usher in a new era. The patriotism and triumphalism of these words reflect an expanding view of the steamship's allegorical significance, which continued to grow at an even more disproportionate rate than the ships themselves. With the giant *Great Eastern* as a benchmark, future vessels would still try to live up to her "wonderment" without consciously replicating any of her failings. The ship, "a giant with the brain of a cretin,"[37] should have been a warning against overreaching known technological limitations. In the short term, she was: Steamers in the 1860s and 70s would grow at a more incremental pace, and not until 1907 would any arrive to eclipse the *Eastern*'s record size. But the idea of ships as "floating palaces," as representatives of their nation's genius, as "contributions to the civilization of the world"—all of these were engendered by the *Great Eastern* and would continue unchecked for the remainder of the century.

More disturbing yet was a shift in the perceived relationship between humankind and nature. Earlier vessels might trumpet their safety mechanisms (in a classic case of closing the barn door after the horse, the Collins Line hurriedly put out an advertisement after the loss of the *Arctic* claiming that "the ships of this Line have improved watertight bulkheads"[38]), yet they were still seen as essentially at the mercy of the cruel sea. But after the *Great Eastern* such attitudes seemed hopelessly arcane. It was telling that in the aftermath of the *Arctic* disaster, sermons commemorating the event acknowledged human error rather than divine retribution as the root cause. The ship was not at fault. This attitude reappeared in the wrecking of the White Star's *Atlantic* off the coast of Nova Scotia in 1871, after which practically everyone—from the marine surveyors to the line to the passengers themselves—seemed at bizarre pains to assert that her foundering was no fault of the ship herself.[39] "She was one of the best built and strongest ships I have ever seen," one surveyor told the disaster inquiry, "She perfectly kept her shape, and I have not seen a leaky rivet or leaky bolt in her hull, or in her upper deck."[40] The court of inquiry agreed and published its astonishing conclusion that "the loss of the *Atlantic* was not through being driven on a lee shore, helpless.... She was run at full speed, engines and boilers all in perfect order, upon well known rocks, in fine weather."[41]

The fantasy of invincibility had taken hold. It was one thing for a ship to be sunk by human error—that, after all, was a culpability confined to the individuals that operated her. But if a ship went down due to some structural or mechanical flaw, or because she had lost some titanic struggle against the elements, it was an indictment on the nation that built her—indeed, of the human race itself.

This transformation in attitude could be charted by looking no further afield than Kensington. After the Great Exhibition ended, there were still a large collection of oddments left unclaimed—because they were impractical, experimental, or simply too big to move. A warehouse full of mechanical curiosities was thus endowed to the Victoria and Albert Museum in 1857, where they were eventually put on permanent display in the ploddingly named "Museum of Patents." The title hinted at its purpose: not to inspire but to invite titters from a new generation. A Cellini goblet might retain its beauty for all time, but an old steam-powered water pump could only become obsolete and eventually absurd. The collection sat unused and largely forgotten until 1883. Then suddenly it was renamed the "Science Collection" and transferred *in toto* to the illustrious South Kensington Museum. Two years later it became the nucleus of the Science Museum, placed on an equal plane with the Arts Collection at the Victoria and Albert, where it remains to this day. The old machines had ceased to be objects of derision, and the Science Museum became a kind of holy reliquary for the worship of mankind's genius.[42]

This veneration of the machines inevitably extended to the men that built them. The first to be apotheosized was, fittingly, Isambard Brunel. Statues of him appeared in London, Bristol, Plymouth, Swindon, and Milford Haven. The Everton Football Club raised a collection to use the *Great Eastern*'s topmast as the flagpole for its stadium at Anfield, where it still stands today. Spurned on by the wondrous feats of men like Brunel and Stephenson, public opinion of engineers and their work began to shift. Earlier in the century, engineering was regarded very much as a *trade*, with all the condescension that term implies. Universities offered few if any courses, preferring to concentrate on traditional disciplines like classics and literature. It was left to "trade schools" to fill the gap. Despite the rigorous training they received, engineers were still looked upon as dirty, oil-stained, too close to the machines they tinkered with. Even aboard ship, a rigorous hierarchy divided the captain from the chief engineer, who was his nominal equal in rank and often received considerably more salary.[43] Engineers ate with their men, kept to their workstations deep within the bowels of the ship, and had virtually no contact with the passengers whatsoever. If the captain was Jupiter, directing things from on high in the bridge, the chief engineer was Vulcan, guardian of the hellish underworld of the stokeholds.

Yet by the second half of the 19th century, attitudes changed. Suddenly great works of engineering were being celebrated—and along with them their creators. Ferdinand de Lesseps and Washington Roebling became heroes of the age. Even the machines themselves became role models, of a kind. Jules Verne describes his hero Phileas Fogg as "a real machine" and means it as a compliment:

He was so exact that he was never in a hurry, was always ready, and was economical alike of his steps and his motions. He never took one step too many, and always went to his destination by the shortest cut; he made no superfluous gestures, and was never seen to be moved or agitated.[44]

Even financiers could bask in this reflected glory. As far away as Valparaiso, a huge crowd—including the president of the republic, officers of the Chilean army and navy, and the ministers of foreign affairs, finance, and justice—all gathered on February 12, 1877, for the dedication of a statue in Plaza de la Aduana to one William Wheelwright, the American businessman who brought the steam to Chile. Don Mateo Clark, the deceased's great friend, declared:

This statue, erected by the people of Valparaiso with the applause of the whole country, will recall to future generations the fact that steamers, telegraphs, railways . . . and other industries in our midst are the work of Don Guillermo Wheelwright, all of them signifying . . . that he had great faith in the future of Chile.[45]

Senor Altamirano, the *intendente* of Valparaiso, took the broader view and spoke of a new and greater age dawning:

Civilizations of the past knew of no other glory than that of the warrior, and the laurel crowns and the cheers of the people were reserved for him. This statue signifies that among us, the old era has closed and the new begun. This is beginning to be understood, and Valparaiso has the honor of taking the initiative in teaching that if glory has its heroes, civilization has its heroes also, and the latter of the real benefactors of humanity. He who, like Wheelwright, eliminated space by land and sea . . . is the true hero of modern times.[46]

The idea that the steamship financier might replace the warrior in the pantheon of human endeavor was only slightly less radical than another introduced around that time: that the engineer might supplant the philosopher. In the pivotal year of 1869, a young scientist named Charles W. Eliot became president of Harvard University, the first to be chosen from outside the humanities. Science, he announced, was "the firm foundation" for humankind's faith in itself, a heretical observation that he hastily amended by adding the words "and the present infinite Creator."[47] Eliot had no patience for the mindset that believed only a working knowledge of Plato and Posidonius made a gentleman. By introducing new scientific courses at Harvard and encouraging other universities to do the same, he set out to dismantle the ingrained prejudice against engineers and their trade:

People who think vaguely about the difference between a good college and a good polytechnic school are apt to say that the aim of the college course is to make a rounded man, with all his faculties impartially developed, while it is the express object of a technical course to make a one-sided man, a mere engineer, chemist, or architect. Two truths are suppressed in this form of statement. First, faculties are not given by God impartially, to each round soul a little of each power, as if the soul were a pill, which must contain its due proportion of many various ingredients. . . . The natural bent and peculiar quality of every boy's mind should be sacredly regarded in his education; the division of mental labor, which is essential in civilized communities in order that knowledge may grow and society improve, demands this regard to the peculiar constitution of each mind, as much as does the happiness of the individual most nearly concerned. Secondly, to make a good engineer, chemist, or architect, the only sure way is to make first, or at least simultaneously, an observant, reflecting, and sensible man, whose mind is not only well stored, but well trained also to see, compare, reason, and decide.[48]

The effect of these words, and the august stature of the man that spoke them, was to create a new kind of Victorian *beau idéal*: the man that made the machine. This was even more radical than it appears, for it also contained an implied challenge. The difference between philosophy and applied science is that the former tries to make sense of the status quo while the latter tries to alter it. Contemplating the wonders of the universe was naturally the province of educated gentlemen; tinkering with it was not. Even the very concept of engineering was vaguely disquieting for some. The purpose of a machine is to improve in some fashion upon the natural order of things. Since, in a Judeo-Christian world, God preordains the natural order, any machine that purports to alter or amend that order risks divine wrath. Recall the immense satisfaction with which Reverend T. J. Greenwood regarded the destruction of the *Atlantic*: There, once again, was proof of the triumph of God's will over mankind's arrogance and folly. Steamships, as objects designed to be set against nature, were natural lightning rods for smiting.

If this concept seems arcane, it is worth pointing out that even as late as 1935 the French Compagnie Generale de Transatlantique sought a special dispensation from the Catholic Church prior to the launching of their 80,000-ton flagship, *Normandie*: "Eminence, those who built this fast and luxurious liner have not committed the sin of pride. They desired that, in international competition, France should be represented by an entry worthy of her."[49] Even the act of christening a vessel, which predates the steam age, began as a kind of ritualized *mea culpa*: begging God's forgiveness for the effrontery of setting a ship against His seas. To this day christenings are traditionally accompanied by a clerical prayer and the words "May God bless this ship and all who sail in her," as the keel meets the waves.

Against the hoary exhortations of Reverend Greenwood and his ilk, Charles Eliot was in effect giving permission for a new kind of worship: reverence of the machine. Such reverence was self-reflexive. By honoring the machine, one honored the person who made it; thus, mankind was in effect worshiping itself. Dr. Eliot would not have used those words, nor—as a good Episcopalian—agreed explicitly with the sentiment, but the result was the same. Glorification of mankind's works inevitably placed them alongside those of God, and the struggle of the engineer was frequently depicted as man against nature.

By the 1880s, this struggle was perceived to have ended, with humankind the victor. In an earlier era, Charles Dickens had marveled at the dichotomy of the Mississippi riverboat: a glittering, gilded saloon resting upon a superheated boiler about to explode. But on a transatlantic liner, the distance from saloon to boiler room was greater, and the luxurious accommodations provided for passengers in the second half of the 19th century belied the very real dangers of the voyage—indeed, the ships' designers went some length to deny the existence of the voyage altogether. Interior architects encouraged the fantasy that passengers never left shore at all, replicating gentlemen's clubs and ladies' parlors and keeping the sea at bay behind tasseled curtains. Inspiration came from grand hotels like the Savoy in London (which, as a novelty, provided electric lifts and private bathrooms for all its guests) and the Astor in New York. "The people who use these ships are not pirates," one architect explained:

They do not dance hornpipes; they are mostly seasick American ladies, and the one thing they want to forget when they are on the vessel is that they are on a ship at all. . . . If we could get ships to look inside like ships, and get people to enjoy the sea, it would be a very good thing; but all we can do, as things are, is to give them gigantic floating hotels.[50]

It worked: The luxury and familiarity of these rooms was soporific, and on a clear day with a quiet sea, one could indeed almost forget they were aboard ship. In the aftermath of the *Titanic*, this fantasy took on darker overtones, as one chronicler in 1912 described:

For there is one thing that the designers of this sea-palace seem to have forgotten and seem to be a little ashamed of—and that is the sea itself. . . . True, there is a smoke-room at the after extremity of the deck below this, whose windows look out into a great verandah sheeted in with glass from which you cannot help looking upon the sea. But in order to counteract as much as possible that austere and lovely reminder of where we are, trellis-work has been raised within the glass, and great rose-trees spread and wander all over it, reminding you by their crimson blossoms of the earth and the land, and the scented shelter of gardens that are far from the boisterous stress of the sea. No spray ever drifts in at these heights, no froth or spume can ever in the wildest storms beat upon this verandah. Here, too, as almost everywhere else on the ship, you can, if you will, forget the sea.[51]

The author has a point. In a very real way, the rooms the shipowners provided for their passengers framed the experience for them—reinforcing the idea that accidents were not only impossible but unthinkable. How could such a lovely place, with its damask draperies, ormolu clocks, Aubusson carpets, and delicate Louis XIV paneling plunge headlong into the cold black sea? *Titanic* survivors would later recall the unreality of it all: John Jacob Astor and his bride sitting on mechanical horses in the gymnasium, clad in their lifejackets; four Philadelphia businessmen playing cards on a sloping baize table in the Smoking Room; Irish immigrant girls pausing on their way to the boats to gape, open-mouthed, at the splendor of the First Class Dining Room, its tables set for breakfast.[52]

As the latter half of the 19th century waned with no further sea disasters, the safety of ships seemed self-evident as well. When the Guion liner *Arizona* struck an iceberg traveling at full throttle in 1879, newspapers on both sides of the Atlantic focused on the ship's resiliency instead of the folly of her speed; Guion even used the near disaster in its advertisements.[53]

By the 1880s, steamship lines confidently claimed mastery over the elements. "The voyage is now made with the regularity of a ferry," one declared, "the steamers moving almost upon a timetable. . . . As steamers have become more rapid with the growth of engine power, they get more independent of the elements. The winds and seas remain practically the same, but ingenious machinery and improved methods are more and more mastering the forces of nature."[54] This was nonsense. Ships still grounded, lost their bearings, broke their shafts, collided in the fog, became encased in ice, caught fire, or barreled through storms that sent them hundreds of miles off course. Some, of course, sank. The forces of nature were never entirely mastered, and even in a relatively mild midwinter gale, passengers would have cause to curse that same line's sanguine claim to have perfected "an effective method of suppressing much of the ship's rolling."[55]

Though much of this apparent confidence could be discarded as fatuous publicity, it was grounded by a genuine conviction that technology had conquered the sea. "I cannot imagine any condition which would cause a ship to founder," one captain told reporters around the turn of the century. "I cannot conceive of any vital disaster happening to this vessel. Modern shipbuilding has gone beyond that."[56] The words were no less remarkable than the speaker: It was Captain E. J. Smith, later master of the *Titanic*.

At some point in the latter half of the century, a new term appeared in the Atlantic lexicon. Shipbuilders, professional journals, and even the steamship lines themselves began to advertise the "unsinkable ship." It is not entirely clear which ship first bore this moniker. The *Great Eastern*'s cellular hull might (reports varied) have been dubbed "practically unsinkable" at the time of her launch, though there would be scant opportunity to test that proposition. Cunard, Inman, and White Star liners of the 1870s heavily advertised their safety features but came just shy of pronouncing their ships unsinkable—which, given the loss of the *Atlantic*, was probably just as well. The first definite mention arrives in 1889, with the advent of Inman's *City of Paris* and *City of New York*. "The builders," a promotional pamphlet of the time declared, "impressed with the paramount duty of securing the nearest approach to absolute safety, have made an unsinkable ship. They meet the dangers of the seas, not only by the best known appliances, but by other methods novel in shipbuilding."[57] As proof, it went on to describe with haunting familiarity the bulkheads and watertight doors that would be cruelly mocked a few decades later:

The hull has a complete double bottom, so that no dangerous result can come from grounding, the inside hull being a full protection.... Should a collision occur, by which one or two, or even three of these compartments are filled with water, the buoyancy of the ship would not be materially affected. A hundred feet of the bottom or sides might be torn away and she would still float.[58]

The *City of Paris* and *City of New York* were lucky. Both went on to long and profitable careers, and the most interesting thing to happen to either came in 1912, when the *New York* was pulled by the suction of the *Titanic*'s propellers and nearly collided with the larger ship in Southampton. Only the quick movements of the *Titanic*'s tug escorts prevented a sailing day disaster; the *New York* sailed another ten years, the *Titanic* another four days.

The veneration of the machine, as an ideology, had good innings: Begun in the 1850s, it outlasted the Victorian Era by eleven years. It perfectly fitted a new, progressive, "go ahead" age—an era of limitless optimism that made the grim warnings of Reverend T. J. Greenwood seem like sour grapes. God was not absent from this mechanized age, yet nor was he a menacing figure waiting to smite humankind's feeble attempts at progress. The stern judge of the Old Testament had been replaced by the loving father of the New: supportive, benevolent, proud of His creation and *their* creations. The more wondrous they were, by this logic, the more proud He would be. The possibly apocryphal statement given to a *Titanic* passenger on sailing day, "God himself could not sink this ship,"[59] carried with it an unspoken addendum: God would not *want* to sink the ship, even if He could.

Against this unassailable optimism, even moderate voices of caution—like those following the *Arctic* disaster—were ignored. Equipped with faster engines and longer hulls, ships raced more than ever before. In January 1896, Captain John Jamison of the American Line flagship *St. Paul* sighted his arch nemesis, the Cunarder *Campania*, gaining on his vessel from astern. He immediately ordered all possible steam. Both ships were roughly 400 miles from New York. According to the *Campania*'s captain: "We kept following her, but did not have her abreast until 1 o'clock pm. We steamed on until about 8:30 pm, when we ran into the fog, and then ran at a fair speed until 1 o'clock this morning." What "a fair speed" was Captain Walker did not say, but it was clearly enough for them to maintain a comfortable lead. When the fog thickened, however, Walker prudently slowed down and eventually anchored outside the approaches at Sandy Hook, waiting for it to lift. He assumed *St. Paul* had done the same. "The fog lifted this morning at 9:30 o'clock, we then got underway. I had no idea of where the *St. Paul* was until the lifting of the fog, and I then saw her on the beach."[60] Captain Jamison of the *St. Paul*, desperate to steal a trick against his rival, had torn through the fog at full speed and run his ship right up the eastern branch of New Jersey. The salvage costs were frightful, but at least there was no loss of life.

Even when ships did not race each other, they raced against the clock. The vessel with the fastest time would get the lion's share of passengers, even if she beat her rivals by less than an hour. Yet, once again, technology erected a barrier. The reciprocating steam engine, which had driven every ship since the *Great Western*, could only do so much. This lesson was aptly demonstrated by the Hamburg–American liner *Deutschland* in 1900. Above 15 knots, the vibration of the engines and the thrashing of the propellers turned the 700-foot ship into a giant tuning fork. Passengers complained, threw up, complained again. The cabins nearest the screws were abandoned by the second night out. *Deutschland* got her speed record and never raced again. A few years later her engine power was halved, three of her boilers removed, and she was sent on long, lazy cruises to the Caribbean.[61] Hamburg–American Lines learned its lesson and left the field to other competitors. The competitors themselves, having reached a solid wall of technological progress, circumvented it by introducing the turbine engine to ocean liners in 1904. The race went on.

Contrary to popular misconception, the *Titanic* was not trying to break any records. She was running just over 21 knots when she struck the berg—as fast as at any time during her voyage but not as fast as she could go if pushed. White Star, like Hamburg–American, had long since abandoned the speed race. Nevertheless, the ship's officers inherited the mindset of the age, which counseled boldness rather than caution, plowing manfully ahead regardless of any obstacle. An iceberg in the mid-Atlantic was rare: The most dangerous spots were the approaches to shore, where marine traffic was the greatest. "Again and again," one historian writes, "in the vicinity of the Lizard, Wolf, and Bishop Rock, fishing vessels have been within an ace of being sent to the bottom by some

'Ram-you-damn-you' liner driving on at a rate of knots in thick weather."[62] Of these, none was more dangerous than the Grand Banks, a fog-bound patch of sea with dangerous shoals and hundreds of vessels all converging at any given time. A diary entry from the Red Star liner *Westerland* in 1897 provides a harrowing example of one of the many near misses that could, in a matter of seconds, have become disasters:

At about 1:30 on Saturday the 17th while many of the passengers were at luncheon I sat on deck playing cribbage with Mr. Alexander, a jaunty man from Staten Island. A whistle was heard so close to our side that everyone sprang up, before we could reach the side of the ship a huge red hull loomed up out of the mist so close that I could have pitched an apple onto her deck.... Every breath ceased almost in horror as she quietly, quickly came down upon us, but not a sound but the smack of the water and our captain's powerful voice calling out his orders to both ships. Mrs. Morrel was with me, her son dragged her away from the side & she me. I saw a huge prow pointing for amidships, waited for the collision but, in God's mercy, she sheared off a few feet from us, gracefully & silently zigzagging away.[63]

Not to worry, a pamphlet for the Inman Line said breezily:

As we swiftly cross the banks of Newfoundland, there are vessels all around us.... Most of them are fishermen—little schooners rocking upon the waves, with a fleet of dories trailing behind.... We pass close by one or two of them, and see their trawls and ready baited hooks in the dories, and the crew give us a cheer, although we gaze upon them rather with a feeling of pity at the enforced hardships of their lives.[64]

Contrast this idyllic scene—the condescension of which is almost palpable—with another. In Rudyard Kipling's *Captains Courageous*, young Harvey Cheyne opens the story by announcing, in a fog-bound liner's smoking room, "Say, it's thick outside. You can hear the fish-boats squawking all around us. Say, wouldn't it be great if we ran down one?" Some time later, cast adrift and rescued by one of those very fishing boats, he has the opportunity to reflect on his callousness:

Harvey heard the muffled shriek of the liner's siren, and he knew enough of the Banks to know what that meant. It came to him, with horrible distinctness, how a boy in a cherry-colored jersey ... had once said it would be "great" if a steamer ran down a fishing boat. That boy had a stateroom with a hot and cold bath, and spent ten minutes each morning gazing over a gilt-edged bill of fare. And that same boy ... was up at four of the dim dawn in streaming crackling oilskins, hammering, literally for dear life, on a bell smaller than the steward's breakfast-bell, while somewhere close at hand a thirty-foot steel stem was storming along at twenty miles an hour! The bitterest thought of all was that there were folks asleep in dry, upholstered cabins who would never learn they massacred a boat before breakfast.[65]

In fact, the passengers would be lucky if a fishing trawler was all they struck. At the British inquiry following the *Titanic* disaster, Lord Mersey asked Charles Lightoller, the ship's second officer, "When a liner is approaching ice, is it usual to reduce speed?"

"I have never known speed to be reduced," Lightoller answered, "in any ship I have ever been in, in fair weather."

Some time later, opposing counsel tried again.

"What I want to suggest to you is that it was recklessness, utter recklessness, in view of the conditions which you have described as abnormal, and in view of the knowledge you had from various sources that ice was in your immediate vicinity, to proceed at 21.5 knots?"

"Then all I can say is that recklessness applies to practically every commander and every ship crossing the Atlantic Ocean."[66]

Lightoller need not have worried. The inquiry ultimately found the disaster occurred due to "a combination of circumstances that never occurred before and never can occur again," a comforting description that absolved all parties, but one. That last, of course, was the Almighty. Just as insurance adjusters ascribe an "act of God" to a natural event devoid of human foresight or culpability, the British public seemed anxious to believe that nothing short of divine intervention could have sunk the *Titanic*. "By the mysterious will of God," one clergyman intoned, "the ship struck the berg."[67] This was a neat inversion of an old idea. In Reverend Greenwood's day, the wreck of the *Atlantic* signified the frailty and folly of all human creation. The *Titanic*, however, was seen as the hapless victim of forces beyond human control. The difference is subtle but telling: In the former, the guilt lies with mankind; in the latter, with fate. Thomas Hardy developed this theme in a poem composed in memoriam of the disaster, in which the ship and the berg are bound by some dark destiny beyond human understanding:

And as the smart ship grew,
In stature, grace and hue,
In shadowy silent distance grew the Iceberg too.

Alien they seemed to be:
No mortal eye could see
The intimate welding of their later history...

Till the Spinner of the Years
Said "Now!" And each one hears,
And consummation comes, and jars two hemispheres.[68]

The idea of an unforeseeable disaster borrowed from old Calvinist notions of predestination and left the cult of technology largely unscathed. By this logic the *Titanic* was an aberration, not the natural result of decades of recklessness. Mankind was not to blame, any more than the engineers that designed the ship, the owners that managed her, or the officers that drove her through the night at full speed. It was unfortunate, yes, indeed, but no one's fault.

This was not, however, the only view. Naturally, there were those who borrowed Reverend Greenwood's words and decried the sinking as divine punishment. A thorough examination of the sermons of the day, however, reveals something more profound: The *Titanic* disaster, like the *Arctic* before her but much more so, provided a moment of clarity and self-realization. Like a ship passing out of fog, for a brief time the phantasmagoria of steam evaporated, and the denizens of the age saw it for what it was. "Should we denounce," Reverend William Moss of the Washington Heights Presbyterian Church asked rhetorically, "the corporations that vie with one another for supremacy on the ocean, and to whom—it would seem—human life is cheap compared with speed and the emoluments of the fastest steamship service?"[69] No matter that the *Titanic* and her owners were not trying for a record. "The contagion of speed was upon her, for she was almost at her speed limit in a dangerous region, of which her officers had been warned." But the owners alone were not at fault. Like Reverend Weiss in 1854, Reverend Moss turned to the zeitgeist of the age:

And the fact is driven home to us today that as an age, as a nation and as individuals, we lack moral vision. We worship success. We worship money. We worship luxury. We worship display. We worship the material. We worship the ephemeral.... In other words, we worship speed.[70]

Just as Reverend Moss correctly faulted humanity's infatuation with speed, Reverend Barth of Safenwil, Switzerland, condemned the veneration of the machine for what it was. Yet he was careful not to count himself among the Luddites:

I fear that in many church pulpits today it will be claimed that such advances made in the perfecting of technology are somehow ungodly or even demonic, that a disaster such as this reminds us again that God will have none of it. The simple minded will draw the conclusion that it is a sin to build ships this big and to journey across the sea in them. Quite the reverse, I am saying. It is entirely God's will that the world's technology and machinery attain higher degrees of perfection.[71]

Thus far, the reverend could have been preaching for the cult of technology. "But," he added, "I nevertheless get the impression that in this disaster God has intended to show us once more that he is the boss. This is what I mean by that: there is a way of using technology that cannot be called labour any more, but playful arrogance."[72] Arrogance was the *mot juste*. The *Titanic* disaster was not an aberration, nor a divine judgment. It was the natural result of a technological fantasy that had begun over half a century before; had been nourished by generations of designers, engineers, owners, and advertisers; and had been received as truth by an avid public that had come to expect miracles—a paradox that could never be sustained without some tragic result.

Among the most clear-eyed observers of the tragedy was Joseph Conrad, who as a former merchant seaman had watched the phantasmagoria of steam take hold. "All the people on board [the *Titanic*] existed under a sense of false security," he wrote soon after the disaster. "And the fact which seems undoubted, that some of them actually were reluctant to enter the boats when told to do so, shows the strength of that falsehood. . . . These people seemed to imagine it an optional matter."[73] Summing up, he described the *Titanic*'s much-vaunted system of watertight doors, as well as the hoopla surrounding her introduction, as a "technical farce."

If farce it was, the farce was over. However one chose to regard the disaster, the undeniable fact of 1,600 souls perishing in a calm sea, with dozens of ships about and yet not enough lifeboats to reach them, was more than enough to quash the cult of technology. The spectacle of steam, both the exhibition and the race, had contributed to the tragic result. The exhibition of the *Titanic* as a mechanical wonder, an "unsinkable ship," had doomed her no less than the transatlantic race that compelled ships' masters to maintain full speed whatever the cost. Both these facts were known, and the repercussions were immediate. Seamen on the *Olympic, Titanic*'s sister ship, refused to leave port unless more lifeboats were added. When the Hamburg–American liner *Imperator* appeared the following year, her upper decks carried no less than eighty-three lifeboats and collapsibles, with a giant searchlight mounted above the bridge to detect icebergs.[74] Masters were given strict instructions to slow their vessels in case of fog, ice, or other hazards, and followed them—for the most part. The Atlantic race would continue but under monitored conditions. Never again would two ships steeplechase to port like the *Campania* and the *St. Paul*. When the *Queen Mary* crossed for the first time in 1936, she deliberately slowed down in a patch of fog and lost her chance to take the record from the French *Normandie*—an action that her owners, the Cunard Line, wholeheartedly approved. Ships would continue to grow in size, speed, and luxury (the current record holder, Royal Caribbean's *Allure of the Seas*, boasts 225,282 tons, against which the *Titanic*'s 45,000 seems almost quaint), yet they would never hold the symbolism of Honor and Glory crowning Time.

Indeed, once the inevitable finally happened, it seemed as if warnings and prognostications lay everywhere on the ground. Some were truly prescient. A novel published in 1898 depicted an "unsinkable" ocean liner of some 800 feet long wrecking against an iceberg on her maiden voyage. Loaded with wealthy, smug passengers and sent heedless into an ice field one cold April night, the loss of the ship was meant to be a parable for the fragility of the age. The title was *Futility*, and the author, Morgan Robertson, named his fictional vessel *Titan*. Robertson's depiction of the ship's much vaunted safety devices could have been lifted almost intact from *Shipbuilder* magazine, some fourteen years later:

From the bridge, engine-room, and a dozen places on her deck the ninety-two doors of nineteen water-tight compartments could be closed in half a minute by turning a lever. These doors would also close automatically in the presence of water. With nine compartments flooded the ship would still float, and as no known accident of the sea could possibly fill this many, the steamship *Titan* was considered practically unsinkable.[75]

In 1911, just as the *Olympic* was preparing to depart on her maiden trip, Rudyard Kipling offered a more subtle critique of the cult of technology. Titled "The Secret of the Machines," its most commonly excerpted stanzas seem to offer up a paean of their own:

You can start this very evening if you choose
And take the Western Ocean in the stride
Of seventy thousand horses and some screws!
    The boat-express is waiting your command!
    You will find the *Mauretania* at the quay,

Till her captain turns the lever 'neath his hand,
And the monstrous nine-decked city goes to sea.[76]

Modern authors often quote this passage on its own,[77] yet the "secret" of these wondrous devices is revealed at the end. Speaking for the machines, Kipling cautions:

But remember, please, the Law by which we live,
We are not built to comprehend a lie,
We can neither love nor pity nor forgive.
If you make a slip in handling us you die!
We are greater than the Peoples or the Kings
Be humble, as you crawl beneath our rods!
Our touch can alter all created things,
We are everything on earth-except The Gods!
> Though our smoke may hide the Heavens from your eyes,
> It will vanish and the stars will shine again,
> Because, for all our power and weight and size,
> We are nothing more than children of your brain![78]

. . .

Spectacles helped launch the steamships, in more ways than one. They conditioned the British and American public to regard the vessel as something wonderful, almost magical, whose capacity for delight was second only to its utility for service. None of these claims was expressly untrue. Steam and spectacle went together perfectly, but there was a caveat. The spectacle had to impress. It could not be the same trick as before. In practical terms, this meant ever larger, faster, more luxurious, more powerful vessels.

To their credit, the need to astound encouraged Victorian engineers to seek new technologies to augment the existing wonder of the engine itself. The iron hull and screw propeller were undoubted advances. Yet neither had the visual impact of scale: a massive liner sitting on the blocks, waiting for launch. The *Great Britain*, the first "wonder ship," set the bar impossibly high. A commercial and in many ways technical failure, she was nevertheless the first ship to be allegorized as a floating symbol of nationhood—a heavy burden for her and subsequent liners. The spectacle was thus no longer just about inspiring wonder, but encouraging pride in national achievement. Technology, politics, and patriotism emerged as a welded mass in the aftermath of the Great Exhibition of 1851, and the result was the *Great Eastern*.

Now the phantasmagoria of steam had reached a tipping point. More spectacle than ship, the *Great Eastern*'s abortive career illustrated the dangers of overreaching merely to satisfy the public's need to be amazed. But the lesson was not read. Technological fantasy overcame reality—in the novels of Jules Verne and in the minds of the Victorian public. Fired by a bullish view of human progress, engineers, shipowners, and the public itself accepted as truth the concept that science could conquer nature. As ships became larger and faster, as their interior appointments grew more luxurious, it seemed as though some technological Rubicon had been crossed. Thus we can draw a direct line from the failed experiments of the *Great Britain* and *Great Eastern* to the monumental folly of the *Titanic*.

Besides the exhibition, there was the race. No speed record could stand unchallenged for long, since the fastest ocean liner or Mississippi flatboat could be assured the lion's share of trade. Races fascinated the public, as any sporting event indubitably would, and encouraged people to regard the ships as so many horses at the starting gate. Having secured the public's interest, shipowners had to keep it, and thus the vessels were subjected to grueling, useless tests of speed that overtaxed their fragile engines, ruptured their boilers, and sent them careening into rocks or sand banks or other ships. To be fair, the speed of such vessels was wondrous in itself. Locomotives, though faster, lacked the majesty of a ship: Countless passengers describe the shock of leaving the warm, gilded comfort of the lounge and emerging on the windswept deck of a liner moving at 20 knots. It was as if the Astor Hotel had broken free of its foundation and was hurtling through the firmament. One historian has noted the dichotomy of a photograph from the turn of the century: Cunard's brand-new flagship tied up at the pier, glistening with fresh paint and smoke pouring out of her funnels, greeted by a fleet of horse-drawn taxis.[79] To a society that still relied on the same daily transport as the Romans, mechanized speed was intoxicating.

Even set against the grim accounting of the *Arctic, Atlantic, Titanic,* and scores of other ships (and hundreds more of smaller craft) that were sacrificed to the public clamor for speed and wonder, the spectacle remained a success. For every flatboat that burst her boilers, another crossed the finish line in triumph. The triumphs, ultimately, outweighed the failures, and apotheosized dubious entrants like the *Great Britain* and *Great Eastern* after the fact. Steamships became absorbed within a larger narrative of triumphant progress and, more specifically, nationalism. As steam became a yardstick of human achievement, a corollary asserted itself: Nations or peoples devoid of steam were lagging behind. Thus the spectacle can be credited for another ideology, far more durable and with more devastating consequences than the veneration of the machine or obsession with speed: Steam as civilization. Recall that the original purpose of the *Great Eastern* was to shore up Britain's control over India—a single ship that could save the raj, provide a town's worth of settlers, or an entire regiment of troops, as needed. Vast in scale and concept, the *Great Eastern* was a product of imperial thinking, arguably the first explicit melding of steam technology and empire. Failure that she was, the potential was still there. As the image of the P&O or Orient liners arriving in some far-flung locale became synonymous with the arrival of civilization, it is hard not to see the ghost of the *Great Eastern* looming behind. The spectacle was being exported and used to justify imperialism.

Spectacle moved steam, and especially steamships, to the center of Victorian consciousness. They were more than ships: Over time, they became floating allegories. The meaning of the allegory was kaleidoscopic. At any given moment, the ship could represent national pride, international amity, technological supremacy, progressive utopia, triumph over nature, the march of civilization, or all of the above. Thus, thinking back to the 1843 crowd at Bristol, the *Great Britain*'s hull becomes a blank canvas upon which the crowd projects whatever image, or meaning, they wish to see. Yet regardless of their choice, the result is always a mirror of themselves. More than any other physical object, the ship came to embody the totality of the Victorian mind: its perceptions, prejudices, recklessness, daring, innovation, vainglory, optimism, and hope.

PART II

Tourists

5
ORDINARY ESCAPES
American Steamboats and the Masquerade of Class

HANNAH CULLWICK WAS A DRUDGE. Much of her life was spent on her knees: scrubbing floors, polishing boots, and cleaning the grates of middle-class families throughout London. Chances for escape were rare, and treasured. One came in the fall of 1867. "It was to be the last excursion from Margate to the Crystal Palace," Hannah writes in her diary, "and the fare there & back was less than one way by train to London & so I was to go by it." She could not take a leave of absence from work, not in 1867; instead, she quit. "The Missus paid me too, & wish'd me all good wishes & ask'd me to write to her & told me not to be afear'd of sending to her for a character when I wanted one. I thank'd her & said I was really sorry to leave, but this chance of the excursion I better not miss."[1]

By this time the Great Exhibition was long since closed, but the Crystal Palace remained a spectacle worth seeing. Dressed in a "stiff frock, green plaid shawl & black bonnet," Hannah boarded the excursion train at 10 o'clock; by early afternoon, after a transfer at Penge "with the rest of the excursionists," she arrived at the object of her pilgrimage. Curiously, her diary becomes mute at this point. Hannah "went into the Palace & sat, & walk'd about" but recorded none of her impressions of the place. "About six o'clock I came away—got my bag & bundle from the cloakroom and started..."[2] Was it worth giving up her place of work? She does not say.

This brief escape from daily life seems to have planted a seed in her consciousness, all the same. In a diary whose entries nearly always begin with some variation of "Lit the fire & clean'd 3 pairs of boots, Swept & did the dining room glasses & inside windows," rare moments of freedom were a cause for celebration, and nearly all of them began with some kind of travel. On the train to Margate or the ferry across the English Channel, Hannah was given permission to abandon her identity and indulge in the fantasy of another life. What must it be like, she asks herself, for the wealthy ladies and gentlemen for whom such rides are a daily occurrence? There is a wistfulness in these accounts, and a measure of guilt as well. On holiday with her young charges, she writes:

I carried their carpet bag through the station, & it is such a large fine one. I took the tickets for 'em—paid 7 lbs for two tourist tickets. It was more money than I'd ever paid at once for anybody. I saw 'em in the first class carriage & told Master Teddy & Charly how much more nice that was than my hard seat was. . . . The carriage waited for me & the porters was quite civil to me 'cause they saw that [I was in first class] & so I guessed why everybody is so civil to ladies & gentlemen. *It must be nice after all to have such comfort, & for all to be obliging to one, but I don't envy 'em at all, for if I was a lady & had such a lot o' fine things, I think I should be afraid I was never humble enough in God's sight.*[3]

Besides an escape from daily chores, travel also afforded Hannah a rare opportunity to see a greater world than the hearths, floors, and boots of her employer's home. She missed nothing, scrupulously recording every conversation on board the train, every passenger she sat with, and, most particularly, everything she saw. Since these moments were so infrequent, she was often astonished at the rapid changes that steam and industry wrought on the landscape. "Had a pleasant journey & look'd out at the country," she records during a visit to relatives in 1874. "It was all nice till we got near Birmingham & passed W. Hampton—that is black & smoky wi' so many pits & chimneys about. The poor folks stood on the backs & I look'd at 'em well to see what they wore & all that." Even her childhood home had not escaped unscathed: "We got to Shifnal Station. . . . [I] saw that they'd cut the oak tree down in the field where we help'd father to work & couldn't help wondering how things was changed since then."[4]

Exciting as these excursions were, it was not until she was a married woman some years later that Hannah took the journey of her life: a channel boat to France. This was quite another matter. In England, even on excursion or visiting family, Hannah Cullwick was instantly identifiable for what she was: a cleaning woman. Her clothes, speech, and manner gave her away at once. In France, however, the rules of caste and society were different enough that she could effectively pretend to be anyone she liked. The prospect thrilled and terrified her. "It seems strange just now to me," she writes, "after all these years o' being a servant that I should go to France & travel about with M. [her husband], stopping at the best hotels & all as if I was ever so much a lady *in reality.*"[5]

The occasion was her honeymoon. Her relationship with her husband was a complex one, but the disparity between their respective stations—he was a gentleman—meant that in public with him Hannah often felt as if she were assuming a role not her own. This feeling was intensified on the Continent, where no one knew her at all. The double shock of being wholly outside her own surroundings and unrecognized for what she was led to a curious and rambling entry that was nevertheless profound:

Massa said I behaved very nicely all through, at the grand hotel too where there was many real ladies about. He said that he wasn't once asham'd of me, & of course I'm glad of it, but it's all the same to me being *this* or that.... And that when I'm with M. & have to remember I'm in disguise it would be no wonder if I felt conscious & ashamed of myself as being *unfit,* & knowing I was a servant myself all the while the chambermaids or waiters bow'd to me and call'd me "Madame."[6]

The pleasure Hannah derived from escape—both from her daily life and indeed from the strictures of her class—was a familiar one. The Duke of Wellington was quite correct in his gloomy prediction that steam would "encourage the lower classes to move about," but even he could not have foreseen the (for him) even more pernicious threat of steam travel: It gave the lower classes a temporary reprieve from their own selves. Even if it was merely traveling between one kind of work and another, the ferry or train ride was a period of enforced rest, where the passengers could do nothing but relax until arriving at their destination. Ensconced in an elegant railway carriage or a trim cabin aboard a ferry, dining on white tablecloths, taken out of their daily lives and thrown in with a group of other passengers who knew nothing about them, ordinary men and women relished the opportunity to assume different roles.

The principle is familiar to us today: Celebrity Cruise Lines, for example, recently had as its motto "On here, you're a celebrity." So it was for Victorian travelers. The price of an excursion ticket to the Great Exhibition, the channel boat to France, a trip down the Mississippi, or the night boat from New York to Boston was within reach of most incomes. Steamship and railway companies were aware of the escapism their journeys provided. Catering primarily to the working and middle classes, steamers nevertheless boasted grand lounges, elegant dining halls, even orchestras to serenade their proletarian clientele.

As we saw in Chapter 2, Thomas Cook pioneered the working-class excursion by offering cheap package rates to the Great Exhibition in 1851.[7] It is no accident that this should be the very thing that first wooed Hannah Cullwick; by the 1860s and 70s, such excursion rates were common throughout England and the United States. Exhibitions and World's Fairs continued to be the biggest draws, offering a democratic spectacle open to all. In 1893, young Clarence Day—a New York aristocrat temporarily short on funds—took the

Erie Special Excursion to see the Chicago World's Fair. The experience was less than ideal:

> It took that train three days and two nights, if I remember correctly, to get to Chicago. We stopped at every small station. . . . Of course, the train had no sleeping cars or diner—only day coaches. There was quite a crowd of us in them, men, women and children. . . . All the windows were open, it was so hot. We were coated with coal dust. The washroom got out of order and had to be locked. The little drinking tank was soon empty. Most of us had nothing to eat, and we slept sitting up. But it was fun. Nearly everyone but the overworked trainmen was good-natured and friendly.[8]

That anyone could be cheerful under such circumstances is proof enough of the powerful lure of the excursion. Even in cramped and uncomfortable surroundings, passengers still felt they were on an adventure. A Marxist might argue, however, that by providing these brief escapes, steam travel was as instrumental in reinforcing class boundaries as offering release from them.[9] The experience it offered was both temporary and illusory: After a night of dining in the grand saloon and taking their ease on the promenade deck, most passengers returned to the drudgery of their daily existence on shore. Of what value, then, was the trip? Was it merely an opiate for the working classes? I will suggest instead that it offered them a new and different way of *defining* their own class. The ferry ticket was an *entrepôt* into a greater community. Beyond escapism, it allowed passengers to feel they belonged to a kind of high society: broader and less restrictive than that found in their hometowns. The particular vantage of steamship travel—looking down from the upper deck—reinforced this sense of separateness from shore and fellowship with other passengers.

Such escapes were more plausible in America, where the lines between classes were comparatively fluid (though still present, as we shall see). Moreover, ferry travel became an integral part of American identity in a way that no other nation shared. The Mississippi steamboat not only opened the riverbanks to new settlement but became a symbol of an advancing civilization. Their opulence, too, was allegorical: Contrasted with the rough towns along the river (and the rough lives of most inhabitants), they seemed to offer a vision of "civilized" society that was both fantastic and aspirational.

In this new community onboard, race became a fixed point of division even as class distinctions melted away. Cosseted in luxurious surroundings, white travelers were encouraged to look down in bland superiority upon the native and black peoples clustered in steerage, as well as the still-untamed landscape around them. To the north, ferries plying the route between New York and Boston sold a different kind of fantasy. Theoretically patronized by both ordinary passengers and the very rich (though considerably more of the former), these ships bridged the gulf between the new-money aristocracy of post–Civil War New York and the less fortunate remainder. Like the Great Exhibition and subsequent World's Fairs, they offered a spectacle of high society that was as seductive as it was fleeting. For one night, like Hannah Cullwick in Paris, the hard-boiled New England fisherman or Brooklyn Heights office clerk could relax in the same tufted lounge as a Vanderbilt or Rockefeller. In both the Mississippi and New York boats, ordinary people were offered a chance to take part in an extraordinary community: The steamboat not only became a vehicle for transport, but wish fulfillment. Its central place within American culture was thus assured.

. . .

The Mississippi River, where the steamboat came into its own, was an imponderable. Unlike the majestic Ganges, the mysterious Rhine, or the romantic Seine, the Mississippi never failed to disappoint. Foreigners traveled thousands of miles to stare at its muddy banks, frothy and sullen, and left embittered. In compiling material for his *Life on the Mississippi*, Twain was amused to discover their litany of grousing. With heavy irony he included it all: Frances Trollope commenting she "had never beheld a scene so utterly desolate as this entrance to the Mississippi"; Charles Dickens sneering at "an enormous ditch, sometimes two or three miles wide, running liquid mud . . . the banks low, the trees dwarfish, the marshes swarming with frogs . . ." And so on. The most charitable description came from Captain Frederick Marryat, another Englishman, who called the Mississippi "The Great Sewer" and wrote that it was not "an angel descended for the benefit of man, [but] a devil, whose energies have been only overcome by the wonderful power of steam."[10]

That was the crux of the matter. In a single decade steam transformed the Mississippi into a thoroughfare, with people and goods traversing north and south. After Fulton's unsuccessful attempt to monopolize the trade ended in 1817, dozens of wildcat steamship firms sprang up almost at once. Cotton and lead were the cash commodities, but speculators soon found there was nothing that, if it could be moved, could not be sold somewhere. The impact on Mississippi life was similar to that of California during the Gold Rush. Little towns now dotted the riverbanks, doing a brisk trade with itinerant boats that passed through each day. Some of these—St. Louis, Memphis, Vicksburg—flourished and became civic powers in their own right. Hundreds of others appeared and vanished like mirages. Returning many years later, Mark Twain spied old Marion City: "When I first saw Marion City thirty-five years ago, it contained one street. . . . It contains but one house now, and this one, in a state of ruin, is getting ready to follow the former five into the river."[11] He was further chagrined to hear that Alexandria, an even larger burg, was under water.

Steam created these communities and vitalized them. Without it, they could not survive. Young Sam Clemens observed this phenomenon before he fully understood what it meant. As an adult he left a depiction of his boyhood home, "the white town drowsing in the sunshine of a summer's morning,"[12] alerted from its slumber by the arrival of a steamboat:

The town drunkard stirs, the clerks wake up . . . every house and store pours out a human contribution, and all in a twinkling the dead town is alive and moving. Drays, carts, men, boys, all go hurrying from many quarters to a common center, the wharf. Assembled there, the people fasten their eyes upon the coming boat as upon a wonder they are seeing for the first time. And the boat *is* rather a handsome sight, too. She is long and sharp and trim and pretty; she has two tall, fancy-topped chimneys, with a gilded device of some kind slung between them; a fanciful pilot-house, all glass and "gingerbread". . . . Ten minutes later the steamer is under way again, with no flag on the jack-staff and no black smoke issuing from the chimneys. After ten more minutes the town is dead again, and the town drunkard asleep by the skids once more.[13]

It was not strange that the steamboats exerted an inexorable pull on him. Few Americans have been so infected with wanderlust as Twain, and it is quite possible that it came to him from the daily contact with those wondrous, mysterious boats. His first passage was a revelatory experience, and one that would color his accounts for the rest of his perambulatory life: "I was a traveler! The word had never tasted so good in my mouth before. I had an exultant sense of being bound for mysterious lands and distant climes which I have never felt in so uplifting a degree." Yet paradoxically there was also the feigned ennui of a tourist gazing down at the hordes beneath his majestic perch on deck. "As soon as I knew they saw me I gaped and stretched, and gave other signs of being mightily bored with traveling."[14] These two contradictory images would come to define not only Twain himself but the American tourist: exhilarated yet detached, gazing down in wonderment yet gazing downward nevertheless. The steamboat offered passengers a new and different vantage. Railway cars and carriages moved through the landscape, but the boat glided above it. As ships grew, deck upon deck, the distance between observer and object lengthened, until finally all port cities looked much the same: a shed, a crane, and a teeming throng of anonymous humanity scurrying about below.[15]

Steamboats held another attraction, as they were by far the grandest things on or near the Mississippi. Most passengers who crossed their threshold had never seen anything so posh. Mark Twain deferred to Dickens's opinion of the Mississippi, but when the crusty Englishman took issue with steamboats, declining to call them "floating palaces," Twain rushed to their defense:

If Mr. Dickens was comparing these boats with the crown jewels, or with the Taj, or with the Matterhorn, he was right. But to the great majority of those populations . . . spread over both banks between Baton Rouge and St. Louis, they were palaces; they tallied with the citizen's dream of what magnificence was, and satisfied it.[16]

In truth, Dickens was less disappointed by the steamboats than mystified. Accustomed to deep-keeled sailing vessels and channel boats, the steamboat's flat bottom—so perfectly designed for the Mississippi—seemed utterly bizarre. "If the native packets I have already described be unlike anything we are in the habit of seeing on water," he wrote, "these western vessels are still more foreign to all the ideas we are accustomed to entertain of boats. I hardly know how to describe them." Nevertheless, he tried:

In the first place, they have no mast, cordage, tackle, rigging, or other such boat-like gear; nor have they anything in their shape at all calculated to remind one of a boat's head, stern, sides or keel. . . . There is no visible deck even: nothing but a long, black, ugly roof, covered with burnt out feathery sparks; above which tower two iron chimneys, and a hoarse escape valve, and a glass steerage house.[17]

A drearier depiction of the Mississippi steamboat has never been penned. Of the grand saloon Dickens said nothing, and the one advantage of his stateroom was that it occupied a choice position near the stern; he had been told the steamboats "generally blew up forward."

Indeed, "the citizen's dream" of "magnificence" was not Dickens's, or any European's for that matter. By the mid-19th century the riverboats had become garish to the point of absurdity, and vastly overscale. Their flat-bottomed hulls obviated the most difficult problem of marine design: how to cram a luxury hotel into a semi-cylindrical tube. As the century progressed, Mississippi steamboats added tier upon tier of decks and filled them with parlors, music rooms, dining halls, and calliopes. Ladies had their own retiring room in the stern, with plate-glass windows overlooking the great churning wheel.[18] By 1852 the *average* length of a steamboat's main salon was 200 feet. In comparison, the Cunard liner *Persia*, introduced four years later and the largest steamship in the world, boasted a great cabin of 75 feet.[19]

Days spent on the river were primarily gastronomic, with passengers finishing one leisurely meal only to lurch back soon after for another. Ship menus hinted at culinary delights beyond the imagination of anyone save royalty. But some of the names were suspect. This excerpt from a January 1851 menu aboard the *Ben Franklin* was typical:

Calves' Head a la Torrul

Giblets a la Glassey

Bone Ducks a la Chamford

Chickens a la Diable

Venison a la Crapsden[20]

Unlikely as it was for Devil Chickens or Crapsden Venison to appear *à la carte* at Delmonico's, it was at least aspirational. But the society did not live up to the surroundings. Diners ate with their knives and then picked their teeth, called out loudly to stewards, belched and spit tobacco juice into nearby spittoons. Sometimes they missed. The talk was of politics, often colored with profanity. In some instances there was no talk at all, just bovine concentration on the food. "The fact was," one captain recalled, "that most of the passengers had never in all their lives lived so well."[21]

If the world of the steamboat seemed glaringly different from the rough-and-tumble towns on the riverbank—or the people who inhabited them—it was deliberately so; 19th-century Americans never fully overcame the feeling that they lagged behind their Old World cousins culturally, and nowhere more so than in the hinterlands. Without the comfort of an established aristocracy to define the rules, Mississippi River society was cobbled together from an admixture of speculators, wealthy farmers, mill owners, and shipping magnates. Foreign visitors were appalled to see them aping English gentry, without the slightest conception of its mores. Dining in the gilded saloon of a steamboat, one lamented "the total want of all the usual courtesies of the table, the voracious rapidity with which the viands were seized and devoured, the strange uncouth phrases and pronunciations."[22]

With gloomy relish, Charles Dickens described passengers sucking on their knives as they decided what to eat next, and heaping great quantities of "beet root, shreds of dried beef, complicated entanglements of yellow pickle, maize, Indian corn, apple sauce, and pumpkin" into a great coagulated mass, then wolfing it down. "There is no conversation, no laughter, no cheerfulness, no sociality, except in spitting." He was also less than impressed with steamboat society. Promised a rich Creole tapestry of humanity, he found instead a boring collection of tradesmen:

The people are all alike, too. There is no diversity of character. They travel about on the same errands, say and do the same things in exactly the same manner, and follow the same cheerless round. All down the long table there is scarcely a man who is in anything different from his neighbor.[23]

Perhaps it was fortunate that Dickens's dinner companions had no notion of how they looked and acted. Steamboat society demanded that passengers rise to its level, and most cheerfully tried to comply. As such, steam was at the same time a harbinger and a promise: It brought "refined" delights to the new settlements and promised that they too would one day reach its pinnacle of urbanity. The effectiveness of this approach was apparent in the response. Within a few years the finest houses along the Mississippi River all sought to emulate the steamboats, with gingerbread moldings, iron filigree, and even funnel-shaped chimneys. Garish and ludicrous though they might be, steamboats set the standard. "A steamboat coming from New Orleans brings to the remotest village of our streams," one contemporary wrote, "and the very doors of our cabins, a little Paris, a section of Broadway, or a slice of Philadelphia."[24]

Decor was intended not to welcome, but to overwhelm. This meant acknowledging their gin-palace notions of finery. As such, "steamboat Gothic" came to mean anything excessively adorned, gilded, and ostentatious. "When he stepped aboard a big fine steamboat," Twain wrote, the passenger "entered a new and marvelous world":

Gilt acorns topping the derricks; gilt deer-horns over the big bell; gaudy symbolical picture on the paddle-box... curving patterns of filigree work touched up with gilding, big chandeliers every little way, each an April shower of glittering glass drops... in the ladies' cabin a pink and white Wilton carpet, soft as mush, and glorified with a ravishing pattern of gigantic flowers.[25]

It is not clear whether Twain is deliberately mocking this catalogue of grotesques or is in earnest. Either way, the greater question is: Why were they there at all? Whom were they trying to impress, and for what purpose?

Much of it was simple one upmanship. The fastest and most luxurious steamer drew the most passengers and consequently was a floating advertisement for the firm. But economics alone cannot explain it. As with ocean liners, the greatest profits for steamboat owners came not from First Class but from deck passengers. Like human cattle they were corralled on the boiler deck, standing awkwardly amongst bales of cotton, shipping crates, and firewood. Despite their profitability, owners paid hardly a thought to them, concentrating instead on furnishing ever more opulent interiors for their middle-class clientele.[26]

The real reason was empire. It may seem strange to envision the Mississippi territories as colonies, but for much of the 19th century that is precisely what they were. Their settlement followed the same pattern that would be repeated throughout much of Africa: Subjugate or eradicate the indigenous populations, encourage emigration, and build. Into this wild landscape the steamboat was the floating embodiment of expanding civilization. Wherever it touched, whoever crossed its threshold and witnessed the wonders therein, was instantly drawn into the "civilized" world it represented. In the words of historian Walter Johnson:

Steam power, in these accounts, became a sort of alibi for imperialism.... The confrontation of steamboat and wilderness, of civilization and savagery, of relentless direction with boundless desolation, was called "Progress." And progress was measured in what Twain referred to as the steamboat's "time-devouring" capacity—which others, using a more conventional formulation, termed "the annihilation of time and space."[27]

Johnson terms this phenomenon the "steamboat sublime." The word pops up everywhere in memoirs, diaries, and articles of the era. One contemporary observer rhapsodizes, "There are few objects more truly grand—I almost said sublime—than a powerful steamer struggling with the rapids of the western waters," while another writes that the Mississippi steamboat "carries one's imagination to the verge of the sublime."[28] In this context, the sublime is not merely beautiful: It is the juxtaposition of one object against a very different background. Gaudy as the Mississippi steamboats became, in form and function they remained essentially floating warehouses. Their sublime quality is measured against the roughness of the landscape and of the people within.

The impression left by such images is of steam conquering vast tracts of empty wasteland. But the land was not empty. The advance of steam coincided with the Indian Removal Act, which saw tens of thousands of Native Americans forcibly exiled from their lands and sent west. Many of these were displaced from the Ohio Valley and Mississippi; indeed, a central purpose of the act was to clear the banks of the Mississippi for settlement.[29] The brutality by which this was accomplished sometimes moved even foreign observers to protest. An English travel guide writer—who had never been to America—pitied the "wandering savages" and their fate. Like some fantastical mythic creatures deforested out of their habitat, they seemed to be on the verge of extinction:

> Once there were a great many, now there are but few; and there are fewer and fewer every year, and so it is probable at last there will be none at all. And why have they become so few? Because white men have come and taken possession of their lands—the grounds where they used to fish.[30]

While Charles Dickens might be appalled at their recklessness and other visiting Europeans bemoan their destructive effect on the native races, for most Americans the allegory of the Mississippi steamboat was quite the opposite. Not only was it set against the savagery of the landscape, but also the perceived savagery of those whom it displaced: "It is needless to do more than mention the Indian canoe, the smallest and rudest of boats, [to suggest that] the introduction of the steamboat upon the western waters . . . contributed more than any other cause" to the civilization of the west.[31] Aboard, there was also an element of the "racial sublime."[32] White patrons enjoyed luxe cabins and saloons on the upper decks, from which they could gaze down at the Indians and slaves gathered below at the bow and stern. Coming into port, a similar scene was enacted: Passengers looked down from a great height at the busy work of the shore, much of which was done by slaves. The senses of distance, detachment, and superiority were all heightened by this unique vantage.[33]

And yet, as with the society of the Mississippi Valley itself, a current of anxiety coursed underneath. The steamboat—so vast, powerful, and beautiful, the very image of progress and civilization—was in fact a floating incendiary waiting for the chance to ignite. The fiery glow that smoldered beneath its layers of white-painted decking, which disturbed Dickens even if he did not complete the allegorical connection, was obvious to others: "[A] river god . . . a huge demon of the wilderness," one observer describes it, "bearing fire in her bosom, and canopying the eternal forest with the smoke of her nostrils." A steamboat barreling up the Mississippi was a spectacle in every sense, yet for many of those gathered along the riverbank—Native Americans, slaves, and even some anxious whites—it was a "spectacle of holy terror."[34]

By the 1840s and 50s, a community of travelers had developed that relied on the Mississippi steam packets and rode them regularly. "Packet people," as they were called, ranged from ordinary farmers carrying their product to market to more colorful characters like John A. Murrell and the quasi-legendary Mike Fink: riverboat men who transitioned from rafts to steam and brought their particular brand of coarse humor and violence with them.[35] The gilded parlors of the steamers also gave rise to gambling, both legitimate and not. Of all the images of the Mississippi boats this is by far the most durable, surfacing in countless novels and films such as W. C. Fields's *Mississippi* and Mel Gibson's *Maverick*. Even one contemporary fictional description (Melville's *Confidence-Man*) picks up the theme:

IN THE CABIN. Stools, settees, divans, ottomans; occupying them are clusters of men, old and young, wise and simple; in their hands are cards spotted with diamonds, spades, clubs, hearts; the favorite games are whist, cribbage, and brag. Lounging in armchairs or sauntering among the marble-topped tables, amused with the scene, are the comparatively few, who, instead of having hands in the games, for the most part keep their hands in their pockets.[36]

The reputation of such ships as gambling halls, however, was overrated. As one historian points out:

The river boats never ran daily pools, nor regular betting on how many miles the boat might go in a day's run. . . . Occasionally someone would offer a bet in the making or failure to make a certain landing by some given hour, but it was a haphazard thing. The journey was too short . . . passengers coming on board for a few hours or often only for one night.[37]

The spiritual center of the Mississippi boat was its saloon. There were usually not one but two, rigidly divided between a ladies' parlor at the stern and a gentleman's lounge midships. The sexes comingled in the dining saloon, if the boat was large enough to boast one, but rarely elsewhere. The shortness of the trip precluded the creation of any kind of closed community onboard, as one might find in ocean crossings of more than a week, and the passenger list was an ever-changing kaleidoscope as some departed and others arrived with each landing along the river. Few knew another, and few would ever see one another again. Thrown into the convivial salon or dining room, for most passengers a trip on a Mississippi riverboat was a chance to shed their provincial identities—if only for one night.

The fluidity of identity aboard the riverboats became the subject of Herman Melville's last novel, *The Confidence-Man: His Masquerade*, published in 1857 at the height of the riverboats' popularity and set aboard one such vessel, the *Fidèle* ("fidelity" in French). She presents a broad face to the observer, "a great white bulk [that] might at distance have been taken by strangers for some whitewashed fort on a floating isle," yet inside is full of secrets: "From quarters unseen comes a murmur as of bees in the comb. Fine promenades, domed saloons, long galleries, sunny balconies, confidential passages, bridal chambers, staterooms as plenty as pigeon-holes, and out-of-the-way retreats like secret drawers in an escritoire."[38] The steamer in Melville's imagining becomes a metaphor for the many-sided nature of the human soul concealed behind a blank visage. Moreover, the honeycomb and escritoire imagery suggests that the vessel is also a kind of repository: Where else but on a steamship could so many diverse people (and their secrets) be contained?

FIGURE 8. The accurately titled "high pressure" steamer *Mayflower*. Such craft were a common sight on the Mississippi and served as the model for Herman Melville's *Fidèle*. SOURCE: Library of Congress LC-DIG-pga-00775.

The Confidence-Man steps on board and at once appears to be a white canvas personified: "a man in cream colors. . . . His cheek was fair, his chin downy, his hair flaxen, his hat a white fur one, with a long fleecy nap."[39] Indeed, that is the role the Confidence-Man will serve in this story, changing shape and presenting a different identity to each of his interlocutors, who are thus "taken into his confidence" and reveal themselves to him. This literary device allows for a kind of Canterbury Tales to ensue, as each passenger-character steps forward into the light to tell their story. Taking inspiration from numerous trips on the Mississippi himself, Melville lists an astonishing variety of persons one might encounter on board, which also reflects the unique heterogeneity of delta culture:

Natives of all sorts, and foreigners, men of business and men of pleasure; parlor men and backwoods-men; farm-hunters and fame-hunters. . . . Fine ladies in slippers, and moccasined squaws; Northern speculators and Eastern philosophers; English, Irish, German, Scotch, Danes; Sante Fe traders in striped blankets, and Broadway bucks in cravats of cloth and gold; fine looking Kentucky boatmen, and Japanese-looking Mississippi cotton planters; Quakers in full drab, and United States soldiers in full regimentals; slaves, black, mulatto, quadroon; modish young Spanish creoles, and old-fashioned French Jews. . . . In short, a piebald parliament, an Anacharsis Cloots congress of all kinds of that multiform pilgrim species, man.[40]

Only on a Mississippi steamer could such a collection be found. How much or how little one wished to believe of their tales is left to the reader—indeed, that is the whole point. If you see a man standing behind a counter in a butcher shop and he tells you he is a butcher, you have every reason to believe him. But if you encounter the same man on board ship, what evidence have you save his word? That paradox fascinated Melville, and he explored it in depth. No one is identified by name but rather by their identifying characteristics.

There is, for example, the "gentleman with gold sleeve buttons," who accosts the Confidence-Man and declares that he had the distinction of presenting his invention at the Great Exhibition in London:

I went to exhibit an invalid's easy-chair that I had invented. . . . My Protean easy-chair is a chair so all over bejointed, behinged, and bepadded, everyway so elastic, springy, and docile to the slightest touch, that in some one of its endlessly-changeable accomodations of back, seat, footboard, and arms, the most restless body, the body most racked, nay, I had almost added the most tormented conscience must, somehow and somewhere, find rest.[41]

Melville was certainly lampooning the more absurd gadgetry that debuted at the Exhibition (one wonders if he himself ever saw Colonel Lloyd's storm leeches), but there is more than that. The characters paraded before the blank slate of the Confidence-Man, and thus before the reader, are not merely caricatures but *self-created* ones. They present an image of themselves for display. The true self is that which exists within its natural habitat—the shopkeeper in his shop, and so on. But when he is no longer there, what precisely is he? And how will others recognize him?

The idea of a community of strangers *en voyage* has been employed by many authors. In Agatha Christie's *Murder on the Orient Express,* for example, M. Bouc declares:

"Ah, for the pen of a Balzac! I would depict this scene.... All around us are people of all classes, of all nationalities, of all ages. For three days these people, these strangers to one another, are brought together. They sleep and eat under one roof, they cannot get away from each other. At the end of three days they part, they go their several ways, never, perhaps, to see each other again."[42]

Yet there is also an element that is unique to the Mississippi steamer, and nothing else. Such vessels—plying their trade up and down the river, stopping at innumerable ports to pick up goods and passengers and deposit others—came to reflect, for Melville, the fluid nature of the river itself. The cliché about a river never being in the same place twice thus becomes a metaphor for human relations:

Though her voyage of twelve hundred miles extends from apple to orange, from clime to clime, yet, like any small ferryboat, to left and right, at every landing, the huge Fidèle still receives additional passengers in exchange for those that disembark; so that, though always full of strangers, she continually, in some degree, adds to or replaces them with strangers still more strange; the Rio Janeiro fountain, fed from the Cocovarde mountains, which is ever overflowing with strange waters but never with the same particles in every part.[43]

Melville's steamboat cavalcade was not well received by critics, and even today it has practically vanished alongside his other works. In truth, it is hard to read. The world it describes is so completely gone that much of the satire falls on deaf ears, and many of the characters he presents seem almost cartoonish. Minorities are minstrel versions of themselves; unlike white men and women, their color denies them the freedom to adopt self-created personas. Yet its very obscurity is one of the reasons *The Confidence-Man* is so valuable: There are few other depictions of this lost world, and none that so thoroughly examines the motives and identities of steamboat culture. Since journeys on the Mississippi were brief, few passengers bothered to write about them. The kaleidoscopic steamboat society that Melville describes can only be seen from afar, which is the vantage of the novelist. He shrewdly depicts it as a masquerade: a plush salon full of an ever-changing cast of characters each wearing a mask of their choosing. Steamboat voyages allowed passengers to engage in wish fulfillment—becoming any character they wished, transcending social barriers at will. It was pure escapism, and it transformed the steamboats from necessary transport into fantasy communities that reflected, as if in a fun-house mirror, society ashore.

. . .

Though not as celebrated as the Mississippi, the northeastern route between Fall River, Boston, Newport, and New York City was no less vital, or colorful. The ships of the Fall River Line shared the tiered white decks of their southern compatriots, but otherwise were designed for a very different kind of service. Deep-keeled, with a high freeboard, sharp prows, and side paddles rather than stern-wheelers, they plied the often dangerous coastline from Massachusetts to New York. Unlike the bales of cotton stacked along a flatboat's decks, they carried more passengers than cargo; they were, indeed, the first true commuter ferries.

Early vessels reflected this fact. There was little ornamentation wasted on the *Firefly*, Robert Fulton's first entrant on the New York–Boston line. For travelers, the advantage of steam was not luxury but regularity. The sailing packets that previously monopolized the route could take anywhere from 18 hours to a week to reach their destination. At a cost of 10 dollars, no small amount in those days, the passenger was given a cramped berth shared with at least six of his or her fellows and took meals in a windowless hearse of a room with an oil lamp swinging above. The first steamboats were hardly more comfortable, and sometimes not even as fast (packet masters occasionally offered to transport their passengers free of charge if they did not "beat the steamboat"), but they left and arrived at regular intervals, a crucial advantage for those who had business or travel connections in New York.[44]

Within a few decades, however, the austerity of these ships gave way to ostentation that was scarcely less impressive (or overblown) than the Mississippi boats. Of the *Empire State*, built in 1848, one English observer wrote, "Cleopatra might envy the splendor of this floating palace."[45] On the Atlantic such descriptions were commonplace (Cleopatra's barge seemed a perennial reference point, despite the fact that no one really knew what it looked like), but for a coastal steamer—or "night boat," as they came to be known—it was novel. This reflected the increasing popularity of the service, and the need for more passenger capacity. Captain Lauchlan MacKinnon, an English visitor to New York in the 1850s, marveled at the spectacle of all the ferries in the harbor. "An unprejudiced mind cannot avoid being struck with amazement at the progress of the United States," he wrote:

Magnificent houses rise as if by magic; mammoth ocean steamers are completed with astonishing celerity. . . . River boats, nearly four hundred feet long, appear to glide like meteors on the surface of the Hudson and East Rivers. Place one of these on end alongside St. Paul's Cathedral, and its foremost extremity would nearly reach the noted ball and cross![46]

The sea change came after the Civil War, as it did for nearly all steam travel. Day ferries had "warm rooms for passengers, each passenger having a partitioned seat. A large cabin is set apart for ladies, another for gentlemen, who smoke there if they please."[47] The fare was 1 cent. Now, with New York burgeoning, the night boats became a crucial link between the metropolis and the northeastern corridor. Unlike the railroad, their only competitor, the steamers were rarely delayed, never cramped, and always comfortable. Instead of a hard bench seat, the passenger received a cabin: small, to be sure, but with a trim bed and a washstand nearby. Passengers journeying southward often came loaded with dozens of trunks, en route to the New York piers and on to Europe or elsewhere. In early summer, the northern route carried the wealthy to their summer homes in Newport or Hyannis and the middle class to the New England coast for seaside holidays.[48] The lustrous names of Vanderbilt, Astor, Berwind, and Oelrichs appeared on passenger lists often enough for ordinary mortals to book passage on the chance of spotting a "celebrity."

Advertisements emphasized the exclusive nature of their clientele. "Of the interior arrangements, decorations, and all the furnishings of the *Pilgrim*," one proclaimed:

It can only be said that they are indeed palatial, with all that can be implied by that term. Her grand saloons, cabins, staterooms, social halls, dining saloons, offices, every provision in fact, are equal to anything found in the fitting of the most elegant caravansary. . . . A thousand persons present in her grand saloons at one time serve only to animate the scene without the least appearance of crowding. . . . Here one meets the elite of every land. In the grand saloons of an evening the recherché orchestral performances (a feature of this Line) attract audiences representing the wealth and culture and fame of every nation and people.[49]

In truth, most passengers were nothing of the kind. This was implied by the statistics of the blurb above. "A thousand persons" might find comfort aboard the *Pilgrim,* but Mrs. Astor's fabled ballroom had space for only 400. How could a vessel be vast and yet exclusive at the same time?

Another promotional pamphlet, published in 1894, had a try at reconciliation:

With regard to the assemblages gathered on board these steamboats—what city or watering place hotel in any section of the country can present the same in greater variety of elements, characteristics and quality of patrons? Here are found representatives of the wealth, culture, intelligence and development of the human family from every part of the world, in associations made up of every grade and class of social elements, except the lowest.[50]

Now the reader is more confused than ever. The steamer appears to be a kind of world's congress, containing within itself the full spectrum of respectable society. Representatives of wealth, culture, and intelligence are easy enough to define, but what of "development of the human family?" And what did it mean that every class was represented, "except the lowest"? Lowest by whose standards?

Clearly the marketing effort here was undermined by its attempt to satisfy every superlative. The Fall River Line ships *were* grand, and famous persons did indeed book passage on them, but the eager celebrity seeker who embarked on the *Pilgrim* hoping to share a butter plate with John Jacob Astor would likely find his fellow travelers much the same as him: commercial travelers, businessmen trying to catch a Europe-bound ship from the Chelsea piers, bond or Bible salesmen, bank clerks and their families on holiday, Providence cousins visiting relatives in the big city, lobstermen delivering their catch to market, and so on. Many of these made the trip dozens if not hundreds of times, and gradually a community developed on board ship that—while not "the elite of every land"—was congenial and solidly middle class. Menus featured New England specialties: oyster stew, steamed clams for 25 cents, broiled lobster for 75, Indian pudding for dessert.

The *Fall River Line Journal* first appeared in 1879 and was delivered under stateroom doors every day for fifty-six years afterwards. Surviving copies suggest a great deal about the persons reading them. The front page of one early edition is crowded with advertisements: Dobson's Boston Carpet Store, William Bourne & Son's Pianos, French's Hotel in New York City featuring "all modern improvements including an elevator." Next, rather incongruously, is an engraving of the main saloon of the *Bristol*, the very ship on which they were now traveling. A trick of perspective makes it seem larger than the Hall of Mirrors at Versailles, which must have been disconcerting to compare with the undeniably grand yet more modest reality around them. After that are a few brief snippets of "news," mostly of the social variety. The back page is given to "Paddle Wheel Splashes," a collection of dubious jokes and anecdotes rendered with a heavy Victorian hand: "A landlady said that she did not know how to make both ends meet. 'Well,' said a boarder, 'why don't you make one end vegetables?'"[51]

Taken in sum, the *Fall River Line Journal* suggests a very different sort of community than the "wealth and culture and fame of every nation." Passengers were affluent enough to consider buying a piano, yet earthy enough to enjoy jokes such as "The postage stamp knows its place after it has been licked." They were being consciously reminded of the grandeur of their vessel even as they traveled aboard her, and they were encouraged to take part in an imagined community that extended from the aristocratic doings of those in the society columns all the way down to themselves. The fact that both classes met—theoretically, and sometimes actually—on board the Fall River Line ships seemed to give the *hoi polloi* a temporary pass into a world of grand society that they would regretfully depart when the *Bristol* reached dock.

The lines went to great lengths to encourage this fantasy, making every traveler feel part of an exclusive, though transient, society. In 1869, the Fall River Line and its rival the Bristol Line were both purchased by one of the most colorful characters of the Gilded Age, Jim Fisk. Partner to Jay Gould (with whom, later that same year, he would try to corner the gold market and thus send the U.S. economy into a panic), Fisk began his career as a street peddler in Brattleboro, Vermont. By 1869 he was the very image of a bloated capitalist that cartoonists would lampoon for decades: a vast, ungainly man in a loud suit with a colored silk shirt and a pearl stickpin as big as a marble. But Fisk was a born promoter, and he understood precisely what the Fall River Line was selling.

The two ships built under his direction, *Bristol* and *Providence,* rivaled anything on the Mississippi. Their saloons were cavernous spaces two decks in height, with a broad atrium that led to 220 cabins for over 800 passengers. A grand staircase tricked out in gold filigree led down to the dining saloon. Brass bands greeted travelers as they came aboard. Fisk even installed 200 canaries in gilt cages about the ship, following a trend ashore (Democratic Party boss William Tweed had dozens of them twittering around his Tammany office). "What are those huge castles rushing madly across the East River?" one awestruck observer asked.[52]

The pageantry extended to Jim Fisk himself. Determined that no passenger should feel anything other than special, Fisk created a character for himself of "the Admiral." Donning a dark blue uniform heavy with gold braid, he appeared on the gangway every evening when the ships left New York. Fisk greeted the ladies, shook hands with the gentlemen, and gave imperious orders to a factotum at his elbow. He remained on the bridge "piloting" the *Bristol* until they reached the entrance to the East River. Then he departed, with flourishes, into a waiting tug. This spectacle continued nightly until Fisk was shot in the stomach at the Grand Central Hotel in 1872.[53]

The ships themselves became larger and grander. "Reference has been made," one pamphlet proclaimed,

to the steamboats as "great floating hotels" and the term is not a misnomer.... There are indeed few hotels on the land that can surpass these vessels in accommodations and

FIGURE 9. The *Pilgrim*, Fall River Line. "Night boats" were a vital link between New York and New England ports, providing not only transport but an escape into a luxurious enclave normally reserved for the privileged few. SOURCE: Library of Congress LC-DIG-pga-00740.

provision for and entertainment of guests.... Altogether [the boats] can provide appropriate and desirable sleeping places for upwards of 1,000 persons at one time.... What grand hotel on land can do better?[54]

But the steamboats were not floating hotels. A traveler on shore would choose a hotel based on its social status, and the grandest hotels prided themselves on exclusivity. They would no more wish to serve 1,000 guests than augment a feeding trough in the dining room or cattle stalls in the bedchambers. The need to provide "appropriate and desirable" accommodation for that number of patrons—who themselves ran the full gamut of social class—imposed exigencies on the ships that meant they could never rise to the service and luxury of even a moderate hotel.

They could, however, present a simulacrum of grandeur in their public rooms. A period brochure for the *Commonwealth* seems to promise a kind of maritime tour through three centuries of architecture:

Stepping aboard the steamer, you enter the quarter-deck.... The style of this room is modern English, the woodwork being oak.... Abaft the lobby is the library. Its decoration is of the period of Louis XVI. The trim is old ivory. The moldings and cornices are embellished with gold.... From the quarter deck an imposing staircase leads to the Saloon Deck. Here is a beautifully decorated saloon in the period of Louis XV.... The second or gallery deck of the steamer forms a balcony around the saloon. There is also a mezzanine gallery where the orchestra holds forth. The supporting piers of the Grand Saloon are enriched at their angles with twisting columns. The capitals of these columns are reproductions from the Church of San Marco.... Strolling aft through the Gallery Saloon, you pass the Adams Saloon which is furnished in prima vera to resemble old satin wood, with panels of green ornamentation.[55]

It was probably just as well that passengers were given this primer. My own grandparents, members of the self-titled "swamp Yankee aristocracy," traveled frequently on the *Commonwealth* and described her as "big" and "fancy." Even the copywriter was rather boggled at this pastiche of styles. The "Adams saloon" was likely named for the neo-Classical architect Robert Adam (no "s"), not—as the writer seems to think—for the patriotic Adams family of Braintree.

In actual fact, passage aboard the night steamers was a strange combination of the grandiose and spartan. The dining saloon aboard the *Priscilla* of 1895, for example, was Moorish, with white tablecloths, real silver, and a small shaded lamp on each table. In size and splendor it was hardly distinguishable from any transatlantic liner. An orchestra serenaded passengers from an alcove above their heads. But the menu ran to plain New England fare: roast beef and mussels with stewed fruit and pudding for dessert. Breakfast, taken on the fly as the ship docked in Boston, was juice, eggs, waffles, or flapjacks drowned in maple syrup—all for 50 cents.

The *Priscilla*'s cabins, like all in the Fall River Line, were "a keen disappointment."[56] On entering the vessel and presenting a dollar fifty to the chief steward, passengers received a large brass key with their stateroom number marked on the plate. Navigating through endless deep-carpeted corridors, one finally found the correct door and on entering discovered a tiny white-painted bedchamber roughly 7 feet square. Two narrow berths were stacked at one side, looking more like bookshelves than beds. Except in the most expensive accommodation, there was no window. A metal grate above the door ventilated the room—and also carried in the sound of drunken revelers lurching down the hallway at night. A porcelain sink dispensed cold seawater. Stowed beneath the lower bunk were two lifejackets and a chamber pot. The *Priscilla* had exactly one bathroom for its thousand passengers, divided between men and women and located amidships. It had neither tub nor shower. Passengers, spending only one night aboard, were expected to perform their ablutions on shore.[57]

The dichotomy between public grandeur and private austerity was mandated, in part, by economics: If 1,000 paying guests were crammed into the hull, large staterooms were clearly out of the question. A similar dynamic operates on the mass-market cruise lines of today, like Carnival or Royal Caribbean. But there was more to it than that. There are clearly two very different kind of experiences being offered, corresponding to public and private selves. In the grand Louis XVI lounges and dining rooms, passengers were encouraged to live out the fantasy of celebrity and wealth. This, of course, was the public self. This was the shipboard community, a shared experience of luxury and indulgence that required each passenger—as on board the Mississippi steamboats—to live up to expectations. Yet those expectations were never too high for even the humblest passenger to reach: The Fall River Line did not try and mystify its guests, for example, with complicated French dishes or dozens of little forks arranged next to their plates. Good, plain food was sufficient.

Alone in their cabins, passengers shed this persona and became again their normal selves. There was no community here, no artificial standards to aspire to. The ships' cabins were exactly what a dollar fifty should buy and suited for exactly the kind of clientele they attracted. This is not to suggest that every passenger was happy with the 30 inches of bunk space provided; rather, they did not expect much else. The fantasy ended at the cabin door.

Nor were the New England boats free from the racism that pervaded their Mississippi cousins. Although nearly all the stewards were African American, the rest of the crew was not. Hiring policies rigidly forbade them in any other capacity but service. Blacks were not expressly prohibited to book passage, but on arriving at the pier might find the ship "overbooked." Even if successful in gaining a cabin, they were not allowed in the dining hall or lounges. As aboard the Mississippi boats, the aristocratic fantasy such rooms provided was clearly not a multiracial one. This was consistent with attitudes ashore. As an English observer in the 1850s described it:

There are no slaves in the Northern States, but there are many blacks there; and perhaps you think they are kindly treated as they are not slaves. Far from it. They are not beaten, it is true, but they are despised and insulted in every possible way. . . . The blacks may not ride in the same carriage on a railway as the whites, so a separate carriage is provided for them. . . . In the Southern States it is common for masters and mistresses, when they are going on a journey, to shake hands with their black slaves at parting; but no such kindness is ever shown to black servants in the Northern States.[58]

North and south, steamboats became vehicles for a fantastical escape from ordinary life. The luxe and grandeur of their public rooms raised most passengers well above the station of their caste and offered them a momentary glimpse of a privileged world. For one night they shared the same space as the wealthiest of the land, and thus became part of a shipboard community that transcended—temporarily—the strictures of class that bound them ashore. In fact, the fleeting nature of these experiences added to their magic, like Cinderella at the ball. As the bridge between two very different lifestyles, steamboats could lay claim to democracy even as they reinforced class distinctions. The ordinary passenger would come away from a night aboard feeling privileged to have rubbed shoulders with the good and great without experiencing any of the jealousy that such an encounter might cause on land. Beyond that, both kinds of steamboats became allegories for civilization triumphant, modern technology bringing light to darkness, as the Fall River Line itself argued rather grandiosely in 1894:

As has often been written and said, "History repeats itself"; if not in the exact duplication of events, still in the way of names and kindred characteristics: an in the present time history writers take note of a *Pilgrim* and a *Puritan* [Fall River Line steamboats], equally representative of daring and lofty enterprises, and more closely allied in working out a destiny than were the ancient worthies bearing those same titles in the seventeenth century.[59]

If surviving descendants of the Puritan pioneers felt aggrieved at having their "city on a hill" supplanted by a ferryboat, it was nothing compared to the cultural transformation that steamboats brought to the Mississippi. There, "civilization" took on even starker social overtones. The juxtaposition of their gilded rooms against the rude savagery of the river inevitably invited comparison between white and brown and red peoples, with the latter at the distaff end. Looking down from the railing at the slaves and Indians gathered below, white passengers were encouraged to regard their privileged quarters as a kind of natural right. The allegory of civilization's struggle with barbaric nature, common throughout steamship lore, acquired an extra dimension on the Mississippi: Here nature acquired a face, and it was Native American:

They [the steamboats] overwrote the history of conquest with the history of technology. They transformed the history of capitalism into the history of technology, the results of incentives and investment in inventions. They were bright, didactic bubbles floating on top of the muddy tide of the history of the Mississippi Valley.[60]

The identification of technology as a shared "civilizing" experience, and one that allowed temporary transgression of class norms, bound the steamships even closer to the societies they carried. To this day, the memory of such vessels is inextricably linked with luxury and excess. In their own age, they brought the phantasmagoria of steam to the *hoi polloi*, which showed its gratitude by granting them a central place within local culture. Mississippi boats not only created and sustained communities along the river but on board—distinct, but still reflective of and co-dependent with one another. In the Northeast, steamers served as nexus between the exclusive world of New York's Gilded Age aristocracy and the ordinary traveler. Concealed by their surroundings and the "masquerade" of anonymity, ordinary travelers became, for one night, extraordinary.

6

ONE SMALL IRON COUNTRY
Social Hierarchies on the North Atlantic

THE MOST TALKED-ABOUT EXHIBIT in the Transportation Building of the 1893 Columbian Exhibition was a segment of an ocean liner, thoughtfully provided for the fair by the American Line and the shipbuilders William Cramp & Son. At 70 feet long, 35 feet wide, and fully to scale, it towered over all. "This is such a novel display," the official guidebook noted, "and of so much interest to the multitudes of our people who have had no opportunity to visit such a ship afloat, that it is worthy extended description."[1] And so it was:

> The floor line of the building comes just where the twenty-six foot water line of the ship would be, so there is as much of it above the floor as there will be above the water at her draft on sailing.... As it is now, the first or promenade deck is more than twenty-five feet above the floor, and the top of the funnel is yet fifty-three feet above this. This serves to give some idea of the actual height of these transatlantic liners.[2]

From the starboard side the ship appeared solid, a black iron wall studded with rivets and pocked with portholes, capped by a band of cream-painted superstructure. Electric lights twinkled behind the glass where the First Class saloon would be, real teak railings ringed the promenade deck, and "just aft of the bridge and on top of the deck house is a life-boat ready for launching."[3] Yet the real wonder came when the observer began to circumnavigate the hull. It was vivisected, opened up like a giant doll's house and glowing with incandescent light. "The visitor passing through this exhibit will see the model-room, steerage compartment, first-class compartment, dining saloon, promenade deck, library and smoking room. The visitor can thus obtain a perfect idea of the size, furnishings and style of the ocean liners."[4]

In fact, they would learn more than that. The catalogue of rooms, beginning with steerage and ending with the First Class library and smoking room, roughly follows the eye as it travels upward, starting at the waterline and ending with the spire of the ship's funnel. Consequently, the American Steamship Line had produced a perfect facsimile of Victorian class divisions, life-sized and ready to be inhabited by actual representatives of each caste. First Class was on top, naturally, followed by the purgatory middle layer of Second Class, and finally steerage. Standing on the ground looking up, First would have seemed as lofty and remote as a fairy kingdom; Second was still above their heads, but not by so much; steerage was right at eye level with those most likely to inhabit it. Only the mephitic underworld of the boilers was omitted—legitimately so, since it lay beneath the waterline, but also because it might remind visitors that this miracle of 19th-century innovation relied on the sweating, heaving strength of 300 stokers shoveling coal. There was such a thing as being *too* technically accurate.

The idea of ships as floating microcosms is hardly novel. In the wake of the *Titanic* disaster, English author Filson Young depicted in Marxist terms the strata on board:

If, thinking of the *Titanic* . . . you could imagine her to be split in half from bow to stern so that you could look, as one looks at the section of a hive, upon all her manifold life suddenly laid bare, you would find in her a microcosm of civilized society. Upon the top are the rulers, surrounded by the rich and the luxurious, enjoying the best of everything; a little way below them their servants and parasites, ministering not so much to their necessities as to their luxuries; lower down still, at the base and foundation of all, the fierce and terrible labor of the stokeholds. . . . Up above are the people who rest and enjoy; down below the people who sweat and suffer.[5]

Young was writing at the end of an era, just two years before the cataclysm of the Great War that destroyed the fragile social hive he describes so well. By 1914, ships had reached a greater degree of social stratification than they had ever known or ever would again. They were more than microcosms: They were the only place on earth where the extremely rich, the poor, and the middle class met in such close proximity for the same basic purpose. The nearest second would be a church, though even in that egalitarian haven one found divisions. The elites of New York customarily purchased pews in the front of the nave, while the middle classes milled about in the back; servants sat in the galleries out of sight. The working classes were nowhere to be found. Traditionally Catholic, Jewish, or other faiths besides Protestant, their churches were in their own neighborhoods; even by 1900, it was not unusual for residents of the Lower East Side to never travel more than fifteen blocks their entire life.[6] Nor were they encouraged to do so. But on a ship, the classes were confined barely inches apart: A single closed door might separate First from Second Class, or Second from Third (steerage). Outdoors, the privileged looked down from the promenade deck onto the fore and aft well decks, where steerage denizens gathered to escape the stifling gloom below. Sometimes the upper-deck passengers threw coins.

In the previous chapter we considered how steamships, specifically coastal and river ferries, could be a means for transcending class. On the Atlantic, however, steam travel reinforced class distinctions. Gathered together "in one small iron country on the deep," as Robert Louis Stevenson described it,[7] the presence of persons from widely divergent social castes compelled steamship companies to create artificial barriers to separate and segregate them. These barriers had the effect not only of reproducing hierarchies ashore, but heightening them, transforming passengers into caricatures of themselves: carefree, lustful, unwashed emigrants; social-climbing middle class; bloated capitalists gorging themselves on delicacies and tossing crumbs down to the downtrodden steerage passengers below. Theoretically compartmentalized, each found ways of interacting with the others, and such interactions replicated (often starkly) conditions ashore. For First Class passengers, the voyage reinforced their sense of entitlement and privilege. For Second Class, it stoked their social ambitions. For emigrants in steerage, it offered a grim preview of what their lives would be like once they reached shore.

But it was not always so. In the early days of steam navigation, the difference between First Class and steerage might be nothing more than a bulkhead and a complimentary blanket. It took ships of commensurate size to replicate a full range of social divisions, and it was not until late in the 19th century that the technology existed for such vessels to be built. At first, it seemed unlikely that rich and poor would ever cross in the same vessel. Nearly a decade after the introduction of the *Great Western,* steamships remained exclusively marketed to wealthy clientele. Emigrants did not need to reach New York all that quickly, and in any event could not afford the privilege. No less an authority than Samuel Cunard dismissed the possibility of turning steamships to the emigrant trade: "It is so very expensive."[8]

Emigrant ships were often cargo vessels whose lower decks had been hastily scrubbed out (or not) and filled with straw pallets. The emigrant was expected to bring his or her own bedding, eating utensils, and sometimes even food. There was no segregation of married and single travelers, no bathing facilities, and no heat. Typhus, cholera, and dysentery were rampant; up to half the passenger load could be wiped out before the ship reached port. Shipping lines were indifferent. Reform-minded parliamentarians in London and Washington urged the passage of emigration acts to inspect and certify such vessels: The laws were duly passed, then withered away in desuetude. Examining officials were bribed; honest inspectors found hostility at both ends of their job. Until the 1840s, however, the horrors of emigration were mercifully confined to a small number of passengers.[9]

The Great Famine of Ireland, which began in 1846, turned the trickle of transatlantic emigration into a flood. It also provided the impetus for emigrant shipping lines to reconsider steam navigation: With hundreds of thousands of potential passengers waiting at the pier, so to speak, sailing ships that meandered across the Atlantic in 6 to 8 weeks were no longer a profitable or efficient solution.[10] A fast steamship with ample capabilities could ferry up to 500 steerage passengers in just 14 days, bring cargo back to England, then turn around and do it again.

The Inman Line, founded in 1850, attempted the experiment. They purchased the brand-new, iron-hulled, and screw-driven steamer *City of Glasgow* and converted her to carry 400 emigrants in what had previously been the cargo hold. An additional 137 cabin passengers were accommodated in a deckhouse at the stern. The ship was a tremendous success, traveling at full capacity on almost every voyage.[11] William Inman himself took passage as a steerage traveler *manqué* and wrote up a report on the conditions. The *City of Glasgow* was not fast or fancy, but she paid. Traveling at a sedate 10 knots, her engines consumed just 20 tons of coal per day against the Cunard speed queens' 75. The experiment worked.[12]

Other companies followed suit, haltingly. There was snobbery among shipping lines: As late as the 1870s many still advertised "No Third Class Passengers" as a selling point for their ships, as if the presence of such people on board—even down below and out of sight—was somehow a contaminant.[13] The Anglo-American press, which avidly greeted every new steamer and wrote up columns of shipping news, barely acknowledged the Inman Line or others like it. When the *City of Glasgow* disappeared with some 480 passengers on board in March 1854, it received only a few lines of press.[14] Yet when the Collins liner *Arctic* sank a few months later, in September, it was front-page news for days. That suited William Inman just fine. Unlike Collins, which saw itself destroyed by unfavorable publicity, the emigrant lines went right on virtually undisturbed by disaster. The *City of Philadelphia* was wrecked on her maiden voyage; a few years later, the *City of Boston* vanished, like the *Glasgow*, without a trace. Few cared, including the Inman Line itself. If one ship sank, another would be built. If some passengers drowned, others would take their place.

Despite traveling with them, William Inman continued to regard his charges as "cargo"[15] and treated them accordingly. He segregated men from women and kept married couples midships as a natural buffer—a pattern that would continue on ships right up to the *Titanic* (where single men, housed in the bow, were obliged to walk nearly the entire length of the ship down a broad corridor known as Scotland Row to reach the General Room at the stern).[16] Passengers got porridge for breakfast, "mess beef" for dinner, and gruel afterwards.[17] If this was not to their liking, they had no one to complain to. Even so, and with a safety record that would make other companies blanch, Inman kept filling his ships. In the Irish countryside, touts traveled through villages distributing leaflets that promised luxurious and safe accommodations for "a halfpenny a mile."[18] As a final stroke of brilliance, William Inman routed his liners through Queenstown (Ireland) instead of Liverpool, thus draining the fount at its source.

In 1879, English novelist Robert Louis Stevenson tried to book steerage from Glasgow to New York on board the Anchor liner *Devonia* as a kind of social experiment. Friends, colleagues, and the Anchor Line itself gently intimated to him that this was simply not done. No gentleman of independent means would ever travel anything other than First Class. Both sides insisted, and after some wrangling Stevenson accepted a berth in Second—but with the proviso that he could, if he wished, spend his days amongst the common herd in steerage. From this vantage, halfway in between two worlds, he was able to provide one of the only surviving 19th-century accounts of life below decks.

The first striking observation was how close these worlds were to each other. "Through the thin partition" that separated his cabin from the open stalls, "you can hear the steerage passengers being sick, the rattle of tin dishes as they sit at meals, the varied accents in which they converse, the crying of their children terrified by this new experience, or the clean flat smack of a parental hand in chastisement."[19] Second Class passengers enjoyed marginally better food: "Irish stew, sometimes a bit of fish," served in an actual dining room—spartan, but clean. "In my experience, the principal difference between our table and that of a true steerage passenger was the table itself, and the crockery plates from which we ate."[20] Steerage passengers ate from a communal trough and had neither plates nor cutlery unless they brought their own. They were also expected to supply their own bedding. As a Second Class passenger, Stevenson was given a tiny cabin with a washstand; his companions slept in long dormitory rows of bunks. But the most telling difference between Second and steerage had nothing to do with the food or surroundings. "In the steerage cabin," writes Stevenson, "there are males and females; in the second cabin ladies and gentlemen."[21]

If the line between Second and steerage was a single partition, from First it was a metaphorical gulf. Ships like the *Devonia* were designed with a complex series of baffles, one-way doors and trick staircases aimed at preventing steerage from gaining access to forbidden parts of the vessel. As ocean liners grew, these subterfuges became increasingly complex.[22] Nevertheless, though separated rigidly below, on deck, First and steerage passengers occasionally encountered one another. Stevenson was astonished at how he had seemingly diminished in their eyes. Clean, shaved, and wearing his usual clothes, the simple line of demarcation between his portion of the deck and theirs transformed him. "[T]here was no recognition in their eye," he writes. "They gave me a hard, dead look, with the flesh about the eye kept unrelaxed." One such encounter left him particularly disturbed:

My height seemed to decrease with every woman who passed me, for she passed me like a dog. This is one of my grounds for supposing that what are called the upper classes may sometimes produce a disagreeable impression in what are called the lower; and I wish someone would continue my experiment, and find out exactly at what stage of toilette a man becomes invisible to the well-regulated female eye.[23]

It was a gaze that the other steerage passengers would come to know well; unlike Stevenson, most would encounter it the rest of their lives. We have only his word that the ruse worked and he was "taken for a steerage passenger," but given the rarity of the experiment it seems likely enough. "The sailors called me 'my man,'" he professes proudly, "my comrades accepted me without hesitation for a person of their own character and experience."[24] In fact, traveling in Second Class may have aided his disguise: An English gentleman in reduced circumstances might find himself thus, but it was improbable he would have traveled in anything less.

Still, this was a very different group than one might expect. We might describe 1879 as a transitional year in American emigration: The Irish potato famine had ended, but the brutal pogroms in Russia and eastern Europe that sent millions of Jews across the Atlantic had only just begun. The passenger load on the *Devonia* was thus a polyglot of nationalities: "Scots and Irish in plenty, a few English, a few Americans, a good handful of Scandinavians, a German or two, and one Russian." They were not a prepossessing lot. In spite of trying to understand their ordeal, Stevenson dismissed his traveling companions as "family men broken by adversity, elderly youths who had failed to place themselves in life, and people who had seen better days. . . . We were a shipful of failures, the broken men of England."[25]

It is hard not to detect a glint of that same "hard, dead look" in Stevenson's own eyes when reading descriptions like these. Nevertheless, his account is all the more remarkable for its rarity: As an "amateur emigrant," he is able to preserve a certain detachment from both his confrères and alleged superiors, providing an equally clear picture of both. Despite earlier reservations, Stevenson eventually accepted his traveling companions on their own terms and was accepted in turn. A man who once told an audience "one of the truest ladies in Bournemouth, Mrs. Waats, is at this moment washing my study windows"[26] can perhaps be forgiven for expressing himself in platitudes:

> It seemed no disgrace to be confounded with my company; for I may as well declare at once I found their manners as gentle and becoming as those of any other class. I do not mean that my friends could have sat down without embarrassment and laughable disaster at the table of a duke. That does not imply an inferiority of breeding, but a difference of usage.[27]

Victorian egalitarianism had its limits. "Kind hearts are more than coronets" was a useful aphorism that could be applied liberally, from Zambezi tribesmen to the poor of Liverpool; it confirmed the essential humanity of the intended without threatening the status quo. Robert Louis Stevenson was not a revolutionary, and his account was not meant to be a call to arms. His portraits of the people he encountered were sympathetic yet tinged with condescension. It is all the more remarkable, then, to note how he depicts an unusual foray from the upper classes midway through the voyage. One Tuesday morning the weather cleared, and the steerage passengers enjoyed themselves after their fashion: singing, dancing, playing cards, and dominoes. Stevenson himself was rolling cigarettes for a newfound acquaintance who lacked the skill. Then, suddenly, the mood changed. Stevenson's description of what happened next deserves to be quoted in full:

> Through this merry and good-hearted scene there came three cabin passengers, a gentlemen and two young ladies, picking their way with little gracious titters of indulgence, and a Lady-Bountiful air about nothing, which galled me to the quick. I have little of the radical in social questions, and have always nourished an idea that one person was as good as another. But I began to be troubled by this episode. It was astonishing what insults these people managed to convey by their presence. They seemed to throw their

clothes in our faces. Their eyes searched us over for tatters and incongruities. A laugh was ready on their lips; but they were too well-mannered to indulge it in our hearing. Wait a bit, till they were all back in the saloon, and then hear how wittily they would depict the manners of the steerage.... Not a word was said; but when they were gone Mackay sullenly damned their impudence under his breath; but we were all conscious of an icy influence and a dead break in the course of our enjoyment.[28]

There is much to consider in this passage. First is the obvious irony: Stevenson harshly condemns these interlopers transgressing the boundaries of class for their own amusement, but does so from the vantage of one who traveled incognito himself in order to both observe and depict the same scenes. Beyond that, however, there is a conflict of perception. Steerage was a closed community: Isolated from the rest of the ship, it was almost as if the other classes did not exist. That illusion was shattered, and the passengers were forced to regard themselves outside their own experience—not as individuals, but as objects of curiosity.

At the same 1893 World's Fair that displayed a bisected ocean liner, an even more spectacular display was a genuine Dahomey village brought over intact from West Africa, complete with tribesmen. Its location gave some indication of its intent: not in the Anthropology Building, but right on the Midway Plaisance alongside the belly dancers and the Ferris wheel.[29] New York socialite Clarence Day visited and recorded his impressions: "I could reach out and touch them as they stalked about, scowling," he marveled. "And whenever they did I could hear them muttering things to themselves."[30] It would not take much imagination to guess at what they were muttering, given the provocation. The official guide to the fair was more circumspect. "There are forty women and sixty men in the village," it reported. "The various dances and other ceremonials peculiar to these people are exhibited.... They also sell unique products of their mechanical skill." The description closed with an interesting note:

During the later months of the Fair it was found necessary by the management of this enterprise to place a strange placard just outside the entrance. It was a request to all visitors that they refrain from questioning the natives of the village in regard to past cannibal habits of themselves and their ancestors, as it was very annoying to them.[31]

It was probably just as well. When Clarence Day returned to New York, his father demanded his impressions and offered his own: "I was interested in those filthy Hottentots. How people can live in that disgusting manner I don't understand. I didn't know it was allowed."[32]

On the *Devonia*, the steerage passengers became Dahomey. Being regarded as objects of ridicule was their first introduction to the New World, and it was a disturbing one. "Day by day, throughout the passage," Stevenson writes, "this knowledge grew more clear and melancholy."[33] It was also a reminder of the close proximity of the other worlds on board ship, and how they might be transgressed in one direction but not another. Beyond the socialized strata of the decks, ocean liners were metaphorical of the struggle their emigrants would soon face: a world full of doors that opened for others but not for them, of stairs that led in only one direction, of baffles and buffers designed to keep them in their place.

In moments of crisis, these distinctions surfaced most tellingly. As the White Star liner *Republic* sank in 1909, First Class was loaded into the boats, then Second, and finally Third. Three years later, after the general alarm was given on the *Titanic*, stewards knocked on First Class cabins but barged into Second Class and tossed lifejackets onto the beds. Steerage got no warning at all. As the lifeboats were being lowered, a handful of Second Class passengers were told that their lifeboats were "on their own deck," but this was still better than steerage, which remained for the most part locked behind grill cage doors until all the boats were gone. The barriers between First and Third were so efficiently maintained that, despite the rule of women and children first, a greater percentage of First Class men survived than Third Class children.[34]

Robert Louis Stevenson's account, *The Amateur Emigrant*, was never published in full during his lifetime. His own father tried to buy out an advance release of the first few chapters, convinced it would be a social disaster if it became widely known. Indeed, despite Stevenson's protestations that he was not a radical, in the context of its day it was a radical book. In an age of reform, there was no shortage of texts depicting life among the lower classes. But this was different: Life aboard ship was an occasion for reveries on the beauty of nature, the power of the machine, the pleasant society of one's fellow passengers. In the annals of travel literature that emerge from this era, these are the themes that are invariably raised. If any chronicler happens to notice the emigrants below, it is merely to observe how very cheerful they seem. In a buttoned-up era, sounds of unrestrained merriment below could provoke real wistfulness. As one passenger on Inman's *City of Boston* writes:

Just so many of the jolly though uncleanly denizens of the steerage as can find place in the lower gangways huddle there then, smoking, chaffing, skylarking, erewhile dancing—while the saloon passengers look down from the railings above, sometimes not half so happy, and often, I think, aching to have the privilege of joining in the rough amusements...[35]

Indeed, sometimes it seemed from above as if steerage was one giant deck party, as much for the entertainment of upper-deck voyeurs as the emigrants themselves. The possibility that they gathered on deck because their actual quarters were uninhabitable seems not to have occurred to anyone in First Class. "On Saturday afternoon the steerage passengers had a ball," a passenger on the *Adriatic* noted in 1884, "to the great amusement of us on the saloon deck. Very merry they were until sunset, when, according to inexorable rule, the men were relegated to one end of the ship, and the women to the other."[36] Perhaps these revels might have seemed too bacchanalian, for "when Sunday came, one or two well-meaning enthusiasts among our party, anxious for the welfare of the emigrants, tried in the afternoon to get up a sort of informal prayer meeting. But the wind got up at the same time, and the rain came down in torrents, so that the whole affair was a fiasco."[37]

The lure of the lower classes was so great that some shipping lines felt obliged to post notices. "Commanders are requested to discourage communication between saloon and steerage passengers," one read, "for should it become known to the Health or Quarantine Officers that such communication has existed... saloon passengers would probably be made subject to quarantine." Another sounded as if it could have been placed outside an enclosure at the London Zoo: "The passengers of First and Second Class are requested not to throw money or eatables to the steerage passengers, thereby creating disturbance and annoyance."[38]

Despite these warnings, upper-class invasions persisted. Passengers who had never been to Limehouse in London or Five Points in New York could nevertheless indulge the well-known practice of slumming, and then retreat within moments to the cosseted luxury of their own quarters. "In this connection," an etiquette book advised,

it cannot be urged too strongly that it is a gross breach of the etiquette of sea life, and a shocking exhibition of bad manners and low inquisitiveness, for passengers to visit unasked the quarters of an inferior class.... The third class passengers... expect to have the privileges and privacy of their quarters respected also.[39]

There were other, more salacious motives for these incursions. It was well known among gentlemen travelers that the ladies in steerage could neither afford nor desire the elaborate corsetry and layered garments of the middle classes. Steerage women wore simple garments that gave a better sense of the body beneath, and a bare shoulder or unshod foot—or even an exposed suckling breast—was not uncommon. An account of the Inman liners, published in 1875, provides a description of one such "colleen" in steerage so vivid as to be almost pornographic:

> She was a tall, round, bonny wench. She had a pair of large hazel eyes in her head, and that same head was covered with rich auburn hair, and it was very long and very thick, and the beauty of it was that it was scrupulously clean.... Her nose ran straight down from her forehead, and seemed quite to belong to her spotless face, the skin of which was a fleshy, whity brown, especially the white.... She had a small mouth with a row of even teeth in it, which went to show how very red her lips were...[40]

Unless as an object of amusement, sexual arousal, or moral reform, saloon passengers had little use for those below them. A diary entry from the *Celtic* at Queenstown in 1880 summed up the prevailing attitude: "A great many emigrants came on this afternoon, and a sorry looking crowd they are."[41] Genuine interactions were brief or nonexistent and were colored by the prejudices of the age. "One of these asked me if I knew of any work for him in New York," the *Adriatic* passenger—an Englishman—dubiously claims, "when an Irish emigrant, overhearing our conversation, exclaimed, 'Oh, the divil take the work! It's not that I want, it's the money.'"[42]

The general attitude of the American and British public was that Atlantic emigration was a form of charity dispensed by kindly shipowners to their childlike charges. The fact that these charges paid for their tickets, just like any First Class grandee, was quite forgotten. One contemporary author dedicated his book on transatlantic travel to "that generous and far-sighted shipowner, William Inman ... the first to send steamers to Ireland to take on board poor passengers, thereby sparing them the expense and misery of an extra channel voyage."[43]

Since few of the emigrants spoke for themselves, it was left to others to speak on their behalf. After a wild winter storm on the *City of Berlin*, the steerage passengers allegedly presented their captain with a written commendation and a request that he appear before them in the steerage saloon so that they could express their gratitude in person. The captain's speech therein was even more implausible:

> I can assure you it is not me, or my ship's company you have to thank, it is the good ship. She is sixteen years old, she has been faithfully built and well fastened, and has always been well found. Had it been your misfortune to have been in one of those steamers built during the last ten years [for other companies] ... nine out of ten of you would have drowned.[44]

When emigrants did have the rare opportunity to speak in their own voice, few of their listeners liked what they heard. Complaints of poor food quality, inadequate ventilation, physical or sexual abuse by the crew, or dangerous conditions on board were alike dismissed as so much ungrateful whining.[45]

If they did not know it already, emigrants soon realized that the company cared nothing for them at all and was only interested in their welfare as far as keeping them alive (most of the time) and healthy (if practicable) until they reached New York. On the *Veendam* in February 1898, a sudden calamity forward alarmed the predominantly Polish Jewish passengers. The response was predictable:

It was after 5 o'clock on Sunday that there came a terrific crash. We did not know what was the matter. The women sprang from their cots, forgetting their seasickness, and began to rush about shrieking in alarm. We asked to be told what the trouble was, but received no information.... Suddenly one of the officers appeared in steerage and ordered all the men on deck. We obeyed and were put to work on the pumps.[46]

Inasmuch as it was possible, steamship lines pretended the emigrants did not exist at all. A glossy brochure published by the Inman Line in 1889 is indicative. It ran some fifty pages, with illustrations. Over half of that number was devoted to lavish descriptions of First Class. Of steerage there is no mention whatsoever. The only sign that such ships even carried them is found in the foldout plan for the new liners *City of New York* and *City of Paris,* tucked at the end of the brochure. It is a fantastically detailed schema, copied directly from the builder's plans, which not only shows every chair in the dining room but every bed in the cabins and every commode in the lavatories. Fore and aft on the main and upper decks, however, there is a curious white space, devoid of any ornamentation or detail. It is denoted with a single word: "Emigrants."

On the other hand, Second Class received this chaste and modest paragraph:

The excellent accommodations for second cabin passengers are a special feature of these ships, being equal to the first cabin of most vessels, and more complete than anything heretofore attempted. These passengers are carried on the same deck as first cabin, and have a special appropriation of the after and finest portion of the promenade deck.... A plentiful supply of baths with hot and cold water and lavatories is also provided; and, in fact, their staterooms and other accommodations are superior to those first cabins of many steamers.[47]

It is interesting to note that the many excellences of Second Class, having "equaled" First on other ships at the beginning of the paragraph, become "superior" to it by the end. The unspoken subtext was that not only were the accommodations equal to First Class, the passengers therein would be also. Just a decade later, this was a far cry from the "modified oasis in the very heart of the steerages"[48] that Robert Louis Stevenson encountered on the *Devonia*. Here Second Class is a plainer facsimile of First, for a respectable clientele. The repetition of this theme in the passage quoted above is typical: Advertisements for Cunard, White Star, Hamburg–American, and scores of other firms all promised that their Second Class accommodations rivaled First in other ships—which makes one wonder to which ships they referred.

This reflected a conundrum for copywriters. First and steerage sold themselves, being marketed for luxury and economy respectively, but how to describe the charms of Second? The answer came by assuring the would-be passenger that there was no step-down in traveling thus: "As good as First" meant those who chose it were of the same caste as First Class passengers—or at least aspired to be. Positioned halfway between the aristocrats and the *hoi polloi*, Second Class passengers wished to feel they were closer to the former than the latter. Shipping companies capitalized on this social-climbing aspect. When the *Lusitania* appeared in 1907, *Engineering* magazine took pains to denote that the Second Class dining room and smoking room were Georgian, with "a very beautiful sideboard of mahogany," while the drawing room was "in a grey tone, and of the Louis XVI style. The rose of the carpet and curtains, the satin-wood furniture, and the general grey of the walls, make an admirable contrast."[49] Of Third, it said merely that the "advance of accommodation" was "as marked as in the cases of first and second-class" and mentioned that the dining room was finished in polished pine.[50]

Denizens of Second Class might imagine themselves almost on par with First, yet despite their proximity barriers were present. Architects often relegated them to a separate deckhouse on the stern, detached from the rest of the superstructure; Cunard ships invariably followed this pattern until the 1920s. There, in the admittedly less desirable space over the churning propellers, was a scaled-down replica of First: cabins on the main deck, dining saloon on the upper deck, smoking room, lounge and ladies' writing room on the promenade deck, wrapped with a teak walkabout that, if not quite as long as First, nevertheless gave Second Class passengers a brief turn under a sheltered eave overhead.

Separate but not beneath, on an equal plane but rather out of things, their position on the ship gave some indication as to how the shipping lines regarded them—and how they regarded themselves.

When shipping lines had to market to both First and Second Class simultaneously, a kind of schizophrenia ensued. Were Second Class passengers close cousins to First or objects of curiosity like steerage? Inman Line, for one, couldn't quite make up its mind. The result was a masterpiece of condescension:

> The mainmast rises through the afterpart of the promenade deck-house, while at some distance further astern, a railing crosses the deck to divide off the second cabin space.... [T]hese second cabin passengers have an accommodation exceeding in comfort and actual luxury anything heretofore provided for them, with a broad stairway leading down to their dining-saloon. The people from the first cabin walk back here, and envy them this wide and level deck, which is just the place for a dancing floor.... A hundred or more passengers are reclining in chairs or lying about this spacious deck getting much the most comfortable trans-Atlantic passage they ever experienced. They nurse their babies, gossip and sing with music and games, and have generally that very good time which people in their walks of life know so well how to enjoy.[51]

Some distinctions were reinforced by the passengers themselves. The line between First and Second was not as easily drawn or uniformly enforced as First and Third; until the Great War, it was customary for the two classes to worship together on Sunday in the main saloon. Parents traveling First might send their children along in the relative economy of Second and still be assured of almost the same level of care. It was also not uncommon for Second Class gentlemen—if reasonably young and unattached—to be discreetly invited to fill out dancing cards in First Class on gala nights. Notwithstanding these occasional transgressions, passengers traveling in First Class were encouraged to believe that they were a breed apart.

This extended not only to the prestigious Atlantic run but the smaller, shabbier vessels that plied the far-flung routes of empire. Early in the 20th century, English author Somerset Maugham set his short story "P&O" aboard one such steamer making its long trek across the Indian Ocean. With Christmas approaching, the passengers began preparations for a fancy dress party in the saloon. Then a social conundrum arose:

> A meeting was held of the first class passengers to decide whether the second class passengers should be invited, and notwithstanding the heat the discussion was animated. The ladies said that the second class passengers would only feel ill-at-ease. On Christmas Day

it was to be expected that they would drink more than was good for them and unpleasantness might ensue. Everyone who spoke insisted that there was in his (or her) mind no idea of class distinction, no-one would be so snobbish as to think there was any difference between first and second class passengers as far as that went, but it would really be kinder to the second class passengers not to put them in a false position.... The scheme was at last devised to invite the second class passengers, but go to the captain privily and point out to him the advisability of withholding his consent to their coming to the first class saloon.[52]

One can imagine the saloon in which this fictitious exchange might have taken place: damask draperies, mahogany-paneled walls, a harbor scene framed above a carved marble fireplace. The rarified air of First Class seemed to encourage this kind of insularity.

Though advertisers sold the idea that such interiors were intended to remind passengers of home, this was nothing more than pandering to their egos: Unless home was in Newport or the Gold Coast, few even in First Class regularly encountered such luxury.

The need to impress, and to fill ever-expanding interiors without becoming monotonous, produced a pastiche of conflicting styles that if replicated in a private home or even a hotel would have seemed absurd. Even contemporary chroniclers found it all a bit much. "The various apartments," one wrote,

are decorated in almost as many styles and combinations of styles as there are rooms to be adorned. Every monarch's reign, and every period of history of every civilized nation ... have been laid under contribution by the designers of furnishings who seem to regard history from the point of view of its reproductiveness in the matter of mural adornments, the shape of chair legs, the picturesqueness of sideboards, and the scheme of architecture of bedsteads.[53]

Just as Second Class passengers were expected to live up to their surroundings, so too were those in First. But the subtext was different: Instead of offering a vision of a world to aspire to, First Class rooms seemed to reinforce a sense of entitlement; you were there because you *belonged* there and deserved nothing less. The effect on the passengers was empowering and overwhelming at the same time, and might even tempt them to forget their proletarian roots, if they had any:

All social classes of passengers and all tastes in surroundings and furniture are catered for. If a good democratic citizen of the United States thinks he can enjoy his voyage better in an Empire suite of rooms, or a French republican likes a royal suite of one of the

Louis monarchs; or an ardent German Socialist suddenly evinces a desire to travel in luxury in an Imperial suite or one named after some Teuton hero or other; whatever the taste, the steamship company will welcome and make them comfortable, as long as they pay in advance.[54]

The same pragmatic commercial thinking that filled the cattle stalls in steerage operated here as well. First Class was luxurious because it had to be: With more and more shipping lines appearing on the Atlantic, competition was fierce. Not every ship could be the largest or fastest (distinctions they would soon lose anyway), but each could still lay claim to some item of luxury that no other could match. The American Line, for example, heavily advertised the introduction of air mattresses on the *St. Louis* of 1893: Compact, storable, theoretically adjustable to the desired firmness of the occupant via a steward and his pump, they were in fact nothing more than pneumonic rubber bladders that stank and released their contents in flatulent spurts. After a few voyages, they were replaced.[55] Their existence, however, indicated the willingness of the steamship companies to try almost anything to seduce First Class passengers. The commercial equation was a simple one. "Space on a steamship has an economic and commercial value," R. A. Fletcher wrote early in the 20th century,

and no one knows this better than the steamship owners. They understand perfectly, much better than the public, that if the public wants space it must pay for it. . . . The greater the space and the more numerous the luxuries, the higher the prices that may be charged and the greater the number of people who will be tempted to pay them.[56]

As layer upon layer of decks were added to steamships, First Class grew even more remote and exclusive. Hamburg–American pioneered extra-tariff grill rooms aboard their ships in 1905; other companies answered with private dining areas within their suites. Now the very rich could isolate themselves not merely from the lower classes, but from other First Class passengers as well. Those determined to make an excursion down into steerage had to contend with innumerable blind alleys and obstacles in their path. By the turn of the century, naval architects finally achieved what they had been aiming for all along: Passengers from different classes could embark on the same ship without ever coming into contact with one another. Companies even staggered boarding and disembarkation times: Steerage boarded first and exited last; First Class was the opposite. The "hive" that Filson Young describes in 1912 was actually a series of distinct layers with almost no contact between them.

Yet by then it no longer mattered. Fifty years of coexistence aboard the Atlantic steamers had already worked its way into the Victorian/Edwardian psyche, and arriving passengers of each class would continue to have roles pressed on them that were inherited from previous generations. White Star Line's coy decision to name their "millionaires' ships" *Olympic* and *Titanic* made explicit a reality that had been present for some time: First Class passengers were made to feel like gods dawdling on Mount Olympus, gazing down from lofty heights with disdain or amused tolerance at the groundlings below. The privileges of their class were constantly reinforced, from the size of their cabins to the thread count of their pillows to the number of forks at dinner. Most of all was the service: a ubiquitous presence waiting to answer every demand, reasonable or not. Not everyone in First Class was J. P. Morgan or the Duke of Kent, yet the price of a steamship ticket allowed the passenger to indulge that fantasy in surroundings eminently suited for the purpose.

Beneath or behind them (depending on the vessel) was Second Class, the bourgeoisie. Populated for the most part by perfectly ordinary, respectable travelers, its metaphorical position midway within the social strata made it an uneasy kind of purgatory, neither one thing nor the other. Steamship companies did a credible job of reassuring passengers that their median quarters were *almost* as good as those above, but one could never quite forget that somewhere else on the ship—quite often very close—were people whose success in life exceeded one's own, and they were reaping the rewards. The archetypal middle-class tragedy of keeping up with the Joneses was thus played out on every voyage.

Finally there was steerage. The millions who embarked seeking a better life, greater freedom, or more social mobility in America were instantly confronted with a system designed to keep them penned in the lowest, foulest quarters on the ship. They were not only forced to endure the privations of poor food and inadequate lodging, but also the pitying or prurient gaze of those up above.

Whatever their background, the ocean crossing would become their first introduction to the Anglo-American class system. Passengers in First and Second Class understood this system, and their place within it; if anything, the voyage merely served to remind and reinforce that knowledge. But steerage passengers had to be educated. Witness, for example, the gradual disenchantment of Robert Louis Stevenson's fellow travelers. "Emigration," he wrote, "from a word of the most cheerful import, came to sound most dismally on my ear. There is nothing more agreeable to picture and nothing more pathetic to behold."[57] By journey's end the reality of their situation had come home. Optimists among them might regard the voyage as the last gasp of the oppressive Old World they left behind; others soon disabused them of this notion. Sitting on deck, writes Stevenson, "We discussed the probable duration of the voyage, we exchanged pieces of information, naming our trades, what we hoped to find in the new world, or what we were fleeing from in the old; and, above all, we condoled together over the food and the vileness of the steerage."[58]

Nevertheless, for all the rigidity of their separation, First, Second, and Third were all bound on the same journey and experiencing it together. There were moments of transcendence. Standing alone on the *Devonia*'s deck after nightfall, Stevenson felt for the first time the enormity of the enterprise:

The engine pounded, the screw tossed out of the water with a roar, and shook the ship from end to end; the bows battled with loud reports against the billows: and as I stood in the lee scuppers and looked up to where the funnel leaned out, over my head, vomiting smoke, and the black and monstrous topsails blotted, at each lurch, a different crop of stars, it seemed as if all this trouble were a thing of small account, and that just above the mast reigned peace unbroken and eternal.[59]

7

VANDALS ABROAD
Travelogues and the Pleasure Cruise

IN OCTOBER 1868, Mark Twain was about to embark on a six-month lecture tour when a thought occurred to him. The original title of his lecture, "Innocents Abroad," struck him as incongruous. "Dear Sir," he wrote his publishers:

If I have heretofore told you the title of my proposed lecture I beg to alter it. I had not then written the lecture. I have just finished writing it now, & it has taken a little different shape from what I had expected—so I now call it "The American Vandal Abroad." I am one of those myself.[1]

From innocents to Vandals is a telling change. Twain must have had second (or third?) thoughts later on, for when the collection of his speeches was finally published in 1869, the original title was restored. In a sense, both terms were accurate. The passengers of the *Quaker City* were innocents, or at least novices, turned loose on the capitals of Europe (Twain himself was less so, having completed numerous journeys on both the Atlantic and Pacific). Yet they were also, indisputably, Vandals. "Your genuine Vandal is an intolerable and incorrigible relic gatherer," Twain lectured his audiences. He or she is also, apparently, immune or inured to Old World culture. On seeing Da Vinci's *Last Supper* for the first time: "The Vandal goes to see this picture—which all the world praises—looks at it with a critical eye, and says it's a perfect old nightmare of a picture and he wouldn't give forty dollars for a million like it."[2]

Twain's hesitance on nomenclature reflects a deeper ambiguity about the character of the American Vandal—or, as he would later be titled, the American tourist. As a group they were easy enough to identify. Vandal, said Twain, "best describes the roving, independent, free-and-easy character of that class of traveling Americans who are not elaborately educated, cultivated and refined, and gilded and filigreed with the ineffable graces of the first society." They were, in the words of one historian, "well-heeled rubes"[3] of at least middle-class means whose sudden influx of disposable income allowed them the purchase of a steamship ticket. This ticket became an *entrepôt* into a higher strata of society than would be available in Duluth or Des Moines, and the return home promised

FIGURE 10. Samuel Clemens, alias Mark Twain, at the time of his travels recounted in *Following the Equator*. SOURCE: Library of Congress LC-USZ62-5513.

bragging rights for months.[4] "Doing" Europe, as opposed to the more serious expeditions of the Grand Tour (which usually meant a year or longer abroad) was a relatively cheap and easy way to attain cultural refinement.[5]

From whence did these creatures come? Literally and figuratively, the steamships brought them. As the arctic social chill from the Civil War began to thaw, passenger trade on the Atlantic blossomed. Ships were larger, faster, safer, and most importantly cheaper than ever before. New lines—Inman, White Star,

Allan—emerged to challenge Cunard's supremacy on the Atlantic, resulting in a rate war not unlike airline deregulation in the 20th century.[6] Thomas Cook, emboldened by the success of his Great Exhibition excursions, combined steamship tickets with sightseeing at each port and created the first package tours. Similar to our own generation, lower fares and package tours encouraged a new breed of traveler. Politics at home and abroad also favored making the trip. England and the United States were reconciled, albeit reluctantly, after the Confederacy's nearly successful efforts to achieve British recognition. The Continent was at peace, most of the time. In the United States, the war had made fortunes and consolidated many others, and now a new generation of Americans sought enrichment—and bargains—abroad.[7]

Steamship companies welcomed their trade but were not above a few Twain-like barbs at their expense. The Hamburg–American Line published a caustic little cartoon on their liners; one wonders how the "Pa Venu" on board took to it. The scene is a ship's dining saloon, richly furnished:

PURSER (*making "dinner talk"*): Glad you made your mind up to come back with us, Mr. Venu. Did you go everywhere you intended?
PA VENU: Yep, didn't miss nothin'. Went all through Italy, 'n' all over.
PURSER: You spent some time at Venice, of course?
PA VENU: Nop. Meant to, but when we got thar, ther' was this flood or somethin', and the hull place was under water. Everybody goin' round in boats. So we cleared right out.[8]

For all their gaucherie, Mark Twain had sympathy for the Vandals. "I am one myself," he wrote, and meant it: Vandals might be coarse, uneducated, boorish, and prejudiced, but there was no greater cure for all those ills, he thought, than travel in a foreign land. At least the Vandals were curious, which distinguished them from their mud-bound ilk: "You never saw a bigoted, opinionated, stubborn, narrow-minded, self-conceited, almighty mean man in your life but he had stuck in one place ever since he was born," Twain told his audience. In fact, he concluded his lecture with an extraordinary and un-ironic bit of proselytizing that could have been written by the Cunard Line itself:

If there is a moral to this lecture it is an injunction to all Vandals to travel. I am glad the American Vandal goes abroad. It does him good. It makes a better man of him. It rubs out a multitude of his old unworthy biases and prejudices. It aids his religion, for it enlarges his charity and his benevolence, it broadens his views of men and things; it deepens his generosity and compassion for the failings and shortcomings of his fellow creatures. Contact with men of various nations and many creeds teaches him that there are other people in the world besides his own little clique, and other opinions as worthy of attention as his own.[9]

This benign vision spoke more of Twain than his subject. The sentiment recalls Herman Melville, who in an earlier decade wrote that "Travel to a large and generous nature is as a new birth. Its legitimate tendency is to teach profound personal humility, while it enlarges the sphere of comprehensive benevolence until it includes the whole human race."[10] Melville delivered that lecture in 1859, yet the world he described—the world of the traveler—was infinitely different than that of Mark Twain, despite less than a decade separating them. While there can be no question that travel broadened Twain in all the ways he describes,[11] a closer inspection of his fellow Vandals often reveals just the opposite. "Cast into trouble and misfortune in strange lands," Twain writes, "and being mercifully cared for by those he never saw before, [the Vandal] begins to learn the best lesson of all . . . that God puts something good and something lovable in every man His hands create."[12]

But that was just the problem. This new generation of Vandals was *not* cast into misfortune in strange lands. They descended on those lands from the hermetic comfort of a steamship, experienced a day's worth of minor irritation, and got back on the ship with great relief in time for dinner. Recall James Gordon Bennett's belief, voiced on the maiden arrival of the *Great Western* in 1838, that steam travel would ultimately conquer "odious misconstructions and paltry jealousies" between peoples, bringing humanity closer to a holistic oneness. Thirty years later, Mark Twain seems to embrace that concept. An English visitor to America in the 1880s echoed both men when he advised his compatriots:

Every Englishman who can spare the time and the money—the latter being a very important factor in the enterprise—should visit the great English-speaking nation on the other side of the Atlantic. He cannot fail to return with his mind enlarged, his sympathies quickened, and his Old World ideas of hospitality greatly extended.[13]

Yet in fact the opposite was true: Despite the real potential for steam travel to bring cultures into contact and connection, in practice it often drove them further apart. It allowed the world of the traveler—with all its bigotry and conceits—to move with them. American Vandals (and their British cousins) could "do" Europe, or anywhere else for that matter, and still return home with nothing but a few souvenirs and all their worst prejudices confirmed.

Mark Twain was hardly the first to exhort his countrymen on the broadening aspects of steam travel. As early as 1844, William Makepeace Thackeray extolled the delights of a sea voyage to new lands:

It was so easy, so charming, and I think profitable . . . that I can't but recommend all persons who have time and means to make a similar journey—vacation idlers to extend their travels and pursue it: above all, young well-educated men entering life, to take this course, we will say, after that at college; and, having their book-learning fresh in their minds, see the living people and their cities, and the actual aspect of Nature, along the famous shores of the Mediterranean.[14]

Of course, Thackeray was being subsidized by the P&O Line to say that. Yet the choice of words was revealing: "easy, charming, profitable." The central idea was that travel need not be *travailler*, hard work, but rather a boating holiday for well-heeled collegiates and "vacation idlers."

It was not always so. Before the advent of steam, the traveler abroad faced innumerable delays, obstacles, irritations, and even calamities. Sea travel was subject to fickle winds that could keep a ship becalmed for weeks or blow it hundreds of miles off course. Sailing schedules were nothing more than a name, for captains had to await favorable conditions before setting off. Overland travel was even more arduous. This was typically undertaken on large carriages called "diligences" (similar to the American stage coach), which connected most of the major cities of Europe through a circuitous route that took their passengers over countless miles of bumpy roads. Diligence passengers typically spent up to sixteen hours a day locked in a small, heaving box with as many as ten other persons, bouncing along on hard horsehair benches. There were no lavatories, and meals and ablutions would have to wait until the coach arrived at a local inn for the night. Highwaymen lay in wait all along the route. An account from the era is evocative:

INSIDE.—Crammed full of passengers—three fat fusty old men—a young Mother and her sick child—a cross old maid. . . . Awake out of a sound nap with the cramp in one leg and the other in a lady's bandbox—pay the damage for gallantry's sake—getting out in the dark at the half-way house, in the hurry stepping into the return coach and finding yourself the next morning at the very spot you had started from the evening before—not a breath of air—asthmatic old woman child with the measles . . . unpleasant smell—shoes filled with warm water . . .[15]

Those travelers who wished to explore lands beyond Europe were strictly left to their own devices. There were hardly any guidebooks or atlases. Local travel had to be arranged on the fly with whomever and whatever conveyance could be found. This precluded all but the hardiest and most adventurous souls, those for whom adversity was a stimulant. It also meant that "pleasure" travel was a contradiction in terms: one traveled for necessity, not pleasure.[16]

The Hamburg–American Line, writing smugly from the vantage of 1873, took pity on these early pioneers. "Who," it asked rhetorically, "when settling down to a sumptuous dinner in one of the palaces on wheels of our railways, thinks of the scanty meals, hastily taken at miserable roadside inns in former days? Who, when ensconced in one of our magnificent Drawing Room Carriages, and reclining on its elastic cushions . . . cares now-a-days for the thousand petty annoyances our fathers experienced?" And yet those memories were not far off: "it is not over thirty years," the pamphlet proclaims, "since a person undertaking a tour . . . was subjected to all these hardships":

Should it then be a matter of surprise that our fathers abhorred traveling, and only ventured on a journey when it was really indispensible? Leaving the exploration of distant climes to more adventurous spirits, bold and daring enough to face the perils and hardships of a voyage across the seas, to be imprisoned for long and tedious months in cabins in which they could not stand erect and wholly destitute of comfort . . . at other times have patience wholly exhausted by waiting for weeks for a favorable breeze to carry them through a channel or a strait that may now be passed in as many hours.[17]

This was not to say that conditions hadn't improved, even before steam. Like Donald McKay's stunning clipper ships, diligences reached the apogee of their design at the exact moment of their obsolescence. By 1830, British coaches had springs and tufted seats and a patented device to keep the wheels from flying off (some improvement!). Instead of rocks and ruts, they traveled over level macadam for much of the route, often at speeds of 12 miles an hour.[18] Coaching inns might not be luxurious, but they had a long enough pedigree that some had become institutions in themselves. Things were improving on the Continent as well. Passengers in France or the German principalities could elect to make their journey by canal barge on the Rhine or Seine: infinitely slow—especially upstream—but smooth.

Nevertheless, no one wrote of the joys of travel in those days, at least not of the journey itself. Joy lay in encounters with locals, unexpected moments when the barriers of language, class, and climate suddenly dissolved, and one experienced the warmth of shared humanity that had so moved Bennett and Twain. Such experiences could not be predicted, scheduled, or planned for. They simply happened. The ideal traveler, then, was hardy, indefatigable, curious, and—most important—open-minded.[19]

Such adventurers often kept records of their voyages, and even as early as the 17th century they discovered that others wanted to read them. The pirates Francis Drake and William Dampier both published accounts of their travels round the world—and recouped their reputations thereby. In the early 19th century, travel writing came into its own, most particularly in America. Washington Irving's *The Sketch Book of Geoffrey Crayon* and James Fenimore Cooper's *Gleanings in Europe* were early examples, followed soon thereafter by Henry Wadsworth Longfellow's *Outre-Mer* and Ralph Waldo Emerson's *English Traits*. By the end of the century the genre had exploded, with such diverse literary lights as Harriet Beecher Stowe, Nathaniel Hawthorne, Frederick Douglass, Lydia Sigourney, Margaret Fuller, Henry James, and Julia Ward Howe all publishing memoirs of their travels in Europe, not to mention political figures like Thurlow Weed, William Henry Seward, Horace Greeley, and President Ulysses S. Grant.[20]

In most early accounts the transatlantic voyage is dispensed with hurriedly. At their best, ocean voyages by sail were long, tedious, and boring. From a literary point of view, it made sense to pass rapidly over them unless something notable occurred. Washington Irving described a thrilling mid-ocean rescue, while other authors related wild storms, wreck sightings, near misses, and the occasional "uncouth porpoise."[21] The ocean had long been a source of literary inspiration, albeit mostly from the vantage of shore. On board it was a different matter. "Let me assure you," Harriet Beecher Stowe confided, "that going to sea is not at all the thing that we have taken it to be. . . . The one step from the sublime to the ridiculous is never taken with such alacrity as in a sea voyage."[22] She goes on:

In the first place, it is a melancholy fact . . . that ship life is not at all fragrant; in short, particularly on a steamer, there is a most mournful combination of grease, steam, onions, and dinners in general, either past, present, or to come, which, floating invisibly in the atmosphere, strongly predisposes to that disgust of existence . . . which makes every heaving billow, every white-capped wave, the ship, the people, the sight, taste, sound and smell of everything a matter of inexpressible loathing! Man cannot utter it.[23]

Mrs. Stowe uttered it at some length. Yet in the decades that followed steamships grew ever larger and grander, ever more removed from the locales they visited. Travel writing reflected this change; everything seemed to have sped up, even the books themselves. The titles were suggestive: Horace Greeley apparently only had time for a few *Glances at Europe*; Eratus Benedict saw things at full gallop in *A Run Through Europe*; and Francis C. Sessions floated over all *On the Wing Through Europe*. Possibly the most direct of all was Edward Everett Hale, who (perhaps unconsciously) reduced the Old World to a quantifiable commodity in *Ninety Days' Worth of Europe*.[24]

Even within this comparatively narrow selection, there are enormous differences in how the crossing is described. Greeley and Benedict, traveling in the 1850s, echoed Mrs. Stowe in her litany of miseries and wrote primarily of storms, icebergs, and seasickness. "So long as I was able," Greeley laments,

I walked the deck, and sought to occupy my eyes, my limbs, my brain, with something else than the sea and its perturbations. The attempt, however, proved a signal failure. By the time we were five miles off the Hook, I was a decided case; another hour laid me prostrate, though I refused to leave the deck; at six o'clock a friend, finding me recumbent and hopeless in the smokers' room, persuaded and helped me to go below. There I unbooted and swayed into my berth, which endured me, perforce, for the next twenty-four hours. I then summoned strength to crawl on deck, because, while I remained below, my sufferings were barely less than while walking above, and my recovery hopeless.[25]

Yet by the time Francis Sessions made the same trip three decades later, a transformation had occurred. There is no mention of illness or discomfort; instead, the first chapter is given over entirely to the wonders of the ship and the pleasures of a transatlantic voyage:

We were only eight days in crossing the ocean in the *City of Berlin*, a splendid floating palace. . . . She is the largest steamship afloat, except the *Great Eastern*, and is nearly as long as the distance from Broad to State Street in front of our Ohio state house in Columbus. . . . Every morning a salt water bath, in marble bathrooms supplied with hot and cold water, could be enjoyed; whist eating and drinking—in fact the entire *menu*—was all that a hungry voyager could desire. One of the pleasures on board was to examine the novelties of the ship, and promenade the long upper and lower decks.[26]

Mark Twain, more perspicacious than any of these authors, nevertheless reveled in the steamships' evolution. He loved watching the broad band of a departing city disappear on the horizon, the sense of freedom and release. "No telegrams could come here," he wrote in 1877, "no letters, no news. This was an uplifting thought. It was still more uplifting to reflect that millions of harassed people on shore behind us were suffering just as usual."[27]

Twain was fascinated by new technology; indeed, investment in it would cost him his entire fortune. As a traveler on all the oceans of the world, he was able to chart the transformation of steamships with great precision. On the Cunarder *Batavia*, which carried Twain across the Atlantic in 1873, cabins were lit by candlelight (shared, in true Scottish fashion, between two rooms and extinguished promptly at 11 o'clock) and passengers entertained on long, hard benches in the saloon. Still, the author had only praise for the ship and its crew. He quoted approvingly Samuel Cunard's famous instructions to his captains, "Your ship is loaded, take her; speed is nothing . . . safety is all that is required" and added his own postscript that "the Cunard people would not take Noah himself as first mate till they had worked him up through all the lower gates and tried him ten years or such matter."[28]

Twenty years later, his allegiance shifted. Coming over on the new German liner *Havel*, he found her in every way superior to the poor old *Batavia*. Now passengers sat on comfortable swivel chairs, ate French delicacies instead of "boiled codfish, boiled potatoes, boiled beef," and retired at night to steam-heated rooms lit by incandescent bulbs. Twain was delighted by the smoking room, the sofas, the "Sabbath stillness" of the engines and the men that operated them. He called her "the delightfulest ship I was ever in," and wrote to a friend that if he could manage it he would happily ferry back and forth on her forever. In an article entitled *About All Kinds of Ships,* written in 1893, he paused for a moment to consider how far they (and he) had come:

In all ways the ocean greyhound of today is imposing and impressive to one who carries in his head no ship pictures of a recent date. In bulk she comes near to rivaling the Ark; yet this monstrous mass of steel is driven five hundred miles through the waves in twenty-four hours. . . . I was a passenger in the excursion tub *Quaker City,* and on one occasion in a level and glassy sea it was claimed that she rattled off two hundred and eleven miles between noon and noon, but that was probably a campaign lie.[29]

The sense of wonderment conveyed in this passage is reminiscent of Twain's description of the Mississippi riverboats; indeed, few people of the century had experienced as many different kinds of steam vessels as he. It is interesting to note that his enthusiasm for them remained unalloyed, even as his attitude towards their passengers, and the nations they represented, soured. He apparently did not perceive that, just as the ships themselves grew and grew, so too did the insularity of the people therein. As steam travel opened new continents for tourism, it created a paradox: The more Americans learned about the world around them, the more aggrandized became their sense of self. Seeing the world from a giant steamship fostered this attitude. The more perceptive amongst them saw, as Twain did, where all this would lead. "If you talk with Europeans," one journalist advised, "it is always nice to give them fresh impressions of just what's the matter with their country and with them."[30]

Sometimes that sense of superiority was so ingrained as to be physically dangerous. A midcentury author recounted the experience of encountering officialdom in the Levant:

A tall, grave Turkish officer, dressed in the blue frock-coat and straight trousers of his uniform, advanced to our Sagamore [American guide] and bade him dismount. "For what reason?" asked our resolute chieftain, without offering to stir from his saddle.

"A new system of passports has been instituted, and yours must be examined."

"Who has ordered it?"

"His Excellency, the pasha."

"Well, send the pasha to me!" thundered the Sagamore, and, putting spurs to his horse, he pranced over the clattering pavement.[31]

By the time Mark Twain arrived on the scene to lampoon it in 1869, steamships had already begun to transform the travelogue genre. If they could not remove the discomfort of seasickness, the mortal fear of storms, or the tedium of days at sea, they at least ameliorated them. Greater comfort and faster passages, as well as the novelty of traveling on board a vast technological wonder, made the crossing an event in itself—worthy of recording. Passengers, as Thackeray observed, were finally at leisure to enjoy and observe their surroundings, and one another. The effects percolated through travel writing over much of the century. Writers began to focus as much on their fellow passengers as on the sights they encountered. Confined for days or even weeks with a random assembly of strangers, they also rediscovered a kind of rude democracy that seemed to fulfill the cross-cultural connections Mark Twain promised. "We had about twenty English passengers," Isabella Bird recorded, "the rest were Canadians, Americans, Jews, Germans, Dutch, French, Californians, Spaniards, and Bavarians":

Some equality was preserved in this heterogeneous assembly. An Irish pork-merchant was seated at dining table next to a Jew who regarded the pig *in toto* as an abomination—a lady, a scion of a ducal family, found herself next to a French cook going out to a San Francisco eating house.... The most conspicuous of our fellow-voyagers was the editor of an American paper, who was writing a series of clever but scurrilous articles on England, from materials gleaned in a three weeks' tour![32]

The transformative effects of steam on travel writing—and on the travelers themselves—were not immediately apparent.[33] Indeed, the first lengthy account of such a voyage, penned in 1842, was enough to discourage anyone from attempting it. Despite their penchant for self-promotion, steamship companies stumbled upon their most valuable mode of advertisement by pure accident. This was the celebrity endorsement. To be sure, the idea was already there: In the days before trademarking, Queen Victoria unwittingly leant her name and image to a range of products from Pears' Soap to Golfer's Oats to Frank Rippingille's Patent Cooking Stoves. Yet to drum up business for the new steamships, something more would be needed. It was not enough for a celebrity to merely visit the ship; the person must experience her as a passenger. This would not only give the celebrity the opportunity to describe her many excellences firsthand but would reassure the traveling public that steam was a safe means of travel.

In 1842, the public was sorely in need of reassurance. In March the previous year, the largest and finest steamer in the world, *S.S. President,* embarked from New York with the famous Irish actor Tyrone Power[34] on board and disappeared forever. After weeks of waiting in vain, the British and American press began to speculate wildly on the ship's probable demise. "Wonderful disclosure!" declared one overeager pamphleteer: "The mystery solved!!, or Narrative of Dr. M. Lorner, one of the passengers of the Steam Ship *President,* which vessel left New York, bound for Liverpool, March 11, 1841, since which time, until recently, nothing has been heard respecting her fate."[35]

This was not the kind of publicity the companies had in mind. When Charles Dickens booked passage on Cunard's flagship *Britannia* in January of 1842, the tragedy was still fresh enough for many to wonder if he was taking his life in his hands. After only three years of operation, Cunard had not yet acquired its legendary reputation for safety. The *Britannia* was considered a fine vessel, but so too had the *President.* Dickens's ostensible purpose in traveling westward was to give dramatic readings of his works to American audiences and settle a royalties dispute with his New York publishers. In actuality, he intended to capitalize on the gaucherie and quaintness of his hosts by writing a humorous travelogue of his journey on the American continent.[36]

If we are to believe his account, Dickens chose the *Britannia* for the same reason as most passengers: He read the brochure. At Cunard's London office he was presented with an image of the main saloon, "a chamber of almost interminable perspective, furnished ... in the style of more than Eastern splendour, and filled ... with groups of ladies and gentlemen in the very highest state of enjoyment and vivacity."[37] A builder's model of the vessel showed a trim packet with elegant lines, gold filigree about the stern, and an aura of competence. The actual vessel, encountered at Liverpool, seemed to live up to expectations:

And there she is! All eyes are turned to where she lies, dimly discernible through the gathering fog of the early winter afternoon; every finger is pointed in the same direction: and murmurs of interest and admiration—as "How beautiful she looks!" "How trim she is!"—are heard on every side.... We are made fast alongside the packet, whose huge red funnel is smoking bravely, giving rich promise of serious intentions.[38]

Yet what seemed grand and powerful from alongside (and in the Cunard offices) gave way to a darker and dingier reality once aboard. The vaunted saloon was nothing but "a long, narrow apartment, not unlike a gigantic hearse with windows in the sides; having at the upper end a melancholy stove, at which three or four chilly stewards were warming their hands."[39] Passageways were narrow and unlit save for a single oil lamp at each end. The air stank of body odor, machine oil, and bilge: "that extraordinary compound of strange smells which is to be found nowhere but aboard ship."

Dickens's cabin was an even greater disappointment. He begins his *American Notes* with a grim surprise: "I shall never forget the one-fourth serious and three-fourths comical astonishment with which, on the morning of the third of January, eighteen-hundred-and-forty-two, I opened the door of, and put my head into, a 'state-room' on board the *Britannia* steam packet."[40] Promised a large and comfortable berth, he found instead an "utterly impracticable, thoroughly hopeless and profoundly preposterous box" with two tiny berths covered with thin mattresses "like a surgical plaster." Nothing smaller had ever been made for sleeping, Dickens declared, except a coffin. Coffins and hearses seemed much on his mind as the *Britannia* left harbor, and for good reason: It was January, the worst month to travel on the North Atlantic, and somewhere amidst the ice floes and storm-tossed seas was the wreckage of the *S.S. President*.

The voyage bore out his worst fears. They were barely out of the channel before the first storm hit, and kept with them for days on end. Dickens's wife was desperately seasick, and he himself was "not ill but going to be." He passed the time by measuring out calomel and other remedies; none of them worked. The sounds of the ship—creaking, groaning, moaning—made him think, yet again, of death. The steam engine under his feet terrified him: "fire in hiding, ready to burst through any outlet, with its resistless power of death and ruin." One morning he awoke to find an inch of seawater sloshing around on the cabin floor and all his possessions soaked. Thinking the ship was going down, he stopped a steward in the passageway and demanded to know what was happening. "Rather a heavy sea on, sir," came the laconic reply.[41]

Halfway across the storms moderated, and boredom set in. Dickens's account of listless days at sea would be familiar to generations of travelers:

> The captain being gone, we compose ourselves to read, if the place be light enough, and if not, we doze and talk alternately. At one, a bell rings and the stewardess comes down with a steaming dish of baked potatoes, and another of roasted apples; and a plate of pig's faces, cold ham, salt beef; or perhaps a smoking mess of hot collops. We fall upon these dainties; eat as much as we can (we have great appetites now); and are as long as possible about it. If the fire will burn (it *will* sometimes) we are pretty cheerful. If it won't, we all remark to each other that it's very cold, rub our hands, cover ourselves with coats and cloaks, and like down again to doze, talk and read.[42]

After two weeks the *Britannia* arrived in Halifax and promptly ran aground. The engine shuddered to a stop, and Dickens observed several seamen remove their shoes in preparation to swim ashore. The captain fired rockets into the air, but there was no reply. Finally, after a melancholy night, the ship floated free. Two days later they reached Boston, where Charles Dickens gratefully disembarked. He returned home by sailing packet.

The journey, published later that year in *American Notes for General Circulation*, would become famous. Dickens's humorous depiction of the *Britannia*'s failings provided fodder for generations of historians to deride the early steamers as uncomfortable and dangerous, most often in comparison to the sybaritic delights of later ships.[43] One such irresistible statistic: The whole of the *Britannia* could fit within the *Queen Mary*'s First Class dining room. Even today aboard the *Queen Mary 2* there is a panel depicting Dickens's "preposterous" cabin, with a short excerpt from his *Notes* alongside.

What was more significant to his contemporaries, however, was that despite the cold and discomfort, the *Britannia* carried him safely across the Atlantic through one of the worst storms on record. The Cunard Line, for one, never pretended to do anything else. "There were no napkins at our table," one passenger reported,

and when our passengers made a sort of protest to the Company in regard to what we considered hardships... old Mr. MacIver [one of the Line's founders] replied that going to sea was a hardship, that the Cunard Company did *not* undertake to make anything else out of it, and that if people wanted to wipe their mouths at a ship's table they could use their pocket handkerchief.[44]

When a company employee suggested replacing the hard padded benches in the *Britannia*'s saloon with armchairs, as most other lines had done, MacIver threw the man out of his office.[45]

As an advertisement for the Cunard Line, Charles Dickens's experience was lacking. But the potential for publicity was still there: If he had enjoyed his voyage, the boon for the Cunard Line might have been enormous. Even as it was, Dickens's caustic review did not discourage many passengers. A few years later, in 1844, the Peninsular and Oriental Steamship Line decided to leave nothing to chance. The company offered William Makepeace Thackeray free steamship tickets from Cornhill to Cairo if he would agree to write up his experiences. A favorable review for the line was taken for granted. Thackeray agreed, and thus began one of the earliest press junkets on record.

Thackeray might not have had the celebrity status of Charles Dickens, but he was a rising star. Known principally for his satirical articles in *Fraser's Magazine* and *Punch*, he had recently published his most successful novel to date, *The Luck of Barry Lyndon*. A short, round man with a fondness of sweetmeats and a penetrating glare, Thackeray is commonly credited with popularizing the word *snob* (in reference to others, not himself). In 1844 he was still three years away from the meteoric success of his greatest novel, *Vanity Fair*. He was witty, intelligent, and hungry in several senses of the word. In sum, he was a perfect choice for the P&O Line.

Since blatant flattery by a well-known personage might seem suspicious, Thackeray gave himself a *nom de plume*, M. A. Titmarsh, and took pains at the outset to disavow any ulterior motive for his *Notes of a Journey*:

These important statements are made partly to convince some incredulous friends—who insist still that the writer never went abroad at all, and wrote the following pages, out of pure fancy, in retirement at Putney; but mainly, to give him an opportunity of thanking the Directors of the Company in question for a delightful excursion.[46]

Even contemporary readers might be skeptical of such sentiments, and it is probable that "Mr. Titmarsh" anticipated his readers would see through this obfuscation. Very likely they did not care. The point was the journey, and Thackeray proved just as adept a travel writer as Dickens had been, albeit with a more whimsical flair. "On deck beneath the awning," he lyricizes one sleepless night en route to Smyrna:

I dozing lay and yawning; It was the grey of dawning, Ere yet the sun arose; And above the funnel's roaring, And the fitful wind's deploring, I heard the cabin snoring, With universal nose. I could hear the passengers snorting, I envied their disporting: Vainly I was courting, The pleasure of a doze.[47]

Thackeray followed the P&O on its longest uninterrupted route (without overland connections), journeying from England to various ports in Spain, Greece, the Ottoman empire, and the Middle East, terminating at Cairo. The passenger compliment was the usual mix of clergymen, empire builders, and locals using the ship to ferry from port to port. Thackeray was one of a handful of genuine tourists, perhaps twenty in all. Biased and blinkered by the need to repay his debt to P&O, his *Notes* are nevertheless a fascinating record of one of the earliest pleasure cruises ever undertaken. What is so shocking is their familiarity: Much of what Thackeray experienced en route came to define steam tourism, and many of these themes survive even now.

Take, for example, Mark Twain's optimistic words of the broadening effects of travel. Twenty-five years earlier, Thackeray had a very different view and his proved more durable. In common with most cruise passengers today, he lamented that the short stay in each port barely left enough time to touch the major sights, much less engage in any meaningful way with the citizenry. And after a while all ports started to look the same: a city hall, a market square, bronze statues of the local nabobs. Travel, which should be exploration, became a chore:

A great misfortune which befalls a man who has but a single day to stay in a town, is that fatal duty which superstition entails upon him of visiting the chief lions of the city in which he may happen to be. You must go through the ceremony, however much you may sigh to avoid it; and however much you know that the lions in one capital roar very much like the lions in another; that the churches are more or less large and splendid, the palaces pretty spacious, all the world over; and that there is scarcely a capital city in this Europe but has its pompous bronze statue or two of some periwigged, hook-nosed emperor, in a Roman habit, waving his bronze baton on his broad-flanked brazen charger.[48]

To be fair, there was no mistaking Constantinople for Deptford. But the question was, by the time Thackeray and his fellow tourists arrived at their destination, would all capacity for wonder be leeched out of them? "Are we so blasé," Thackeray worried, "that the greatest marvels in [the world] do not succeed in moving us?" In a word, yes. Having journeyed some 4,000 miles across the Mediterranean and into the very heart of the mysterious Levant, he finally stood before the object of his travels. "My sensation with regard to the Pyramids was that I had seen them before; then came a feeling of shame that the view of them should awaken no respect." His letdown is a familiar one; in a world that was already becoming acclimated to print culture, icons lost their mystique. Many years later, in 1912, English dramatist Maurice Baring spotted the Rock of Gibraltar from his porthole and exclaimed: "It looks exactly like the advertisements of the Prudential Life Insurance Company!"[49]

William Thackeray was a professional satirist of the upper classes, so one could argue he was paid to be blasé. But what of his fellow travelers? "Trinity College, Oxford, was busy with the cold ham," he reports, describing each by his antecedents:

Downing Street was particularly attentive to a bunch of grapes; Figtree Court behaved with decent propriety; he is in good practice, and of a Conservative turn of mind, which leads him to respect from principle *les faits accomplis*: perhaps he remembered that one of them [the Pyramids] was as big as Lincoln's Inn Fields. But, the truth is, nobody was seriously moved.[50]

To his credit, Thackeray seems saddened by this. Why come halfway round the world only to be underwhelmed? With an unusually clear gaze, he contemplated the parochial nature of the English tourist. Was it really surprising that such an insular, ignorant people would fail to be reduced to silent awe in the face of the monumental? It was not their fault, Thackeray decided:

What is the reason that blundering Yorkshire squires . . . should think proper to be enthusiastic about a country of which they know nothing; the mere physical beauty of which they cannot, for the most part, comprehend; and because certain characters lived in it two thousand four hundred years ago? What have these people in common with Pericles, what have these ladies in common with Aspasia (O fie)? Of the race of Englishmen who come wandering about the tomb of Socrates, do you think the majority would not have voted to hemlock him?[51]

In truth, Thackeray was no better himself. He could solemnly admire the Greek, Turk, Jew, or Egyptian, as long as they were dead. The living specimen appalled him. Rolling back in a hired diligence from the Acropolis, he caught sight of a band of locals and wondered how "yonder dirty, swindling, ragged blackguards, lolling over greasy cards three hours before noon, quarrelling and shrieking, armed to the teeth and afraid to fight, are bred out of the same land which begot the philosophers and heroes."[52] That was apparently as close a contact as he could bear, for when a party of Jews and Muslims came aboard at Smyrna, all attempts at light irony were set aside:

The sailing of our vessel direct for Jaffa brought a great number of passengers together, and our decks were covered with Christian, Jew, and Heathen. . . . The dirt of these children of captivity exceeds all possibility of description; the profusion of stinks which they raised, the grease of their venerable garments and faces, the horrible messes cooked in the filthy pots, and devoured with the nasty fingers, the squalor of mats, pots, old bedding, and foul carpets of our Hebrew friends, could hardly be painted by Swift in his dirtiest mood, and cannot be, of course, attempted by my timid and genteel pen.[53]

So much for the broadening effect of exposure to other cultures. Thackeray's attitude is of a man whose house has been invaded, and for the remainder of the *Notes* he makes frequent references to the "dirty Jews" that disturb his sleep, interrupt his walks along the deck, and parade their "disgusting habits" in front of him. The sanctity of the ship was lost. This was no small matter, for the P&O liner had become a bastion of insular Britishness. Readers of a certain generation might recall David Niven's Phileas Fogg ordering roast beef and suet pudding on a sweltering ship bound for India. "All that food on an 'ot day," the steward laments.

But P&O made no concessions to climate, or patronage. Near Aden, Thackeray reprints with approval the day's menu: "Mulligatawny Soup; Salt Fish and Egg Sauce; Roast Haunch of Mutton; Boiled Shoulder and Onion Sauce; Boiled Beef; Roast Fowls . . ."[54] Caustic as he may be of his fellow Britons, they are the only passengers he deigns to speak with throughout the entire cruise. The ship, which in truth was little more than a glorified ferry for local trade, is transformed into a national symbol. On seeing another vessel go aground in Vigo:

We Britons on board the English boat received the news of the "Groenenland's" abrupt demise with grins of satisfaction. It was a sort of national compliment, and cause of agreeable congratulation. "The lubbers!" we said; "the clumsy humbugs! There's none but Britons to rule the waves!" and we gave ourselves piratical airs, and went down presently and were sick in our little buggy berths.[55]

Again and again, Thackeray reinforces the notion of the ship as "home." It is comfortable, familiar, civilized, British—in short, everything that the world outside is not. When Thackeray returns from a day of riding along dusty roads and enduring the unwanted attentions of natives, it welcomes him back with beef tea and Yorkshire accents and Church of England services on Sunday. Little wonder he was so outraged when the party of "foreigners" embarked. The ship is sanctuary. Indeed the only unreserved praise in the whole of the *Notes* comes for the P&O liner and its crew. While much of this can be credited to the financial arrangement between Thackeray and the line, it is hard not to impute a genuine fondness in passages like this:

In the week we were on board—it seemed a year, by the way—we came to regard the ship quite as a home. We felt for the captain—the most good-humoured, active, careful, ready of captains—a filial, a fraternal regard; for the provider, who provided for us with admirable comfort and generosity, a genial gratitude; and for the brisk steward's lads—brisk in serving the banquet, sympathizing in handing the basin—every possible sentiment of regard and good-will.[56]

Evelyn Waugh once wrote, "Every Englishman abroad, until it is proved to the contrary, likes to consider himself a traveler and not a tourist."[57] Travelers explore, seek out new experiences, immerse themselves in the culture and customs of their hosts. Tourists are conveyed from place to place in a pack of like-minded nationals and expect all things to be done for them. Their culture comes in small doses, which can be washed off as easily as port dirt in the ship's sluice bath afterward. As historian Chloe Chard describes it:

The romantic approach defines this adventure as one that entails crossing symbolic as well as geographical boundaries, experiencing travel as a means of self-exploration and self-realization, and encountering various forms of destabilization and danger. The approach of the tourist, formulated in opposition to this romantic outlook, recognized the possibility that the traveler may be drawn into plots of transgression and destabilization, but insists that it is still feasible to keep any major threat to the self and to identity at bay.[58]

William Makepeace Thackeray and his compatriots were very much tourists. The *Lady Mary Wood* and *Tagus* kept them insulated from the places they visited, allowing them to observe without gaining any real understanding. Consequently,

Thackeray's descriptions of such places are often superficial, photographic. One can read the whole of *Notes of a Voyage* and still have only the barest glimpse of what they looked (or sounded, or smelled) like.

The most in-depth depictions are of his fellow passengers and the ship itself. This is not surprising, given the mode of transport. Waugh also wrote about traveling aboard a steamship: "I soon found my fellow passengers and their behavior in the different places we visited a far more absorbing study than the places themselves."[59] Thackeray would have agreed with that sentiment. He undertook the voyage of a lifetime and returned to England confirmed in all his worst prejudices. He then conveyed those prejudices to the reading public, which accepted them as truth. What choice did they have? After all, he had been there.

. . .

Englishmen might balk at the title of tourist, but Americans had no such compunctions. The first Americans to "cruise" through Europe were a grisly sample of the breed. More important than encountering new cultures was, for them, the opportunity to hold each up in unfavorable comparison with America and shine its beacon hard into uncomprehending eyes. Their steamer, the aptly named *Quaker City*, left New York for a six-month tour of the Old World and the Holy Land on June 8, 1867. Amongst them was Mark Twain.

Twain was by far the most traveled of his compatriots.[60] He had already embarked on tours across the United States and through the Pacific, as a reporter for the *Sacramento Union*. It was ironic and prescient that his first visit outside the United States should be to a place that would soon become its first overseas colony: Hawaii. Unlike his later voyages, however, this time Twain traveled by sail. The two-week voyage took twenty-eight days, with fourteen spent becalmed in the middle of the Pacific. It was enough to instill a lifelong loathing for sailing packets over steam. Writing on the deck of a steamship many years later, Twain commented, "I hear no sea-songs in this present vessel, but I heard the entire layout in that one."[61]

Arriving in Honolulu in March of 1866, Twain discovered a kingdom in transition. The Sandwich Islands, as they were called, were no longer isolated: In 1851 missionaries Samuel Castle and Amos Cooke had set up a trading post that soon expanded into a vast conglomerate involved in everything from railways to pineapples. Honolulu transformed almost overnight from a forbidden royal enclave to a bustling metropolis. According to Twain, captains and missionaries formed one-half its population, foreign (mostly American) merchants another quarter, and native Hawaiians the remainder. King Kamehameha V sported a Van Dyke and English tweeds; his sister combed her dark hair in careful imitation of the young Victoria.[62]

America's presence could be felt everywhere, from the stout brick churches to the Sailor's Home. As a neophyte traveler, Twain wrote approvingly of Hawaii's westernization and discovered that there was nothing more pleasing to American readers than to hear, first, that foreigners wanted to be like them and, second, that they weren't. A note of insularity crept into his dispatches. Hawaiians, he reported, were happy, pagan, childlike, but—like their aboriginal cousins in North America—savages. While deploring missionary attempts to civilize them, Twain was hardly less contemptuous of the people themselves. "The missionaries have Christianized and educated all the natives," he wrote. "All this ameliorating cultivation has at last built up in the native women a profound respect for chastity—in other people."[63]

Twain's attitude toward the natives he encountered, and towards himself, would eventually transform. But he was still very much confirmed in these parochial opinions when he embarked on an even more ambitious journey in 1867. The voyage of the *Quaker City* was unique in that for the first time in American history the entire Grand Tour would be accomplished from the deck of a single steamer, an idea borrowed from Cornelius Vanderbilt's celebrated yachting tours on the *North Star* (although not from Thackeray's voyage, which had not made much of an impression in the United States).[64] There would be no connecting trains, no queues, no disagreements with taxi men, no dirty or bug-infested hotels. Passengers would disembark, see the sights, and get back on again that evening.

Twain was captivated by the thought of it, especially the ship itself. He and his fellow passengers "were to sail away in a great steamship with flags flying and cannons pealing, and take a royal holiday beyond the broad ocean."[65] The choice of words is revealing. By removing the Grand Tour to a steamship, it gave the whole excursion the feel of an imperial procession. Passengers would descend amongst the throng, be whisked away to whatever cultural wonders awaited them, then carried back up and aboard. The palpable distance from deck to pier reinforced their detachment. In a word, they were not traveling *through* Europe but *above* it. It was the first American pleasure cruise and a model for all to come.[66]

Yet in contrast to the modern cruise passenger, Twain's companions were a sober and forbidding lot.[67] The excursion had originally been organized by the famous 19th-century clergyman Henry Ward Beecher, and thus the whole of the

European tour was merely a prelude for what followed: the Holy Land. Reverend Beecher backed out at the last moment, citing other commitments, but that did not prevent the ship's complement from resembling a Chautauqua revival tent. Liquor and mirth were in short supply, and one passenger gravely advised the captain to halt the vessel's progress mid-Atlantic, on the Sabbath.[68]

Solemn as his companions might have been, like the Hawaiian natives they made excellent copy. The dislike Twain felt for most of them, and they for him, kept a healthy detachment between writer and subject. Twain whiled away his time on deck, observing and taking notes. Within a few days, he had already identified several distinct groups. First were the Divines, who brought to pleasure cruising the grim determination of Wesleyan missionaries. Next were the Old Travelers, who claimed to have been everywhere already and delighted in instructing those who had not. In an age before Kodak slides, these bores had to content themselves with spinning long and spurious tales. "We love the Old Travelers," Twain wrote. "We love to hear them prate and drivel and lie.... Their central idea, their grand aim, is to subjugate you, keep you down, make you feel insignificant and humble in the blaze of their cosmopolitan glory!"[69]

Similar were the third group, the Continentals. These had become so enraptured with foreign phrases and customs that they adopted them, only to trot them out for their companions when they returned. "I love this sort of people," Twain wrote, though he didn't. "A lady passenger of ours tells of a fellow-citizen who spent eight weeks in Paris and then returned home and addressed his dearest old bosom friend Herbert as Mr. 'Er-bare'!"[70] If Americans were quickly developing an insufferable reputation abroad, it was no worse than they enjoyed after they returned home. Mark Twain was forced to endure their company on a short train ride from New York to Boston. Pouring out his rage for his readers, he asked rhetorically,

Have you ever seen a family of geese just back from Europe—or Yurrup, as they pronounce it? They never talk *to* you, of course, being strangers, but they talk to each other and *at* you... till you are sick of their imbecile faces and relentless clack, and wish it had pleased Providence to leave the clapper out of their empty skulls.[71]

After reconstructing a dialogue filled with allusions to "Count Nixkumarouse" and "that nahsty old tub, the *Ville de Paris*," Twain dismissed them as "a *nahsty* family of American snobs, and there ought to be a law against allowing such to go to Europe and misrepresent the nation."[72]

The temptation for going native ran strong, even in staunch Calvinist breasts. When the *Quaker City* left Tangier, her passengers arrayed themselves in fezzes; in Constantinople they turned out in turbans, tunics, and harem pants. "Oh, we were gorgeous!" But clothes can be discarded. More insidious was the disposition among some Continentals to become so enamored of foreign mores that they rejected their own. For Twain, a patriot, these were ludicrous: "It is not pleasant to see an American thrusting his nationality forward *obtrusively* in a foreign land, but oh it is pitiable to see him making of himself a thing that is neither male nor female . . . poor, hermaphroditic Frenchman!"[73]

Worst of all, in Mark Twain's opinion, was the last group. He had no name for them, and they were perhaps too numerous to classify. But their behavior was unmistakable: Twain was seeing the very first Ugly Americans. Symptoms manifested themselves before they had even made it across the Atlantic. "We were troubled a little at dinner today," he wrote in his journal,

by the conduct of an American, who talked very loudly and coarsely, and laughed boisterously where all others were so quiet and well behaved. This fellow said: "I am a free-born sovereign, sir, an American, sir, and I want everybody to know it!" He did not mention that he was a lineal descendant of Balaam's ass, but everyone knew that without his telling it.[74]

Things only got worse once they reached Europe. The first encounter with "furriners" led some Americans to forsake their nationality and others to rigorously and unnecessarily defend it. The two were not incompatible: Throughout his life Twain often felt the lure of exotic climes, yet held tight to his American identity. This tension was expressed in his writing, particularly his tendency to compare foreign wonders with American landmarks—usually unfavorably. Thus Venice was a "funny old city" that reminded him of an overflowed Arkansas town, and the Great Pyramid was very fine, but not so impressive as Holliday's Hill in Missouri![75] Partly this was a sop to his readers, wearied by travelogues that read like panegyrics, but not entirely. Comparing great monuments with local wonders belittled the former and aggrandized the latter.

For Twain, this leveling seemed only fair. Why should Europe hold claim to all the culture and beauty and history in the world? Why should Lake Como be infinitely superior to Lake Tahoe, simply because it is Italian? In Italy, too, he discovered his nemesis: Michael Angelo. According to the guides, every significant article in Rome had been designed by him: "He designed St. Peters; he designed the Pope; he designed the Pantheon, the Tiber, the Vatican, the Coliseum.... I never felt so fervently thankful, so soothed, so tranquil, so filled with a blessed peace, as I did yesterday when I learned that Michael Angelo was dead."[76]

If Twain and his companions were expected to evince wonder at these marvels, they reacted by vowing never to show any emotion whatsoever. Like comparing Venice to Arkansas, this was a conscious rejection of the idea that the Old World had anything to teach the New. Twain's motives were mostly benign—the natural irritation of a tourist surfeited by too much culture (a complaint still uttered by holiday seekers today) combined with latent patriotism and the fear that if he surrendered to these seductions he too might end up a "hermaphrodite."[77]

Others had darker impulses. The bigoted, insular American that saw everything and absorbed nothing was much in evidence. Indeed, for many it seemed as though his only reason for embarking was to pour scorn on the locals he encountered. Some of this came from prejudices nursed at home, suddenly confronted by peoples that neither understood nor condoned them. Americans seemed particularly prone to these gaffes. "Vulgar, vulgar, vulgar," Henry James described them. "Their ignorance, their stingy, defiant, grudging attitude towards everything European, their perpetual reference of all things to some American standard ... these things glare at you hideously."[78] On a Caribbean cruise in 1914, for example, a company of Midwesterners were brought ashore to meet the president of Haiti, only to flee in disgust when they discovered the president was black.[79] For many of the passengers of the *Quaker City*, every dark face or "heathen" custom was an opportunity to reassert their patriotic rectitude. "The people stared at us everywhere," said Twain, "and we stared at them. We generally made them feel pretty small, too, before we got done with them, because we bore down on them with America's greatness until we crushed them."[80]

Mark Twain and his fellow voyagers were learning to think like imperialists. The central idea was that they, and not those whom they encountered, occupied the mythic "center." In fact it moved with them. Therefore everyone they met was a foreigner, despite the reality that the Americans were standing on someone else's soil and were, consequently, foreigners themselves. This insularity did not make their reactions uniform. One might greet the foreigners with missionary zeal, as potential converts either to Protestantism or, more broadly, American ideals. Another dismissed them as in every way inferior and unworthy of conversation, much less conversion. Such disregard did not extend, however, to business transactions. Twain was amused to observe that those passengers who harbored the most disdain also drove the hardest bargains and came back to the ship perversely proud that they had "put one over" the natives. What was not bought was stolen: Passengers whittled off chunks from an alleged true cross, pocketed relics of pottery from Pompeii, and shamelessly snatched up goodwill gifts from naïve locals. Mark Twain secreted a stone from Solomon's temple as a gift for his mother, though he felt bad about it afterwards. When he referred to himself and his party as Vandals, after the hordes that sacked Rome, he was not kidding.

There was nothing singular in any of this behavior. In fact, judging by the graffiti etched into the walls of many of the sacred places they visited, Americans had been coming and leaving their mark for some time. The stereotypes observed by Twain were not just on the *Quaker City*; they predated the voyage, and regrettably sometimes still hold true. The uniqueness of the *Quaker City* voyage lay, first, in the presence of a chronicler who depicted them with such savage accuracy that they are recognizable for readers today. Second, and just as exceptional, was the *Quaker City* herself.

Previously, Americans abroad could never entirely distance themselves from the locales they visited. It was impossible to feel detached from Morocco, for example, if one ate and slept and performed one's ablutions there. While grand hotels might protect guests from the alien clamor outside, no amount of velvet drapery could convince Minnesotans that they were still in Duluth. But a ship was a different matter. Now the mythic center that moved with Twain and his fellow tourists was not mythic but actual: the steamship. By living aboard the vessel, traveling upon it from place to place, and descending only briefly into foreign climes, passengers could reasonably feel that they had never left home. Like Jules Verne's "Propeller City," the vast steamship was a floating, moving island.

Except that it did not move: Places came to it. Anyone who has experienced a pleasure cruise knows this sensation. Each day, a different city. Passengers disembarked after breakfast into waiting jitneys, were carried off into the town for a day's excursion, and arrived back that evening. The sights and sounds and smells of the ship were familiar and welcoming. Whatever horrors one endured on shore—avaricious guides, pushy peddlers, disappointing vistas—disappeared on descending to dinner and finding the ship's orchestra playing popular tunes, the dining steward pulling back one's chair, and friends waiting to swap stories. Best of all, the hum of conversation was reassuringly American. Coming back from a long day at Leghorn, Twain spoke words familiar to generations of cruise passengers thereafter:

We never entirely appreciated before what a very pleasant den our stateroom is, nor how jolly it is to sit at dinner in one's own seat in one's own cabin, and hold familiar conversation in one's own language.... We are surfeited with Italian cities for the present, and much prefer to walk the familiar quarter deck.[81]

The *Quaker City* was embassy, sanctuary, and avatar. For the first time, American tourists could preserve the fiction that they remained "at home" while the world moved past them. They could visit foreign lands without enduring the inconveniences of total immersion; whether arriving in Constantinople or St. Petersburg or Jerusalem, the fixed center was the *Quaker City*, which remained unchanged and reassuringly American. With its vaulted rooms, tufted cushions, and beveled mirrors, it also presented a physical embodiment and omnipresent reminder of America at its best. For those who enjoyed holding up other nations in scornful comparison, this was an unexpected boon. How could any city, with its litter and paupers and dirt, compare with the antiseptic charms of the steamship?[82]

A floating city also gave its passengers a shared sense of identity. "Home again!" Twain wrote gleefully after returning from a three-week excursion. He marveled at how quickly the passengers had become a family, even including himself: "The seats were full at dinner again, and the life and bustle on the upper deck in the fine moonlight at night was like old times—old times that had been gone weeks only, but yet were so crowded with incident, adventure and excitement that they felt like years."[83] Considering that these were the same God-botherers Twain had disparaged just weeks before, it was clear that being aboard ship worked its alchemy on them all. Passengers on a steamship invariably formed close bonds, a consequence of spending nearly every waking hour together. Indeed the society of the ship became their whole world, as one author has commented:

[T]he tentative formation of groups and experimental alliances, the rapid disintegration of these and re-formation on entirely new lines; and then that miracle of unending interest and wonder, that the faces that were only the blurred material of a crowd begin one by one to emerge from the background and detach themselves from the mass, to take on identity, individuality, character, till what was a crowd of uninteresting, unidentified humanity becomes a collection of individual persons with whom one's destinies for the time are strangely and unaccountably bound up; among whom one may have acquaintances, friends, or perhaps enemies; who for the inside of a week are all one's world of men and women.[84]

Now, on a pleasure cruise, this camaraderie was juxtaposed with a kaleidoscope of unfamiliar faces. It was natural, and inevitable, for the American passengers to band together against these foreign intrusions: a phenomenon that, writ large, would one day be termed "us versus them." William Makepeace Thackeray had expressed himself in almost exactly the same words, twenty-five years before:

We all left the house of entertainment joyfully, glad to get out of the sun-burnt city and go HOME. Yonder in the steamer was home, with its black funnel and gilt portraiture of "Lady Mary Wood" at the bows; and every soul on board felt glad to return to the friendly little vessel.[85]

Whatever faults Mark Twain found in his fellow passengers, he came away from his voyage on the *Quaker City* enraptured by the ship and the community it fostered. His concluding comments in *The Innocents Abroad* were a powerful testament to the nexus between the imperial imagination and steam:

When I travel again, I wish to go in a pleasure ship. No amount of money could have purchased for us, in a strange vessel and among unfamiliar faces, the perfect satisfaction and the sense of being *at home* again which we experienced when we stepped on board the *Quaker City—our own ship—*after this wearisome pilgrimage. It is something we have felt always when we returned to her, and something we had no desire to sell.[86]

Were the Vandals also innocents? If innocence is ignorance, they were. Tourists of the steam age traveled more widely and in greater numbers than ever before, yet remained woefully ignorant of the places they visited. Pa and Ma Venu "did" Yurrup, collected souvenirs, took "snaps" of the locals, and returned to their homes confirmed in their prejudices. The experience was no longer the locale, but the ship itself. Greater comfort and service accentuated the feeling of "coming home" after a frustrating day ashore. Familiarity of language, like-minded passengers, and Anglo-American fare turned such vessels into floating embassies that carried their nationalities wherever they went. Even the most objective observers, Thackeray and Twain, succumbed to their delights. It was impossible to resist. In Thackeray's case, his prejudices were not only confirmed by steam travel, but disseminated to a wider reading public. This was the same as one who returns from a voyage abroad and tells one's neighbors that everything was as dirty, avaricious, uncomfortable, and uncivilized as expected. Not only has the experience failed to broaden the traveler, it compounds the ignorance of one's listeners by validating their chauvinism. As steam travel ascended, and more and more people took their holidays abroad, this phenomenon increased.

"The blissful isolation of a cruise," one 19th-century passenger wrote, "is not seriously interfered with when the ship stops at port. The visits are too brief to allow local, contemporary reality to disturb our detachment."[87] Naturally, not all travelers were boors. Those who were genuinely curious and open to new cultures now had greater opportunity to satisfy such desires. Mark Twain was perhaps the most developed—and certainly the most articulate—of this type. He was circumspect, self-aware, to a degree almost unique in his time. His writing evinces an understanding that there were animals on both sides of the zoo fence. When Twain spoke of himself and his party as "innocents," he referred to the best, rather than the worst, within them: "not elaborately educated," but adventurous and warm-hearted. Yet in almost the same breath he disparaged these selfsame compatriots as narrow-minded, greedy, indifferent, and outright hostile to the new, the ancient, the foreign. This is a curious dichotomy in all of Twain's travel writing: the ideal versus the real. Sometimes it is applied to the expectation surrounding a place or event, with humorous results.[88] But one cannot escape the impression that Twain expected more from his fellow travelers and was continually disappointed.

To the extent that Dickens, Thackeray, Twain, and other travelogues were read, they shaped the public's perception of 19th-century travel and the lands they encountered. The authors' perceptions, in turn, were shaped by steam. *Schadenfreude* might not have been identified in this pre-Freudian age, but it was certainly experienced. Whether viewed from the Olympian perspective of a ship approaching harbor, brief descents into the hugger-mugger of the street, or glorious return to the civilized succor of one's cabin and compatriots, the vantage of steam travel was an appealing one for traveler and reader alike. It was the vicarious pleasure of looking *down*.

8
THE DOLLARS ARE COMING
Steam Tourism and the Transformation of Space

IN 1883, *Appleton's European Guide Book* published its nineteenth edition. In a neat, travel-sized binding, it offered advice on choosing hotels, arranging railway timetables, securing a passport, changing currency, finding a luggage porter in Zurich—in short, everything a traveling American would need to survive a brief excursion abroad. It began, appropriately, with the steamship trip across. "There is little difference in point of safety and comfort between the ships of various lines," it advised, as "most of them are of recent construction, are believed to be seaworthy, and are under the command of competent seamen. The dietary leaves little to be desired."[1] As if acknowledging the brevity of this counsel, it added that "full information in relation to steamers will be found in the official advertisements of the companies" that both preceded and followed the text.

Thus within its covers *Appleton's European Guide Book* managed to replicate one crucial element of the Grand Tour: Europe and all its wonders were bracketed, literally and figuratively, by the steamship crossing. In an age of heavy metaphor, this one was especially leaden. Historian William Stowe described guidebooks as liturgy for the high ritual of American travel, providing "an order of worship at the shrines of the beautiful, the historic, and the foreign, telling the potential tourist what kind of behavior is appropriate at each site and indicating what kind of fulfillment to expect from it."[2] As the first point of contact between American tourists and their destination, guidebooks not only told them what to expect but framed the entire experience: go here, don't go there, look at this, ignore that. Things to look at included cathedrals, monuments, public parks, and "curiosities." Things to ignore included private homes (unless palatial), neighborhoods, factories, public markets, and the poor. Indeed, as evidenced by the guidebooks Baedeker's, Putnam, Park, Morford, Fetridge, and Appleton, there was no poverty in Europe to speak of—at least, none worth noticing. A similar kind of narrative framing appears in the railway timetables section. A short stopover in Manchester, for example, doomed the town to become known for its lavatories and tearooms rather than any cultural significance. The exigencies of time and the railroad made tough choices necessary, and the guidebook was there to advise—politely, but with authority—on which places were more worthwhile than others.[3]

The authors of such texts were acutely aware of the effect of steam on this travel bonanza. "If the social history of the world is ever written," said *Putnam's Magazine* in 1868, "the era in which we live will be called the nomadic period. With the advent of ocean steam navigation and the railway system began a traveling mania which has gradually increased until half the earth's inhabitants, or at least its civilized portion, are on the move."[4] Beyond the hyperbole, that last qualification—"its civilized portion"—is revealing. Steam travel was not just a means of conveyance, but a new form of human progress: civilization on the move. It was perhaps for this reason that travel in this era became invested with artistic and even religious symbolism.[5] As Stowe has written:

European travel in the nineteenth century was a highly conventional activity, controlled at one level by the layout of transportation networks and a list of canonical sights, at another level by the socially sanctioned purposes of travel . . . a kind of secular ritual, complete with prescribed actions, promised rewards, and a set of quasi-scriptural writings.[6]

The role of the steamship in this pilgrimage is indicated, not merely by the bracketing of advertisements in Appleton, but their wording as well. If Appleton was saying, in effect, that most steamships and steamship lines were roughly the same, the lines themselves begged to differ. Sybaritic passengers were extolled on the virtues of the Guion Line: "These Steamers . . . are furnished with every requisite to make the passage across the Atlantic both safe and agreeable, having Bath-room, Smoking-room, Drawing-room, Piano and Library . . . the Staterooms are all on Upper Deck, thus ensuring those greatest of all luxuries at sea, perfect Ventilation and Light." Conversely, nervous first-timers might be reassured by Cunard's terse "NOTICE: With a view of diminishing the chances of Collision, the steamers of this Line take a specified course for all the seasons of the year." Adventurers would be drawn to the exotic delights of the Anchor Line and its "route of unequalled interest, usually comprising the Ports of Lisbon, Gibraltar, Genoa, Leghorn, Naples, Messina and Palermo. . . . Passengers visiting the HOLY LAND can be conveyed by Indian Steamers to Port Said." Reluctant patriots were assured by the struggling American Line that "the accommodation for all classes of passengers is equal in elegance and comfort to any of the European Steamship Lines," while the National Steam-Ship Company appealed bluntly to a different sort of zeal: "OUR CUISINE IS OF THE HIGHEST ORDER."[7]

The success of these blandishments could be measured by the exponential number of passengers each line carried. Every year dozens of new liners joined the ranks of their sisters, and the size and carrying capacity of these vessels grew astonishingly fast as well. As early as 1850, one prominent New Yorker noted the proliferation of steamships in harbor and accurately predicted what was to come:

> Everybody is so enamored of [steam] that for a while it will supersede the New York packets—the noblest vessels that ever floated in the merchant service. Our countrymen . . . will rush forward to visit the shores of Europe instead of resorting to Virginia or Saratoga Springs; and steamers will continue to be the fashion until some more dashing adventurer of the go-ahead tribe shall demonstrate the practicality of balloon navigation, and gratify their impatience on a voyage *over,* and not *upon,* the blue waters in two days instead of as many weeks.[8]

The post–Civil War generation of middle-class Americans followed the trail set by Mark Twain and other early pioneers in steam tourism. Twain himself exhorted them to travel, in the belief that it would erase old prejudices and foster amity between nations. That was a high ambition, which even the guidebooks seemed to shrink from. The advice contained therein was more appropriate to a steam-driven age: how to arrive on time, see as much as possible in a given timeframe, and move on expeditiously to the next city or sight with a minimum of fuss.[9] Hamburg–American Line's *General Information for Passengers,* distributed on board its ships in 1874, conveniently listed railway schedules between most of the capitals of Europe in its appendix.[10] Could these two aims—one philosophical, one practical—be reconciled? Or did the mode of conveyance dictate a kind of tourism antithetical to Twain's vision?

One thing was certain: Whatever else might be selected or modified en route, the steamship voyage across was the one inescapable element. Years later Ed Wynn would get a laugh out of audiences when he advised them, "Say, next time you go to Europe, don't forget the boat trip!"[11] Until the 1870s this was a necessary evil, a rite of passage to be overcome. Family and friends gathered at the pier not to say bon voyage but Godspeed. As late as 1878, *Ocean Notes for Ladies* was still advising passengers to dress in their best, since a body washed ashore in fine clothes would receive better care.[12] Yet even by then things had begun to change. White Star Line's *Oceanic* of 1870 ushered in a new era by moving the deckhouse to the center of the vessel, rather than at the stern. Cabins were fitted more like a decent hotel ashore—fine linens, steam heat, individual lights, and a bell push for the steward—than the cramped, heaving box that tortured Charles Dickens. One impressed traveler wrote,

> Messrs. Ismay, Imrie & Co., the spirited owners of the White Star Line of Steamships, have revolutionized not only the time taken for the voyage, but have in every way so added to the comforts and convenience of their passengers, that the end of even an only tolerable passage is viewed with regret.[13]

Following suit, other lines would soon introduce all manner of improvements designed, as the Guion Line said above, to make the voyage "safe and agreeable." Some became necessitous: refrigeration for cold storage, electric lights, deck railings, foghorns. Others, like the hydraulic barber's chair aboard the *Teutonic* or the *Adriatic*'s tiny swimming bath, were mere novelties. But they spoke to a larger truth: Steamship travel was becoming *fun*. "These improved facilities," a Red Star Line pamphlet declared in 1883, "have materially tended to promote travel between America and the Continent of Europe."[14]

That much was indisputable. But then the line went on to make a larger claim for democratic travel: No longer were such vessels the playthings of the rich, and "a sojourn in the Old World is becoming not alone 'the proper thing to do' but a general movement." More ships meant more berths, and lower fares. While some lines still maintained the fiction that they catered exclusively to titled aristocrats and robber barons at cut-rate prices, the Red Star Line's advertising was refreshingly honest:

> The natural restlessness of the American people, their spirit for investigation and enterprise and thirst after knowledge have done much to break through these society rules, and since it has become a fact that a three month's trip in Europe can be accomplished for *less* than it would cost the sojourner at a home watering resort for a month's stay, Americans of every station of life from the banker to the mechanic can now be found admiring the beauties of the birth place of arts, science and literature.[15]

Witness the delicacy of the copywriter's art: Not only do Red Star Line ships cater to shop mechanics, but they do not presume that the mechanic is any less possessed of aesthetic sensibilities than the millionaire banker. Both are joined at the rail, so to speak, in their earnestly American "thirst after knowledge." Taking passage on a Red Star ship thus becomes an act of egalitarian rebellion, "breaking though society's rules" in a Pygmalion-like conquest of fine art and culture. The blurb is equally pitched to appeal to Yankee parsimony: Such a priceless experience, which *seems* extravagant, can be gained for less than the cost of staying at home! And how long would the nervous machinist, grocer, or clerk need to be away from his shop? "A few weeks' sojourn in the cradle of civilization suffices," the pamphlet assures them. It was a perfect inversion of the Grand Tour: Instead of a year-long rite of passage for wealthy bluebloods, the European "sojourn" is recast as a few weeks' holiday for the restless proletariat. The success of such advertising was immediate and colossal.[16]

Besides escapism, rebellion, and thrift, steamship lines also began to pitch the voyage to Europe as a cure-all. This was the era of the patent nostrum, and practically anything could be marketed as "good for all that ails you," even a week tossing and turning across the Atlantic. To counter the health faddism of Battle Creek, the springs at Carlsbad, or the pine-scented air of Baden Baden, the steamship offered its own curative: "In the sultriness of the American Summer," an Inman Line brochure purred,

What is better than the whiff of refreshing salt air? For exhausted nature, no tonic equals a sea voyage. When the ordinary watering place has lost its charms, and the purse maybe have been a trifle lightened by the excursions of fashionable recreation, there is nothing promising a more health-giving return on the investment, than a journey over the sea, with the wonders and magnificence of the Old World on splendid exhibition when the voyage is over.[17]

Some steamship lines went so far as to solicit endorsements from prominent medicos. Once again, the tactic worked: By the end of the century, for those who could afford it, "a good long sea-voyage" was a common prescription for frazzled nerves.

Besides Europe, the other great draw was the Holy Land, as it had been for Thackeray and Twain. Though not obliged to visit the roots of their faith, as Muslims were, good Christians in both England and the United States welcomed the relative security and comfort the steamers provided.[18] Prior to their introduction, journeying to the Middle East was little different than a medieval pilgrimage. Though encouraged by generations of clergy and missionaries that "the Land where Word-Made-Flesh dwelt among men must ever continue to be an important part of Revelation,"[19] the actual visitor was less overcome by the spirituality of the place than the extraordinary inconveniences involved in getting there, and disenchantment in the result. Returning pilgrims complained of the heat, dreadful food, saddle sores, fleas, bedbugs, and avaricious locals. "No country will more quickly dissipate romantic expectations than Palestine—particularly Jerusalem," wrote Herman Melville. "To some the disappointment is heart sickening."[20] He offered his opinion that Jesus Christ should, if the place suited the man, have been born in Tahiti.

Yet the magic of the steamship cruise meant that by the later decades of the 19th century, one could experience the Holy Land without having to deal with any of these nuisances—or at least for only a very short time. Debarking on shore, passengers were met at once by liveries that carried them safely to the sights of interest, complete with English-speaking guides and, if necessary, bodyguards. Meals, ablutions, and rest all took place on the vessel, which became a kind of floating inn and embassy. The concept was wildly popular. Certain steamship lines—P&O and Orient Line in Britain, Anchor Line in the United States, and eventually the Hamburg–American Line of Germany—began advertising such cruises in the newspapers. The concept of cruising, in fact, was born out of necessity: A point-to-point voyage from Liverpool or New York to Jerusalem, even if completely booked, could not make a profit given the length of sea time and amount of coal consumed. Moreover, no ship until the *Great Eastern* (or after her, until almost the turn of the century) could carry enough coal in her bunkers to make the entire trip without refueling. Consequently, ships stopped at a multiplicity of ports along the way, collecting some passengers and depositing others, taking on cargo and delivering the mails, and refueling.

But for the passengers who booked a complete passage, such frequent stops could seem irritating or inefficient—like taking the local instead of the express. Gradually, with help from Thomas Cook, steamship lines repackaged such voyages as journeys of exploration, wherein each port offered a new opportunity for some cultural, historical, gastronomical, or commercial experience.[21] The short duration in port—usually just enough for the ship to unload, reload, and set off—meant that touring passengers had to content themselves with the briefest acquaintance with the locale. Canny steamship lines began contracting with local tour guides to streamline the experience; by century's end, it was common to see a line of hired jitneys waiting on every pier. The idea was that passengers should never leave the protective hand of the company, even when amusing themselves ashore. By co-opting the tours, the line not only made a profit but ensured that their wayward charges would all make it safely back to the ship on time. Passengers, meanwhile, enjoyed the convenience of remaining within their own social groups. The system worked beautifully for all concerned and still does today. Though their ultimate destination still beckoned, for most tourists the experience became the journey itself, and thus the pleasure cruise was born. Insulated both at sea and on shore, passengers could now "see" Europe, the Holy Land, or anywhere the steamships traveled, all without leaving the comforting, amniotic bubble of the ship.

Shipping lines, sensing that they were on to something, began advertising cruises on board their own ships. There was a certain confidence in this tactic: If passengers had a miserable voyage, why would they willingly elect to book another? But conversely, if one enjoyed oneself, why not extend it with even more time aboard ship? Passengers waking up on board the *Deutschland* in April 1908 found the ship's newsletter, *The North German Lloyd Bulletin,* on their breakfast trays. In some ways it resembled a typical paper: There was sporting news communicated via wireless, social announcements, stock reports, and the "Monthly and Weakly Wit," which read:

"Can February March?" asked the punster with a sickly smile.
"Perhaps not," replied the quiet man, "But April May."
"June know this ought to be stopped? July awake nights, August chronicler, to arrive at this conclusion?"[22]

Before any of this, however, was a six-page article complete with half-page photographs, advertising "NORWAY AND THE NORTH CAPE." "To meet the desires of an ever-increasing number of tourists who wish to make the trip to the beautiful Northland," the line announced, "the North German Lloyd Steamship Company has determined to assign one of its largest steamers to this service." What follows is a detailed description, not only of each port of call, but the ease and comfort with which passengers will be taken there. Steam launches whisk them from the ship to the pier, where luxury coaches tour Stavanger or ascend the Geirangerfjord. Steam trains chuff up and down the cliffs at Flaam, delivering passengers back on board in time for supper. Unlike a self-guided expedition, only a minimum of exertion is needed—or sometimes none at all: "On the projected voyage of the *Grosser Kurfuerst* the traveler is afforded an opportunity of seeing the wonders of nature in all their pristine majesty, while comfortable seated in a deck chair."[23] Despite the wonders of nature on display, it is clear that the real destination is the ship herself:

The *Grosser Kurfuerst,* which has been selected for the splendid excursion cruise to Norway and the North Cape, is a twin-screw passenger steamship of 13,182 tons and of modern construction. . . . The saloon, vestibules, lounges, drawing rooms, reading rooms and smoking rooms are all on an ample scale, insuring adequate comfort to a full complement of passengers. . . . The high standard of excellence always maintained by North German Lloyd is assurance that every passenger will be made comfortable and given all possible care and attention.[24]

Perhaps indicative of Germany's imperial aspirations, throughout the *Bulletin*, the line reinforced the impression that steam cruising had conquered the globe. After smugly announcing in one of its "news items" that the Lloyd fleet exceeded the size of some navies—including the United States and France—the *Bulletin* went on to list "Round the World Tours" via America, Japan, and Australia, noting that "steamers of the China service now stop at Algiers." Not only had the world been conquered, but it had been done suavely. Passengers could journey to such exotic locales as Ceylon or Malta without abandoning a fraction of their comfort or security. Travel, which had once been exploration, now became an extended social call. Included in its "Information for Passengers" section at the back was this telling notice:

EGYPT AND THE ORIENT: In addition to the Alexandria service by steamers of the North German Lloyd . . . connections can be made at Genoa or Naples with North German Lloyd Imperial Mail steamers that call at these ports on their way to Egypt. The ships in this service are magnificent types of the most modern construction. The chief characteristic, after their size and solidity, is their great comfort, which pervades all their interior arrangements and furnishing.[25]

Whatever their ultimate destination, neophyte tourists came to regard the crossing over as the start to a jolly adventure. For most Americans, the adventure began in New York City. Arriving by rail or night boat from all over the United States, passengers spent a sleepless night in one of dozens of hotels near the piers before setting off the next morning. As a transportation hub, New York's status as the unofficial capital and official gateway to the New World continued to grow throughout the second half of the 19th century. Arriving as an "amateur emigrant" in 1879, Robert Louis Stevenson recorded the wonder and apprehension with which his fellow passengers regarded the sprawling city:

As we drew near to New York I was at first amused, and then somewhat staggered, by the cautious and the grisly tales that went the round. You would have thought we were to land upon a cannibal island. You must speak to no-one in the streets, as they would not leave you till you were rooked and beaten. You must enter a hotel with military precaution; for the least you had to apprehend was to awake the next morning without money or baggage . . . and if the worst befell, you would instantly and mysteriously disappear from the ranks of mankind.[26]

Yet it need not have been so. At the dawn of the steam age, other cities seemed just as likely to inherit the title. Intense civic pride in Savannah prompted the first steam transatlantic crossing in 1818; promoters were certain the notoriety would make their Georgian city the new capital of American trade. It didn't work out that way, even though the *S.S. Savannah* attracted her own share of spectacle and even hosted President James Monroe on a short cruise around the Tybee lighthouse.

Then the focus shifted to Boston, which seemed to have a more respectable claim. Boston had long been the hub of northeastern trade, edging out Newport in the 18th century and holding its own until well into the 19th. Samuel Cunard thought well enough of the city to make it the American terminus for his first ships, even when the intense cold of winter hampered their service. Boston was justly proud of the honor and repaid it. In February 1844, when the *Britannia* became trapped in ice within Boston harbor, a brigade of citizenry chipped away a channel for her to escape. The event made headlines, and Currier & Ives published a special print commemorating it. Cunard was honored but wary; one year later, in spite or because of this incident, he transferred the ships to New York.

This was as an acknowledgment of commercial as well as meteorological realities. To the north, the Allan Line and Canadian Pacific tried to convince passengers to forsake New York for Quebec. The Canadian route, they argued, shaved off almost a day of travel time. It didn't matter; passengers still chose the longer route. Finally, in the most heartbreaking example of civic overreach, Portland, Maine, in 1859 constructed a vast pier—the largest in the world—to accommodate the new *Great Eastern*. But by the time the ship made her maiden voyage one year later, the Portland plan was abandoned in favor of New York. The pier sat unused for years, except for fishing boats.

Why did New York succeed? There are many factors, but one of the most elemental is steam. Steam ferries brought passengers from their Brooklyn brownstones to offices on Wall Street; elevated railways allowed for the creation of commuter suburbs in the Upper East and Upper West Sides, and finally all the way to Harlem, Queens, and the Bronx.[27] New York expanded because it was allowed to expand, facilitated by the steam engine; and to fill its tenements came a steady flood of immigrants. They were delivered, of course, by steamships.

This resolves itself into a chicken-and-egg problem: New York's reputation as an immigrant hub drew more and more steamship companies to route there, but the immigrants themselves had been delivered by those steamships in the first place. However it began, this was the cycle that created modern New York. By the mid-19th century, its reputation preceded it. "New York is the chief city," one English guidebook told its readers, before getting rather carried away: "It is much more beautiful [than London], for it has neither smoke nor fog, but enjoys clear and brilliant sunshine. In warmth it is like Spain or Italy."[28] Much of this sunny view might be owed to the fact that few travelers made the Atlantic crossing in wintertime.

By 1880, Cunard, White Star, Inman, North German Lloyd, Hamburg–American, the French Line, and a dozen other firms all had their American headquarters in New York and routed their ships through the Manhattan piers. They built grand edifices along the waterfront and placed builder's models of their newest ships prominently in the windows, along with sailing schedules and ticket kiosks. The result was much the same as what JFK airport has created today: New Yorkers, with unparalleled access to transportation, became inveterate travelers. New money after the Civil War fostered a new generation of potential tourists. Mark Twain, visiting the city in 1867, could already sense that something was changing: "The old, genuine, traveled, cultivated, pedigreed aristocracy of New York," he wrote, "stand stunned and helpless under the new order of things. They find themselves supplanted by the upstart princes of Shoddy, vulgar and with unknown grandfathers."[29]

The old aristocracy was not as stunned or helpless as they appeared. Let's consider two such Knickerbocker families, both inveterate travelers, before going on to examine the greater traveling public that used New York as its starting point. The implication of Twain's comment is that "traveled, cultivated" families will somehow behave better abroad than their rough-lettered usurpers. Later he makes this explicit:

New Yorkers are a singular people, somehow or other. Here, in their own home, they have the name among strangers of being excessively unsociable; but take them in any part of the world, outside their State limits, and they are the most liberal pleasant and companionable people you can find.[30]

If so, these would be ideal candidates to challenge the mantle of "Ugly American." But we shall see.

The Days were not the most notable scions of New York, but they were representative of the breed. "Not wealthy, but comfortable," as one of their in-laws described them, they included in their ranks Benjamin Day, founder of the *New York Sun*, and his grandson Benjamin Henry Day, who provided illustrations for Mark Twain's *A Tramp Abroad*. Neither rich enough to rank alongside the Vanderbilts nor poor enough to be memorialized by Jacob Riis, they were just the kind of solid, unremarkable, upper-middle-class New Yorkers who might otherwise have disappeared from history were it not for the chronicles of their eldest son, Clarence.

In his memoirs he provides a rich depiction of coming of age alongside the city itself. Joining his father on an outing downtown, for example, they alight from the Elevated into a "tangle of little streets" that would hardly be familiar to readers even a few decades later:

Most of the business buildings were old and many of them were dirty, with steep, well-worn wooden stairways, and dark, busy basements. Exchange Place and Broad Street were full of these warrens, and there were some even on Wall Street. The southern corner of Wall Street and Broadway was one of the dingiest. Father raised his cane and said as we passed, "That's where Great-Aunt Lavinia was born."[31]

Like many New Yorkers of his stature, Father—Clarence Day Sr.—joined the throng of tourists bound for Europe after the Civil War. His first voyage came in 1869, and his motives were typical of the age. "He had several things to attend to in Europe," Clarence Jr. writes. "He went to the best watchmaker in Switzerland. . . . After getting just the right watch, he went to London to get proper clothes." Clarence Sr. returned well satisfied with the experience:

Father came back from his first trip to Europe with his watch and his good clothes from Poole like a Columbus who had discovered a pleasant and useful new world. He had taken his ease in its cities, he had enjoyed the orderly loveliness of The Hague and the solid richness of London, and everywhere he had seen what taste and time could do for homes in the country. He had no wish to live among Europeans for he looked down on them, somehow, but he respected them too for the contributions they had made to his comfort.[32]

This was a rare acknowledgment of an established truth: With the advent of regular steam travel, American tourists began mining the Old World. Clarence Day's expedition pales in comparison to the orgiastic buying sprees of J. P. Morgan, for example, but the principle is the same.

Having been exposed to "their cookery, their wines, and their manners," Clarence Sr. resolved to return a year later. "He wanted to see more of Europe," writes his son. "Also he wanted some shirts."[33] Embarking on the *St. Laurent* of the French Line, a new vessel with the novelty of a screw propeller, Day encountered an old friend, Alden Stockwell. This, too, was typical. Despite all the talk of the democratization of travel, crack steamers still drew from a relatively select group wealthy enough to afford a First Class ticket. Since this represented only a tiny fraction of the populace, it was not surprising they should know one another. This "Vanity Fair afloat," as one writer termed it, persisted until the First World War.[34] On board the *Titanic* in 1912, there were so many close friends among the First Class passengers that Mrs. Churchill Candie referred to them, collectively, as "our little coterie."[35]

On the *St. Laurent*, Day not only found Stockwell but Stockwell's young niece. A romance flourished: "He promenaded the deck with her on breezy days, with her veils flying and her skirts billowing out, and on foggy days he placed her chair where the cordage and yards wouldn't drip on her. He brought her hot cups of tea." After a suitable courtship in London and New York, Lavinia Stockwell became Mrs. Clarence Day. They honeymooned, naturally, in Europe. By now, Paris was embarked on the era that would later be known as the Belle Epoque, yet Mr. Day remained largely impervious to its wonders: "The Shah of Persia and his glittering court were guests of the government, a whole hotel had been reserved for their use, and the city was being given over to illuminations and fetes. . . . But Father said it would take more than a Shah to thrill him. He said the Shah was a nuisance."[36]

By 1874, the year Clarence Jr. was born, the Days had established themselves as a cosmopolitan New York household. Clarence Sr. continued to have his clothes sent from Poole's of London and indulged his love of French cooking at Delmonico's. The family made regular trips across the Atlantic. In the mid-1880s, Vinnie Day left for a several-month excursion that took her throughout the continent and down the Nile in a *dahabeeyah*. Nevertheless, even thousands of miles from home, she remained encased in the same close-knit circle of New York society:

Some of her letters told us how she was constantly meeting people she knew, not only on the ship but at every port where . . . she went ashore. "Your mother has the damndest number of friends I ever heard of," said Father. "She's everlastingly meeting some old friend or other wherever she goes. I never see people I know when I'm traveling. But there isn't a city in Europe where your mother wouldn't spot a friend in just five minutes." And when a letter came saying she had just climbed Mt. Vesuvius and had found old Mr. and Mrs. Quintard of Rye at the top, peering down into the crater, Father said that upon his soul he never knew anyone like her.[37]

There is a great deal contained within these vignettes. If the Days were indeed representative of the moderately well-off, sophisticated American gentry that began to travel *en masse* after the Civil War (and they certainly considered themselves to be), several distinct trends can be identified. First is the objectification of Europe as a source—not of enlightenment or knowledge, but acquisition. Mr. Day approved of European watches, clothes, food, and manners and disapproved of Europeans. The condescension of this might have been apparent to his son but not to him. Certainly not every American tourist saw transatlantic travel in such material terms, as we shall see, yet there is something novel and revealing in Mr. Day's attitude: With Europe just a week away by steamer, buying sprees of this kind became common. Before the advent of steam, the length and risks of a transatlantic crossing meant it was contemplated only out of necessity. Sometimes that necessity was spiritual: a need to acquire knowledge and exposure to a greater world.[38] But one does not go on a pilgrimage to buy shirts.

As steam travel became the norm, transatlantic journeys were undertaken for simpler pleasures. One could now arrive and tour the Continent and take back only what one wished—a watch, a vase, a suit of clothes—and not any excess exposure to "foreign" culture.[39] The presence of foreign items in the home became a mark of sophistication, just as were foreign dishes served at meals and foreign wines in the cellar. In the novel *Salvage*, published in 1880, Elizabeth Wormeley Latimer writes, "The leading interests in daily life in America are connected with the Atlantic Ocean.... The ocean is a highway which brings everything most delightful to an American's home ... an American's news, letters, books, clothes, prima donnas, fashions, ancestors, and church associations all come ... from across the seas."[40] But that did not mean that families like the Days regarded themselves as Francophiles or Anglophiles. "He liked to live well," writes Clarence Jr. of his father, "and he wanted us to live well too."

Secondly, when they traveled, the Days moved in a protective circle of fellow Americans, many of whom they knew beforehand. The crossing over became the means whereby a new community was established from myriad preexisting ones: clubs, auxiliary guilds, church membership, and so on. The steamship was the locus. Newly arrived on board, travelers at once consulted the passenger list to see whom they knew and who might be worth knowing (Mr. Day actually saw his friend Stockwell on the pier, but otherwise he would quickly have found the name on the register). "The first thing one does on coming aboard," an English academic wrote, "is to scrutinize the party with whom he is to spend the next twelve days. In our case, certain groups very soon began to attract more than common attention."[41]

Despite all being in the same class of stateroom and thus theoretically entitled to the same common areas, there were fixed rules for claiming acquaintance. An etiquette book of the day offered the following hypothetical icebreaker: "Mrs. Brown, I saw your name in the passenger list and I am going to ask you to let me introduce myself to you on the strength of my long acquaintance with and great affection for your sister, Mrs. William Barr, of Cleveland."[42]

There are two assumptions at work here: first, that the world in which the speaker and Mrs. Brown move is both small enough for there to only be one degree of separation *and* for that fact to be known to one or both parties; second, that if the speaker were not fortunate enough to know Mrs. William Barr of Cleveland (and be aware of her familial relations), he would have no business intruding himself upon Mrs. Brown. Perhaps it would be more accurate to say that not one but multiple communities were quickly established on board ship, each with rules of membership as rigid as a Mayfair club.

The diary of Boston socialite Marian Lawrence Peabody offers a revealing example. Aged 21 at the time of her crossing on the *Umbria* in 1896, she found herself accosted on deck "by one of those awful Cook's tourists [who] asked me if I hadn't thrown up yet and related his experiences before I could get away from him." Fortunately it was not all package tourists on board; a group of Yale men were traveling also, and Miss Peabody gratefully fell in with them. Less than one day out of port, she had already found her community. "In the evening our particular group gathered in the saloon—the Howlands, Brink Thorne, Cheney, Mr. Amory Gardner, Cecil Baring and George Booth—and had roast beef sandwiches and drinks, about 11 o'clock at night."[43]

The diary of a wealthy Philadelphian, Mrs. Finlay MacLaren, gives insight to how extraordinarily compact this society was. On boarding the Liverpool-bound Inman liner *City of Chester* at New York in 1880, she reckoned the voyage a failure since "there are not many on board whose acquaintances we care to make [except] some friends of Mr. Will Miller's, and Mr. and Mrs. Wilbur, and

Mr. Reading, all of Philadelphia."[44] Returning a few months later on the White Star *Celtic*, she was even more disappointed:

> There is no-one we know except that there is one gentleman Mr. Mortimer who crossed with us in August. He is now accompanied by his sister and her husband, Count and Countess von—. A family of Hamiltons sat near us at table—father and mother and his daughter, the latter with a display of diamond rings on their fingers.[45]

The absence of the countess' name was deliberate; perhaps Mrs. MacLaren couldn't pronounce it (the brief comment does, however, underscore the predilection among wealthy Americans to acquire titles from the impoverished aristocracy; one does not need to know the name of the count and countess to infer certain things about their financial arrangements). The ostentatious Hamiltons are equally unknown to us, but clearly not to Mrs. MacLaren.

Even ships bound for more obscure ports invariably produced at least one common acquaintance. Leaving a cold New York winter for Puerto Rico in February 1882, Mrs. MacLaren was delighted to find a familiar face:

> Donald MacLaren came to bid us goodbye, bringing me a bunch of paints and Fanny an illustrated paper and two magazines. Before he left, he met a friend on deck to whom he introduced us, Mr. Sinclair of Philadelphia, a friend of Bess Simons and a classmate of Will Robinson. He was very polite and agreeable.[46]

These communities, once formed, became prophylactics against the "foreignness" of foreign travel. Whether packaged together by Thomas Cook or forming their own coteries, the steamship crossing gave passengers a week to insulate themselves within their cliques. Turned loose on the capitals of Europe, they naturally chose to stay at the same hotels, dine in the same restaurants, take excursions together. There could be no greater testament to the insularity and protectiveness of such groups than the fact that Clarence Day allowed his wife to travel alone without him—in an age when most proper New York ladies did not even venture above 14th Street unaccompanied.

Another such prominent New York family, more familiar to most readers, was the Theodore Roosevelts. The Roosevelts and the Days moved in the same tight circles of New York society: Corrine Roosevelt Robinson lived in the brownstone adjoining Clarence Day's. While principally remembered for the presence of their youngest son, Theodore Jr., the record of the Roosevelt family's travels offers a fascinating glimpse into the emergence of the modern tourist. Theodore Sr., the patriarch, was the trailblazer. He had journeyed across the Atlantic several times, first as a lad of 19 in 1851. His letters home were full of detailed descriptions of each place he visited. It was the year of the Great Exhibition, and Paxton's stunning Crystal Palace merited an especially long screed (the Roosevelts were in the window glass business). His brother Robert chided him to spend less time staring at buildings and more "conversing with, and seeing the bent of the minds of other people." But if young Theodore was more interested in Notre Dame than the peasants huddled around it, he was no different from most tourists seeing Europe for the first time—then and now.

Later, as an adult, this indifference seemed to have been replaced by extraordinary compassion. Theodore Roosevelt served on the board of numerous charities, several of his own founding, including the Children's Aid Society. He was instrumental in raising New York's consciousness to its urban poor and by all accounts was a passionately devoted philanthropist. One friend recalled him as "a bright, cheerful man with an intense sympathy with everything you brought to him. He loved children especially."[47] If so, Theodore Roosevelt was very much a representative American, as other nations believed them to be. "The Americans are very benevolent," one midcentury English guidebook declared. "They love to do good, and among other things they have asylums for the blind, and hospitals for the sick, and refuges for the destitute; and they make even their prisoners comfortable—perhaps *too* comfortable."[48]

In 1869, Theodore Roosevelt Sr. put business and philanthropy aside and took his family on a Grand Tour that would bring them across the Atlantic and through all the capitals of Europe. The year was significant—indeed, for steam travel, it was probably the most significant year of the 19th century. The year also marked the opening of the Suez Canal and of the first transcontinental railway in the United States. It was the year that the *Great Eastern* laid the transatlantic cable. In France, Jules Verne completed his manuscript for *20,000 Leagues Under the Sea*. In Northern Ireland, construction began at Harland & Wolff shipyard on the *Oceanic*, the first modern ocean liner. On May 10, 1869, ironclads of the Imperial Japanese Navy completely overwhelmed the smaller, weaker vessels of Ezo Republic at Hakodate—a battle that many historians would rank alongside Hampton Roads in its demonstration of novel steam technology.

Other, more tangential events would also have lasting consequences. In New York, the Roosevelts' hometown, a deal was finally reached to replace the steam ferries with a bridge stretching from Brooklyn Heights to lower Manhattan. On

September 24, "Black Friday," Jay Gould and "Admiral" Jim Fisk (of Fall River Line fame) would try to corner the gold market, causing a financial panic that shattered the Grant administration and left lasting scars on American finance. Finally, perhaps most relevant here, 1869 was the year that Mark Twain published *Innocents Abroad* and, as will be recalled, Clarence Day Sr. embarked on his first transatlantic shopping spree.

The Roosevelts—father Theodore, mother Mittie, and three children—departed New York on the *Scotia* on May 12. Their choice of ship was revealing: The *Scotia* was the flagship of the Cunard Line, a large and plush vessel with ample First Class accommodation but also the last Cunarder to be fitted with paddles instead of screws. Her reputation for safety was so great that the *Nautilus* tried to ram her in Jules Verne's 1870 novel, only to have the *Scotia*'s water-tight compartments keep her afloat. She was, therefore, both a comfortable and conservative choice.

Arriving in Liverpool, the Roosevelts remained in England for several weeks, long enough for Mittie to outfit her children (and herself) in the latest London fashions, and then departed for Antwerp, Amsterdam, numerous cities in Bavaria and Prussia, Switzerland, Paris, Milan, Venice, Florence, and finally Naples. There a curious incident took place. Theodore Sr., patron of children's charities, whom his own family called "Greatheart," is seen throwing pennies into a crowd of Neapolitan beggar children. One of the boys grabbed more than his share, and, according to the diary of his own son, Roosevelt "beat him till he cried."[49]

What are we to make of this? The diary entry offers no context, but passes on briskly to other sights encountered that day. This sudden act of cruelty appears nowhere else in the family's surviving papers. It made no impression at all. Nor did another event, which took place some weeks later. Again, a crowd of Italian beggars pesters the Roosevelt family, this time women and children. "We hired one to keep off the rest," young Theodore Jr. writes in his diary. "Then came some more fun." Father Roosevelt purchased a basket of cakes, and the crowd gathered round. "We tossed the cakes to them and fed them like chickens with small pieces, and like chickens they ate it. Mr. Stevens kept guard with a whip with which he pretended to whip a small boy." At least Mr. Stevens, unlike Mr. Roosevelt, was only pretending. The "fun" became progressively more demeaning, as "we made them open their mouths and tossed the cake into it. For a 'Coup de Grace' we threw a lot of them in a place and a writhing heap of human beings [snatched it up]." The explicit comparison between humans and animals is disturbing enough, but the true "Coup de Grace" came at the end: "We made the crowds . . . give three cheers for the U.S.A. before we gave them cakes."[50]

Nearly every recent biography of Theodore Roosevelt Jr. includes this scene, yet biographers never quite know what to make of it. Here is Greatheart behaving very badly, "strangely out of character,"[51] without any rational explanation. The crowd is reduced to beasts, while Greatheart and his fellow tourists gleefully taunt and humiliate them in the act of dispensing "charity." Even the last reference to "the U.S.A." is telling in itself: The crowd is reminded that it is *American* charity and is expected to grovel accordingly. Not long after this second incident comes a third, mentioned only briefly in Corinne Roosevelt's otherwise adoring memoir of her brother. Again in Italy, the elder Theodore and their traveling companion Mr. Stevens are seen gleefully washing the faces of dirty street urchins—with champagne.[52]

There is a wealth of material here, but I will confine myself to a few general observations. First, it is very hard to imagine Roosevelt Sr. behaving this way with American children, however destitute. Indeed there is no record of such a kindred incident in all the many years he spent doing charitable works in New York City. We must assume, then, that he is taking license granted to the tourist abroad to behave in ways that would be anathema at home.[53] Witness the fact that the others in the party are doing the same. Even by 1869 the Continent (and Italy in particular) was gaining a reputation as a place where Americans could indulge their prurient desires. As one historian describes it, "Traveling Americans used Europe as a stage to enact their personal and social fantasies."[54] These could run the gamut from the sort of cheery cruelty encountered above to all-out debauches in nearby Capri, where wealthy industrialists kept a harem of boys for their own gratification.[55]

Second, Roosevelt's son (who already at the age of 11 was a keen and insightful observer) offers these vignettes with seeming approval. His father, who never did anything without some moral exemplar attached to it, is demonstrating how one treats "foreigners," even when on their soil. The callousness would be shocking, yet no one in the party appears to be shocked.

Third and finally, Papa Roosevelt's behavior might have been unusual for him, but it was entirely typical of the breed. Generations of American tourists would bemoan the poverty they encountered in their travels, yet nearly always as an annoyance rather than a crippling social condition. Beggars were a particular irritation, crowding round, obscuring one's path. Thackeray noted ruefully that he and his fellow passengers had hardly landed on the "juicy sand" of Vigo before they were "surrounded by a host of mendicants, screaming, 'I say, sir! Penny, sir! I say, English! Penny!' in all voices, from extreme youth to the most lousy and venerable old age."[56] Tales of this kind were common, as were those of locals abasing themselves for spare change. According to *The Graphic* 1875 steamship traveler's guide:

> The most amusing sight in Aden is the crowd of Somali boys who swarm in their canoes round a newly-arrived steamer, all crying out "I dive, I dive, yessir me dive!" On a small coin being thrown out they plunge after it, splashing, dashing, scrambling, overturning canoes, and generally seize it as it sinks.... Upon landing, one hideous little imp attached himself to each of us, following us everywhere until we left, where we heard a great jabbering for "baksheesh."[57]

Not everyone was amused. When Nelly Bly arrived in Aden in 1889, she noted grimly that,

> Hardly had the anchor dropped than the ship was surrounded with a fleet of small boats, steered by half-clad Arabs, fighting, grabbing, pulling, yelling in their mad haste to be first. I never in my life saw such an exhibition of hungry greed for the few pence they expected to earn by taking the passengers ashore.... This dreadful exhibition made me feel that probably there was some justification in arming one's self with a club.[58]

Repeated exposure made passengers jaded. Even the most altruistic of them balked at the ubiquitous poverty they encountered in Europe and elsewhere, the constant clamoring for "baksheesh." After all, it was not their country; it was not their fault. They did not come here to be pestered. They just wanted to see the Parthenon and get back on the boat. One cannot help but think of Robert Roosevelt's naïve advice to his brother to "converse with the people" instead of touring the architecture, and one cannot entirely fault Theodore Sr. for ignoring it.

Contemporary attitudes rendered Victorian tourists even more callous to suffering than their cognates today. To their minds, poverty was a moral condition, not a social one. Even charitable Theodore was not immune to this sort of thinking. And it was only too easy to impute low morals on a crowd of "foreigners" who were impolite enough to press their poverty in your face and demand that you do something about it. Even in the Holy Land, where Christ's teachings might have been more prevalent, such attitudes persisted. Jerusalem and Palestine were popular destinations for early cruisers: they were, in fact, the *raison d'être* for the *Quaker City*'s tour. Yet the people that lived in them seemed encumbrances, all the more so when they seemed to play cynically on the devotion of the pious. In *Oriental Acquaintance*, published in 1856, American author John William De Forest described one such encounter:

And one fine morning in early March we had everything packed up, called our tribe together, mounted our horses and set out for the holy city. "God preserve your eyes!" shouted the beggars with sore optics or none at all, as we rode by them. "God keep your children!" screamed women, holding out disgusting babies to attract our pecuniary commiseration.[59]

The attitude of the local population was always assumed to be avaricious, even when at their most welcoming. One could often not tell the difference. Disembarking in Haiti, lady passengers were greeted with a polite if ingratiating demand: "*Bonjour mademoiselle! Vous êtes très jolie! Donnez-moi un sou.*" As one author has written, "The first encounter was charming, the second disillusioning, the third ignored."[60] The tourist abroad could only endure so many of these disappointments before the whole world began to look like an Arab bazaar full of sharp-eyed traders out to bilk them. Passengers on a P&O liner in the Far East caught sight of a group of natives greeting them on the pier with dance and song. "I wonder what the tune is?" one wondered. His friend answered him, "They are playing, 'The Dollars Are Coming.'"[61]

This cut both ways. As author John Malcolm Brinnin notes, on a cruise the only likely contact between tourist and local would be some minor purchase ashore—a transaction that was unlikely to raise the opinion of either party for the other. "Bargaining for an article and paying for it, [the tourist] might for a moment be pleased to think that he had participated in the exotic, without losing control of his own prerogatives."[62] This is a familiar phenomenon: One need only remember Clarence Day Sr. sampling the wares of each nation, or the unsavory glee of Mark Twain's fellow passengers as they "put one over" on the locals. As the century wore on, these attitudes became even more entrenched. Ships became self-contained worlds with only intermittent outside contact, and the experience of travel transformed.[63] Again, according to Brinnin: "The memories one might bring back from a cruise shifted from what one *saw* in Malta or Martinique to what one *did* at the Captain's Reception or the Crazy Hat Parade. The essential experience of a cruise lay not in the people you saw on land but the people you met on board."[64]

The choice of ship—its newness, size, nationality, and character—also helped fashion the communities created aboard. On arriving aboard the French liner *Lafayette* in 1870, May Alcott, sister of Louisa, was horrified to discover that the crew and most passengers were, in fact, French. She so "dread[ed] the French waiters" that she took most of her meals below decks and was further chagrined by the food. "The French messes on board nearly kill me," she wrote her sister, "and I shall never learn to like the horrid soups." Yet by the end of the week May found herself enjoying the cosmopolitan company and confessed herself delighted when a joke "convulsed the table." "We shall . . . be quite Parisian when we return," she wrote brightly.[65]

Increased comfort on board was always relative. Sometimes unexpected hazards came from foreign languages or unfamiliar dishes; more often, it was nothing more or less than dirty weather. For all their shaded lamps and tasseled armchairs, ships at the end of the century rolled just as much as the *Britannia* of 1840. It would not be until the introduction of stabilizers in the 1950s—ironically, at the very end of steam ocean travel—that the problem was finally eradicated. Until then, passengers who believed the steamship lines' advertising puffery often had cause to regret it.

In an 1883 edition of *Frank Leslie's Illustrated Newspaper,* a full-page cartoon entitled "Experiences During a First Voyage in an Ocean Palace" poked gentle fun both at the lines' boastful claims and the foolish souls that accepted them. "The First Morning Out" shows two young American ladies being tossed around their tiny cabin like ragdolls, pummeled by their own hairbrushes and baskets of fruit bearing "bon voyage" wishes. A steward appears and pronounces the weather "a little fresh" (just as Dickens's steward had done) while the purser twirls his cigar in elaborate indifference. The lower panel shows one of the ladies lying supine on the deck, swaddled in blankets and obviously seasick. "The American female takes her ease," the cartoon slyly notes, while nearby two English ladies "take a constitutional," bent nearly double by the roaring wind.[66]

As much as they might have damned the advertising firms on shore, once at sea there was precious little to do but endure. Dirty weather drove passengers inward, and boredom made them seek entertainment and diversion from one another. On long passages, this sense of community increased. A fascinating account of the *S.S. Great Britain*'s later years survives in the diary of one Mary Crompton, passenger on an epic crossing from Melbourne to Liverpool in 1866. Arriving on board, she and her husband did what all newly arrived passengers do: They began making themselves at home. "We spent most of our time putting the cabin in order," she writes in her diary. "It is a comfortable little place about 9 ft by 6 ft.... Joe had the lower berth enlarged and we only use the top one to keep things in.... No 2 is a sofa all nicely padded, over it a shelf with a ledge where we keep all our books, and a candle lamp is fixed to the side of the cabin."[67]

Properly nested, they began to explore the ship. The *Great Britain* had been in service for over twenty years and was a far cry from the glittering spectacle encountered at Bristol. Still, to a young woman from the Antipodes, it was enough to impress:

The saloon is very large. There are six tables, all covered with red cloths, with long seats on each side padded in crimson velvet; the walls are painted in small panels.... I don't sit in it very much except at mealtimes and for a short time in the evenings; it is very draughty and people will sit there with hats on and it provokes me.[68]

Out at sea for weeks at a time with no distractions and the same people day after day, such minor irritations could flare into conflagration. To this day, crewmen on round-the-world cruises dread the long passages of sea time between Asian ports, which are commonly termed "Hate Weeks." Seemingly trivial matters suddenly became flash points. Once, on a three-week voyage from Los Angeles to Auckland aboard the *Queen Elizabeth 2,* I went down to the passenger laundry room to find two elderly women screaming and flinging clothes at each other. Historian John Maxtone-Graham describes another incident on the *Rotterdam,* when a German woman believed herself snubbed in the lounge and clobbered the other woman "with one roundhouse swing of her evening purse."[69]

Such minor irritations aside, Mary Crompton and her husband quickly became part of the *Great Britain*'s social set. The passengers, it seems, wasted no time in organizing themselves. "We had a general meeting in the saloon to consider how we might amuse ourselves during the voyage," Mary reports. "It was resolved that if possible one evening every week some of us should combine to entertain the others with music, reading, etc.... Dr. Sanger volunteered, he is that very queer looking old man that Effie saw on board the Coorong. I don't much admire him but he has a good voice, sings a comic song with great spirit." Soon even these reservations were abandoned. In a later entry, she admits: "Dr. Sanger is getting up 'Bombastes Furioso'; I take the part of Disdaffena, we are very busy with rehearsals every day."

Other details hint at a community that was all the more tight-knit for its transient nature. Even with a home that was only 9 feet by 6, Mary and her husband asserted the proprietary rights as hosts. "Leonard Fosbery got a teapot full of champagne for us after we left off dancing," Mary records of one convivial night, "[and] then we had Miss Farrar and Mr. Allfrey to a biscuit and cheese supper in our cabin." In the end, after over a month at sea, it was time for the community to disperse. Relief comingled with sadness as the ship arrived in Liverpool. Mary's diary closes with a poignant scene: "At last we got away in one of the steamers but it was a grief to leave the beautiful ship: the Captain stood on his bridge and gave a hearty cheer to which we responded again and again."[70]

Mary Crompton's experience was representative. On long voyages, the most pressing need was to stave off boredom. Holidays were celebrated to the hilt, even rather contentious ones. An American passenger on a British steamer in 1875 lamented that there were no revelries on the Fourth of July, but he amended his entry the next morning to admit that "we had some singing and speeches this evening in honor of the 4th; I had almost despaired of any celebration at all, but better late than never."[71] A few years later, on the Inman liner *City of Chester*, this initial hesitance among British crews to celebrate the loss of the American colonies seemed to have been overcome: "A beautiful day—celebrated the Fourth this evening; we had speeches and quite a lovely time generally."[72] With British lines eager to please but unsure how to do so, the results were sometimes uneven. Consider this scene from a diary entry on board the Cunarder *Servia* in 1874: "On account of being the 4th of July the saloon was decorated with flags. The sailors amused us by dressing themselves as a donkey and bearers, and went through the saloon. Also had music."[73]

Most days, however, passed in a literal and figurative fog. Tedium and seasickness made the hours drag. The diary of Elizabeth Van Der Peyser, a loquacious young New Yorker, becomes almost telegraphic as the voyage progresses:

Sunday June 28: The weather lovely, we are well so far. How long it will last I cannot tell.
Monday June 29: I am sick as I can be. Cornelia and mother also sick. Gus well.
Monday July 6: Anything to pass the time. It is rather tedious when one is not well, and the weather unfavorable. For amusement I read "The Tour Around the World in 80 Days". Quite good.[74]

Companies did what they could, and passengers themselves were eager for any distraction. Thus communities that might have developed naturally were rushed into existence at once by the necessity to keep oneself amused. "Life on board the *Adriatic* was relieved of its monotony," one passenger wrote in the 1880s, "by the active interest taken by the purser and the doctor in getting up games on deck, in which the English were always ready to join."[75] More elaborate games occurred on the Cunard steamer *Europa* in the 1850s. Discovering that they had on board none other than the impresario P. T. Barnum, the passengers made him the fixture of their "fun":

Anyone who has made a voyage knows that a never-failing expedient for passing the time is to hold a mock court of justice; and on this occasion you may be sure Mr. Barnum was brought to trial. The indictment was an able analysis of Mr. Barnum's Autobiography, but it was eclipsed by the evidence of one of the witnesses, who had thrown the principal incidents of the work into doggerel verse. Mr. Barnum spoke for an hour in his defense, with such ability, earnestness, and eloquence, that he carried his acquittal by acclamation. He proved that every walk of life has its share of deceiving the public; the only innocuous deceit being that which he has always practiced, professional deceit.[76]

But the creation of a shipboard community was more than fun and games. Mrs. Crompton's indebtedness to the crew, her identification with her peers, and the almost instantaneous creation of a distinct society with general meetings, resolutions, and so on are all reflected in a short excerpt from the log of the Collins Line steamer *Atlantic,* dated June 21, 1856. After a successful crossing, the passengers presented Captain Eldridge with a memorandum of almost parliamentary exactitude:

Whereupon the committee after returning reported the following: Resolved, that the vigilant attention of Captain Eldridge to his duties as said master of the vessel has at all times given us confident assurance of his strength and our safety, while his gentlemanly deportment and polite attention has contributed to the comfort of all.... Resolved, that we have entire confidence in the stability of the ship and machinery and cannot but express our satisfaction in the discipline observed in every department. We can therefore recommend her with confidence to the traveling public. Resolved, that a copy of this resolution now adopted, signed by the offices of this meeting, be presented to Capt Eldridge, accompanied by the signatures of the passengers.[77]

If the ship was the locus, or center, all around became a void. Unlike trains passing through the landscape, there were no markers on board ship to indicate passage through time and space. It simply left one place and arrived in another.

The effect on the passengers was to turn them even more inward. The ship became not only their home but their whole reality. As Washington Irving described it,

There is no gradual transition by which, as in Europe, the features and populations of one country blend almost imperceptibly with those of another. From the moment you lose sight of the land you have left, all is vacancy, until you step at once until you step on the opposite shore, and are launched at once into the bustle and novelties of another world.[78]

This isolation, which in an earlier era drove some sailors mad, was marketed by the steamship lines as yet another perk of the sea voyage:

The steamer has gone away from the land, and the light blue sky and dark blue ocean meet all around, in the great expansive and almost limitless circle of the horizon, without a spot to break the line bounding the vision. The ship and her company have become all the world to those on board, and thus cut off from everything outside, the voyage is an enforced idleness.[79]

If the ship became the reality, all else—even its destination or the ports it visited—was merely transient. Cut off from the world, steamship passengers formed unique communities and embraced the experience of living within the confines of a steel-walled universe.

English tourists bound for the Continent were denied this weeklong transatlantic bonding, yet the proliferation of cruises in the 19th century meant that they, too, began to experience Europe and elsewhere from the deck of a steamer. As the century wore on, the effects of steam tourism began to work on the national consciousness of Britain and the United States, until even those who had never taken a voyage abroad found their opinions of the world shaped by it. Favell Lee Mortimer, an Englishwoman and successful author of numerous children's books, turned her hand later in life to writing travel guides. *Near Home, or, The Countries of Europe Described; Far Off Part I: Asia and Australia Described;* and *Far Off Part II: Oceania, Africa, and America Described* were all midcentury bestsellers, full of anecdotes, descriptions and practical advice. Mrs. Mortimer's enthusiasm was unhampered by the fact that her adult travels consisted of exactly one weekend trip to Edinburgh.[80] Her sources were passengers: friends, relations, acquaintances, and other published accounts. It is their vantage that permeates her descriptions, as here:

Some places look pretty at a distance which look very ugly when you come up to them. Lisbon is one of those places. If you were to cross the Atlantic in a ship, and go up the broad river Tagus, you would soon see Lisbon. . . . When you first see Lisbon, the white houses glittering in the sun, the balconies adorned with flowers and shrubs, and the lovely orange groves,—you cry out "What a beautiful city!" But when you have landed on shore . . . the streets are full of litter and rubbish; and troops of dirty dogs are seen on every side, and very unpleasant smells come from the houses.[81]

Compare this passage with the account of an actual passenger arriving in Rangoon: "As the steamer nears the quay at Rangoon, the city, which was so ethereal and so delicately hinted at when viewed from a far away reach of the river, becomes every moment grosser and more commonplace."[82] This keen sense of disappointment arises from a certain amount of fantasizing. The traveler, having built up in her mind a mythical and wholly unrealistic image of the exotic destination, encounters it on the horizon like Bali Hai. After weeks at sea, the voyage acts like a whetting stone against these fantasies, sharpening them to a fine point. But arriving on shore, what reality could ever match the heavy weight of expectation? After a day or so dropped into the hugger-mugger of the stalls, the traveler returns home disenchanted.

Mrs. Mortimer, at the receiving end of these accounts, reflects them in her guidebook. Even Constantinople, which had enraptured visitors for centuries, is exposed as a sham: "Like many other towns it looks beautiful at a distance, but turns out, when you arrive there, to be very unpleasant."[83] This lofty perch also allowed her to pass judgment on the citizens within. The Turks, for example, "are so grave they look wise. But how can a lazy people be really wise? They like to spend their time eating opium, sipping coffee, and sitting still."[84]

The ignorance and insularity of such pronouncements takes the modern reader's breath away. There is not a culture on earth that cannot be dismissed by a few pithy sentences. The Burmese, for example, "are a blunt and rough people . . . they are very deceitful, and tell lies on every occasion; indeed, they are not ashamed of their falsehoods. They are also very proud, because they fancy they were so good before they were born into this world." For sheer mendacity, however, the Burmese had nothing on the Egyptians: "It is a rare thing in Egypt to speak the truth. There was an Egyptian, by trade a jeweler, who was a man of his word. His countrymen were so much surprised to find he spoke the truth constantly that they gave him the name of 'The Englishman.'"[85]

Where was this bile coming from? Consider the sources Mrs. Mortimer had available to her. Though born to an upper-middle-class family, she spent most of her life as a parson's wife in a windswept corner of Shropshire, hundreds of miles from London and its great libraries. Even if she had had access to their books, they would not have helped her much. Tomes describing each nation would have focused more on geography than personal habits and in any case would likely be years out of date. Mrs. Mortimer would have wanted the most current information. For this, she would necessarily rely on her friends and neighbors who had been abroad. There are traces of anecdotal reportage: Stories of being haggled to death in Morocco or accosted in Florence factor heavily in her accounts. But as it was unlikely that the Shropshire gentry ventured as far as Tokyo, she would also draw perforce from published travelogues (if she could find them), accounts in newspapers—in short, anything current.

Yet when these sources dried up, as they certainly must have, what remained? Only the kind of general understandings and prejudices common to most ordinary Englishmen and women regarding "abroad." Very likely Mrs. Mortimer could no more have said where her opinions came from on such diverse places and topics than any ordinary pub-dwelling xenophobe. Hence, as a travel guide Mrs. Mortimer is a disaster, but as a representative of British attitudes she is pure gold. "Superficial, incomplete, and trifling" were some of the criticisms given of *The Countries of Europe Described* when it first appeared, but none of the editors took issue with the basic assumptions underlying it.[86]

Besides the Olympian vantage of a ship approaching harbor, the snapshot impressions Mrs. Mortimer provides of other peoples are clearly drawn from the brief, frenetic, and usually pecuniary encounters made by tourists. From lazy Spaniards to duplicitous Arabs and rude Chinese, Mrs. Mortimer's world is populated exclusively by gorgons whose only aim is to waylay, mislead, swindle, or corrupt the morals of the English traveler. Not even the destitute escaped her censure. Italian beggars followed one from place to place, she reports (just as they did the Roosevelt family) but when finally given money, "they are not as thankful as Irish beggars are."[87] The leitmotif that runs throughout Mrs. Mortimer's works is as simple as one of her children's books: England is the greatest nation on earth, and the English traveler abroad must expect to be continually disappointed. Or, as one historian puts it:

When the typical British subject went abroad, he naturally assumed that nothing would quite measure up to what he had left behind; nothing would be as pleasurable or comfortable as it was at home. His breakfast tray would carry neither eggs, grilled sausage nor an intelligible morning paper; peckish at four o'clock, he would be left at the mercy of people just awakening from siesta, dubious bistros advertising "Tea Within." He expected on the whole to rough it and forebear, to tolerate all those things of which he could not approve, from Spanish brandy to German feather beds.[88]

Blind to their own insularity, Britons were quick to point it out in others. Near the end of the century, a British consular officer in Venice admitted the traveling American bemused him. "One wonders what idea they have in traveling," he wrote, "Their interest seems to be principally motion; and when they find themselves out of railway carriages, they are at a loss for employment."[89] This was unfair. The American tourist, or the British tourist for that matter, was simply following the path laid down for him. As historian Stephen Prickett writes,[90] there is something powerfully symbolic about a railroad track. One cannot deviate from it; all travel is reduced from exploration to fixed schedules and locales. This was equally true of steamships, which carried passengers through the "void" and deposited them—briefly—in exotic locales. Thus steam marks the division between two very different kinds of travel: the rough but romantic, and the smooth but sterilized. The gains for the traveler from the latter included safety, security, speed, efficiency, comfort, and the ability to insulate oneself from the irritating, dangerous, or "foreign." The losses were freedom and the joy of discovery.

One could argue that this was a false dichotomy: hardy souls still eschewed the railway carriage and traveled the Continent by horse or even—as in our own age—bicycle. They could still be thrilled at the Matterhorn or struck dumb by the beauty of the *Pietà*. Nor was there any rule mandating that mechanized transport instantly transformed one from a traveler into a tourist. Even Mr. Cook's much-maligned holidaymakers experienced moments of wonder. Nevertheless, the most ardent romantic still had to arrive there by ship, and the voyage over had an indelible effect on shaping their impressions of what was to come.

Steam cruising also facilitated the proliferation of a new kind of tourist, one who preferred their culture in packaged, carefully siphoned quantities and reveled in the detachment from locale that such travel provided. Instead of braving the new and unknown, passengers could now preserve not only their postcard-like impressions of destinations, but their preconceptions and prejudices as well. Travel, which Twain, Melville, and others had taken to be universally broadening, contracted to exact dimensions of a steamship's hull. The communities created therein remained intact even when ashore. The ship was the reality; all else, the world itself, became a phantasmagoria of images sliding under the projectionist's scope as the ship moved from place to place.

As ships grew larger and more luxurious, more emblematic of the nations they represented, the metaphorical distance between themselves and the places they touched lengthened apace. William Makepeace Thackeray identified this phenomenon as early as 1844:

Wherever the captain cries "Stop her!" Civilization stops, and lands in the ship's boat, and makes a permanent acquaintance with the savages on shore.[91]

The idea that the opposite might be equally true apparently did not occur to him.

PART III
Imperials

9

TIFFIN FOR GRIFFINS
Educating Imperial Administrators on the Long Voyage

AT THE CLOSE OF HIS SEMINAL, multivolume work on *Indian Shipping*, published in 1912, Dr. Radhakumud Mookerji allowed himself a moment of regret. Having traced the history of his people's maritime enterprise from the earliest dhows to the present, he gave a brief requiem for lost glory. "Thus has passed away one of the great national industries of India after a long and brilliant history," he wrote sadly. "It was undoubtably one of the triumphs of Indian civilization, the chief means by which that civilization asserted itself and influenced other civilizations. India is now without this most important organ of national life."[1]

It would not have been proper for Dr. Mookerji (Premchand Roychaud Scholar, Calcutta University, and professor of Indian history at the National Council of Education at Bengal) to lay blame at any particular source, especially when the likely imperial culprit had founded both of his academic institutions and was currently paying his salary. He did, however, note rather broadly that the "sea borne trade of India is continually expanding, with the result of increasing our dependence on foreign shipping."[2] That was a telling word choice: Did "foreign" shipping include the dozens of P&O and British India liners currently clogging the harbors at Bombay, Madras, and Calcutta? Or the hundreds of English steam freighters that daily arrived bearing cloth, coal, and sundries? Or indeed the hundreds more of river vessels, chugging along the Ganges and the Indus, all operated by subsidiaries of those august companies in London? Mookerji, prudently, did not elaborate.

And yet it had only been one year since the great Delhi Durbar, where King George V appeared in person as Emperor of India, wearing a crown specially made for the occasion. Every maharajah in the nation arrived to pay homage, along with thousands of lesser supplicants. The pageant, meant to be a display of Eastern splendor, instead recalled a ruder time when the earls of Mercia, Northumbria, and Wessex laid their crowns before the feet of William the Conqueror.[3] No Indian gentleman, especially one as astute and well connected as Dr. Mookerji, could be ignorant of the Durbar's message.

In previous chapters we examined how the spectacle of steam conditioned

Victorians to regard it as a harbinger of civilization, and how the experience of traveling on board shaped their perception of other cultures. In this final section, both themes are combined: The spectacle of steam is exported, and it is used to carry imperial administrators to their new posts overseas. For the latter, the voyage over shaped their understanding and perception of empire (and their place within it) even more profoundly than cruising transformed Anglo-American travel. Some elements were shared: Brief interactions with avaricious locals at coaling ports reinforced preexisting prejudices, while once again the ship served as a floating avatar of British nationhood, mores, and customs. Yet these passengers were not holidaymakers. As the first contact with the world the empire builders would soon inhabit, the vessel became a locus of transition from England to colonies—physically, of course, but psychologically as well. Along the way, the administrators were exposed to new and distinctly "foreign" words, foods, customs, experiences, and climate, while always reminded of the paramount importance of retaining their British identity. The great fleets of P&O, British India, Orient, and others became the lifelines of empire (just as Isambard Brunel had hoped, but not in the way he imagined) and *de facto* training schools for the next generation of imperial administrators.

More broadly, the spectacle of steam became a fixture within the moral universe of imperialism. The effects of introducing 19th-century technology to the empire by fiat has been well examined by other scholars;[4] steamship transport, specifically, has received somewhat less attention—at best a chapter within a larger narrative that includes telegraphs and railways. Not that its importance has been underestimated, as Ben Marsden and Crosbie Smith write:

The distinctive features of the widely scattered island empire of Queen Victoria invite a revisionist account in which the Empire ceases to be regarded merely as the sum of the disparate parts but can be better understood by focusing on those physical and symbolic systems which, for a time, gave it unity amid diversity and made it what it was. Nothing exemplified better these bonds, embodied in space, than the engineering artifacts that were the iron steamships of the Victorian age.[5]

My purpose here is not to revisit covered ground but to consider how the concept shaped the Victorian/Edwardian imperial imagination. If steam was a spectacle signifying human progress, then the arrival of a steamship in a "barbaric" land could have only one symbolic meaning: the spread of civilization. The spectacle, in short, was now being exported. In 1890, for example, Robert

Baden-Powell noted approvingly that East Africa, which had known nothing but "piracy and the slave trade," was now (thanks to the African Steamship Company) "within the range of civilized travel."[6]

The image was seductive: The ship—paint gleaming, smokestack churning, the very embodiment of progressive technology—is set against the coarse, lush landscape. P&O used it in their advertisement posters for years, often adding a few fawning natives just for good measure. Transportation as civilization was a compelling concept because it seemed—like the machine itself—to be immune from subjectivity. Steam power was not religious dogma, but a tool that mankind had fashioned for its own good. Like hospitals and schools, it was regarded as "good" imperialism.[7] This view, however, emerged from the cult of technology that (as we saw in Chapter 4) grew up around the device and obscured its limitations. As the belief in technological infallibility collapsed in 1912, one remnant survived: the concept of transportation as civilization. In other words, even if Edwardians no longer believed that steam would lead the way to a future utopia for themselves, they continued to espouse the idea for their captive peoples.

Ultimately, as we shall see, some began to question this steam-powered morality. As doubts grew about their mechanized age—and the progressive axioms underlying it—so too did concern over whether imposing it on subjugated cultures was a moral imperative or a mortal sin. Mark Twain, following Phileas Fogg's route around the world in 1897, lamented the effects of technological imperialism even as he marveled at the wonder of the ships that bore him from one colony to the next. Jules Verne himself came to despise the mechanical world he had envisioned: From the marvels of the *Great Eastern* in 1869 he finally arrived at the horrors of a dystopian *Propeller Island* in 1895. The phantasmagoria of steam, which had been a vision of wonderment and delight, became a nightmare.

This Huxleyian future seemed remote in the 1850s, when the more immediate issue was not steam technology's limitations but how to maximize its potential. The problem of governing India, tied to the greater problem of imperial governance as a whole, came down finally to the exigencies of distance. Generations of civil servants agonized over how to manage an empire that theoretically spanned the globe yet was connected by only the most tenuous of threads: wind power and frail wooden hulls.[8] The impracticability of communication left colonial administrators stranded, failed to replenish needed reserves of munitions and militia, and had already helped deprive Britain of her most valuable possession second to India, in the American War of Independence.

This bureaucratic quandary had a mechanical solution. Almost since its advent early in the century, British traders and statesmen had pondered how to create a regular steamship service between England and her possessions abroad. In the records of the British Library are dozens of memoranda, some dating as far back as 1822, on the "steam question" for India. A public meeting held in London in that year enthusiastically endorsed the idea (over a decade before the *Sirius* departed on her transatlantic run) but offered few concrete proposals.[9] At almost exactly the same moment, a cadre of Calcuttan businessmen created the Society of the Encouragement of Steam Navigation Between Great Britain and India. Prominent among them was the Nawab of Oudh, whose yacht was the first steam craft in India. Together they raised a handsome sum of £5,000, which was used to finance the construction of the *Enterprize,* a tiny vessel of only 464 tons. She was dispatched, rather precipitately, on her maiden voyage from London in the fall of 1827. The *Enterprize* reached Calcutta 113 days later, having run out of coal and exhausted both her supplies and her crew. So began and ended India's only chance to have a role in her own maritime destiny, at least for another century.[10]

The voyage was a signal failure, but it demonstrated a few useful principles: First, if any steamship were to undertake the trip, it would have to be specially constructed for long distances, extreme heat, and severe weather; second, even more crucially, there would have to be coaling stations all along the route. Since neither existed, the plan was shelved.[11] Yet the dream still tantalized: Lord Bentinck, Governor General of India, saw in steam the possibilities of consolidating his own dominion. Typically, he described it as for the Indians' own good: Steam travel was "the great engine of working moral improvement.... [A]s the communication between the two countries shall be facilitated and shortened, so will civilized Europe be approximated, as it were, to these benighted regions."[12] The annihilation of space, in other words, with a vengeance.

A decade later, the building race between the *Great Western* and *British Queen* inspired Parliament to take up the matter again.[13] By now the bottleneck had reached crisis levels: English cotton exports to India, which had been 817,000 yards in 1814, reached 24 million in 1824, and doubled again by 1837.[14] Pressed by city merchants who wanted a more reliable trade with Bombay and Calcutta, the government approved a plan to establish a permanent route and then threw the contest open to the most attractive offer. The lucky winners were a consortium of local merchants with scant experience but plenty of capital, who gave themselves the title of the Peninsular & Oriental Steamship Company.[15]

The company (which was the line later carrying William Makepeace Thackeray) had modest aims initially: Its first ships, *Don Juan* and *Tagus* (one of the ships that carried Thackeray), terminated their voyages at Gibraltar. The admiralty contract to carry the mails required not only a fleet of fast ships to reach Alexandria, but overland service to Suez (the canal not yet being built) and onwards, by a second fleet, to Calcutta.[16] The logistics were diabolical. Coaling stations would need to be established every 500 miles or so along the route, the coal itself brought out to these supply stations ironically by sailing ships. The overland passage could not be accomplished without the consent and aid of the pasha of Egypt, which did not come cheap. Then, having arrived upon the distaff side of the continent, P&O ships sailing to Calcutta would be in direct competition with the formidable East India Company, whose packets had held dominion over the Indian trade since the reign of Elizabeth I.[17]

Against these obstacles, both logistical and human, P&O dispatched two superb vessels, the *Hindustan* and *Bentinck*, in 1843. The first passenger steamships expressly designed for the tropical trade, they were fitted with watertight compartments, iron bulkheads, and cabins that opened directly onto the deck, the better to take advantage of light and fresh breezes. The dining saloon, likewise, had ports on either side that could be ventilated to catch the fickle crosswinds.[18] The magnitude of P&O's enterprise did not go unnoticed. The *Illustrated London News* lauded their "patriotic efforts to shorten the distance between Europe and the East" and the "vast benefit conferred upon Great Britain and her Oriental possessions." It devoted an entire issue to describing the many wonders of these new steamers:

They are fitted up with every attention to comfort and convenience: and, above all, light and ventilation, so desirable in tropic climates, have been abundantly provided. . . . Venetian blinds are inserted in the upper part of the doors, and, wherever possible, in the sides of the cabins also; and plates of perforated zinc, and all manner of contrivances, are introduced to ensure a constant circulation of refreshing drafts of air. . . . The decorations of the saloon consist of several highly interesting views of Cabul, Ghunzee, etc., painted, or rather enameled, on slate. The gildings are gorgeous, and all the fittings are correspondingly superb.[19]

It could be fairly said that these early vessels were in many ways more practical for the Indian trade than those that followed a generation later. They were not bastions of empire—not yet—and hence their designers saw no need to replicate the claustrophobia of a London club in 110-degree heat. Light and airy, they embraced their "Oriental" character, as the depictions of Far Eastern ports in the saloon suggested. They were also unique in employing local crews. This fact, born of economy, gave P&O liners an exotic dash that often represented passengers' first encounter with non-white peoples. While the officers remained British, deck and engine hands were recruited from East Africa, with stewards from Goa. The African crew was particularly prized: As Muslims, they were mercifully immune from the perils of drunkenness endemic to the British sailor. They could also better handle the ferocious heat of a stoking furnace in tropical conditions; the *Illustrated London News* noted approvingly that "some of them will work half an hour in such a place as the stokehole and come up on deck without a drop of perspiration on their dark skins."[20] Goanese stewards were predominantly Catholic—a legacy of Portuguese occupation—and thus marginally more acceptable to the insular British traveler than "pagan" Hindus. The line established a training school in Goa that also served as a recruitment office; it remains open to this day. Thus was established a long tradition of Indian service on board P&O ships, often passed down as a familial trade from father to son.[21]

Early travelers were, for the most part, enchanted by this exoticism. "Through the ports one could see the moon shining on the sea," one wrote rapturously,

while from the lower deck came the muffled throb of tom tom accompanying a weird, minor crooning song from some of the fourth class passengers, who seemed to be voicing all the despair of Africa.... Who would not rather sail the tropical seas in the rottenest craft afloat than cross the Atlantic in the finest ocean greyhound?[22]

Even the exposure to new (and, in the parlance of the age, heathen) faiths could offer moments of surprising grace:

There are many Mahommedans among the Lascar deck crew and deck passengers who never fail to say the sunset and sunrise prayers ordained to the followers of the Prophet. At the appointed time, off go their shoes, their faces are turned towards Mecca, their turbans and pugerees laid aside, the enjoined genuflections performed.[23]

How bizarre and wondrous this ritual must have seemed to one accustomed to the dry liturgy of Anglican prayer!

By 1845, P&O's success emboldened them to extend their reach to China.[24] The *Lady Mary Wood*, which had also carried Thackeray, was put in service between Calcutta, Singapore, and Hong Kong. By the early 1850s an additional route was augmented to Australia, and thus the company had drawn its thin contrail lines in the seas connecting nearly all of Britain's imperial possessions in the East.[25] This hegemony did not go unchallenged for long. Rival firms, and their agents, accused P&O of lateness with the mail, of overloading their ships with cargo at the expense of passenger comfort, even of using the grand saloon of one vessel to store opium bound for China.[26] All of the charges were probably true, but, set against the sheer logistics of P&O's round-the-world operations, seem niggling.

Nevertheless, by midcentury the strain on the company was beginning to show. Members of Parliament accused it of inefficiency, even fraud, and began demanding monthly representations as to its operations. Recall from Chapter 2 that it was around this time when a parliamentary committee formally reconsidered the possibility of breaking the line's monopoly: It was then that the Eastern Steamship Line submitted its doomed proposal. But P&O emerged victorious, for the moment. In 1854 the company purchased an entire city block on Leadenhall Street in London, which became the site of its new offices. They were directly across from those of the East India Company, and one story taller—as if inviting a dare.[27]

Then, in 1857, came the Indian Mutiny. The shock of its outbreak—and the surprising difficulties that the British encountered trying to suppress it—demonstrated only too well the inadequacy of the present state of imperial shipping. Brunel's *Great Eastern* was a radical attempt to turn the entire system on its head. Instead of sailing through the Mediterranean and then passing overland (a cumbersome business at best), the ship's passengers would sail directly to India round the Cape of Good Hope. Instead of constantly bunkering at Port Said or Aden or Galle, which added days to the trip, the *Great Eastern* would carry the coal herself. The plan, as we have seen, was both brilliant and impractical: a simple solution to a difficult problem that—by its failure—reinforced just how monumental that problem was.

If one single ship was not the answer, perhaps a giant fleet would be. From 1859 onward, the P&O Line embarked on an ambitious construction plan, beginning with the *Mooltan* of 1861. Half again as large as any prior vessel in the fleet, she had the first compound engine on the Indian route—a development that not only increased her speed but also reduced fuel consumption. The *Illustrated London News,* which often seemed to be on retainer for the line, professed itself amazed in equal parts by her strength and splendor. It even troubled to note a favorable comparison with another competitor, as yet unvanquished:

Light, however, as she looks, the hull is of enormous strength, and broad diagonal stringers of iron so cross the ship in both sides and deck in all directions that she may be considered, of her size, as strong as the *Great Eastern* herself. Inside she is fitted up with a solidity and splendour, which have not been seen in the finest vessels of this company. . . . The decorations of the state saloon might be pointed to as a model for good taste and elegance of what a ship's fittings would be in this respect.[28]

For all her elegance and innovation, the *Mooltan* was one ship, not five, and barely a fifth the size of the *Great Eastern*. The Company continued to build, and build. In 1865 came the *Niphow, Tanjore,* and *Mongolia*; in 1866 the *Malacca, Geelong, Sunda, Surat,* and *Avoca*; in 1867 the *Travancore, Bangalore,* and *Sumatra*. The combined tonnage of the fleet in 1854 was a mere 58,185 tons; by 1912 that number had increased to 538,875.[29]

Nor were they the only lifeline of empire. Another consequence of the mutiny was that the British government was no longer willing to trust P&O with a monopoly: Now it would grant lucrative mail contracts to all comers, and a plethora of new firms rushed to take advantage of the admiralty's largesse. British India was the first to break P&O's hold, with a fleet of combination passenger/freighters that specialized in transporting commodities like timber and rice, as well as migrants between India, China, and the Malay states. The Blue Funnel Line inaugurated direct service from Liverpool to Hong Kong in 1865, challenging not only P&O but the Chinese clipper trade as well. Admiralty mail contracts also provided early subsidies for the Glen, China Mutual, Union, Castle, and African Steam Ship companies, all entering service in the critical years of 1860–1875.[30] This massive influx of tonnage not only transformed Britain's relationship with her colonies, but the colonies themselves. The ships' constant need for fuel turned traditional ports like Bombay, Calcutta, and Cape Town into coaling stations; others were constructed virtually anew for that purpose, including Karachi, Dakar, Port Said, Singapore, and Hong Kong.[31]

While not the only nation plying their ships along these routes—the French Messageries Maritimes and German Norddeutscher Lloyd both made respectable showings—the British firms had the inestimable advantage of purchasing British coal. Though not as beautiful as Aztec gold or Italian marble, Britain's plentiful supply of those dark, smutty rocks gave it near domination in the creation of collier ports, which in turn fueled the nation's trade at vastly lower prices than their German or French competitors. This advantage could not be underestimated, for it ensured British supremacy for as long as they controlled the coal and the refueling stations.[32] The ability to set prices and control supply would later establish the fortunes of men like Andrew Carnegie, John D. Rockefeller, and J. P. Morgan: Here, the British used it to consolidate an empire.

In addition to coal, there was speed. On the North Atlantic—despite all the furious competition—speed was a negligible commodity: The difference between the fastest and slowest steamers from Liverpool to New York would mean, at most, a single day's travel. But on the long route to India, China, or Australia, faster engines could shave off whole weeks. More important yet, they ensured regular and swift communication between mother country and colony—for the first time in history. In 1872, one London newspaper put it baldly: "Iron and steam power, which Great Britain possesses most abundantly, are now the rulers of the sea." The companies themselves were acutely aware of their importance to the empire. A passenger's guide published by the Orient Line used a familiar phrase to describe it:

Increased size of ships has been accompanied by increased engine power, with a consequent increase of speed and steadiness . . . When the Orient Company first began to carry passengers, the average duration of the voyage to Adelaide was about fifty days. Now the average of, say, the *Orphir*, is thirty-four days. The Cape has been brought within half the distance in time that it was from us thirty years ago, and on all the routes of ocean traffic a similar acceleration of speed has taken place. Thus the new ships seem to be *conquering space itself*, and under their giant strides the very world grows smaller.[33]

By 1869, with the opening of the Suez Canal, these ships were central to the maintenance of Britain's overseas colonies. Moreover, as the metaphorical and actual links between home and abroad, they became loci of transition for men and women taking up the business of imperial rule. Coming onboard at Tilbury, the ship was their first introduction to the people, culture, and climate of the British empire. The weeks-long crossing was thus a cathartic experience—framed and managed by the ship's décor, food, service, and of course the passengers themselves—no less than the gradually warming weather en route, tensions of close confinement, brief coaling stops in exotic ports, and the almost mythical prospect of arrival in a strange land.

Oddly, though, the memoirs of these imperial administrators rarely devote much time to it. Most begin with the arrival itself, first impressions of Bombay or Ceylon, and immersion within an alien culture.[34] The ship seems to be a last vestige of the world they left behind: comfortable, familiar, British—and boring. Weary from weeks on sea, they are only too glad to leave it at the pier. Yet even if they did not acknowledge it, the voyage over was of paramount importance. It conditioned them to the mores, rituals, and even language of the world they would soon inhabit and reinforced their conviction in the rightness of their task. They were not the same people who embarked in England. In a few short weeks, it made them imperials.

Most of those taking up administrative positions in the empire were young men, usually unmarried, drawn from the middle and upper classes of English society. Few had been abroad further than the Continent; almost none had been to India or the Far East.[35] Until the moment of their departure, their knowledge was confined to Henry Morton Stanley's accounts or the tales and poems of Rudyard Kipling. Representations of empire were almost always rendered in gorgeous colors, yet these young men must also have been aware of the dangers: disease, revolt, the occasional wild animal. Some might have relations or older friends who had returned from an overseas posting, but this was not always the best source of information. The archetype of the imperial boor—a retired colonel, say, of the Hussars—would quickly become a fixture of English fiction. Garrulous, insistent, peppering his speech with words like *howdah*, *shufti*, and *memsahib*, he bored unwilling listeners with endless tales of elephant hunts and sultry nights on the veldt.[36] While clearly a caricature, it nevertheless suggests a romanticized vision of empire propagated even by those with experience in it.

The uncertainty of the neophyte empire builder was reflected by his choice of what to bring with him. Besides several complete wardrobes, the traveler was also expected to pack hunting rifles and revolvers, cartridges, foldable furniture, a writing desk, several pairs of spectacles, tooth and flea powder, mosquito netting, replaceable boot soles, and—if the gentleman was so inclined—enough rubber prophylactics to last his entire duty abroad. If he happened to be married, the decision of what to bring was often left to his wife, with varying results. A passenger on the Elder Dempster liner *Abosso*, bound for equatorial Africa, found himself "in a cabin littered with steel boxes and helmet cases. . . . My wife insisted that I should take an eiderdown and plentiful supplies of Cooper's Oxford Marmalade and Lux and Epsom salts."[37] It is worth noting in passing that the ignorance reflected in such choices was not confined to Far Eastern travel. Mr. Frederick Lort-Phillips, bound for New York City on the *Majestic* in 1892, wrote confidently, "As we expected to mix with the inhabitants of the wild and wooly west, we had brought with us such weapons as we thought would help us in preserving our lives." These included two hunting knives and a revolver. Mr. Lort-Phillips also attempted to grow a beard, the better to blend in.[38]

For those taking up residence in tropical climes, the Orient Line offered a few suggestions: "White is the best color for clothes, black the worst. Sun helmets and light shoes with rubber soles for the deck should be provided for enjoyments' sake."[39] London tailors advertised "India outfits": a complete wardrobe including four suits (two linen, one serge, one light flannel), pajamas, white linen dress shirts, umbrella, pith helmet and a mystifying object called a "cholera belt."[40] An early guide recommended even more impedimenta: "swinging cot, hair mattress, feather pillow, ship couch or sofa, case of blacking, brushes, footbath and tin can for water; 48 longcloth shirts, 24 longcloth full front nightshirts, 24 Indian gauze waistcoats, 128 nightcaps . . ."[41] How the aspiring traveler was supposed to convey this menagerie to the pier, or from it, is not known. Still, nothing could beat Mrs. Wilson's solemn advice, in *Hints for the First Years of Residence in India*, to bring a cast-iron tub for bathing—English iron being of better quality than inferior local zinc.[42]

Arriving at the pier in Tilbury, the scene was sheer chaos. Veterans of England's much-vaunted public schools must have experienced a familiar pang: They were leaving home again, and this time for as long as eight years—or, perhaps, forever. Imminent departure from England brought out a welter of conflicting emotions. One had to find his way to the assigned cabin, reserve his table in the dining saloon, ensure that the trunks marked "Wanted On Voyage" did not end up in the hold, pay the deck steward a handsome bribe to secure a good chair (Port Out, Starboard Home, or POSH, was the rule), and greet his new cabin mate, with whom he would be sharing a 9 by 9 box for the next three weeks.[43]

Finally, of course, it was time to say goodbye. The lengthy term of service often made these departures especially poignant. The parting scene, which deserved to be played in a solemn funereal hush, was indecently loud. "All was hurry and confusion on board," one P&O passenger recorded:

Passengers crying and lamenting and leaving their friends and relations, some hunting their luggage without effect, pigs grunting, calves bellowing, cocks crowing, geese screaming, crew drunk, officers swearing, steam blowing off, other passengers seeking after their berths—in short, a thousand like this, which made all confusion and riot.[44]

There would be little chance to see the ship herself, other than a black, salt-streaked iron wall butting up against the pier. Hence the transition from shore to vessel was so abrupt as to pass almost unnoticed; it was not until the liner began to head out into the channel that the reality of what was happening finally set in. Joining his tablemates for dinner, the new arrival would experience two things for the first time: Indian service, and the bizarre patois of the empire builders. For in addition to himself and his fellows, there would also be other, seasoned passengers returning to India or elsewhere in the empire after a sojourn at home. "They spoke a language all their own," one newcomer marveled.

An evening drink, for example, was always a sundowner. A drink at any other time was a *chota peg*. One's wife was the *memsahib*. To have a look at something was to have a *shufti*. . . . Something of poor quality was *shenzi*. Supper was tiffin and so on and so forth. The Empire builder's jargon would have filled a dictionary.[45]

Likely the first word he would learn of this strange new language was his own title: griffin. Barbarized from the Welsh name Griffith, it was first applied to supposedly ignorant Welshmen arriving in India for the first time and eventually grew to encompass all new arrivals. Griffins were plebes, and needed someone to show them the ropes.[46] That education began on board, at once. Anglo-Indians, judges, military officers, consuls, station chiefs, policemen, doctors, sisal traders, customs agents—and their wives—all took it upon themselves to help guide the young man.

A very young Roald Dahl made the voyage to East Africa in the twilight days of empire, but his observations en route were reflective of the Victorians as much as their successors. "More English than the English, more Scottish than the Scots," he wrote, "they were the craziest bunch of humans I shall ever meet."[47] Some of their zaniness was traditionally blamed on the climate (English eccentricity in the tropics was a well-known phenomenon, inspiring Noel Coward's famous ditty "Mad Dogs and Englishmen"), yet the remainder, Dahl discovered, had much to do with the absolute power these individuals enjoyed in their colonial roles:

It would seem that when the British live for years in a foul and sweaty climate among foreign people they maintain their sanity by allowing themselves to go slightly dotty. They cultivate bizarre habits that would never be tolerated back home, whereas in faraway Africa or in Ceylon or in India or in the Federated Malay States they could do as they liked.[48]

One Anglo-Indian major and his *memsahib* ran naked along the decks at first light; Dahl's cabin mate sprinkled artificial dandruff on his shoulders to convince others that his hairpiece was genuine; and gentle, elderly Miss Trefusis expressed a mortal horror at her own toes—only her African servant was allowed to touch them.

This fact hints at another new experience for the griffins: observing how the colonials treated those that served them. Goanese stewards were invariably called "boy," regardless of age, while at dinner the Anglo-Indians often simply clapped when they wanted something. This peremptory manner was contagious: Soon the griffins themselves would be loudly ordering their *chota pegs* and demanding another serving of curry at tiffin. The experience of native service, a prelude to what they would encounter on shore, was both empowering and exotic. Just as the veteran administrators instructed them on their new language, the ship also became a training ground for the next generation of imperial overlords. "It was rather wonderful for me," Dahl admitted, "to be thrust suddenly into the middle of this pack of sinewy sunburnt gophers and their bright, bony little wives, and what I liked best about them was their eccentricities."[49]

The surreality of the passengers—seemingly normal Englishmen, but with a hint of sun-stroked madness within—was reflected by the ship itself. Aware that their patrons would be spending weeks at sea, P&O and other lines fashioned comfortable, familiar interiors intended to remind them of home. There was a ladies' parlor done in stifling chintz and tassels, a gentlemen's smoking room in dark woods and animal hides, and a saloon amidships for the enjoyment of both sexes, designed to emulate the most proper of English drawing rooms. As time went on, these interiors came to reflect growing confidence in the empire, until they became almost caricatures of Britishness abroad. Consider this depiction of an Orient liner from 1888:

The saloon of the *Austral* is a magnificent chamber. It measures about 40 feet each way, and will hold about 120 people at dinner together. The sides are in walnut, paneled with beautiful carving, and the columns which support the roof are in an old English pattern. In all the Arms of the Company may be found with their lion and kangaroo supporters, and the motto PAR NON LEONINA SOCIETAS.[50]

"The lion is no match for civilized society." Yet an observant eye noted certain oddities. Above almost every door was an ornamental grate, the better to increase the flow of air between rooms; most public rooms and staterooms opened directly onto the deck, eschewing interior passages that would inevitably become claustrophobic en route. As the weather grew hotter, crewmembers began affixing tin shovel-like devices to all the portholes, called wind-scoops.

But the most striking addition were so-called *punkahs:* long sheets of linen or brocade suspended above each room with ropes at both ends. Goanese servants held the ropes and gently swayed the curtain, circulating the air. The result might seem negligible (as one author notes, *punkahs* moved air but did not cool it[51]), yet the sight was at once exotic and impressive. There was something almost decadent in watching the native servants engaged in this tedious work: It brought to mind the sultan dallying in his harem. To the rare passenger from the American South, it would have seemed doubly familiar; Louisiana plantations had a similar device, manned by slaves.[52] The companies eventually sensed this Oriental pageant had outlived its utility. A steamship guide at the turn of the century boasted:

The Company have rejected the "punkah" as out of date, and other mechanical contrivances on account of noise and other objectionable features. Absolutely noiseless electric beeswing fans depending from the ceiling, each stretching out some five feet, circulate the air in a thorough and agreeable manner.[53]

FIGURE 11. British Orient's *Ortona* (1899), typical of the dozens of ships that maintained the link between Britain and her empire. SOURCE: Author's collection.

As the *punkah* swayed gently overhead, griffins sat down to the first of a seemingly endless stretch of meals. With few other distractions on board, eating took up a considerable portion of the day. The breakfast bugle tooted at 8 AM precisely; slugabeds had only an hour to shave and dress before it ended. Latecomers could console themselves with bouillon and sandwiches on deck at 11, or wait until a full lunch spread at 1. Then came that most quintessential of institutions, high tea, at 4, and dinner at 6. Fruit, dessert, and spirits came out at 9.[54] Little wonder many passengers complained, at the end of three weeks on-board, of feeling "flabby and cramped."[55]

Early vessels carried a complete menagerie of live animals on deck: sheep, calves, pigs, and chickens, all lowing mournfully. Those of a morbid turn of mind could watch their numbers steadily deplete as the ship made her way towards Aden: One passenger noted approvingly that at a single meal he and his companions feasted on "ducks, fowls, tongues, hams with lobster salads, oyster patties, jellies, blanc-manges and dessert."[56] After the advent of refrigeration, the livestock pen mercifully disappeared. P&O even installed an ice-making plant at Suez, the better to keep their foodstuffs (and passengers) cool. The company was justly proud of this innovation, and boasted of it in their brochures:

Nothing of late years has contributed more to the comfort and luxury of life on board ships in the tropics, next to the increase in the size of vessels and their speed, than the refrigerating machinery with which they are fitted, and which enables the traveler to enjoy the comforts of a European climate in the tropics, and vice versa. It is among the curiosities of history appertaining to the Company that the profit obtained on the considerable sale of liquors which takes place on board their ships barely pays for the cost of refrigeration, and, viewed in this light, the Company does not derive a sixpence of benefit to their own exchequer from that department of their business.[57]

Menus on board reflected the same duality as the ship and passengers, albeit with mixed results. On the one hand, British standards of cuisine were rigidly enforced despite the increasing heat. There was something almost masochistic in the expectation that passengers would enjoy "porridge, fresh fish, beefsteak, or mutton chop" for breakfast, "cold fish, sardines, herring or lobster salad, two dishes of cold meats, and jams" for tea, or the tour de force of dinner: "soup, joint, two entrees or one entrée and poultry, pudding, a sweet dish, and dessert."[58] Some diners, especially those "gophers" who had already become accustomed to the more sensible Indian diet, rebelled. "High Tea in Second Class is a deliberate insult to the common sense of Anglo-Indians," a group of them wrote in complaint, "who are in constant combat with the dyspeptic incidents of life in the East." They spelled out the indictment in nauseating detail:

> You expect them to sit down at the close of the day, under the inaction of shipboard life, to slabs of cold meat and greasy imitations of Melton Mowbray pies, with no condiment but bread, director's jams, and dissolving butter, washed down by decoctions of tea. . . . Dairy and meat at the close of an inactive day on a tropical sea are physiological incompatibles and directly invoke a fit of dyspepsia.[59]

The companies listened. From the 1880s onward, menus were altered to reflect the maturity of the empire itself. No longer carrying the first generation of griffins out to the dominions, P&O, Orient Line, and British India ships now just as often catered to Anglo-Indians who had spent much of their life in the tropics. For the newcomer, therefore, the bill of fare for breakfast and dinner also included such novelties as chutney, poppadum, chapati, candied mangoes, and curries made with lamb, chicken, fish, and vegetables. Curry spice not only concealed the pungent flavor of meat left to slowly congeal on long voyages, but it also drew heat from the body. The Orient Line passenger's guide put it in clinical terms:

> In a medium climate with an ordinary diet an adult produces enough heat to raise the body in half an hour nearly 2 degrees Fahrenheit. It is clear then that it is as necessary to reduce internal heat production in a hot climate as to increase it in a cold one. Therefore the amount and quality of food must vary according to climate.[60]

Shipboard meals thus became the griffin's first exposure to such exotic and yet practical cuisine, and the response was almost universally favorable (so much so, in fact, that not only have such items become a staple of British cuisine, they remain perennial favorites aboard P&O ships to this day). The clash of cultures must have seemed at times profound: proper Englishmen and women in full evening dress, dining on richly colored and flavored Indian delicacies served by native stewards in a room that could have been lifted bodily from Brown's Hotel in Mayfair. Nor were the British ships the only ones to maintain cultural standards. A frequent traveler to East Africa commented in 1900:

> The Austrian Lloyd Lines are the favorite with the British officials on the East Coast. Of the Messageries boats I know little except that they undoubtedly have an excellent table. . . . You always feel safe on a German ship, even if you do have veal and pork served in the Red Sea with the thermometer hovering near the hundred mark.[61]

After a bumpy crossing through the Bay of Biscay, life on board settled into an unvarying routine. The day began with a good-humored Ro-Sham-Bo with one's cabin mate over who would dress first. Cabins were small and spartan, even in First Class, and the majority of space was taken up with the large, brass-handled trunks that contained daily clothes; the rest could only be accessed by visiting the luggage room, a cumbersome business that often entailed long queues before dinner.[62] An 1891 illustration for P&O tried to make light of the difficulties in assembling one's wardrobe within a heaving cabin. The gentleman begins by extracting his shirt, only to be attacked by his own suitcase as the ship rolls. He is then seen groping towards the sink, one arm in a shirtsleeve and the rest thrown over his head like a monk's cowl. The next frame was of a straight razor lolling menacingly in a basin full of water; what came next was too graphic to depict. Finally he appears on deck, hair somewhat rumpled, tie askew, but reasonably correct in dark suit and waistcoat.[63]

The gentleman's choice of attire hints at another anachronism. For most griffins, their only exposure to hot weather was a mild English summer. Passing through the Red Sea, they encountered a sticky, wet, still heat that was an assault upon the senses. Collars and shirtfronts wilted, layers of cloth chafed against the skin. Passengers began to smell. Public rooms reeked of sweat and stewed meat. The ship, which had never felt large, now contracted uncomfortably until it seemed as though the cushions on the sofas or even one's own mattress conspired to make one miserable. "The *Victoria,*" wrote Nellie Bly in 1889,

is said to be the finest boat on the P. and O. Line, still it could not be more unsuited for the trip. It is very badly planned, being built so that a great number of cabins inside are absolutely cut off from light and air. It is a compliment to call them cabins as they are really nothing more than small, dark, disagreeable, and unventilated boxes.[64]

Desperate for relief, passengers drowsed under an awning on deck. Yet at no time did they vary their dress. An 1875 etching from *The Graphic* displays a coterie of First Class passengers on the *Sumatra*'s top deck in the Red Sea. It is Sunday, and the captain is reading service while the others follow in their prayer books. Someone has brought up the saloon piano. Ladies are dressed in corsets, bonnets, and layers of voluminous petticoats. Most dresses appear to be light colored, but one lady—perhaps a widow—is all in black. The men concede even less to the climate: boiled shirt, necktie, vest, dark suit, and polished patent leather shoes are *de rigeur*. They are hatless, but that might owe more to the reverential scene than to the heat.[65]

Images like this were intended to reassure those at home in the unshakable propriety of empire: A tranquil domestic tableau transported to circumstances that were anything but ordinary meant that the English would uphold their faith and their manners, whatever the circumstances. Somerset Maugham's famous short story, "The Outstation," features a colonial administrator who invariably dresses for dinner, despite being the only Englishman on the island. He explains this behavior to a visitor:

For three years during the war I never saw a white man. I never omitted to dress on a single occasion on which I was well enough to come in to dinner.... When a white man surrenders in the slightest degree to the influences that surround him he very soon loses his self respect, and when he loses his self-respect you may be quite sure the natives will soon cease to respect him.[66]

On P&O liners, the performance of dress was as much for one another as for the Goanese that served them. It reminded the griffins of their place and what was expected of them. Stiff-upper-lip fortitude in the sweltering heat was just one of the ways that imperials demonstrated their mastery over the world they surveyed.

Between meals, passengers read or paced the deck, played cards, chatted, or dozed. With so many young men all traveling together, it was inevitable that there would almost immediately be a games committee, with regular sporting events scheduled every day except Sunday. P&O ships lacked the broad decks of the Atlantic liners: Denied their traditional promenade, griffins and others had to invent more compact means of exertion. There were tug-of-wars, ring tosses, skittles, potato sack races, egg-and-spoon relays, quoits, and that inevitable shipboard standard, shuffleboard. Prizes were awarded.[67] The ubiquity of games on board was yet another means for Victorian and Edwardian men to assert their masculinity and continue the tradition of competitive sport begun at school. Thus such games were not merely ways to pass the time, but reassertion of one's identity through familiar ritual. Those rituals would become even more comforting as the ship passed further into the unknown.

Even if one did not compete, he could at least bet on the outcome. Passengers bet on everything: the ship's speed, tomorrow's weather, the probability that the pilot at Aden would have a beard, and so on. This suggests another endemic quality of the sea passage: boredom. "Really one day passes so much like another," one passenger confided in her diary, "that there are few interesting items to note."[68] The heat made everyone listless and drowsy; the inevitable monotony of sea and sky—and the same group of people—could be maddening. Rudyard Kipling crossed on the British India liner *Africa* in 1889, and commented ruefully: "We are now running down to Penang with the thermometer 87 degrees in the cabins and anything you please on deck. We have exhausted all our literature, drunk two hundred lemon squashes, played forty different games of cards, organized a lottery on the run, and slept seventeen hours out of the twenty-four."[69]

Companies did all they could to ensure passengers' comfort on the long voyage. The Orient Line, P&O's chief competitor on the Indian trade, promised luxury and tranquility even as they acknowledged (in the past tense) some of the seedier aspects of Far Eastern travel:

Great progress has been made in late years in the art—for it is an art—of building and organizing passenger steamers. . . . Since the publication of the second edition some of the most magnificent ships have been launched, giving passengers examples of the highest pitch of perfection yet attainable. For comfort, we must refer the reader to pages 3–6 where we describe two or three vessels in which also electric light, the refrigerator, and in the tropics the punkahs worked by steam do all that is possible to annul the ordinary discomforts of a voyage. Here are no swinging, ill smelling oil lamps, no tough salt junk, no foul air, but good ventilation, fresh meat, ice *ad libitum,* and the soft steady light of electric lamps.[70]

In reality, the ships were not luxurious or even—for the most part—comfortable. Nor was the service as reliable as companies claimed. While Orient Lines employed Goanese stewards, P&O kept with Englishmen and women. The results were mixed. American journalist Nellie Bly was so put off by the curtness of the staff aboard the *Victoria* that she spent three pages castigating them, concluding wrathfully:

Travelers who care to be treated with courtesy, and furnished with palatable food, will never by any chance travel on the *Victoria*. It is all rule and no practice on that ship. The impudence and rudeness of the servants in America is a standing joke, but if the servants on the *Victoria* are a sample of English servants, I am thankful to keep those we have, such as they are. I asked the stewardess to assist a woman who looked as if she was dying of consumption, to the deck with her rugs, only to be told in reply, that she would not help any one unless they came and requested her to do so.[71]

Cabins became dark, ill-smelling sweatboxes at nightfall; so many passengers took refuge on the upper decks that the crew began laying out mattresses there every night. And, despite their best efforts, vermin proliferated. The Duchess of Buckingham and Chandos, traveling on P&O's *Arcadia* in 1892, handled one such incident with aplomb: "One night I was just going to bed when a large rat came into my cabin and began to hop all over my things.... I was dreadfully frightened by this unwelcome visitor, but refrained from screaming, as I fled down the passage in my night dress. My maid was still more unfortunate, as her rat went up her petticoats."[72] Even disturbances like this, however, gradually became part of the tapestry of shipboard life. "I used to have a horror of rats," one South Pacific passenger confided to his diary, "but here I soon became used to them." As indeed he might:

The first night I slept on board I smelt something very disgusting as I got into my bunk, and at last I discovered that it arose from a dead rat in the wainscot of the ship.... But there are plenty of living and very lively rats too. One night a big fellow ran over my face, and in a fright I cried out. But use is everything, and in the course of a few more nights I got quite rid of my childish astonishment and fear at rats running over my face. Have you ever heard rats sing? I assure you they sing in a very lively chorus; though I confess I have heard much pleasanter music in my time.[73]

Nevertheless, there was something rather wonderful about this "old paint-peeling tub," as Dahl described it. For all the anachronisms of the Anglo-Indians—the absurdity of dressing for dinner in 100-degree heat or the banality of deck conversation—the experience of leaving England and sailing for the unknown was immeasurably liberating. "Give me the freedom and cockroaches of the British India," declared Kipling, "where we dined on deck, altered the hours of our meals by plebiscite, and were lords of all we saw."[74] This sudden license was a foretaste of what they would experience in the colonies, where they would likewise regard themselves as "lords" of their imperial dominions.

As on transatlantic vessels, new cliques quickly sprung up among the passengers. With a mix of Anglo-Indians, griffins, tourists, and even the occasional Indian, Lascar, or Malay, it was harder to maintain the traditional barriers of class and station. Newly formed groups tended to be more heterogeneous, often comprised of old-hand colonial administrators and their families, newly arrived griffins anxious for instruction, unmarried ladies traveling alone (many of whom were on the lookout for a husband among the griffins, so common a sight that they were collectively referred to as the "fishing fleet"),[75] and perhaps even a distinguished Asian or Indian potentate and his entourage. Indeed, the forced congeniality of a ship's saloon often invited encounters that might take weeks to effect on shore, or not occur at all. Some English passengers delighted in meeting other races; others were horrified at the close proximity. A titled Englishwoman on the *Cambodge* in 1884 remarked disgustedly that the Ethiopian woman at her table was "black as soot,"[76] while Thackeray, as will be recalled, regarded every non-white (or even non-Christian) face on the *Tagus* as an invasion of his sanctified space.

Sometimes encounters were best effected at a discrete distance. Passenger Mary Poynter, on the Austrian Lloyd liner *Graz* bound for Bombay, was interested to observe a society where women were even more disenfranchised than her own:

When tired of book and steamer chair we go to the forward railing and look down upon the really "simple life"—upon a venerable green-turbaned haji, just returned from Mecca, saying his prayers in the direction of the city of his pilgrimage; upon the brightly if scantily garbed little companies of natives sitting cross legged. The women sit a little apart.... But that is the life of the eastern women, to sit apart and be obedient to their lords.[77]

For the most part, the three-week voyage offered griffins the opportunity to establish contacts that would invariably become useful once they reached shore. The journey was equivalent to initiation into a new and exclusive club. Once accepted by the group, he could rely on them for introductions later. Playing billiards in the smoking room, relaxing in deck chairs side by side, joining the same cricket team, and taking all their meals at the same table for weeks on end, friendships formed hard and fast.[78] So, inevitably, did enmities. Most surprising, however, were those relationships that seemed to vanish the moment the ship reached port. A young Englishwoman arriving in Bombay was shocked when her best friend on board "left early before breakfast with her husband & never came to see one of us! Queer woman!"[79]

A coaling stop in Port Said was the first exposure to what was described as the "mysterious Orient." It never failed to disappoint. Hawkers swarmed the decks, thrusting everything from beads and curios to squawking livestock into the faces of astonished passengers. If the griffin dared to go ashore, the experience was even worse. "Port Said!" one diarist fumed, "Impressions of filth, uncharm, roguery, poverty, disease, ignorance, nastiness, dirty postcards ... evil looking men who hawked their wares, arguing, haggling, bargaining."[80] In a previous chapter we considered the effects of steam tourism on shore encounters, transforming an immersive experience into a brief commercial foray marked by avarice and distrust on both sides. So it was here. "Port Said affords a display of the West at its worst and of the East spoiled," Frederick Treves wrote in 1903. Like Mrs. Mortimer and generations of tourists arriving by steam in foreign locales, he liked the city best when viewed from offshore: "At the time of sunset . . . the squalid house tops become turrets and battlements of gold. The sky is the color of a yellow rose, the clouds are tinted with lilac."[81]

Before the advent of the Suez Canal in 1869, passengers decamped here for a treacherous weeklong journey overland to join a second P&O vessel at Suez. Even after its opening, a bizarre clause in the line's admiralty mail contract obliged them to forgo the shorter route until this obvious absurdity was amended in 1872. Passengers appreciated the convenience, but the canal itself—a miracle of modern engineering—was no more representative of mankind's genius than Port Said had been of the mysterious East. "Just a ditch, and an ugly one at that," Mr. Seymour Fortescue commented dismissively in 1876.[82]

Some ships forwent coaling at Port Said and waited to reach Aden, in the Gulf of Suez. The most impressive fact about the port was not calculated to delight: It held, at any given time, over 20,000 tons of British coal. This was stored in the hollowed-out husks of cargo ships, lying dismasted at the approaches of the harbor. From there it was brought to the ship in deep-hulled barges called lighters, where sweating crewmen swayed it into the hold one basket at a time, a laborious and dirty process that could take days.[83] Coal dust wafted up and covered the decks, seeped into the ventilation ducts, clung tenaciously to carpets, upholstery, and clothes. Bunkering, as it was called, could consume up to a third the length of the voyage.[84] As the ship lay trapped, it was besieged "with small boats filled with clamoring hoards wishing to sell . . . ostrich feathers, beautiful baskets, many kinds of ivory and silver, draperies of every variety. The people who offered the things were even more interesting than their wares, pawing our sleeves and fawningly striving to attract our attention." And yet: "A rascally, untrustworthy lot they were!"[85]

The passage from Suez to Bombay or Calcutta was undertaken in ever-increasing heat. Tempers frayed, minor irritations flared. Storms at sea provided a welcome relief from the monotony.[86] At last, their destination lay in sight; for most, it came none too soon. "Here we are once more on dry land and I need not say very delighted to have done now with that horrid ship and sea," wrote one disgruntled passenger in 1866.[87] Despite the fact that the opening of the Suez

Canal reduced the London to Bombay voyage from forty days to just fourteen by the turn of the century, even Edwardian griffins expressed themselves profoundly bored and restless by the time they reached India or the Far East. Their response to the voyage was expressed by silence: Few if any recorded it in their memoirs, other than to say it was long.

The magic lay in arrival. Unlike Aden and Port Said, Indian ports were indubitably impressive. Calcutta was both exotic and familiar: White-painted row houses along the wharf recalled Bristol, Chowinghee Street was lined with the brick mansions of the merchant class, and the Maidan was deliberately laid out to resemble Hyde Park. Advertisements in the P&O guide reassured nervous passengers that India, for all its mystique, was not threatening: "Visitors desirous of seeing with comfort all the beauties of the Coast and Inland scenery will find that their natural center is the ILFRAMCOME hotel."[88] Bombay, in contrast, was overwhelming. The Marchioness of Dufferin and Ava, arriving as vicereine in 1885, could hardly put the experience into words:

> I wish it were possible for me to give you even a faint idea of the splendour of the landing at Bombay, but it was such a magnificent sight that it seems almost useless to try to describe it. I believe that we shall never, even in India, see anything to compare with it again. . . . The *Tasmania* anchored at 11 AM; but as we were not to land until 4:30, we remained quietly watching the departure of the other passengers and admiring the splendid harbor in which we found ourselves. It was extremely amusing to see the crowds of boats alongside, full of various coloured people of various business . . . noise and bustle everywhere![89]

The sudden immersion into this brilliant melee helped further banish memories of seasickness, torpid deck games, and greasy cooking smells. Yet the griffins taking up their posts owed more to the crossing than they realized. They had "learned to swagger," one missionary noted, before they even reached dry land.[90]

Despite all the attention given thus far to the trip eastward, it is worth noting that the ships returned to England as well. This time, instead of eager young griffins setting off on a jolly adventure, those who came back were hardened by what they had seen, and done. The experience of relinquishing such power and returning to ordinary life left many feeling rootless, adrift, even emasculated.[91] They did not know what they would find for them at home—indeed, for many, "home" had become their bungalow in Mysore, or a villa in Singapore, or even a cottage at the edge of the African savannah. Hence the voyage homeward was just as cathartic in its way as the voyage out had been: Once again, the ship became the nexus between one life and another, one identity and the next.

Kipling sympathized with these lost souls. In his 1890 poem "The Exiles' Line,"[92] P&O becomes a kind of Charon ferrying ex-imperials across the Styx. Early stanzas convey the suicidal depression that could overtake them as they left the world they had come to love:

The Tragedy of all our East is laid
On those white deck beneath the awning shade—
Birth, absence, longing, laughter, love and tears,
And death unmaking ere the land is made.

And midnight madnesses of souls distraught
Whom the cool seas call through the open port,
So that the table lacks one place next morn,
And for one forenoon men forgo their sport.

How many of these men actually threw themselves into the sea is not known, but the poem's grim tone is evocative of the very real despair that many must have felt. Kipling, a frequent traveler himself, surely witnessed such scenes during his voyages. The poem's conclusion represents a neat and tragic inversion of the bullish optimism of "The White Man's Burden": All the efforts of the empire-builders are mocked by time and stagnation, and the empire itself becomes a slave camp not for the colonized, but the colonizers. All that remains is the ship, chugging its lonely way from the site of one's failed dreams, towards an even greater unknown at homecoming:

The camp is struck, the bungalow decays,
Dead friends and houses desert mark our ways,
Till sickness sends us down to Prince's Dock
To meet the changeless use of many days.

Bound in the wheel of Empire, one by one,
The chain-gangs of the East from sire to son,
The Exiles' Line takes out the exiles' line
And ships them homeward when their work is done.

How runs the old indictment? "Dear and slow,"
So much and twice so much. We gird, but go.

For all the soul of our sad East is there,
Beneath the house-flag of the P&O.

Viewed from a distance, there was little spectacle in a P&O ship. Smaller than the transatlantic liners, dirty with coal smuts and streaked with rust from long weeks at sea, it was an unlikely avatar of imperial domination. Yet if there was something in the dumpy, dowdy, thick-waisted, black-and-dun hull that recalled the aged queen in her widow's weeds, that too had a majesty of its own. Like statues of Victoria herself, the ships were everywhere: No port city would be complete without a P&O or British India liner resting in harbor. This ubiquity was the crux of their importance. For the colonized, the image of the ship was often the most visible symbol of empire, a link between themselves and the mother country. The logistical problem of communicating with Britain's overseas dominions was solved—not with giant steamers like the *Great Eastern* but with a massive fleet of smaller vessels that allowed Britain to be literally everywhere at once: transmitting a constant stream of administrators, munitions, supplies, and soldiers. Hence the fleets of P&O, British India, and the other English firms formed a lifeline to empire: "flagships of imperialism," as one author has termed them.[93]

Crucial as this role was, it was secondary to the cathartic effects of the voyage itself. Passengers might want to put the miserable three weeks behind them, but they remained an indelible part of their imperial experience. The ship became a training ground, introducing griffins to the society they would inhabit and the role they were expected to fulfill. For most, the crossing was their first exposure to the hybrid world of the colonial: trappings of Britain combined with bizarre food, language, and mannerisms. One reinforced the other. The tenacity with which the "gophers" clung to English traits was matched by the aggressive Englishness of their surroundings, yet both served only to emphasize points of divergence: curries for breakfast, *punkahs* wafting overhead, and the constant presence of Goanese servants. The griffin, overwhelmed at first by this new environment, gradually became acclimated to it. The weather warmed by degree, and behaviors or expressions that might have seemed outlandish in Tilbury became logical, even welcome. By the time the ship reached Aden or Port Said, the griffin was already conditioned to regard himself as an imperial master. Truly he might already have done so back in England, but now for the first time that belief was buttressed with actual practice. Brief interactions with the locals at coaling ports disabused Orientalist fantasies, but they reinforced one's conviction in the superiority of the colonizers and the need for keeping order. Once he arrived in Calcutta, Bombay, or Singapore, the griffin was ready.

Coming ashore, he was unlikely to give his ship any fond farewell glances. Yet as the city enveloped him in a cacophony of alien smells, sounds, and colors, the griffin might find himself wistful for the familiarity of the oak-paneled smoking room, the welcome strains of Lehár played by the ship's orchestra. If he chanced to turn back, he would see his P&O liner still at the pier, familiar and yet already distant. Puissant and belching smoke, surrounded by a scrum of dark-complected humanity, she was the very image of civilization in a barbaric land. How could anyone, viewing this for the first time, not be reassured in the rightness of empire?

10 THE FLOATING KAISER
Steamships and National Identity

AT THE CHICAGO WORLD'S FAIR OF 1893, not too far from the American Line's bisected ocean liner, was a display of a different sort. In comparison to the monolithic wonder of a ship rising up above the spectators' heads, North German Lloyd lines opted for a more allegorical approach. A kiosk greeted visitors: an exact replica of the steamship wickets in Lloyd's New York offices. Small and unremarkable beside larger entries for Cunard and White Star, it was fronted by a chalkboard on which vessels and sailing times were recorded. The list was prodigious. Behind the kiosk an enormous globe turned slow gyrations in place. On it were dozens of models representing all the ships named on the board, moved about daily to represent their actual position on the seas of the world.[1] The effect was impressive, and alarming. One could not find a single ocean or sea without some North German Lloyd liner cutting a trail of foam across it. In promotional literature for the line, this ubiquity was even more disconcerting. "Lloyd Fleet Exceeds Some Navies," it declared grandly.

The Navies of not only the United States, but of Germany and France as well, are exceeded in gross registered tonnage by the fleet of North German Lloyd. . . . The gross registered tonnage of the fleet of the North German Lloyd is 792,800 gross registered tons or more than the combined tonnage of the navies of Russia, Italy, and Austria and twice that of Japan. Even upon the present naval programs of the United States, Germany and Japan being completed, the fleet of the North German Lloyd will continue to hold first place.[2]

There was mendacity in these figures (naval fleets had no need for the tonnage of a passenger line or cargo firm, and in terms of *civilian* fleets, North German Lloyd trailed a distant third behind Cunard and Hamburg–American), yet there is a kind of *vaterstolz* as well. Sometime in the late 19th century, just as steam became identified with the spread of civilization, the steamship transformed into a vehicle for nationalism. Liner fleets became avatars for their respective nations' imperial ambitions, as a nation's potency became defined by how far its reach extended. North German Lloyd's rival, Hamburg–American

Lines, made this explicit in their motto: "*Mein Feld Ist Die Welt*," the world is in my reach. The *Imperator* of 1913, their last flagship before the outbreak of war, boasted a bizarre figurehead at the bow: an imperial eagle, wings outstretched, beak straining forward, clutching a globe tightly within its talons.[3]

As technology and nationalism intermeshed, the phantasmagoria of steam entered its final phase. Passenger liners became floating embodiments of their national origin, carrying the flag to their imperial possessions and flaunting it before visitors on board. The German firms, which had emerged late in the century, had the most to prove and were perhaps the most ostentatious in reinforcing the link between themselves and empire.[4] Yet that connection was no less prevalent on board the ships of the P&O, Cunard, White Star, or Orient Line. Thus the disparate themes of steam as wonder, as harbinger of a technological utopia, as ambassador, as both transgressor and defender of class barriers, and as nation builder—all of which had been following their own separate trajectories throughout the century—finally coalesced into a single whole: steam as civilization. This was, however, a very singular view of civilization, combining elements of technological progressivism with the *weltpolitik* of the age. Its spread across the globe, like that of the steamship fleets themselves, was rapid and stunning. It was noted with alarm by some of the same Victorian figures who had earlier been heralds of the steam age: Jules Verne and Mark Twain. Its consequences resonate to this day.

. . .

To comprehend the role of the steamship as imperial avatar, it is necessary to briefly consider other cognates. The diminutive size and functionality of a railway car prevented it from ever becoming much more than it appeared; while the sight of tracks through the jungle was enough to inspire Kiplingesque paeans, trains themselves were not particularly impressive. It was left to the railway terminus to carry the weight of allegory. Unlike trains (or steamships, for that matter), a station had the advantage of permanence; built of iron and stone, it was meant to be a fixed point in the kaleidoscopic universe of rail travel, the place where all journeys began and ended. Early stations tended to reflect the secular worship of steam and its proponents, a phenomenon discussed in Chapter 4. "Cathedrals of the new humanity,"[5] as one author described them, their architecture was self-consciously ecclesiastical. "Railway termini and hotels are to the nineteenth century what monasteries and cathedrals were to the thirteenth century," *Building News* declared in 1875.[6]

The Great Western Line's terminus at Bristol, designed by Brunel in 1840, was a Gothic fantasy whose central spire was deliberately reminiscent of Westminster. Within, vaulted quatrefoil arches enclosed a nave where trains moved up and down like acolytes, and passengers absorbed the scene from long mahogany pews. Paddington Station, at the opposite end of the line, replicated Brunel's transit cathedral on an even grander scale. Its arches were so ennobling that artist William Frith chose them as the backdrop for his famous depiction of *The Railway Station*, juxtaposing their serenity against a confused tumult of London society. Frith was on to something: Railway stations became the locus for a paradoxical ordered chaos, where the flow of humanity was directed along predetermined channels. On the ground, things appeared helter-skelter. But from up above—the window of the station café, say—a magical orderliness appeared. The metaphor of civilization emerging from anarchy was inescapable. The station, meanwhile, maintained an Olympian detachment from the melee even as it orchestrated, godlike, the movements of those within.[7]

As time went on and more routes were added, this concept of deified steam became even more pronounced. Newcastle Central, Huddersfield, and Euston stations, all completed in 1850, were modeled on Greco-Roman temples. "Great, echoing halls of glass and iron, colonnaded, canopied, buttressed, and turreted," they became "living temples to the worship of King Steam."[8] Yet instead of an effigy or statue, the central icon was the station clock. The cynosure of all eyes, it not only directed movement but symbolized order and measured progress. Even as Gothic arches gave way to Vitruvian architraves, the reverence of technology—Honor and Glory crowning Time—continued apace.

By the turn of the century, the relatively modest proportions of a Roman temple could not encompass the crowds within, and a new classical form was needed. American architect Daniel Burnham, whose Roman revivals shaped the Chicago World's Fair, chose the Baths of Diocletian as an inspiration for Washington's Union Station. A few years later, the model was used again for Grand Central Station in New York. Above its entranceway was an unconscious allegorical echo of the *Titanic*'s grand staircase: a station clock flanked by Hercules (strength) and Minerva (wisdom), crowned by triumphant Mercury (speed).[9] The shift in architectural and allegorical models suggested a subtle evolution in the kind of reverence taking place within. Mercury, patron god of travelers, extends a friendly welcoming arm. And the baths—sprawling, sybaritic, imperial—were more fitting for a society that had reached maturity and now permitted itself a certain amount of complacent self-satisfaction. While taking nothing away from King Steam, Edwardians were celebrating the crowd as well.

As railway architecture in England, America, and the Continent transitioned from ecclesiastic reverence to pagan indulgence, an imperial transformation was taking place abroad. Early British stations in India had been, like early P&O liners, sensibly cognizant of climate: cool and lofty pavilions, open-sided to catch the breeze. Following the Indian Mutiny, a new aesthetic prevailed. Stations became enclosed, sweltering, claustrophobic fortresses with arrow-slit windows and thick stone walls. The reason was as much strategic as symbolic: In a small town as well as a large city, the railway station could well serve as a redoubt for Anglo-Indians under siege.[10] For daily commuters, however, the transition from marquee to citadel must have been an uncomfortable one—especially in summer.

In British Africa, stations were deliberately incongruous: a little piece of Southwark transposed onto the veldt. Larger stations replicated English castles, cathedrals, or some combination of the two (as at Alexandria) while smaller ones took their inspiration from the modest platforms scattered throughout Britain. Not even the uniforms of the baggage handlers surrendered anything to locality: Broadcloth and brass buttons were the norm, though some stationmasters were allowed to replace the peaked cap with a more exotic fez. In some cases the railway station not only contrasted with the surrounding landscape but dominated it. The sudden rise of Germany as a brash world power could be seen most clearly in their Africa termini: Kigoma, in German East Africa, and Windhoek, in the west, were smallish towns whose stations could be seen from miles away.[11]

Yet no railway station was more emblematic of the melding of steam and empire than Bombay's Victoria Terminus. In the provinces of Augustan Rome, locals were allowed to worship their deities so long as they included a temple of the divine emperor alongside. In Bombay, the directors of the Great Indian Peninsular Railway chose as their site the traditional holy ground of goddess Mumba Devi, protector of the city. On the ruins of her shrine, they constructed a vast temple to the goddess "Progress," whose colossal 16-foot-tall figure stood atop the station's highest dome, flanked by Engineering, Science, Trade, and other deities. Demigods, in the form of the company directors, peered out of cameos along the principal façade.[12] Out front, guarding the entrance in glittering copper, was a station's namesake. Her disapproving gaze looked outward, which was just as well; the terminus was a riot of styles combining the worst excesses of Romanesque, Gothic, Arabic, English Victorian, and what could only be described as Orientalist—somewhere in between the Houses of Parliament, the Umaid Bhawan, and Brighton Pavilion. It was as if the British empire had taken solidified form, and this was the result.

Given the lavish attention architects expended on railway stations, one might expect a similar largesse for maritime terminals. These, after all, were designed to accommodate thousands of passengers at one time, and vessels up to 800 feet long. The scene at the docks on sailing day made Frith's railway passengers seem quaint: a veritable tide of humanity from every conceivable walk of life—duchesses to stowaways—all deposited on the pier via horsecar or train (some of which ran right into the terminal) in a narrow window of about three hours, along with all their baggage. A Brueghelian scene of such complexity, color, and confusion deserved a grand concourse surrounding it, but that was not what it received.

Throughout the 19th century and most of the 20th, maritime terminals were as barren as stockyards: vast corrals for human cattle that funneled them into place with neither charm nor higher sense of purpose. There were no cherubim dangling from the ceiling, no allegorical images, scarcely any decoration at all. The first purpose-built marine terminal in Southampton was not completed until 1950; it was torn down thirty years later and replaced with a shedlike enclosure that could have been lifted bodily from 1895. Colonial ports offered even less: Despite being the newly arrived traveler's first sight of Bombay, Calcutta, Alexandria, or Hong Kong, the ship terminals were usually nothing more than a corrugated tin roof stretching the length of the dock.

The reason lay with the ships themselves. They incorporated allegorical symbolism within their own hulls; consequently, any such imagery in the terminals would have been redundant. A transformation was taking place in the later decades of the 19th century, as passenger liner interiors came to reflect more concretely the nationality of their owners. As late as the 1880s, this was not the case. The public rooms of all the crack liners on the Atlantic, for example, followed the same basic mold: a high-ceilinged dining room with long tables and swivel chairs, capped by a skylight; a ladies' writing room or parlor in overstuffed chintz; a compact smoking den for gentlemen done in oak, leather, and brass; and a lounge, usually located adjacent to the dining saloon, where couples might gather together for an aperitif before dinner.[13]

It was the German firms that heralded the change. Emerging on the Atlantic in the 1870s, their rise to prominence mirrored that of their nation. North German Lloyd was the first firm to hire shoreside decorators to furnish their ships (a job that, incredibly enough, was previously often awarded to the director's wife), and the inevitable result was a discernible Germanness on board their new liners. The *Lahn*, launched in 1877, was so heavily weighted with allegorical statuary as to make her seem paradoxically small; passengers navigated the overstuffed rooms searching vainly for comfort amidst the ship's pantheonic pretensions.[14] A few decades later, these interiors had become operatic. The First Class dining room on board the *Kronprinzessin Cecilie* matched the Palais Garnier or the Teatro la Fenice pound for pound in gilt *putti*: The three tiers of its atrium were each more elaborate than the next; winged cherubim and pastoral scenes were watched over by allegorical figures in Grecian robes, around whose hems were clustered yet more prancing, pot-bellied fauna.[15] Over all, set like a diadem in a gilded crown, was a bust of the princess herself.

This was not the Germany of beer steins, antlers, and half-timbered Bavarian lodges (those were reserved for the smoking room)[16] but a new imperial *volk*. All the allegorical imagery of the *Lahn, Cecilie*, and other vessels was superseded by a greater mythic narrative: the rise of Germany herself. It was no accident that even the gods looked up to Princess Cecilie in the dining room. Marble and oil paintings of the Kaiser and royal family dominated the entire fleet: Just as the Crown Princess watched over diners as they ate, her mother smiled benignly over card tables in the ladies' writing room[17] while Wilhelm, in full naval regalia, greeted guests with a haughty glare from a portrait on the main stairwell.[18] Yet another imperial bust recoiled from the burr of conversation in the lounge.[19]

Indeed, few places were spared. In a surviving postcard of the ladies' social room aboard the *Kaiser Wilhelm der Grosse,* the old Kaiser himself peeks out at this sacrosanct feminine space from behind a column. This alarming surprise was replicated in a surviving menu cover from 1900. At the turn of the century, menu covers often displayed fantastical maritime scenes designed to convince passengers that they were part of a great adventure. Yet here, other than the company's name atop, there is nothing remotely marine about the image. Instead we are presented with a marble bust of the Kaiser, stern and forbidding, beneath which Victory raises her torch aloft. The drape of her robes and the manner of her upraised arm immediately remind one of the Statue of Liberty, yet she wears no crown and instead of a tablet she holds an engraved shield. The image is heavy and turgid—an odd choice to greet diners, but perhaps an inevitable one.[20]

Passengers coming aboard at Bremerhaven or Hamburg might be excused for thinking they had unwittingly blundered into the Stadtschloss.[21] That was

FIGURE 12. The First Class dining saloon of the *Deutschland* (1900). The room is overwhelmed by the vast heraldic imagery on the far wall, one of many such imperial symbols throughout the ship. SOURCE: Author's collection.

precisely how they were meant to feel: Germany, unified in 1871, could not share the long history and tradition of her rivals. The ships became floating apartments of state, stand-ins for ancient royal palaces. So it was that the *Deutschland*'s otherwise stark dining room was overwhelmed by a bas-relief of winged Victory (or, some might say, Germany herself) trodding triumphantly upon a globe. Twenty feet in height and utterly out of scale, it loomed over diners as if it could crush them at any moment.[22] This monumentalism carried over to the smoking room, where yet another baronial crest held court beneath a barrel-vaulted skylight.[23] Even the Hamburg–American Line's New York offices reflected the patriotic allegorical theme. Naiads riding sea serpents pointed excitedly towards the center of the room, where a vast builder's model of the *Deutschland* glittered under a glass case.[24]

Other countries followed suit, belatedly. Italian ships became repositories for the lost glory that was Rome, and nearly matched the German liners in overly decorated, hideous interiors (Italian liners, unlike the Germans who ultimately embraced clean Bauhaus lines, went right on filling their public rooms with cherubs, statuary, and allegorical murals until the late 1930s; the Colonna Room of the *Conte di Savoia* featured an exact replica of the ceiling in the Villa Borghese, underneath which were several dozen zebra-striped chairs).[25] The French, too, drew their inspiration from past glories. Reaching beyond the horrors of Sedan, the Commune, and the Committee of Public Safety, they resurrected the buoyant serenity of the *ancien régime*. *La Provence*, launched in 1905, stressed intimate, aristocratic luxury over top-heavy grandeur. Passengers entertained one another on needlepoint fauteuils, dined *à deux* at individual tables in the dining room, and relaxed in elegant white-paneled Louis XVI drawing rooms where gilt was reserved for picture frames and cherubim were relegated to the corners.[26]

Conversely, the American Line flagships *St. Louis* and *St. Paul* reflected their Pennsylvanian probity by offering interiors as stark and devoid of frills as a Quaker meetinghouse. Bare walls, wide-plank floors, and gritty, salt-sprayed saloon windows predominated. What decoration that existed was hawkishly patriotic: flag buntings around American statesmen portraits and stained-glass windows depicting harbor scenes in New York and Philadelphia. The one admitted indulgence—a massive and elaborate pipe organ in the grand saloon—seemed to echo those on board an earlier generation of Mississippi flatboats.[27]

Of all the major firms, only the British avoided the temptation to produce interiors that were caricatures of nationhood. True, many liners boasted at least one Adam fireplace or Inigo Jones-inspired lounge, but these were enmeshed within an eclecticism that continued to be a hallmark of British ships until the First World War. Decorators for Cunard's flagships *Campania* and *Lucania*, for example, drew heavily from the Italian and French Renaissance, while offering a sop to English tastes with a Tudor smoking room. There was a certain amount of confidence, not to say smugness, in such choices. The British, who had held maritime supremacy in steam since the advent of the invention, had nothing to prove to their upstart rivals. The ships reflected a different kind of empire: not emergent, but complacent.

This was less true aboard the colonial vessels of the P&O and other lines, as we explored in the last chapter. Such vessels were continually called upon to act as avatars for their nation, and their interiors reflected as much. The rooms constructed to carry England's imperial administrators were self-conscious echoes of previous golden ages: Gothic, Elizabethan, Georgian. They were meant not only to reassure but to remind the griffin that he (and the ship that carried him) was a standard-bearer for empire: "England expects." None of these styles was amenable to the grand opera scale of the German ships. Instead, warm woods and shaded lamps suggested the kind of hominess of an elegant country house or a London club. The obvious locus for imperial symbolism was the smoking room, and that on the Africa-bound *Winchester Castle* was representative of the breed. A half-timbered ceiling, real brick fireplace, oak settles, and mullioned windows raised comfortable images of days spent tramping the moors—though the lack of air conditioning quickly dispelled such fantasies. Yet hung on the wall next to the fireplace was a real, honest-to-God copy of the *real* Round Table at Camelot; the original (of equally dubious provenance) remained at Winchester.[28] Cast thousands of miles from home and unsure of what to expect on arrival, English travelers were comforted by public rooms that reminded them of home even as they reinforced the awesome responsibility of their mission.[29]

Besides interiors, there was also the critical matter of the ship's name. The naming of a ship has always been invested with metaphorical significance; since ancient times it not only identified the vessel but determined its character. In the modern era, christening represents the moment when the giant mass of steel takes to the water for the first time and becomes an actual vessel. Thus "Hull 534" did not officially become *Queen Mary* until the bottle of Australian champagne hit the stem, yet after that moment could never be known as anything else.[30] Few inanimate objects are thus honored: The granting of a name confers a kind of artificial life upon them. Even today, we speak of ships as having careers, even life spans, and nearly always refer to them in the feminine. On board, passengers and crew likewise identify most with vessels that bear proper names; the few companies that bucked this predisposition usually regretted it (in the 1990s, for example, Renaissance Cruises tried the bold approach of naming their vessels *R1, R2*, and so forth; the company folded, for multiple reasons, in 2001).

Choosing a name was thus a delicate business, for it could instantly convey the ship's ownership, nationality, probable route, and personality. Sometimes the message was subtler. White Star Line, founded in 1871, named its first vessel the *Oceanic* and followed it with the trio of liners *Atlantic, Adriatic,* and *Baltic.* These latter were the same as given to the Collins liners of the 1850s. Collins had been the last firm to challenge Cunard's supremacy and still remained, though long defunct, a watchword for luxury. The connection between the two lines was reinforced by the fact that White Star, though it continued the tradition of giving its vessels names ending in "-ic," never produced an *Arctic* or *Pacific*—out of respect for, or perhaps dread of, the lost Collins's ships. When planning began in 1907 for a trio of ocean liners, the largest in the world, the company chose names that looked ahead rather than back and were appropriately grandiose: *Olympic, Titanic, Gigantic.*

Cunard Line's decision to name their first vessel *Britannia* was arbitrary; her sister ship was titled *Columbia,* and naming them after the two ends of their route had a neat symmetry. There was nothing more to it than that; a later pair, arriving in 1848, was even more prosaically christened *America* and *Europa.* The longstanding Cunard tradition of giving vessels names ending in "-ia" was haltingly arrived upon; as late as the 1860s the fleet still included such dissonant monikers as *Aleppo, Balbec, Kedar,* and *Marathon.* Gradually, though, uniformity won out. Later ships not only shared the same suffix, but the names themselves were drawn (as was *Britannia*) from Roman provinces. This was a deliberate choice. As England expanded her empire, many began to speak of a *Pax Britannia* spreading even farther than the ancient *Pax Romana* had reached. Cunard, which had rapidly ascended to become the largest shipowner in Britain, was a vital part of that imperial transformation. Their routes stretched as far as the empire itself—in fact, even farther. Ironically, as the Italian lines loaded their vessels with classical knock-offs, names such as *Samaria, Campania,* or *Ivernia* gently reminded Cunard passengers that *their* ship's nation was the true inheritor of Roman greatness.[31]

The scheme worked brilliantly well, for a time. But there were a fixed number of Roman provinces, and not all of them euphonious. Not long after ships started appearing with names like *Feltria* and *Cephalonia,* the First World War came and culled the herd. Afterwards the company was content to recycle names of previous ships (the *Tyrrhenia* of 1923 was an unfortunate exception) and unbent enough to christen their flagship, not after a province, but after Richard the Lionhearted's long-suffering wife: *Berengaria.*[32]

For the vessels of P&O, Orient Lines, and other colonial firms, a different scheme was employed to convey the nexus between ship and empire. Starting with the *Hindustan* of 1842, P&O named their vessels after imperial localities. As the British empire expanded, so too did the fleet list: *Rangoon, Zambesi, Cathay, Tientsin, Aden, Poonah, Borneo*, and so on.[33] The decision might have been motivated solely by the desire to advertise P&O's extensive routes, yet this alone reinforced the passengers' sense (as well as the public's) of England's imperial reach. Moreover, there was something infinitely reassuring in coming aboard a vessel with a name like *Mirzapore* and finding a full English tea being served in the Georgian lounge. Thus the vessels paralleled Britons' views of empire: The names might seem remote and exotic, but all was reassuringly familiar within.

P&O's naming strategy was so successful that many of her rivals copied it. British India sent forth the *Calcutta, Kapurthala*, and *Waroonga*; the African Steam Ship Company (later Elder Dempster Lines) delighted passengers with such titles as *Yoruba, Sekondi, Mayumba*, and *Coomassie*. There were, of course, some divergences. Castle Line's service to Calcutta and Cape Town was maintained, nor surprisingly, by vessels named after British castles (unlike Roman provinces, this seemed to provide ample selection), while Union Lines chose the unique concept of titling their ships not after locations but the people that inhabited them: *Asiatic, Dane, Mexican, Greek, American, German, Arab*, and the flagship *Briton*. Lest the *Briton* should merely be seen as one among equals, however, there was also a *Celt, Norman, Saxon, Anglian*, and *Scot* to round things out in Britain's favor.

On rare occasions, company directors broke the mold and gave their new ships names that were expressly patriotic, even imperial. The investiture of Queen Victoria as Empress of India in 1876 inspired P&O to christen their next flagship *Kaisar-i-Hind*, which was the Hindi translation of the term. The choice was subtle and revealing: rather than simply title her *Empress of India*, they selected one that would be instantly familiar to Indians yet left most Britons mystified. The intended audience, therefore, was not in London but Bombay—reminding India that the vessels of the P&O Line were a direct conduit between rulers and ruled. Just over a decade later, the occasion of the Queen's Diamond Jubilee prompted P&O directors to entirely abandon traditional titles for their newest "Jubilee" ships: *Victoria, Britannia, Arcadia*, and *Oceana*.[34] By far the largest, fastest, and most luxurious liners placed on the Indian route to that time, they were self-conscious celebrations of empire without even the pretext of deferring to colonial locality. The names would become staples within the fleet, recycled and reused right up to the present day.[35]

Nevertheless, just as they had on board their ships, it was the German lines that most prominently advertised their nationhood through the names chosen for their fleet. North German Lloyd and Hamburg–American both employed vast numbers of ships spanning the globe, in every possible service. With such a large and diverse fleet, any coherent naming scheme was impossible. Instead, both firms focused on their flagships. Near the end of the century, at a time when Germany's imperial ambitions were matched by the expansionist policies of North German Lloyd, the company began naming their largest vessels after members of the imperial family. Thus the record-breaker *Kaiser Wilhelm der Grosse* of 1897 was followed in short order by the *Kaiser Friedrich* (1898), *Prinzessin Irene* (1900), *Kronprinz Wilhelm* (1901), *Kaiser Wilhelm II* (1903), and *Kronprinzessin Cecilie* (1906), as well as a host of lesser princelings that augmented the subsidiary fleet.[36]

Quite often the ship would be christened by the very person named, or at least by a close relation. This was an anomaly rarely seen in maritime history: The honor of having a ship named after one is customarily awarded in memoriam. Passengers might well assume that the vessel was under royal patronage, a belief that was reinforced by the ubiquitous presence on board of Hohenzollern effigies, as discussed above. Indeed, they would not be far wrong. The Kaiser took a great personal interest in the German merchant marine, and it was as much to curry imperial favor as any other reason that the shipping lines chose such names (rival firm Hamburg–American Lines sought three separate times to name their flagship *Europa* but were deflected by the need to flatter the monarch instead). Whatever the impetus, the net result was to interweave the North German Lloyd Line inextricably not only with Germany, but with the imperial family itself.[37]

Hamburg–American Lines followed suit, picking up all the names that their rival had omitted: *Kaiserin Auguste Victoria, Prinz August Wilhelm, Prinzessin Victoria Luise,* and so on.[38] But company chairman Albert Ballin had an even broader vision. If the ships could become avatars for imperial might, why could they not represent the whole of the German people? Thus the first modern flagship of the line, which successfully took the prize for Atlantic speed in 1900, was simply named the *Deutschland*. This would be followed, over a decade later, by the *Imperator* and *Vaterland*: vessels whose names seemed to encompass the German *volk*.

In effect, the German ships of the late 19th and early 20th centuries simply made explicit a reality that had existed for some time. Steamships had become living, working, moving avatars of nationhood, embodying their respective *staatskultur* within and without. For eastbound Atlantic passengers, the ship was their first exposure to the Old World and irrevocably shaped later impressions. Most were favorable. "In the *Havel*," Mark Twain reported, "one can be in several respects more comfortable than he can be in the finest hotels in Europe."[39] Though some passengers despaired the German obsession with body *kultur*, overzealous French service, or the curious English predilection for baked beans at breakfast, companies did everything they could to ease the transition. Instead of concealing their national origins, they flaunted them: "France, you know," an early 20th-century advertisement declared, "really begins at Pier 88!" For passengers on colonial lines, nationalism was conveyed less directly. Exotic names conjured up the mystique of empire, yet the ships that bore them offered traditionally English surroundings. The juxtaposition provided a telling statement on the breadth of Britain's imperial reach.

Through print media, the nexus between steamships and empire reached beyond passengers to the public sphere. As ships grew in size, clever promoters seized on the idea of transposing them against famous monuments: an idea that combined the awe of exhibition with the competitiveness of the race. It was hardly a fair contest. In an age that valued the colossal above all else, steamships were the largest man-made objects in the world. Longer than the tallest skyscraper, heavier than the Houses of Parliament, they not only dazzled with their size—they moved! It was the German firms, not surprisingly, that led the way. An early postcard shows the *Kaiser Wilhelm der Grosse* of 1897 set precariously on her tail and measured against such American icons as Trinity Church, the St. Paul Building of New York, the Capitol, and the Washington Monument.[40] As if in parallel to their worsening naval rivalry, British firms immediately followed suit: The *Mauretania* was stacked against the Great Pyramid at Giza, her sister *Lusitania* wedged uncomfortably in Trafalgar Square, the *Olympic* stood on end and towering over the Metropolitan Life building, the Woolworth building, and the Cologne cathedral.[41] There was more to these comparisons than simple puffery. Such images situated the vessel in a setting of dominance, pitting it not only against other ships but the greatest creations of mankind. The subtext was obvious: The ships had supplanted these earlier wonders and become the true technological miracles of the age.

Even as this occurred, a revolution was taking place in advertising. From the days of the Black Ball packets until the mid-19th century, shipping firm notices consisted merely of a posted bill with a crude image of the vessel and a list of sailing dates below. Even as late as the 1880s, this formula was replicated in the front matter of numerous guidebooks. The rise of poster art, coupled with the growth of package tours and other popular travel, transformed everything. By the 1890s, crude handbills had given way to glorious, vibrant scenes that appeared in magazines, shipping offices, and posted on buildings throughout London, New York, and the Continent. The poster became the vehicle for passenger lines to convey the entire character of their ships, routes, and nationhood. This had to be accomplished with as few words as possible—oftentimes nothing more than the company name. Images were everything.[42]

One early attempt from the 1890s conveys the tentative exploration of a new medium. A P&O liner is viewed as if through a porthole, flanked atop by barebreasted mermaids with flowing pre-Raphaelite auburn locks. One holds a trident, the other a miniature galleon, and the words "China" and "Egypt" appear beside them. "Australia" and "Japan" are represented by miniature globes at the bottom; "India" is at the top, crowning all, even the company name. Within the porthole the ship looms large, dwarfing smaller craft around her. There is no landscape to set the scene, and the little boats are ambiguously foreign: She could be in Port Said, Calcutta, or Rangoon. Exoticism is hinted at but not expressly portrayed; the ship's dimensions are formidable but still to scale. The overall tone is restrained, the theme allegorical: The P&O liner is the center of a world whose outer extremities are still within its scope.[43]

Over time such classical allegory disappeared, and the two subsidiary aspects—the ship and the landscape—came to dominate. German firms were the first, once again, to depict their liners as behemoths. The ship was placed alongside some other craft—a tug, a fishing trawler—and the exaggerated contrast in sizes rendered both objects almost absurd. While earlier images nearly always showed the vessel in profile, later ones adopted the three-quarter view: bow slicing through the waves, superstructure rearing up, funnels scraping the sky. The angle of sight also dropped; one might as well have been a cork floating on the surface of the sea. In the rare instances where the ship was shown in harbor, her decks were crowded with Lilliputian figures rendered as a mass of black dots. In most cases the house flag would be crossed above the image with that of the ship's nationality. The overall impression was one

FIGURE 13. By the end of the 19th century, advertising conveyed a wealth of symbolism. Here the *Kaiserin Augusta Victoria*, a medium-sized ship, dominates the scene, entirely out of scale with her surroundings. SOURCE: Author's collection.

of strength, virility, and dominance—adjectives that were meant to extend to the nation as well.

There were, however, other ways to convey imperial might. An 1898 advertisement for North German Lloyd appears at first to be a perfect inversion of that for P&O: A giant globe occupies the center, and the ships are relegated to the periphery, the four corners of the earth. Yet on closer inspection the globe is a perfect replica of that displayed at the 1893 World's Fair (and indeed was likely inspired by it). Across its broad blue face are dozens of tiny lines, like a net or spider web, representing routes. The ships have not been displaced by the globe; they hold it captive.

A different set of priorities was to be found in the advertisements for the colonial lines. Here the ship falls to the background, replaced by a scene of the mystic Orient. In one poster for the United Netherlands Navigation Company, which serviced Indian and Asian ports, the diminutive liner hovers in the extreme corner of the frame. The central figure is a maharajah traveling atop a gilded elephant with his retinue fanned out around him. Camels and parasols abound. Here the ship seems almost an intruder, an oddly modern and utilitarian note in a scene of gorgeous antiquity. A similar poster for P&O reveals a nighttime vision of a Bedouin campfire: Smoke from the fire trickles upward, forming a parallel line to that rising from the funnels of the P&O ship traversing the Suez behind them. The lights from the ship mirror the stars overhead. One of the Bedouins turns his head to regard the spectacle. Here again the ship is intruder, but her arrival seems to have the same portent as the stars.[44]

The idea of the ship arriving upon some picturesque local scene became ubiquitous, but what was more interesting was the position of the figures. The maharajah in the previous poster barely notices the ship behind him, but in later ones the liner becomes the sinecure of all eyes. Thus the spectacle transfers from shore to ship. Her arrival is wondrous: civilization dropping anchor in a strange and primitive land. There were variants on this theme. One, by far the most common, was to make the ship seem like a conquering giant. The 1902 brochure for Hamburg–American's cruises shows the *Prinzessin Victoria Luise*, a tiny yachtlike vessel of some 4,409 tons, magically engorged into a leviathan cleaving her way through mountains that barely reach her waterline; the Sphinx is submerged at the bottom of the frame. Nor were the Germans the only ones to tinker with forced perspective. An Orient Line poster from the same decade shows the *Orcades* bearing down on some assembled Arab tradesmen as if about to crush them; they are all turned away from the ship, as though fleeing in alarm.

Not all imperial imagery was so heavy-handed. A Dutch firm, Rotterdamsche Lloyd, gave pride of place in their rendering to a young Ceylonese girl with a woven basket. Behind her is a thatched-roof sampan. Above her stands an elegantly dressed European lady in traveling clothes, holding a pair of binoculars to her eyes. The contrast between her starched whites and the girl's simple muslin dress is striking. But the lady is looking away from the picturesque scene at her feet, towards the liner—which rather improbably is moving at flank speed across the frame. Now the spectacle has come full circle. Not only are natives expected to be fascinated by the ship amongst them, but even the *passengers* forsake the wonders of the Orient for the greater spectacle of the ship herself.[45]

In sum, poster art became a means for conveying a plethora of concepts: steam as spectacle, as harbinger of technological utopia, as ambassador, as conqueror, as avatar of nationhood. None of these themes was novel; indeed, we have seen their development throughout the century. Yet the poster could convey with a single image a multiplicity of meanings with hardly any explanatory text. It was efficient and powerful, perfectly suited to the age.[46]

Inevitably, as ships became more and more identified with their respective nations, rivalry between them intensified. This, again, was not entirely new. The same choleric antebellum senators that shouted their support for the Collins Line also, in the same breath, spoke of "the absolute conquest of that man Cunard."[47] National rivalries were an integral part of the racing aspect of steam. From the mid-1850s on, however, Britain enjoyed a near hegemony in that regard, and its rivals were reduced to trumpeting the luxury of their furnishings or table. For them, the only victories to be had were pyrrhic. When, in 1886, the American Steamship Company purchased Britain's Inman Line—along with her two flagships *City of New York* and *City of Paris*—President Benjamin Harrison himself was invited to raise the Stars and Stripes from the *New York*'s stern at Philadelphia. Newspapers depicted the scene more colorfully, with the American buffalo kicking the English lion into the sea. The *City of Paris* and *City of New York* were among the fastest ships of their day, a fact that did not escape the American press. Yet few bothered to note that purchasing the speed record was quite a bit different than earning it.[48]

It was hardly an accident that the first serious challenger to British dominance should bear the name *Kaiser Wilhelm der Grosse*. Though the crown had already passed to his grandson, Wilhelm II, the title still represented a new and assertive superpower on the world stage. Capturing the Blue Riband (a symbolic prize for the fastest transatlantic crossing) from Cunard's *Campania* and *Lucania* in 1897, the new German fleet paralleled in steam what the Kaiser himself was attempting in yacht races against his elderly uncle, the Prince of Wales. Wilhelm cultivated close relationships with the directors of both the North German Lloyd and Hamburg–American lines; they, in turn, cultivated relationships with him. Nor was this phenomenon unique to Germany. In America, Lloyd Griscom, son of American Line's director Clement Griscom, became a fixture of the Republican Party and close advisor to several presidents. In England, both White Star founder Thomas Ismay and Cunard chairman Lord Inverclyde enjoyed close relationships with government. The net result in all three nations was to bind the shipping lines to imperial aspirations, and vice versa.

The consequences were significant. Albert Ballin, chairman of Hamburg–American, was a passionate advocate for naval expansion, and in his own way pressed as hard as Admiral von Tirpitz. But his view was limited in scope to the protection of his ships. "Without the support of a strong fleet," he declared in 1900, "Germany has no real power against the tiniest exotic state which . . . can sneer at obsolete, impotent cruisers. Behind every German vessel abroad must stand a German battleship!"[49] Sentiments like these drove the concurrent construction of merchant and military vessels for all the colonial powers—Germany and England most of all. It was a dangerous causal chain. More ships meant further expansion; further expansion meant eventual collision with another empire. Like seismic eruptions hinting at even greater tectonic shifts, these collisions began

FIGURE 14. "*Mein Feld Ist Die Welt.*" The imperial eagle affixed to the prow of Hamburg–American's *Imperator*, the ultimate symbol of the meld between steamships, empire, and statecraft. SOURCE: Library of Congress LC-DIG-ggbain-14057.

spurting up across the map. Fashoda, Tangier, Agadir, Caracas, Mukden—the very names were redolent of empires stretched so far that conflict between them flared in places unimaginable and often unpronounceable to the average reader.

Albert Ballin had seen where this would lead as early as 1909. Gone was his earlier bullishness on the German navy. "Our relations to England are causing me great concern," he wrote one of the Kaiser's inner circle. "Please use your maximum influence for support of an agreement on naval construction."[50] As managing director of Germany's largest shipping line, his was a unique perspective; running his finger along the globe next to his desk, Ballin saw German sea lanes cross over British, French, Russian, American. An intimate knowledge of every colonial port (geography, language, customs, tidal patterns) made him cognizant of imperial realities, though he rarely ventured further from his desk than the Tiergartenstrasse. Keeping up with his rivals gave him insight into their respective empires as well. As the gaps between them closed, and friction mounted, Ballin became fearful.

Taking matters into his own hands in 1912, Ballin traveled to London and met with the First Lord of the Admiralty, Winston Churchill. He came back elated: "Your Majesty, I bring the alliance with England!" The Kaiser's response was crushing. Ballin was forced to pursue his diplomatic channels in secret, leading some to ironically suppose that he was maneuvering the country into war. "Germany has made an enemy of the whole world through HAPAG [Hamburg–American Lines]," journalist Goerg Schroeder declared, "that is, through Ballin." He was even the subject of a caustic novel *The Struggle for the Sea*; in it, dastardly shipping magnate Moritz Bebacher schemes Germany into declaring war so that his ships will be used as lifelines to the rest of the empire. Ballin sued for libel and won, but his close friends teasingly persisted in calling him Moritz.[51] The novel, utterly meritless from an aesthetic standpoint, was a powerful indicator of how the public imagination had transformed. Instead of engines facilitating empire, imperial expansion had become *causus belli*; steamship lines (and their owners) were viewed with increasing distrust.

The coming of war in 1914 decimated the passenger fleets, just as the previous decade of rivalry had helped create them. Liners were converted into troop carriers, armed merchant cruisers, hospital ships, even aircraft carriers. Their role in the war was as vital as it had been in peacetime. Some of them suffered horrific ends: *Kaiser Wilhelm der Grosse* scuttled; *Campania* sunk by collision with her own escort; *Cap Trafalgar* destroyed in battle with another ex-liner, the *Carmania*. Ships as national avatars had finally achieved an ironic, perhaps inevitable, result. So it was that when a German submarine sank the *Lusitania* in May 1915, the German people celebrated and the Kaiser declared a holiday. The *Lusitania*, along with her even faster sister *Mauretania*, had taken the Blue Riband back from Germany in 1907.[52]

Those ships that survived saw their interiors stripped bare, artillery mounted on shuffleboard courts, grand salons filled with makeshift bunks. German liners left in the relative safety of neutral American ports were seized in 1917 and transformed into troopships. In a symbolic twist that underscored the connection between naming and nationalism, the *Kaiser Wilhelm II* became the *Monticello,* the *Kronprinz Wilhelm* became *Von Steuben,* and *Kronprinzessin Cecilie* the *Mount Vernon.* Strangely, the last member of the family retinue was unchanged, embarking on her first troop voyage as *U.S.S. Kaiserin Auguste Victoria.* The transformation of the *Amerika* was almost as simple, altering a single letter.

Just as the Germans had imbued their national pride into these ships, Americans inverted it and made it their own. Nowhere was this more apparent than in the case of Ballin's flagship, *Vaterland.* American navy men took particular relish in demolishing every trace of Germany within the liner. Portraits of the Kaiser, imperial busts, heraldic crests, Rhineland tapestries, and anything even remotely "foreign" was tossed over the side, joining a pile of smashed detritus on the pier. One observer described it as the "gutting of the German whale."[53] Clearly, once this process was complete, it was inadvisable for her to go to sea as *U.S.S. Vaterland.* The question of nomenclature was so significant that it traveled up the chain of command and finally reached the White House. "Call her *Leviathan,*" President Wilson directed. "It's from the Bible. It means 'monster of the deep.'"[54]

The final irony was cruel. A reparations committee established by the Allies at Paris arbitrarily dispersed the captured German passenger fleet among the victors. Older ships, including the first generation of national superliners like the *Kaiser Wilhelm II* and *Kronprinzessin Cecilie,* were shunted aside to the mothball fleet in the James River for alleged future military use. There they remained for decades, rusting relics from another age, until finally obliterated. As the hapless owners of the *Great Eastern* could have told them, there is nothing so forlorn as a spectacle after it ends.

The fate of the newer German liners was, in the nationalist sense, even more tragic. By 1918 Britain had lost two flagships, the *Lusitania* and *Britannic*. The reparations committee awarded Cunard and White Star the *Imperator* and unfinished *Bismarck,* respectively. The *Vaterland* was given over to the Americans, who kept the biblical name they had selected. By the early 20s all three ships were reconditioned and sailing under appropriate titles: *Berengaria, Majestic, Leviathan.* Though representing different firms, the effect of seeing the trio gathered together on the West Side piers was disconcerting. Aside from a few minor alterations, only the color of their funnels distinguished them. Aboard, the whitewash was even more apparent. Faucets were marked *"Auf"* and *"Zu,"* gauges were similarly mystifying, and no amount of heraldic Olde English veneer could conceal the Bavarian origins of *Berengaria*'s smoking room.[55] Nevertheless, the image of the German *Berengaria* appearing in Cunard colors, with a potted palm standing where the Kaiser's portrait once hung, was as symbolic of victory as the Cenotaph in Whitehall.

There was hollowness in this triumph. In 1886, America had attained dominance over its rivals by purchasing them; in 1919, the Allies achieved the same result through outright theft. Hamburg–American Line was left with a single ship, the rusting and obsolete ex-*Deutschland.* By then Albert Ballin was dead, possibly by his own hand. Though undeniably a victim, he was not a blameless one. Shipping companies like his had worked for decades to link their vessels— symbolically, actually, and in the public mind—with empire. Through their interiors, names, and advertising, they adhered themselves to the imperial state. The English firms had done the same, albeit in more muted tones. Now both sides had reaped the result.

11 SITTING IN DARKNESS
Critiquing Imperialism from the Top Deck

ON STAGE AT THE PARIS OPERA, poor lovelorn Hoffmann is beguiled by an automaton. Blinded by a pair of magical spectacles, he cannot see Olympia's jerking, clockwork spasms. She wheels and pivots around him, out of control, as her maker frantically tries to rein her in. The audience laughs and applauds. Then Coppelius, the villain, appears from the wings. He dashes the spectacles from Hoffmann's eyes, and the truth is revealed. Disillusioned, the lover flees. The first act of the *Tales of Hoffmann* closes with Olympia the automaton dismembered on stage, accompanied by the shriek of demolished springs and raucous laughter of the crowd.

In August 1914, the steam-driven world tore itself apart, facilitated as ever by the engines themselves. Like a Tibetan sand painting, destroyed only when it has reached perfection, the western powers had finally achieved the *summa maxima* of their ambitions. P&O vessels left London and Liverpool each day, often twice a day, bound for every corner of the empire from Fremantle to Mombasa. Cecil Rhodes's vast "Cape to Cairo" railway, linking British possessions in South Africa to Egypt, was nearly complete. Travelers could depart Johannesburg in the morning, pass over the Victoria Falls at tiffin time, and disembark in Rhodesia to watch the sun set over the Matobo hills. The more ambitious could stay on and journey through nearly the whole of the continent in less than five days. Once the line was finished—projections ran to 1916—the British empire would be able to move settlers, military, cargo, and materiel across Africa as easily as from Bristol to Brighton.[1]

The end was sudden and final. After the war, everything would be different. While ships would always bear the symbolic pride of their nations, never again would the unique combination of technology, wonderment, and empire so elevate their status in the public imagination. The veneration of machines was not a uniquely Victorian phenomenon, but its melding with imperial aspirations certainly was. Empire was more than a collection of colored blobs on a map: It was a set of assumptions and understandings about oneself and the rest of the world. Even as it shortened distances, displaced aboriginals, and facilitated the mechanics of imperialism, steam fostered a concurrent sense of the basic "rightness" of these acts. The machine—impersonal, indefatigable, orderly—became a metaphor for the imperial will itself. The process began, as we have seen, with the externalization of wonder. Pride in grandiose vessels like the *Great Eastern*, coupled with the aspirational fantasies of Jules Verne, instilled the belief that technology was the motive force of civilization, and its yardstick. Drunken Bostonians sang loudly, "Oh dear, think of a scheme, odd though it may seem / 'Tis sure to succeed if you work it by steam!"[2]

In the mid-19th century, this awe turned outward: Victorians not only celebrated what they had, but disparaged those who did not have it. As with much of this society, snobbery was coupled with charity: bringing modernity to "those sitting in darkness." Steam leant itself to this task. Unlike other inventions, it was transferable—indeed, it was the agent of transfer. Thus the steamship became the harbinger of civilization, physically and metaphorically. Steam as civilization was such an established presumption that it would take years for the public to accept that it could also be an instrument of barbarism. Even then, such brutality was considered surrendering to the jungle, not a policy carried upriver by ship. Gunboat diplomacy was viewed as a corrective measure, paternalistic and condescending at once. "We should spank their bottoms," Theodore Roosevelt famously said of the Colombian government, as he dispatched the *U.S.S. Nashville* to Panama.[3]

Yet by the end of the century many of those who had watched with awe as steam conquered the world now began to fear the result. Imperial governance seemed to replicate the cold, impersonal efficiency of the engine. Even as steamship lines extolled the exoticism of their destinations, those destinations came to resemble the very places passengers had left. The magic of travel faded rapidly. Railroad tours and cruises turned locals into parodies of themselves. No part of the world was beyond the reach of a society powered by steam, and this fact alone bred a kind of wistfulness for lost mysteries. Ironically, whereas steam power had once been an object of fascination and wonder itself, by the 20th century its very predictability and ubiquity had produced the inverse: The phantasmagoria of steam was replaced by the tedium of timetables. Steam as conqueror brought civilization, but at the expense of wonder and innocence. As Danny Kaye's Congolese "savage" laments in a song from 1947: "They hurry like savages to get aboard an iron train / And though it's smoky and it's crowded, they're too civilized to complain . . ."[4]

As previous chapters examined how steam and empire became entwined in the Victorian imagination, it is fitting to close with the dissenters. Not all of them emerged at the end of the century: Almost from the advent of steam on water, there were observers who saw its devastating potential. While these voices would never overcome the greater chorus, they remained a jarring counterpoint throughout the age.

One such observer witnessed the decimation of the Native American race and recorded disgustedly: "This deep, bloody American tragedy is now concluded. [They acted] not for the Honor of God . . . but in truth, only stimulated and goaded on by insatiable Avarice and Ambition, that they might for ever Domineer, Command, and Tyrannize."[5] It was Bartolomé de las Casas, writing in 1552, yet he might as well have been speaking of the Mississippi in 1840. Just as America pioneered the use of steam on waterways, it was the first nation to use it as an instrument of "civilization." Steam navigation facilitated white settlement along the banks of the Mississippi River; for the first time, with boats moving both up- and downriver, permanent communities could be established. The problem, for the United States government, was what to do with the thousands of Native Americans who currently occupied the land.

A test case occurred in 1832, when the Sauk tribe under Chief Black Hawk murdered twenty-eight Menominee Indians, who had allied themselves with the whites. The Sixth Regiment was sent downstream to retaliate, carried on the steamers *Enterprise* and *Chieftain*. Black Hawk would not stand down, and in fact triumphed in a skirmish against a group of local militia.[6] The governor of Illinois responded by advocating wholesale genocide. "The State is not only invaded by hostile Indians," he proclaimed, "but many of your citizens have been slain in battle. . . . To subdue these Indians and drive them out of the State, it will require a force of at least two thousand mounted volunteers."[7] These were given him, carried on steamboats commissioned by the U.S. Army.

Now that its military potential was realized, the Mississippi became a critical strategic element of Indian removal. Steamboats moved men and supplies downriver to resupply stockades, then carried the wounded or relieved back up North. It was big business for local captains and grew over time. By 1851 the transportation of soldiers on the Mississippi cost the American government some $212,213.90 per annum. Added up, in one decade steamboat captains collectively earned over $3 million from government transport.[8] An attempt was made to use some boats to relocate the Indians themselves, but this was met with ferocious resistance even by those tribes that had acquiesced to removal. Most regarded the steamboat, belching smoke and fire, as a monstrous device. This was taken as further evidence of their backwardness and further justification for removing them in the first place.

One nagging complexity was the presence of witnesses. Innocent bystanders, new arrivals in the Mississippi communities, watched with horror as the Indians in their midst were rounded up and dispatched. In 1837 the Ohio *Reflector* published a scathing condemnation of such practices; interestingly, the victims were none other than the peaceful, much abused Menominee:

> Yes, let it be known that the United States Government, not being able to procure a few thousand dollars of specie from some other cause, has determined to pay its honest debts to the Menominee Indians in this vicinity—in what? In trinkets and calicoes. . . . We cannot view this step on the part of the government in any other light than as an unjustifiable and flagrant infraction of its treaty, a heartless disregard of the aborigines, and of our citizens.[9]

But the U.S. government was unmoved. Most state papers cast the removal in the same light as did the governor of Illinois: Indians were "invaders" to be driven back, not out. The few instances of open resistance were touted as evidence of the basic rightness of this policy. Sometimes the hated steamboats themselves were targeted. In July of 1827, the Gettysburg *Republican Compiler* reported that the Winnebago attacked a military boat carrying stores to Fort Snelling. "At the second attack the Indians got possession of the boat, but the crew afterwards recaptured her. In these several engagements a number were killed on both sides."[10]

Violence without seemed to replicate the inherent violence within: The engine that drove imperialism along the Mississippi was powered by conflagration, expressed its motion through explosive bursts, and remained at all times under intense pressure barely contained. There could hardly be a more fitting metaphor for its surroundings. As Walter Johnson writes:

> Like the fears of slave revolt or class conflict among whites . . . the knowledge that the technologies of dominion and extraction concealed within them mechanisms that could produce disorder and destruction was often pushed to the margins of the account of the Mississippi Valley given by its boosters.[11]

The Mississippi precedent was used to great effect in later colonial empires. The Ganges River in India was often called the second Mississippi, and opening its pathways to commerce became an integral part of the East India Company's commercial and political strategy in the 1830s. The first steamer put in service was named, appropriately, *Lord William Bentinck* after the Governor General of India; the second cemented the link between mother country and colony by titling itself the *Thames*. By the 1840s, the East India Company maintained a sizable fleet of "secret gunboats," carrying neither freight nor passengers, but in effect a private navy securing the Ganges for Britain.[12] "Steamboat imperialism," as one author described it,[13] followed a similar pattern on the waterways of America, Africa, India, and Asia: mapping routes, followed by initial steam exploration, settlement, encroachment, and finally armed defense. Gunboats along the Niger, Yangtze, Indus, and so on moved men, munitions, and materiel to colonial outposts and became the first line of defense both from foreign encroachment and native insurgency. Sometimes their usage bordered on the genocidal: The British Royal Navy regularly sent gunboats up the Niger to decimate villages that had dared to fire their arrows against steam traffic.[14]

The annihilation of space through steam was both invigorating and terrifying to the colonizers. "I can conceive no application," one proponent wrote in 1837, that would gladden the hearts of men like Robert Fulton and James Watts than "seeing the mighty streams of the Mississippi and the Amazon, the Niger and the Nile, the Indus and the Ganges, stemmed by hundreds of steam-vessels, carrying the glad tidings of 'peace and good will toward men' into the dark places of the earth."[15] He was quite right: Fulton himself had seen the potential of steamship imperialism and tried at the beginning of the century to "secure a grant for twenty years" for the Ganges River. He evidently felt the august presence of the British empire looming over his shoulder. "Keep the Ganges Secret," he wrote.[16]

The potential of steamship imperialism was undeniable; its moral efficacy was another matter. The most famous dissent came from Joseph Conrad, who had spent much of his life on steam vessels of one kind or another and understood their power better than most. The boat that conveys his protagonist toward the "Heart of Darkness" was anything but ennobling, and its grim functionality reflected its grim purpose:

This steamboat was exactly like a decked scow.... The funnel projected through that roof, and in front of the funnel a small cabin built of light planks served for a pilot house. It contained a couch, two camp stools, a loaded Martin-Henry leaning in one corner, a tiny table, and the steering wheel.[17]

Instead of becoming a harbinger of civilization, the steamer moves its passengers backward through time. Rather than bringing light to "dark places," it surrenders itself to the darkness. Describing its passage, Conrad evokes the same sense of detachment from one's surroundings that cruise passengers had remarked on for decades. Yet now that detached ignorance becomes a metaphor for the vast unbridgeable gulf between colonized and colonizer, a mutual lack of understanding that was inherently volatile:

The steamer toiled along slowly on the edge of a black and incomprehensible frenzy. The prehistoric man was cursing us, praying to us, welcoming us—who could tell? We were cut off from the comprehension of our surroundings; we glided past like phantoms, wondering and secretly appalled, as sane men would be before an enthusiastic outbreak in a madhouse.[18]

An even more remarkable critique of steam imperialism came from one of the invention's most ardent proponents, whose works had almost single-handedly popularized the cult of technology. In the last decades of the 19th century, the trajectory of Jules Verne's novels moved steadily away from "the unity of mankind," as enshrined in his masterpiece *Around the World in Eighty Days*, towards a dark future of discord and domination. Verne became increasingly disgusted with the imperial world and sympathized—as his own Captain Nemo did—with its oppressed subjects. He was clear-sighted enough to perceive the nexus between technology and imperialism; the same steamships that helped Phileas Fogg circumnavigate the world were also the bonds that held it in check. Indeed, such forces set against the native landscape might even be impious:

The railway, on leaving Benares, passed for a while along the valley of the Ganges. . . . Elephants were bathing in the waters of the sacred river, and groups of Indians, despite the advanced season and chilly air, were performing solemnly their pious ablutions. These were fervent Brahmins, the bitterest foes of Buddhism, their deities being Vishnu, the solar god, Shiva, the divine impersonation of natural forces, and Brahma, the supreme ruler of priests and legislators. What would these divinities think of India, anglicized as is today, with steamers whistling and scudding along the Ganges, frightening . . . the faithful dwelling upon its borders?[19]

One need only consider the original intent of the *Great Eastern*—solidifying Britain's imperial grasp on her dominions, sending whole regiments of troops to quash another potential mutiny—to validate Jules Verne's fears. In later decades his novels became increasingly fantastical and dark. Alongside the wonder of steam technology, these works reflect a growing disenchantment with the world it helped create. In his first appearance, Captain Nemo's origins are left unspecified, his war with humanity sparked by some unknown grievance. A clue is left when he rescues an Indian fisherman from a shark, commenting afterward, "That Indian, sir, is an inhabitant of an oppressed country; and I am still, and shall be to my last breath, one of them!"[20] This is made explicit in the sequel, *The Mysterious Island*, wherein we discover that Nemo was a member of the Indian Mutiny of 1857 (the same that the *Great Eastern* was intended to help prevent) who had lost his family to British marauders.

The theme of revenge against imperialism is revisited in *The Steam House*, where the primary antagonist, Nana Sahib, was an historical character, a leading rebel figure of the mutiny who had disappeared without a trace at its conclusion. "Full of courage and audacity," Verne describes him, "accustomed to face danger, crafty and skilled in the art of baffling and eluding pursuit in every form."[21] The strain of sympathy for Nemo and Nana Sahib is coupled with revulsion for British atrocity. Verne writes trenchantly of one Major Hodson ordering the slaughter of 5,000 unarmed Hindus: "This bloody execution excited the highest admiration throughout the Punjab."[22]

Then there is the remarkable conveyance that is the Steam House itself. The house was nothing more than a carriage on wheels, but pulled by—a locomotive elephant! "The monstrous animal," Verne writes,

> twenty feet in height, and thirty in length, advanced deliberately, steadily, and with a certain mystery of movement which struck the gazer with a thrill of awe. His trunk, curved like a cornucopia, was uplifted high in the air. His gilded tusks, projecting from behind massive jaws, resembled a pair of huge scythes.[23]

There is something ominous in this vision—a mechanical beast whose great size and demonic features recall the worst excesses of Shelley and Poe rather than the unalloyed wonder of the *Great Eastern*. The commentary is subtle, but it is there: an automaton designed by an Englishman to carry other Englishmen on a holiday through India, scything their way through the jungle and crushing anything in their path. They gaze down from a lofty cabin formed of "two pagoda-shaped buildings without minarets, but with double-ridged roofs surmounted by a dome."[24]

Even Verne seems to find the idea of a steam pachyderm faintly ridiculous; the dutiful catalogue of its technical dimensions is almost a parody of earlier attempts:

The tubular boiler is in the fore part of the elephant's body, and the tender, carrying fuel and water, in the hinder part. . . . The nominal strength of the engine is equal to that of eighty horses, but its power can be increased to that of one hundred and fifty, without any danger of an explosion. . . . To complete the marvel of this prodigious locomotive, I must add that it can float![25]

There is a tension here between the "civilized" wonders of steam and the landscape it conquers, and unlike earlier novels it is the latter with which the author sympathizes. By the end of the century, Verne believed that steam had diminished the joy of travel, reducing the landscape to an indistinguishable series of railroad and steamship connections (a lament also voiced by another perambulating contemporary, Mark Twain, as we shall see).

There had been earlier hints of this skepticism: M. Aronnax agrees with Captain Nemo that "steam seems to have killed all gratitude [for the sea] in the hearts of sailors,"[26] while the English tourists aboard the Steam House bemoan railroad travel, "blinded by smoke, steam, dust, and above all by rapid motion!"[27]

This disenchantment reached fruition in Verne's 1895 novel *Propeller Island*,[28] which stands as an ironic counterpoint to *A Floating City*. Now the steamship is so large it has become an island unto itself, populated by American millionaires content to travel aimlessly around the world. These are not dogged adventurers like Phileas Fogg, but idle tourists—indeed, cruise passengers. The story's protagonists are, appropriately, a string quartet brought aboard to entertain. Yet despite the seeming Illyria of the island, a civil war ensues between the Starboardites and Larboardites, and soon the whole vessel is in chaos. In the same decade that Rudyard Kipling intoned "transportation is civilization," Jules Verne suggested quite the reverse.

Verne could only infer the devastating effects of steam imperialism. Mark Twain observed them for himself. In 1895, faced with financial ruin,[29] Twain embarked on his most ambitious voyage yet: a round-the-world tour along the equator. Like Phileas Fogg, Twain would make nearly all the voyage by steam, transferring from ship to railroad across oceans and continents. Weekly dispatches, published in book form as *Following the Equator*, would hopefully rescue his precarious finances. He also hoped to do a little lecturing.

The first stop was familiar, and fateful. Hawaii had greatly changed since his last visit in 1866, and never more than in the previous two years. By that strange organic process found only in fungi and corporations, the Castle & Cook trading post grew into a monolith. Sugar cane supplanted all other crops to become the most profitable enterprise in the Pacific, and now almost all the wealth of the islands was held by a coterie of wealthy American planters and merchants. Led by Sanford Dole (later of Dole Pineapple), this new dollar aristocracy made rapid inroads on the decaying monarchy. In 1887 they forced King David Kalākaua to sign a constitution disenfranchising Asians and other minorities and imposed a hefty property requirement for the right to vote. This excluded nearly everyone but the Americans themselves. Dole and his confrères likened it to the Magna Carta; it would be remembered instead as the Bayonet Constitution.[30]

Five years later, the cabal decided to remove the monarchy and rule outright. The U.S. Navy steam cruiser *U.S.S. Boston* arrived in Honolulu harbor in August 1892, and at precisely that moment the American planters discovered they were living under a barbaric despot. Queen Liliʻuokalani abdicated in January to prevent bloodshed, and Sanford Dole—bewhiskered, waistcoated, looking rather like a scruffy Leopold II—became the first president of the Provisional Government of Hawaii. Thanks to the miracle of the telegraph, his authority was recognized by nearly every western power within forty-eight hours. His ruling council was called, with Jacobin exactitude, the Committee of Safety.

Like everyone else in the United States, Twain had read of the takeover; unlike most, he was disquieted. He longed to see for himself this new, albeit dubious, republic. Ironically, he was never given the chance. A quarantine lay over the island of Oahu when he arrived, and Twain was forced to reacquaint himself with Hawaii from the deck of a steamship. His perspective was correspondingly Olympian: "The silky mountains were clothed in soft, rich splendors of melting color, and some of the cliffs were clothed in slanting mists. I recognized it all. It was just as I had seen it long before, with nothing of its beauty lost, none of its charm wanting."[31]

From that distance Twain could not see the American marines drilling in Kamāmalu (soon, inevitably, renamed Dole Park) or the curfew signs hanging all over town. Martial law was still imposed, the legacy of a brief counterrevolt just months before. He could not have known that Diamond Head, so captivating from this vantage, had been the site of a brief and bloody skirmish between royalists and American military. Least visible of all was the tiny figure of

Lili'uokalani herself, imprisoned like a fairy princess in an upstairs bedroom of Iolani, now chillingly demoted to the "Executive Building." Twain acknowledged the limitations of his vision, while at the same time sparing little sympathy for the lost regime:

A change had come, but that was political, and not visible from the ship. The monarchy of my day was gone, and a republic was sitting in its seat. It was not a material change. The old imitation pomps, the fuss and feathers, have departed, and the royal trademark—that was about all one could miss, I suppose.[32]

The "fuss and feathers" comment is revealing. For Twain, one bogus western government had supplanted another: The fault lay neither with the Americans nor the queen, but rather with her father, that "merry monarch" King David Kalākaua. It was he who, in 1879, embarked on an extensive program to thoroughly westernize the islands. The king spoke grandly of an "imperial" Hawaii, embarked on a tour through Europe to study his fellow royals, and built Iolani Palace in the American Florentine style. If "that imitation monarchy was grotesque," said Twain, it was only because it had allowed itself to become something false.

Mark Twain liked things to appear as they were. He despised pretense, especially when cloaked in righteous sentiment. Anchored off Honolulu and increasingly frustrated, he relied on fellow passengers to educate him on the events that had taken place ashore. What they described, even allowing for their pro-American sympathies, appalled him. The happy, indolent natives of 1866 now writhed under a cheerless oligarchy that engaged in everything from land snatching to secret executions with psalm-singing evangelical fervor. Captain Wawn, the ship's master, spoke with bitterness of missionaries who had gained ascendency amongst the American usurpers, coloring imperialism with humbug piety. Bad enough to steal the islands, Wawn said, but worse yet to claim it was all for the Hawaiians' own good. Twain was persuaded and commented to his readers that the only effect of "civilization" seemed to be instilling such virtues as shame, avarice, and cruelty. Fortunately, none of these was likely to "take" for very long: "Indeed there is only but a single detail of his civilization that can be depended on to stay by [the native]: according to the missionary, he has learned to swear."[33]

Not having seen it for himself, Twain did not feel comfortable passing judgment on the new regime. He opened his dispatch, however, with an oblique non sequitur that made his feelings plain. Writing of Kamehameha III, the 18th-century monarch who united the Hawaiian Islands under his rule, Twain complimented him as a great imperialist:

> He was a remarkable man, for a king; and he was also a remarkable man for a savage. . . . He conceived the idea of enlarging his sphere of influence. That is a courteous modern phrase which means robbing your neighbor—for your neighbor's benefit. . . . The details of Kamehameha's history show he was always hospitably ready to examine the white man's ideas, that he exercised a tidy discrimination in making his selections from the samples placed on view.[34]

Disillusionment came gradually. A born explorer, Mark Twain cherished the moments of first contact, the feeling of arriving upon an unspoiled landscape and experiencing the people therein. It was these he described to readers back home and which accounted for a significant portion of his income. But as his ship took him into more remote regions, Twain realized he was not moving from one isolated community to the next but rather within a handful of vast, omnipresent empires. This became clearer as he was introduced, time and again, both to the imperial masters and the native *ancien régimes* they supplanted. A gentle Fijian diplomat told him what was meant to be a humorous anecdote: When the English commissioner took control of the island in 1858, he tried to assuage the feelings of its late king, Thakombau, by calling it just "a sort of hermit-crab formality, you know." Thakombau was unimpressed. "Yes," he replied, "but with this difference—the crab moves into an unoccupied shell, but mine isn't."[35]

In an astonishingly short period of time, thirty years, that scene was replicated throughout Asia, India, Africa, and the Pacific. By Twain's voyage in 1895, the process was nearly complete. What he did not realize, however, was that the credit for that achievement belonged in part to the ships currently conveying him along the equator. Twain's affection for them was undiminished, and now he had become something of a connoisseur. The tramp *Rosetta* was "a poor old ship, and ought to be insured and sunk," but P&O's *Oceana*, which brought him from Sydney to Ceylon, was "a stately big ship, luxuriously appointed. She has spacious promenade decks, large rooms: a surpassingly comfortable ship."[36] Later on, passing through the Indian Ocean, Twain had the opportunity to compare P&O's service with her chief rival, Union Castle. "The *Arundel Castle*," he said approvingly, "is the finest boat I have seen in these seas, thoroughly modern, and that statement covers a great deal of ground."[37]

It did indeed. Both firms were headquartered in London, just steps from the Colonial Office, but their reach was immense. P&O distinguished itself in 1840 as the first British line to carry mail to Egypt, and it cemented that connection by allowing its flagship *Delta* to be the first commercial vessel to transit the Suez Canal. The canal also determined Union Castle's fortunes. Begun in 1857 to make the long passage from London to Calcutta around the Cape of Good Hope, it curtailed this service after Suez opened to focus instead on Britain's African holdings.[38] Both companies bore mail contracts from the Crown, and both had offered their liners for use as troopships and armed merchant cruisers during the Crimean and Boer Wars. As such, the shipping lines were auxiliaries to the empire, providing commercial and military lifelines that allowed it to function. When Rudyard Kipling called the P&O liners "the most vital link of empire," he meant it in more ways than one.[39]

Twain's experience on board reflected little of this aspect. His comments were those of any passenger: The beds on the *Arundel Castle* were too hard; the *Oceana* had a surprisingly good library. "Friday, December 13," one diary entry read, "Sailed at 3 P.M. in the *Mararoa*. Summer seas and a good ship—life has nothing better."[40] He might not have been aware of it, but the felicity with which he traveled was testimony to the power of a steam-driven empire. Ships like the *Oceana* and *Arundel Castle*, viewed singly, were not particularly impressive. But as part of a fleet, like tiny spiders weaving great and intricate webs, they bound continents and peoples together. Twain's voyage was an unwitting test of their efficiency, and by extension that of the British empire. They were an unqualified success: Phileas Fogg could not have voyaged more swiftly or with a fraction of the comfort.

Mark Twain still found plenty of bejeweled natives to satisfy his readers' taste for the exotic, but these encounters now occurred under the watchful eye of a colonial representative, often within the confines of some Victorian stone-and-mortar edifice. As such, they seemed contrived. Nor was this phenomenon restricted to the Far East. By the turn of the century, the Santa Fe Railroad conveyed so many tourists to view the famous Hopi "snake dance" that the ritual lost all meaning; pottery and jewelry, which the tribe made only occasionally and solely for its own people, became their primary employment. Within a decade the Hopi were transformed into showmen and wage slaves, all to satisfy visitors' insatiable desire for a "genuine" Indian experience and "genuine" souvenirs.[41]

Even when not scrubbed and put on display to amuse the tourists, Twain in his travels found the "mysterious Orient" congregated in disturbingly familiar spaces. The most common of these was the railway station. Here the long benches, station clocks, and rigid timetables of British rail were put to the service of everyone from Zulu tribesmen to Indian Thuggee, with predictable results.[42] The scene depicted by Twain could have served as a metaphor for the conundrum of imperialism itself:

> Inside the great station, tides upon tides of rainbow-costumed natives swept along, this way and that, in massed and bewildering confusion, eager, anxious, belated, distressed; and washed up to the long trains and flowed into them with their packs and bundles, and disappeared, followed at once by the next wave. . . . They hadn't timed themselves well, but that was no matter—the thing had been ordered from on high, therefore why worry?[43]

Like Honolulu, vistas such as this showed their best advantage when viewed from afar. Closer on, the ugliness of empire became apparent. Twain journeyed through India, stopping to inspect the Ganges and the Taj Mahal; he rode an elephant. From there he and his wife journeyed to South Africa, transitioning seamlessly from caste systems to racial segregation. Twain began to notice a recurring theme in all the conquered lands he visited. His white hosts invariably tried to distinguish themselves from the "savages" around them and assumed that he—an American—would prefer their company to the natives'. Twain chafed under this courtesy, especially as he could see all too clearly what lay beneath it. "There are many humorous things in this world," he wrote, "among them the white man's notion that he is less savage than other savages."[44]

Once introduced, it was a theme he would return to again and again: Barbarity, not civilization, was the universal constant. It was a radical concept, the very inverse of imperial thinking. Twain hypothesized that nations actually became *more* barbaric the further they expanded. Nor did he exempt his own people: "In many countries we have taken the savage's land from him, and made him our slave, and lashed him every day, and broken his pride, and overworked him till he dropped in his tracks."[45] By this logic civilization itself (or at least what passed for it) was merely barbarism on a greater scale. The trappings of western influence—"rugs, ices, pictures, lanais, worldly books, sinful bric-à-brac"[46]— reinforced rather than assuaged this impression.

Twain was transforming, and the longer he stayed abroad, the more extreme his ideas became. He turned 60 en route, plagued by carbuncles and exhaustion. A note of weariness crept into his dispatches. It seemed to some readers that he was becoming a cranky old man, harping on the same tired themes again and again.

But Twain had seen things no other living human had. Not just individual acts of barbarity or despotism, but a *pattern*. The ships that moved him from place to place once again framed his perspective. But this time, instead of obscuring the truth, they revealed it. At Ceylon, Twain experienced an epiphany. For the first time, the tourist put himself into the picture. "I can see it to this day," he began,

> that radiant panorama, that wilderness of rich color . . . beautiful brown faces and gracious and graceful gestures . . . free, unstudied, barren of stiffness and restraint, and—

> Just then, into this dream of fairyland and paradise a grating dissonance was interjected. Out of a missionary school came marching, two by two, sixteen prim and pious little Christian black girls, Europeanly clothed . . . oh, they were unspeakably ugly! Ugly, barbarous, destitute of taste, destitute of grace, repulsive as a shroud. I looked at my women-folk's clothes—just full-grown duplicates of the outrages disguising those poor little abused creatures—and was ashamed to be seen in the street with them. Then I looked at my own clothes, and was ashamed to be seen in the street with myself.[47]

After that, it was an effort to return to the breezy manner of the traveling correspondent. *Following the Equator* was not written as an indictment of empire, but it became one nevertheless. Instead of coming upon each foreign land eager to experience the new and exotic, Twain's critical eye searched for evidence of colonial tampering, missionaries, falsity. In one sense, the tour was a success: Royalties from his writings more than satisfied his creditors, and Twain was solvent once more. He also cemented his status as the most famous living American, both at home and around the world. Now he was the most-traveled as well. The image associated with him—white-haired, white-suited, puffing a cigar, and leaning over the railing of a steamship—dates from this time. Still very much alive and prolific, he was acquiring the status of a legend.

But something profound broke within him on his year-long excursion around the world. He returned to personal tragedy: the death of his grown daughter, Susy. She died while Twain was in London, finishing off his tour with a series of humorous lectures. By the time he reached Hartford, she had already been buried.[48] Now his bitterness became more pronounced. Twain's last decade was filled with recrimination—against the world, against himself.

The cynicism of his writings seemed at odds with the age; it was the 20th century, and civilization seemed to have reached its pinnacle. Yet here was Twain, pointedly reminding Americans of things they would much rather forget. In 1901 he raised a dangerous subject in an article titled "The United States of

Lyncherdom." The target was his beloved home state, now sadly changed from the idyll depicted in *Life on the Mississippi*. "And so Missouri has fallen, that great state!" Twain lamented. If lynching black men was to be condoned, Twain wrote, then the United States had better accept once and for all that it was no more civilized than any "heathen" tribe. Why were they sending missionaries to China, when the Chinese had a civilization both immeasurably older and more advanced? "O kind missionary, O compassionate missionary, leave China! Come home and convert these Christians!"[49]

Next he took on the missionaries themselves. Coming upon an interview in the New York *Sun* with one lately returned from China, Twain was stunned to read these words: "I deny emphatically that the missionaries are *vindictive*, that they *generally* looted, or that they did anything since the siege that the *circumstances did not demand*. I criticize the Americans. The soft hand of the Americans is not as good as the *mailed fist* of the Germans."[50] He had heard all this before, in Hawaii. It bothered him then; it outraged him now.

Speaking as one who had seen what imperialism and missionary zeal brought to conquered lands, Twain raged against them. Moving from one empire to the next—British, German, Russian, American—he systematically deconstructed each and revealed the whole for what it was: "a game" played by western powers, with pieces snatched from those they conquered. Addressing himself "to the person sitting in darkness"—that is, to the unconquered native—he cautioned against accepting the fruits of western civilization. Also, the game had been played out: "The People that Sit in Darkness are getting to be too scarce, and too shy. And such darkness as is now left is really of but an indifferent quality, and not dark enough for the game."[51]

But Twain reserved his real ire for his fellow countrymen. The horror was that this new century might follow the same path as the last, aided by new technologies that made the "game" of empire even easier to play. "*Shall we?*" he demanded of them:

That is, shall we go on conferring our Civilization upon the peoples that sit in darkness, or shall we give those poor things a rest? Shall we bang right ahead in our old-time, loud, pious way, and commit the new century to the game; or shall we sober up and sit down and think it over first?[52]

He had no answer, and expected none. Mark Twain was speaking prophecy, gained not from divine insight but a uniquely holistic knowledge. The steamships that facilitated empire bore him along on their courses and revealed to him the full panorama. Yet like many prophets, the breadth of his vision was such that he could not communicate it whole. His life and writings testified to a great truth: The Victorian imagination could not fully comprehend imperialism unless one was willing—like Twain—to see it in all its forms.

Most travelers, however, were content to see the world contract into something recognizable and reassuring. This insularity was so ironclad that expectations for traveling abroad became absurd. While tourists' laments for sanitary plumbing, drinkable water, and recognizable food are endemic, it took a special kind of imperial obtuseness to arrive in East Africa and lament the absence of a Christmas tree: "It was Christmastide when we were there, though in Beira there was no evidence of the season. No church was to be seen; there were no signs of festivity. A steaming apathy pervaded the land and even crept across the brassy waters to our ship."[53]

That "steaming apathy" to civilization characterized many accounts. These "new-caught, sullen peoples, half devil and half child"[54] seemed to resent all that was done for them, and while Mark Twain might regard the sight of a native child in European dress as an indictment of the colonizers, others interpreted it as a lost but noble cause:

Once these Hottentots were a savage people, but now those living near the Cape are not savages. Once they were thickly covered in grease, and wrapped in sheep skins, but now the men wear jackets and trousers, and the women dress in gay-colored cotton gowns, and twist a red handkerchief round their heads. They have even left off their clicking language, and speak Dutch or English in their broken manner. They have left off, also, their savage manners; they used to tear open a sheep with their hands, and suck its warm blood....

But have they left off their wicked practices? They used to drink to excess, and they do so still; they used to delight in idleness, and they do so still; they used to tell lies, and they do so still.[55]

"No more petty rivalries, or national antipathies," James Gordon Bennett had promised in 1838, "no odious misconstructions and paltry jealousies, but a mutual love and respect growing out of an accurate knowledge of one another's good qualities."[56] By century's end his words seemed mocking. "The perfectibility of man" that the steam age heralded was replaced with a more workable concept: "civilization." The former presumed that all humankind would evolve in concert towards a greater end; the latter took as given that some had evolved faster than others, and it was incumbent upon them to bring the stragglers up to par.

Mark Twain's own musings at midcentury that travel "rubs out a multitude of old unworthy biases and prejudices" might have come back to haunt him. Yet even then there remained the hope, if not the expectation. "In Sydney," he wrote in *Following the Equator*, "I had a large dream . . .":

> I dreamed that the visible universe is the physical person of God; that the vast worlds that we see twinkling millions of miles apart in the fields of space are the blood-corpuscles in His veins; and that we and the other creatures are the microbes that charge with multitudinous life the corpuscles.[57]

It was not an entirely original idea: Quakers speak of an "inner light" that represents the presence of God in all living things, and Hindus (Hindoos, Twain called them) also accept the premise that all elements of the universe are particles of a greater whole. But Twain's vision was framed both by the scientific jargon of the age—microbes, corpuscles—and by his own ever-expanding horizons. Steamships had brought him in contact with so many different races and cultures that, more than anyone of his time, Twain perceived the basic universality underlying them all. The boy that wondered what lay beyond the river bend now flung his gaze over the entire cosmos. What he found transcended imperialism and nationhood and argued instead for their antithesis. Different as all peoples were, they were nonetheless bound, and equal. Mark Twain visualized a world where the same technology that allowed one group to subjugate another instead brought them together in a greater community. He would not live to see it, but he was certainly its first ambassador.

CONCLUSION
Transportation Is Civilization

IN 1905, Rudyard Kipling peered into the mists and produced his own vision of the future. The result was exactly what one would expect when the author of "The White Man's Burden" turned his hand to Jules Verne's milieu. *With the Night Mail: A Story of 2000 A.D.* presents a glittering millennium where science, having conquered the sea in the 19th century, has conquered the air by the 21st. Aeroplanes and zeppelins whiz from one continent to another, delivering the mails and transporting passengers. It is a frenetic, exciting, exotic world. But its fascination for us lies in what has apparently *not* changed: Empires remain intact, contemporaries are as enraptured with their machines as before, and the Germans are still making trouble. Most importantly, machines remain the lifelines that keep the whole enterprise going. The monolithic G.P.O. Company, which dispatches the flying ships, is a thinly veiled P&O, and its officers are drawn from the same hardy breed of Englishmen that captained the *Mooltan* over a century before.

As science fiction, the story is lacking: Kipling does not share Verne's passion for engineering detail, and his depictions of "krypton vapours" and "Fleury Rays" read like adolescent fantasy. Yet the assumptions underlying it are revealing. The pessimism of Jules Verne's later works is noticeably absent in Kipling: We are living in a jolly world where the *Titanic* never sank, and thus technological utopia is not oxymoronic. It is dangerous, to be sure (an appendix after the story lists missing airmen, much as *Captains Courageous* closed with a memorial service for drowned fishermen), but thrilling as well. "Man Wanted," one advertisement reads: "Dig driver for Southern Alps with Saharan summer trips. High levels, high speed, high wages."

The prospect of near-instant communication is dizzying, with none of the ominous overtones that a night sky full of dirigibles might produce a decade later (again, like the *Titanic*, there has been no Great War either in the fictive year 2000). Yet within this seeming utopia, Kipling tosses an offhand comment that puts it instantly into stark perspective. The airships are not mere technological marvels but the backbone of empire. The hovering "Mark Boat" occupied by the narrator becomes an avatar for a colonial outstation, as Kipling makes clear:

The Mark Boat hums off joyously and hangs herself up in her appointed eyrie. Here she will stay . . . a court of ultimate appeal-cum-meteorological bureau for three hundred miles in all directions, till Wednesday next when her relief slides across the stars to take her buffeted place. Her black hull, double conning tower, and ever-ready slings represent all that remains to the planet of that odd old word authority. She is responsible only to the Aerial Board of Control—the A. B. C. of which Tim speaks so flippantly. *But that semi-elected, semi-nominated body of a few score persons of both sexes, controls this planet.* "Transportation is Civilisation," *our motto runs. Theoretically, we do what we please so long as we do not interfere with the traffic and all that that implies. Practically, the A. B. C. confirms or annuls all international arrangements and, to judge from its last report, finds our tolerant, humorous, lazy little planet only too ready to shift the whole burden of private administration on its shoulders.*[1]

"Transportation is civilization." With that expression, the future world becomes a dystopia, made no less frightening by the fact that the author himself is unaware of it. For us, "A.B.C." carries unmistakable overtones of Big Brother; for Kipling it meant nothing more insidious than the British empire. To Kipling, and indeed most 19th-century chroniclers, it would seem a logical and welcome result. By the year 2000, in this imagined universe, engineering has conquered every obstacle and secured domination of the world for the European powers indefinitely. What the steamship accomplished in days, the zeppelin does in hours: Thus Brunel's dream of instant and effective communication with Britain's subjugated peoples seems assured. The symbiotic relationship among spectacle, technology, and empire has reached its ultimate potential.

Things did not turn out that way, thankfully. The promised utopia of 19th-century engineers never arrived. In fact, while relics of the Industrial Age are everywhere about, the greatest of them—steamships—are almost utterly gone. *Great Britain* remains encased in glass, but the next survivor from her long line of descendants arrived almost a century later: the *Queen Mary* of 1936, preserved at Long Beach, California. The frugality of the scrapyards allowed for some bits and pieces to be repurposed. The White Star liner *Homeric*'s ceiling now graces a Scottish movie palace, while *Olympic*'s lounge has been reassembled on, of all things, a modern cruise ship; smaller articles, ranging from furniture to butter plates, still turn up at online auctions once in a while. For the vast majority of the vessels mentioned in these pages, however, and hundreds more besides, nothing remains but a few postcards, a menu, and a name.

Gauging their impact of the Victorian imagination is no easy matter, for so few archaeological remnants are left to us. One can still walk into Union Station and commune with the same spirit that its designers intended, yet recapturing that complex emotion for a lost ship is rather like traversing an empty lot that once hosted a World's Fair. Both were fleeting technological spectacles, dazzling at the time but often absurd and anachronistic in retrospect, and neither lasted very long. Daniel Burnham's stunning Court of Honor at Chicago seemed to resurrect the lost glory of Rome, yet was built of wood and plaster and wouldn't survive the year; the steamships' Tudor smoking rooms, Venetian galleries, Louis XIV lounges—even Johannes Poppe's three-tiered dining room on the *Kronprinzessin Cecilie*—were all made with the knowledge that within a single generation they would be torn apart. Carpenters carved their initials on the tops of the *Mauretania*'s columns like tiny time capsules for their sons to discover later—which they did.[2]

Shipping lines perceived and promoted the shared phantasmagoria of the steamship and the World's Fair; one wonders if they sensed the deeper connection between the two. For something made of iron and standing larger than a cathedral, the ships were surprisingly fragile. The phantasmagoria of steam always had a wistful, ephemeral quality: For all the hoopla of each new vessel, the expressions of wonder and incredulity, the sense that "the limits of imagination have now been reached," deep down most spectators knew it was not so. However large or grand or fast the ship before them was, there would inevitably be another even more so thundering down the ways soon after. In the doctrine of technological progressivism, this was as it should be. The spectacle of steam was never embodied by a single vessel, but rather in the progression from one to the next. Just as exhibitions were meant to announce a new arrival, races tracked the march of time and symbolically passed the baton from old to new.

The kindest fate awaiting a ship was obsolescence. Very few achieved a maritime canonization that ensured they would be remembered long after they were gone. Others, failed spectacles like Brunel's *Great Britain* and *Great Eastern*, faced ridicule in their own lifetimes. The majority of them—the *Morea* and the *Laurentic* and the *Saxonia* and hundreds of others—plodded through their active lives without attracting any historical notice whatsoever. Yet each vessel, successful or disastrous, famous or obscure, left its imprint on the zeitgeist of the age. Spectacles conditioned Victorians to accept the steamship as the highest expression of human mechanical endeavor: In a commodified era, they were the largest "things" on earth, and it is important to remember that they were not only exhibited or raced but *sold*. "Steamship companies would fare ill were it not for the publicity department," one chronicler wrote at the turn of the century:

> The manager of this department is responsible for keeping the attractions of his line continually before the public.... He must understand that the public is unforgiving and that if he once lets it become known that he is trying to create a public preference for his line, instead of merely convincing the public that its choice of his line shows commendable and natural intelligence, the public will not fail to remind him of the fact.[3]

This was heady stuff for advertisers: Sell the ship without seeming to do so. As a result, the reams of publicity, the wealth of statistics, the steady stream of hyperbole—these were all absorbed into the public consciousness without the necessary filter to remind them that what they were hearing was, in truth, a sales pitch.

In time this relentless publicity campaign transcended its commercial *raison d'être* and became wedded to even more momentous concepts like nationalism, imperialism, and "the perfectibility of man." The meaning of the spectacle transformed. By midcentury, for example, the *Great Eastern*'s failings not only reflected upon her owners and builders but the nation as a whole. Likewise, steamship disasters became allegories representing a host of complex meanings, mirroring society's relationship with its machines. Disasters were spectacles too, albeit of a different kind: like the launch or the race (or, indeed, the fair), they invited wonder and awe at the greatness of human achievement—in this case, measured by the awesomeness of its fall.

The melding of spectacle and steam not only produced disasters and maritime freaks like the *Great Eastern*, but also stoked a constant public desire for wonderment expressed through the familiar hyperbole of the newest, fastest, grandest, biggest. As steamships grew in size to become the most visible symbols of Victorian engineering, they were invested with the full weight of allegory that such preeminence grants. In an age where even the humblest railway depot or office building was adorned with symbolic imagery—gamboling gods, cherubim, and so on—no man-made creation reflected a broader range of meanings than the steamship. Whether symbolizing transatlantic unity or national pride, modernity or human progress against the cruel elements (or some combination thereof), the ship always seemed to embody the very best of Victorian society. Yet like Hieronymus Bosch's *Garden of Earthly Delights*, the dark inverse of each supposed virtue was never far from sight. Unity was replaced by frenetic competition, national pride with imperial insularity, modernity with disdain for the unenlightened, progressivism with hubris. Even before evaluating the impact of the ships themselves, the power of their allegory is critical to understanding the Victorian mind.

Beyond metaphor, the ships worked an actual transformation on how Victorians viewed the world—and their place within it. First and foremost, they created a new vantage: looking down from the top deck of a steamer. The sense of detachment, of being both above and apart from the *hoi polloi*, of arriving and departing almost magically, all reinforced the ego. Even more than railroads, which moved within the landscape, steamships altered passengers' conception of time and place by taking them out of it altogether: The space between ports was a void. The ship became the entire reality, a self-contained world. Communities coalesced almost instantly. Often these replicated similar social orders ashore; the need to accommodate multiple classes within the same hull turned ships into floating microcosms of Victorian and Edwardian society. The embodiment of class divisions, some journeys also paradoxically allowed passengers to transgress strictures of class. For wealthy yet bourgeois travelers, the purchase of a First Class ticket was an *entrepôt* into high society; for others of more limited means, passage on a night boat or Mississippi steamer offered a brief glimpse into a glittering commercial paradise. Travel, unlike transit, was a form of escape.

The two concepts—spectacle and travel—are not entirely distinct: The ships became floating spectacles, traveling World's Fairs, bringing the wonder of modern technology with them wherever they went. Early cruise passengers like Thackeray intuited this and wrote of the juxtaposition between "civilization" (the ship) and "savagery" (the shore). Ships as avatars of civilization evolved from the technological to embrace patriotic and even xenophobic dimensions. The ship was familiar, recognizably British or American, comfortable, predictable, "home." This was inevitably contrasted with the dirt, poverty, and mendacity of the ports and people it visited. Steam tourism, as we have seen, paradoxically opened up the entire world to exploration yet insulated passengers from it. The need to accommodate a ship's schedule meant that whole cities and civilizations were necessarily reduced to a few landmarks, a souvenir, and perhaps a "native dance" on the pier. Armed with these momentary impressions, passengers returned convinced that they had actually seen the places they visited. Travel, instead of dispelling prejudices, became the means of confirming them.

In later years, this parochial worldview fostered by steam travel became intertwined in the public consciousness with the cult of technology, and the result was steamship imperialism. If steam power was mankind's greatest gift to itself, surely those who possessed it had a moral duty to share it with those who did not. Steam was thus seen as charity given to less-developed peoples, even if it meant displacing or subjugating them. The miraculous nature of steam travel was aligned with cynical imperialism, commercialism, and reformist zeal to produce a panegyric for the age: Transportation is civilization.

By the latter half of the century, steamships had taken on a character of their own, reflecting the identities of their nations and the fragile relationship with their colonies. Sometimes this took almost comical form—Orientalist fantasies coupled with Tudor libraries on the P&O ships, for example—but the overall effect was to reinforce the symbolic connection between Crown and colony and the steamship's pivotal role therein. At the same time, vessels serving colonial ports brought back with them elements of exotic culture, just enough to inspire lurid fantasies and stereotypes. Perhaps most importantly, the ships themselves became a kind of social crucible wherein neophyte griffins were transformed into colonial administrators—exposed to a new climate, new food, and, most critically, the imperial worldview of their fellow passengers—all in the space of a few weeks.

The symbol of the steamship as imperial avatar was so prevalent that in its own age it came under withering attack from writers like Conrad and Verne. These writings are still known to us; why has their subject been forgotten? Why, with so many important revisionist studies emerging on the deleterious impact of Victorian engineering, have the steamships been largely ignored? Again, I believe it comes down at least in part to their total absence from our society. We live in a landscape that is dotted with remnants of the Industrial Age. Factories loom on the outskirts of every city, railways still thread their paths through our towns and our lives. Even in the postcolonial world, many of these relics survive. The Bombay station depicted by Mark Twain still stands and is still bedlam on a weekday afternoon. Cecil Rhodes's great Cape-to-Cairo transit was never finished, but the separate links still function, providing the most heavily trafficked routes on the African continent. Perhaps that is why we have for so long ignored the darker currents underlying the steam era: Its artifacts are both useful and beautiful. To visit a colonial railway station is to experience, fleetingly, the cosseted protectiveness of an empire long since defunct.

Yet the ships cannot participate in this experience, for good or ill. They have vanished so utterly that their impact has been forgotten both by those who would venerate it and those of our generation who have so skillfully deconstructed the heroic myths of other Victorian inventions. Hence, as a profound lover of ships and the sea, for me the act of dragging them into the harsh light of critical analysis has not been an unalloyed pleasure. I justify it on the reasoning that it is better to grant these ships their rightful credit as catalysts and avatars for the Victorian imagination—in all its wonderful and grotesque forms—than to allow them to remain in the Lethe of half-forgotten hagiography.

The steamships may be gone, but their legacy is no less prevalent than other innovations—indeed, more so. The difference is that while one kind of legacy rests on the ground, the other exists solely within our minds. Thus it is very much alive. We are the unwitting inheritors of Victorian attitudes towards travel and foreign locales, which themselves were fostered by the manner of conveyance. If railways seemed to speed up time itself, steamships annihilated it; if trains altered passengers' perception of the landscape, ships did so exponentially by removing the landscape altogether. The sense of detachment—of being ripped from one world and deposited in another with no clear idea of how it was done—is the precursor of modern-day jetlag. It is easy for us to relate to Victorians' shock at suddenly encountering a new culture coming ashore, as it is the same feeling we experience once the airport doors slide open. But while for us it is commonplace, for them it was a new and powerful sensation.

By transforming the way Victorians experienced travel, steamships transformed their understandings of the greater world—usually not for the better. Cities became snapshots; the reality was the ship itself. No other means of transport, then or since, has so entirely divorced its passengers from the places they visit. Beyond cosseting them and keeping their shoreside visits brief, it also created a new community on board as an alternative—a far more attractive one—to the hugger-mugger of foreign locales.

That legacy, too, is still with us. In Europe and America, ocean liners have given way to jets, but Cunard and P&O thrive on the tourist trade. In the morning their ships arrive at harbor, lining the piers of Venice, Gibraltar, Mumbai, Hong Kong. Passengers disembark in hordes. Jitneys await, ready to whisk them away for an afternoon of carefully choreographed, sanitized adventure. Natives dance traditional dances. For all that, however, pesky shopkeepers harass them, poverty-stricken waifs beg for change, and everything has an odd smell. Even colors are different. Yet by 5 PM the jitneys are back, disgorging their load of harassed, overheated, exhausted tourists. In just a few minutes they are back aboard, storing purchases in their cabins and washing off the last trace of port grime. Soon they will be at sea, surrounded by their friends, lulled by familiar music, served rosemary roasted chicken with apple pie for dessert, and all will be well.

NOTES

PROLOGUE

1. Recently the ship's conservators published a wonderful "owner's manual" for the *Great Britain*, detailing in full her construction, career, and restoration. See Brian Lavery, *SS Great Britain, Owner's Workshop Manual: An Insight into the Design, Construction and Operation of Brunel's Famous Passenger Ship* (London: Haynes Publishing, 2012).

2. An eyewitness depiction of the event may be found in the *Bristol Times and Mirror* (*Bristol*: July 20, 1843). See also Christopher Claxton, *History and Description of the S.S. Great Britain, Built at Bristol, with Remarks on the Comparative Merits of Iron and Wood as Materials for Shipbuilding* (New York: J. S. Homans, 1845).

3. *Bristol Times and Mirror*, July 20, 1843.

4. A revealing depiction of the city's transformation midcentury may be found in William Clark Russell, *North-East Ports and the Bristol Channel* (Newcastle-upon-Tyne: A. Reid, 1883), 73–83. See also *Great Western Railway Guide* (London: James Wyld, 1839), 212–220.

5. See Jeremy Caple, *The Bristol Riots of 1831 and Social Reform in Britain* (London: Edwin Mellen, 1990).

6. Walter Benjamin & Rolf Tiedemann, *The Arcades Project* (New York: Belknap Press, 2002).

7. E. P. Thompson, *The Making of the English Working Class* (New York: Random House, 1964).

8. Rudyard Kipling, *With the Night Mail: A Story of 2000 A.D* (New York: Doubleday, 1905), 47. Ironically it is the motto assigned to the Aerial Board of Control, or A.B.C., which rules the fictional future world of the year 2000. Further discussion to follow in the Conclusion.

9. The reference is not accidental. Nationalism and imperialism were deeply interwoven into steam culture, as we shall explore. See Benedict Anderson, *Imagined Communities: Reflection on the Origin and Spread of Nationalism* (revised ed., New York: Verso, 2006).

INTRODUCTION

1. See Christopher Claxton, *The Logs of the First Voyage, Made with the Unceasing Aid of Steam, Between England and America, by the* Great Western, *of Bristol, Lieut. James Hosken, R.N., Commander; also an appendix and remarks, by Christopher Claxton* (London: British Library, 1838). Courtesy of the New York Historical Society. A full description of this event may also be found in John Malcolm Brinnin, *The Sway of the Grand Saloon: A Social History of the North Atlantic* (New York: Delacorte Press, 1971), 66.

2. A more complete account of Webster's speech appears in "On the Beginning of

Transatlantic Steamship Service," *Bulletin of the Business Historical Society* 12, 3 (June 1938), 40–43.

3. Thomas Haliburton, *The Letter Bag of the* Great Western (London: Lee and Blanchard, 1840), 28.

4. Accounts of this incident appear in the *New York Albion*, April 28, 1838, and *New York Advertiser and Express*, April 24, 1838. Courtesy of the New York Public Library, microforms division.

5. See Isambard Brunel, *The Life of Isambard Kingdom Brunel, Civil Engineer* (reprint ed., Cambridge, UK: Cambridge University Press, 2011).

6. Alexis de Tocqueville, *Democracy in America* (New York: Penguin Classics, 2003), 587.

7. See Jack P. Greene, *Negotiated Authorities: Essays in Colonial Political and Constitutional History* (Charlottesville: University of Virginia Press, 1994).

8. Not even Webster himself could escape the phenomenon he described. Samuel Lyman, a contemporary and admirer of Webster, wrote of his farm that "the Northern Railway passes through it near the Mansion House, and several trains of cars, freighted with passengers and products of the country, with merchandise for the people, pass over it daily, almost annihilating time and space . . ." Samuel P. Lyman, *Life and Memorials of Daniel Webster* (New York: D. Appleton, 1852), vol. I, 152.

9. F. Lawrence Babcock, *Spanning the Atlantic* (New York: Alfred Knopf, 1931), 66.

10. Bayard Tuckerman, ed. *The Diary of Philip Hone, 1828–1851* (New York: Dodd, Meade & Co., 1889), 127. Courtesy of the New York Historical Society.

11. Richard White, *Railroaded: The Transcontinentals and the Making of Modern America* (New York: W. W. Norton, 2011), xxix, 149.

12. See Wolfgang Schivelbusch, *The Railway Journey: The Industrialization of Time and Space in the Nineteenth Century* (Los Angeles: University of California Press, 1987); Giordano Nanni, *The Colonisation of Time: Ritual, Routine and Resistance in the British Empire* (Manchester, UK: Manchester University Press, 2014); Michael J. Freeman, *Railways and the Victorian Imagination* (New Haven, CT: Yale University Press, 1999); John R. Stilgoe, *Train Time: Railroads and the Imminent Reshaping of the United States Landscape* (Charlottesville: University of Virginia Press, 2009).

13. One historian in particular has written extensively on the nexus between technology and imperialism. See Daniel R. Headrick, *Power over Peoples: Technology, Environments, and Western Imperialism, 1400 to the Present* (Princeton, NJ: Princeton University Press, 2010); ———, *The Tools of Empire: Technology and Imperialism in the Nineteenth Century* (Oxford, UK: Oxford University Press, 1981); ———, *The Tentacles of Progress: Technology Transfer in the Age of Imperialism, 1850–1940* (Oxford, UK: Oxford University Press, 1988). See also Walter Johnson, *River of Dark Dreams: Slavery and Empire in the Cotton Kingdom* (New York: Belknap Press, 2013). For more studies of the often fraught relationship between technology and society, see Leo Marx, *The Machine in the Garden: Technology and the Pastoral Ideal in America* (Oxford, UK: Oxford University Press, 1967); Samuel P. Hays, *The Response to Industrialism, 1884–1914* (Chicago: University of Chicago Press, 1995).

14. See, for example, Alison Byerly, *Are We There Yet?: Virtual Travel and Victorian Realism* (Ann Arbor: University of Michigan Press, 2012); John Hannavy, *The Victorian and Edwardian Tourist* (London: Shire Library, 2012); Edward Swinglehurst, *Romantic Journey: The Story of Thomas Cook and Victorian Travel* (New York: Pica Editions, 1974).

15. Marjorie Morgan, *National Identities and Travel in Victorian Britain* (New York: Palgrave, 2004), 14.

16. See, for example, Emma Robinson-Tomsett, *Women, Travel and Identity: Journeys by Rail and Sea, 1870–1940* (Manchester, UK: Manchester University Press, 2011).

17. Ibid., 7–8, 16.

18. See John Maxtone-Graham, *The Only Way to Cross* (New York: Barnes & Noble, 1997);————, *Crossing & Cruising* (New York: Scribner's, 1992);————, *Liners to the Sun* (New York: Sheridan House, 1990).

19. The seminal work, however, remains Walter Lord's *A Night to Remember* (New York: Henry Holt, 1955).

20. One notable exception is Freda Harcourt, *Flagships of Imperialism: The P&O Company and the Politics of Empire from Its Origins to 1867* (Manchester, UK: Manchester University Press, 2006), a splendid survey of the linkages between steamships and empire.

21. Michel Foucault, "Of Other Spaces," *Diacritics* 16, 1 (Spring 1986), 24–27.

22. Despite their critical importance, few scholars have studied these oceanic communities, and the handful of titles on the subject are authored by amateur enthusiasts. The most commonly cited was written over forty years ago: John Malcolm Brinnin, *The Sway of the Grand Saloon: A Social History of the North Atlantic* (New York: Delacorte Press, 1971).

23. Marcus Rediker, "Under the Banner of King Death: The Social World of Anglo-American Pirates, 1716–1726," *The William and Mary Quarterly* 38, 2 (April 1981), 203–227.

24. It is worth noting that at least one pair of scholars has gone beyond hagiography to examine the relationship between Victorian engineers and empire. See Ben Marsden & Crosbie Smith, *Engineering Empires: A Cultural History of Technology in Nineteenth-Century Britain* (New York: Palgrave Macmillan, 2007).

25. See, generally, Johnson, *River of Dark Dreams*.

26. Marsden & Smith, *Engineering Empires*, 2.

27. Such an examination is not without precedent. See Edward Beasley, *Mid-Victorian Imperialists: British Gentlemen and the Empire of the Mind* (New York: Routledge, 2005).

28. As Great Britain and the United States were the primary innovators for steam travel, limiting this study to their respective societies seems appropriate. We will, however, consider other nations in the chapters dealing with global imperialism.

29. Alfred Thayer Mahan, *The Influence of Sea Power Upon History, 1660–1783* (reprint ed., New York: Dover, 1987).

30. Charles Robert Longfield Beatty, *De Lesseps of Suez: The Man and His Times* (New York: Harper, 1956), 256.

CHAPTER 1

1. In actuality there was not much chance of that happening: Unlike most ships until the 20th century, and in yet another foresighted innovation, the *Great Britain* was floated out rather than sliding down rails. It was a brilliant innovation by Brunel that he would unaccountably abandon for the much larger, more unwieldy *Great Eastern*.

2. Paul Fatout, ed., *Mark Twain Speaking* (Iowa City: University of Iowa Press, 1976), 274–276.

3. A full account appears in the *Philadelphia Evening Bulletin*, April 10, 1895.

4. Maxtone-Graham, *Only Way to Cross*, 117.

5. For the superstitious, it should be noted that the *Imperator* went on to have a long and mostly happy career, though not for her original owners. After the First World War, the ship was given in reparations to the Cunard Line, who ran her as their flagship *Berengaria* until 1938. The *Bismarck*, likewise christened by Kaiser Wilhelm, became White Star Line's *Majestic* and sailed until 1936. So perhaps the ill omen was not for the ship, but the Kaiser.

6. Nils Schwerdtner, *The New Cunard Queens: Queen Elizabeth 2, Queen Mary 2, Queen Victoria* (Annapolis, MD: Naval Institute Press, 2008), 165. The author can personally attest that video footage of this event was repeatedly—unaccountably—played on the *Queen Victoria*'s onboard television channel, to the great amusement and occasional superstitious terror of her passengers. On my last cruise, in 2012, they had edited out the offending moment.

7. Brinnin, *Sway*, 243.

8. Marsden & Smith, *Engineering Empires*, 7.

9. Quoted in William Rosen, *The Most Powerful Idea in the World* (New York: Random House, 2010), 4.

10. This continued even aboard the ships themselves. Until well into the 20th century, a daily pool was held on most transatlantic liners, with bidders placing bets on the distance covered that day. Steamship lines encouraged this (indeed, the one form of gambling that *was* encouraged) as they routinely pressed their ships to outperform the estimate.

11. Thomas Boyd, *Poor John Fitch: Inventor of the Steamboat* (New York: G. P. Putnam's Sons, 1935), 165.

12. John Fitch, "The Original Steamboat Supported, or, a Reply to Mr. James Rumsey's Pamphlet, Shewing the True Priority of John Fitch, and the False Datings &c. of James Rumsey" (Philadelphia: 1788). Courtesy of the New York Historical Society.

13. Andrea Sutcliffe, *Steam: The Untold Story of America's First Great Invention* (New York: Palgrave Macmillan, 2004), xvii.

14. Rosen, *The Most Powerful Idea in the World*, 277.

15. Frank D. Prager, ed., *The Autobiography of John Fitch* (Philadelphia: American Philosophical Society, 1976), 162–163. Courtesy of the New York Historical Society.

16. Boyd, *Poor John Fitch*, 180. See also Frank Prager, "The Steamboat Pioneers Before the Founding Fathers," *Journal of the Patent Office Society* 37 (July 1955), 486–522.

17. Rosen, *The Most Powerful Idea in the World*, 304.

18. Ibid., 307–313.

19. See William Conant Church, *The Life of John Ericsson* (New York: Scribner's, 1911).

20. G. H. Preble, *History of Steam Navigation* (Philadelphia: Longworth, 1882), 59.

21. *Adams Sentinel* (New York: August 3, 1816).

22. Alice Clary Sutcliffe, *Robert Fulton and the "Clermont"* (New York: Century Company, 1909), 220–221.

23. Walter Nugent, *Habits of Empire: A History of American Expansionism* (New York: Random House, 2009), 65–68.

24. George Byron Merrick, *Old Times on the Upper Mississippi* (New York: Arthur Clark, 1909), 85.

25. S. L. Kotar & J. E. Gessler, *The Steamboat Era* (New York: McFarland, 2009), 17.

26. A fictional but accurate depiction of this process may be found in C. S. Forester, *Hornblower and the* Atropos (reprint ed., New York: Little, Brown, 1999).

27. Mark Twain, *Life on the Mississippi*, in Charles Neider, ed., *The Complete Travel Books of Mark Twain* (New York: Doubleday, 1967), 367. See also William Wilkins, *Charles Dickens in America* (Toronto: University of Toronto Press, 2011).

28. Geoffrey Ward, Dayton Duncan, & Ken Burns, *Mark Twain: An Illustrated Biography* (New York: Alfred Knopf, 2001), 21.

29. Twain, *Life on the Mississippi*, 442.

30. Ibid., 443.

31. Kotar & Gessler, *Steamboat Era*, 140.

32. Twain, *Life on the Mississippi*, 443.

33. William J. Petersen, *Steamboating on the Upper Mississippi* (New York: Dover, 1996), 266–270.

34. See Johnson, *River of Dark Dreams*.

35. Charles Dickens, *American Notes* (New York: St. Martin's Press, 1985), 143.

36. *Carrollton Mirror Extra* (Carrollton: April 3, 1852).

37. For a survivor's account of one such disaster, see P. W. Hall, "A Minute and Circumstantial Narrative of the Loss of the Steam Packet *Pulaski*..." (Providence: H. H. Hall, 1839).

38. Twain, *Life on the Mississippi*, 464.

39. Quoted in Brinnin, *Sway*, 14.

40. Warren Armstrong, *Atlantic Highway* (London: George Harrap & Co., 1961), 13.

41. Brunel, *Life of Brunel*, 233.

42. For a complete schema, see ibid., 131.

43. L. T. C. Rolt, *Isambard Kingdom Brunel* (London: Penguin Books, 2006), 23–34.

44. *Mechanics Magazine* (April 7, 1838).

45. Brinnin, *Sway*, 52.

46. See E. LeRoy Pond, *Junius Smith: Pioneer Promoter of Transatlantic Steam* (New York: Kessinger Publishing, 2007). Not one to leave things to chance, Smith himself also published a compendium of letters supporting his bid for transatlantic steam: Junius Smith, *Letters upon Atlantic Navigation* (London: A. Eccles, 1841).

47. Smith, *Letters*, 10–34.

48. Quoted in Brinnin, *Sway*, 61.

49. *Mechanic's Magazine* (April 7, 1838).

50. Claxton, *Logs of the First Voyage*, 4–29.

51. The little *Savannah* made the crossing eastward in 1818, but she only employed her engines for four and a half hours. In 1833 the Canadian vessel *Royal William* crossed from Nova Scotia to Britain in twenty-five days, but this was not intended to inaugurate a commercial transatlantic service.

52. Quoted in Robert Albion, *The Rise of New York Port, 1815–1860* (New York: Scribner's, 1939), 319.

53. *Evening Post* (New York: April 24, 1838).

54. *Morning Herald* (New York: April 24, 1838).

55. *The Enquirer* (New York: April 24, 1838).

56. *The Sun* (New York: April 24, 1838).

57. *Morning Herald* (New York: April 24, 1838).

58. Tuckerman, *Diary of Philip Hone*, 16.

59. *Evening Post* (New York: April 24, 1838).

60. By the fall of 1838, the matter of steamships' success on the Atlantic seemed already settled. See Ithiel Town, *Atlantic Steam-Ships* (New York: Wiley & Putnam, 1838). Courtesy of the New York Historical Society.

61. Haliburton, *Letter Bag*, 23–24.

62. Tuckerman, *Diary of Philip Hone*, 381. This was hardly the only example of American boosterism for steam. See also "American Steam Navigation: Speech of Hon. George E. Badger, of North Carolina, for the Collins Steamers . . ." (Washington, DC: Buell & Blanchard, 1852), and "American Steam Navigation: Speech of William Henry Seward for the Collins Steamers . . ." (Washington, DC: Buell & Blanchard, 1852). Both courtesy of the New York Historical Society.

63. Cunard Line was the notable exception, instructing captains to value safety above all. This was arguably one reason that the line never lost a life at sea until the *Lusitania* was torpedoed in 1915.

CHAPTER 2

1. See, generally, Anthony Bailey, *Standing in the Sun: A Life of J. M. W. Turner* (New York: HarperCollins, 1997).

2. See Samuel P. Hays, *The Response to Industrialism, 1885–1914* (Chicago: University of Chicago Press, 1995); Leo Marx, *The Machine in the Garden: Technology and the Pastoral Ideal in America* (New York: Oxford University Press, 1964).

3. William Wordsworth, "Kendal and Windemere Railway," (originally published 1844), in Jared Curtis, ed., *William Wordsworth's Last Poems, 1821–1850* (Ithaca, NY: Cornell University Press, 1999), 389–390. See also Stephen Prickett, "Circles and Straight Lines: Romantic Versions of Tourism," in Hartmut Berghoff, Barbara Korte, Ralf Schneider, & Christopher Harvie, eds., *The Making of Modern Tourism: The Cultural History of the British Experience, 1600–2000* (New York: Palgrave, 2002), 69–84.

4. White, *Railroaded*, 141

5. See Haliburton, *Letter Bag*.

6. Ezra Stiles Gannett, *Sermon Delivered in the Federal Street Meeting House, in Boston, July 19, 1840, on the Arrival of the* Britannia (Boston: Joseph Dowe, 1840). Courtesy of the New York Historical Society.

7. Victor Hugo, *The Toilers of the Sea* (reprint ed., New York: Modern Library, 2002), 130–131.

8. Prickett, "Romantic Versions," in Berghoff et al., *The Making of Modern Tourism*, 74.

9. Margaret Carrington, *Ocean to Ocean: Pacific Railroad and Adjoining Territories* (Philadelphia: J. B. Lippincott, 1869), 9–10.

10. Christopher Claxton, *History and Description of the Steam-Ship* Great Britain (New York: J. Smith Homans, 1845), 1. Courtesy of the New York Historical Society.

11. Ibid., 14.

12. Annual Report of the Great Western Steamship Company, March 26, 1840, Isambard Kingdom Brunel Papers.

13. Stephen Fox, *Transatlantic: Samuel Cunard, Isambard Brunel, and the Great Atlantic Steamships* (New York: HarperCollins, 2003), 148.

14. *Mechanic's Magazine* (November 19, 1842).
15. For an operating history of the *Great Britain*, see Claxton, *History of Steam-Ship Great Britain*.
16. William H. Miller, *The First Great Ocean Liners in Photographs* (New York: Dover, 1982), 54.
17. Claxton, *History of Steam-Ship* Great Britain, 24.
18. Ibid., 24.
19. Brinnin, *Sway*, 145.
20. Quoted in ibid., 145.
21. Claxton, History of Steam-Ship Great Britain, 17.
22. Tuckerman, *Diary of Philip Hone*, 260.
23. *Mechanic's Magazine* (March 7, 1846).
24. The *Great Britain* might be the first example of such recklessness, but not the last. The 20th-century Italian superliners *Rex* and *Conte di Savoia* were both hurried into service in the early 1930s by Mussolini's fascist government, anxious to grab the headlines from other national rivals. The *Rex*'s engines failed her in Gibraltar, causing many of her maiden voyage passengers to abandon the ship in fury, while the *Conte di Savoia* blew a 3-foot hole in the side of her hull and nearly capsized before desperate efforts allowed for a temporary patch sufficient for her to limp into port.
25. Claxton, History of Steam-Ship Great Britain, 1.
26. Quoted in Brinnin, *Sway*, 147.
27. Letter to Christopher Claxton, December 11, 1846, Isambard Kingdom Brunel Papers.
28. W. H. Bidwell, ed., *The Eclectic Magazine: Foreign Literature, Science and Art* (New York: W. H. Bidwell, 1850), 135.
29. Quoted in Brinnin, *Sway*, 149.
30. Claxton, History of Steam-Ship *Great Britain*, 28.
31. See Jeffrey Auerbach & Peter Hoffenberg, eds., *Britain, the Empire and the World at the Great Exhibition of 1851* (London: Ashgate Publishing, 2008); Jeffrey Auerbach, *The Great Exhibition of 1851: A Nation on Display* (New Haven, CT: Yale University Press, 1999).
32. See Thompson, *Making of the English Working Class*.
33. See Samuel Smiles, *Industrial Biography: Iron-Workers and Tool-Workers* (Boston: Ticknor and Fields, 1864).
34. Brinnin, *Sway*, 51.
35. Ibid., 51.
36. Paul Young, *Globalization and the Great Exhibition: The Victorian New World Order* (New York: Palgrave, 2009), 23.
37. John Scott Russell, *On the Nature, Properties and Application of Steam and on Steam Navigation* (Edinburgh: Adam and Charles Black, 1841).
38. Fox, *Transatlantic*, 158–159.
39. *The Crystal Palace Illustrated Catalogue* (originally published London, 1851; republished New York: Dover, 1978), xvii.
40. Ibid., xxi.
41. Kate Colquhoun, *The Busiest Man in England: A Life of Joseph Paxton* (Jaffrey, NH: David Godine, 2006), xiii.
42. *Crystal Palace*, xxv.

43. Ibid., xxv.
44. Ibid., iii.
45. Liza Picard, *Victorian London: The Life of a City, 1840–1870* (New York: St. Martin's Press, 2005), 223.
46. Letter from the Duke of Wellington to Lady Salisbury, quoted in Christopher Hobhouse, *1851 and the Crystal Palace* (London: E. P. Dutton, 1937), 89.
47. Asa Briggs, *Victorian People: A Reassessment of Persons and Themes, 1851–67* (Chicago: University of Chicago Press, 1955), 35.
48. *Crystal Palace*, xii.
49. Ibid., iv.
50. *General Information for Passengers by the Steamships of the Hamburg–American Packet Company* (New York: C. B. Richard and Bros., 1873), 3–4.
51. Ibid., 8.
52. William Flayhart, *The American Line: 1871–1902* (New York: W. W. Norton, 2000), 64.
53. *Cunard Line and the World's Fair, Chicago, 1893* (London: E. P. Hodder for Cunard Line, 1893). Courtesy of the Huntington Library.
54. *Rand McNally & Co.'s Handbook of the World's Columbian Exhibition* (Chicago: Rand, McNally, 1893), 36.
55. *Evolution of the Fall River Line* (Boston: Fall River Line, 1894), 1 (emphasis added). Courtesy of the New York Historical Society.
56. *Cunard Line and the World's Fair.*
57. *Rand McNally Handbook of the World's Columbian Exhibition*, 195.
58. Letter to John Scott Russell, July 13, 1852, Isambard Kingdom Brunel Papers.
59. James Dugan, *The Great Iron Ship* (New York: Harper & Bros., 1953), 24.
60. Ibid., 31.
61. See George S. Emmerson, *John Scott Russell: A Great Victorian Engineer and Naval Architect* (New York: Murray Bros., 1977).
62. Quoted in Gerald S. Graham, *A Concise History of the British Empire* (London: Thames and Hudson, 1970), 252.
63. *First Report from the Select Committee on Steam Communications with India, &c.* (London: House of Commons, 1851), v–vi.
64. Ibid., 11.
65. Ibid., 145.
66. Ibid., 362.
67. There is a chill note of prophesy in these words. The *Great Britain*'s iron hull, which robustly survived a year stranded off the Irish coast, would go on to survive almost a hundred years on the rocks of Australia before finally being removed and towed to Bristol in 1970.
68. Ibid., 366.
69. *All About the* Great Eastern (London: W. H. Smith, 1860), 6.
70. Ibid., 6.
71. Ibid., 6.
72. Philip Dawson, *The Liner: Retrospective and Renaissance* (New York: W. W. Norton, 2006), 37.
73. All About the *Great Eastern*, 7.

74. Ibid., 4.
75. Schwerdtner, *The New Cunard Queens*, 19–20.
76. Letter of June 10, 1852, quoted in Brunel, *Life of Brunel*, 290 (emphasis added).

CHAPTER 3

1. This story appears in Julian Evans, *Jules Verne and His Work* (New York: Twayne Publishers, 1966), 33–34.
2. William Henry Webb, *Descriptive Particulars of the* Great Eastern *Steam Ship: With Illustrations and Sectional Plans* (London: Marshall & Sons, 1857). Courtesy of the New York Historical Society.
3. Dugan, *Great Iron Ship*, 2–4.
4. Some early promotional literature still bears the original name. See Samuel Walters, *The* Leviathan *Steam Ship: William Harrison Esqr. Commander; Constructed at the Eastern Steamship Company's Works, Millwall . . .* (London: Lloyd Brothers, 1857). Courtesy of the New York Historical Society.
5. Job 41:1–41:34.
6. Henry Wadsworth Longfellow, "The Building of the Ship," in *Evangeline and Other Poems* (New York: Airmont Press, 1965), 80.
7. Quoted in Dugan, *Great Iron Ship*, 4.
8. Kenneth Allott, *Jules Verne* (reprint ed., Port Washington, NY: Kennikat Press, 1970), 8–15, 66.
9. Circular of March 21, 1853, quoted in ibid., 294.
10. Report on Enquiries Relating to the Draught and Form of the Vessel, October 6, 1852, in ibid., 296.
11. Fox, *Transatlantic*, 161.
12. Letter to I. K. Brunel, November 23, 1853, Isambard Kingdom Brunel Papers.
13. Letter to C. Manby, November 22, 1853, Isambard Kingdom Brunel Papers.
14. Extracts from Memoranda, 1852, in Brunel, *Life of Brunel*, 301.
15. *All About the* Great Eastern, 23.
16. Ibid., 25.
17. William H. Miller, *Picture History of the* Queen Mary *and* Queen Elizabeth (Mineola, NY: Dover, 2004), 34.
18. Ibid., 26.
19. Memorandum on Proposed Arrangements for Launch, September 26, 1857, in Brunel, *Life of Brunel*, 349.
20. Letter from J. S. Russell to James R. Napier, October 30, 1857, quoted in Fox, *Transatlantic*, 165.
21. Dugan, *Great Iron Ship*, 4.
22. W. S. Lindsay, *History of Merchant Shipping and Ancient Commerce* (London: Samson Low, 1874), vol. IV, 516–517.
23. Letter to Samuel Baker, November 14, 1857, quoted in Brinnin, *Sway*, 221.
24. Lindsay, *History of Merchant Shipping*, 518.
25. For a complete description of the failed launch, see ibid., 516–543.
26. *Scientific American* (July 7, 1860), 27.
27. Lindsay, *History of Merchant Shipping*, 521.

28. *Times* (London: January 23, 1858).
29. Quoted in Dugan, *Great Iron Ship*, 37.
30. *All About the* Great Eastern, 18.
31. Brunel, *Life of Brunel*, 408.
32. *All About the* Great Eastern, 28.
33. Brinnin, *Sway*, 234.
34. Dugan, *Great Iron Ship*, 46.
35. *New York Times* (New York: June 12, 1860).
36. *Scientific American* (July 7, 1860), 27.
37. Quoted in Dugan, *Great Iron Ship*, 69.
38. "Visitor's Hand Book, or, How to See the *Great Eastern*" (New York: Baker & Godwin, 1860), 1.
39. Ibid., 9.
40. Ibid., 10.
41. "The *Great Eastern* Steamer: A Song" (1860). Courtesy of the New York Historical Society.
42. *New York Times* (July 8, 1860).
43. Dugan, *Great Iron Ship*, 77.
44. Both the *Harper's Weekly* and the *New York Times* quotes appear in ibid., 79–80.
45. A full account of this disastrous voyage from "A Passenger," first printed in the *Cork Advertiser* (October 1861), appears in Brinnin, *Sway*, 225–229.
46. Quoted in Brinnin, *Sway*, 233.
47. Dugan, *Great Iron Ship*, 191.
48. Evans, *Verne*, 56.
49. Jules Verne, *A Floating City* (New York: Scribner's, 1874), 43.
50. Ibid., 4.
51. Ibid., 9.
52. Ibid., 47.
53. Ibid., 5.
54. Ibid., 211.
55. Ibid., 1.
56. Ibid., 2.
57. Ibid., 46.
58. Ibid., 44.
59. Jules Verne, *20,000 Leagues Under the Sea*, in *The Omnibus Jules Verne* (New York: Blue Ribbon, 1939), 273.
60. Verne, *Floating City*, 45–46.
61. Verne, *20,000 Leagues Under the Sea*, in *Omnibus*, 68.
62. Ibid., 165.
63. Evans, *Verne*, 70.
64. Jules Verne, *Around the World in Eighty Days*, in *The Omnibus Jules Verne* (New York: Blue Ribbon, 1939), 424.
65. Nellie Bly, *Around the World in Seventy-Two Days* (New York: Pictorial Weeklies, 1890). Courtesy of the University of Pennsylvania Digital Library.
66. Ibid.

67. Elizabeth Bisland, *In Seven Stages: A Flying Voyage Around the World* (New York: Harper, 1891), 3.
68. See Bly, *Around the World*.
69. Lindsay, *History of Merchant Shipping*, 513.
70. Ibid., 541.
71. Brinnin, *Sway*, 225.
72. William F. Ainsworth, *All Round the World: An Illustrated Record of Voyages, Travels and Adventures in All Parts of the Globe* (London: William Collins, 1869).
73. Quoted in David Newsome, *The Victorian World Picture* (New Brunswick, NJ: Rutgers University Press, 1999), 125.
74. Quoted in Rolt, *Brunel*, 241.
75. Verne, *Floating City*, 164.
76. Mark Twain, "A Curious Pleasure Excursion" (1874) in Charles Neider, ed., *The Complete Humorous Sketches and Tales of Mark Twain* (New York: Doubleday, 1961), 245.

CHAPTER 4

1. References to the clock are ubiquitous in *Titanic* literature, but a more thorough discussion appears in Tom McCluskie, Titanic *and Her Sisters* Olympic *and* Britannic (New York: PRC Publishing, 1998), 54.
2. *S.O.S. Titanic* (1979).
3. Filson Young, *Titanic* (London: Grant Richards, 1912), 34.
4. Brinnin, *Sway*, 311.
5. "The Cunard Turbine-Driven Quadruple Screw Atlantic Liner *Lusitania*," *Engineering* (1907), fig. 197.
6. "*Imperator*: The World's Largest Ship, Embodying Maximum Comfort and Safety for All" pamphlet (New York: Hamburg-American Line, 1913). Courtesy of the New York Historical Society.
7. Images of these staircases appear in William H. Miller, *The Fabulous Interiors of the Great Ocean Liners in Historic Photographs* (New York: Dover, 1985), 9, 16, 17.
8. Jeffrey Richards & John M. MacKenzie, *The Railway Station: A Social History* (Oxford, UK: Oxford University Press, 1986), 3.
9. For examples, see Dawson, *The Liner*, 70.
10. Geoffrey Marcus, *The Maiden Voyage* (New York: Viking Press, 1969), 298.
11. "The Reverend Ernest M. Stires, of St. Thomas Church, Who preached yesterday on the heroic example of the men who went down on the *Titanic*." Broadside, courtesy of the British Museum.
12. Roger Williams McAdam, *The Old Fall River Line* (Boston: Stephen Daye Press, 1955), 118.
13. Daniel Webster to Fletcher Webster, November 27, 1846, in Edward Everett, ed., *The Writings and Speeches of Daniel Webster* (Boston: Little, Brown, 1903), vol. XVI, 497.
14. *New London Morning News* (New London: December 16, 1847).
15. T. J. Greenwood, "A Sermon in Allusion to the Wreck of the Steamer *Atlantic* on Fisher's Island" (New London: Bolles & Williams, 1847). Courtesy of the New York Historical Society.
16. Ibid.

17. Ibid. (emphasis added).

18. Ibid., appendix.

19. See Alexander Crosby Brown, *Women and Children Last: The Loss of the Steamship* Arctic (New York: G. P. Putnam's Sons, 1961).

20. "Full Account of the Loss of the *Arctic*, with Nearly Three Hundred Lives!: Containing the Statements of Captain Luce, the Officers, and Passengers ..." (Boston: Federhen & Co., 1854). Courtesy of the New York Historical Society.

21. Survivor accounts may be found in the *New York Times* (New York: October 14, 1854).

22. George Templeton Strong, *The Diary of George Templeton Strong* (Seattle: University of Washington Press, 1988), vol. II, 198.

23. *New York Herald* (New York: October 22, 1854).

24. *New York Express* (New York: November 14, 1854).

25. Quoted in Brinnin, *Sway*, 191.

26. John Weiss, "A Discourse Occasioned by the Loss of the *Arctic*," October 22, 1854 (New Bedford, MA: Benjamin Lindsey, 1854), 7. Courtesy of the New York Historical Society.

27. Orren Perkins, "Lessons of the Sea: A Sermon on the Loss of the Steamer *Arctic*, October 22, 1854" (Boston: 1854), 4. Courtesy of the New York Historical Society.

28. Phineas Garrett, et al., *One Hundred Choice Selections: A Repository of Readings, Recitations and Plays* (Philadelphia: P. Garrett & Co., 1891), 81.

29. "American Steam Navigation: Speech of Hon. Thomas F. Bayard, of Delaware, for the Collins Steamers ..." (Washington, DC: Buell & Blanchard, 1852). Courtesy of the New York Historical Society.

30. Weiss, "Discourse," 14–15.

31. Perkins, "Lessons," 5.

32. For more sermons on this theme, see Cortland van Rensselaer, "God's Way in the Deep: A Discourse on the Occasion of the Wreck of the *Arctic*, Delivered in the Presbyterian Church, Burlington, N.J., October 15, 1854" (Philadelphia: C. Sherman, 1854). Courtesy of the New York Historical Society.

33. Ibid., 6.

34. Quoted in R. A. Fletcher, *Traveling Palaces: Luxury in Passenger Steamships* (London: Sir Isaac Pitman, 1913), 38.

35. *All About the* Great Eastern, 12.

36. Ibid., 32.

37. Brinnin, *Sway*, 215.

38. Ibid., 195.

39. For an account of the disaster see the *Times* (London: April 10, 1873).

40. *Papers Relating to the Loss of the Steam Ship "Atlantic,"* Parliamentary Papers (1873), vol. LX, 75.

41. Ibid., 269. Nevertheless, the sinking still attracted considerable press attention and even inspired a rather mournful ballad. A. W. Harmon, "Loss of the Steamship *Atlantic*, from Five to Six Hundred Lives Sacrificed" (Portland, ME: 1873). Courtesy of the New York Historical Society.

42. See Peter Morris, ed., *Science for the Nation: Perspectives on the History of the Science Museum* (London: Palgrave Macmillan, 2013).

43. Fox, *Transatlantic*, 323–324.
44. Jules Verne, *Around the World in 80 Days* (reprint ed., New York: Bantam, 2006), 6–8.
45. Arthur C. Wardle, *Steam Conquers the Pacific: A Record of Maritime Achievement, 1840–1940* (London: Hodder & Stoughton, 1940), 123–124.
46. Ibid., 125.
47. *New York Times* (New York: December 23, 1877).
48. "The New Education," *The Atlantic* (February 27, 1869).
49. Melvin Maddocks, *The Great Liners* (Alexandria, VA: Time-Life Books, 1978), 107.
50. Maxtone-Graham, *Only Way to Cross*, 117.
51. Young, *Titanic*, 36.
52. See Lord, *A Night to Remember*.
53. *New York Times* (New York: November 12, 1879); *Illustrated London News* (London: November 29, 1879); see also Guion Line Papers (1879).
54. *The Magnificent New Steamships* City of New York *and* City of Paris: *A Pleasant Journey Over the Sea* (New York: Gillis Bros., 1889), 12.
55. Ibid., 17.
56. Lord, *A Night to Remember*, 21.
57. *Magnificent New Steamships*, 6. See also *Marine Engineer* (London: April 1, 1888).
58. *Magnificent New Steamships*, 7.
59. Lord, *A Night to Remember*, 34.
60. *New York Times* (New York: January 26, 1896).
61. A comparison study of the ship before and after conversion may be found in Miller, *The First Great Ocean Liners*, 6–7.
62. Marcus, *Maiden Voyage*, 292.
63. Diary of Helen Newell, July 1897. Courtesy of the New York Historical Society.
64. *Magnificent New Steamships*, 37–38.
65. Rudyard Kipling, *Selected Works* (New York: Gramercy Books, 1982), 441.
66. *Report on the Loss of the "Titanic" (S.S.)*, Her Majesty's Stationery Office (1912), notes 14414–14425.
67. Marcus, *Maiden Voyage*, 287.
68. Thomas Hardy, "The Convergence of the Twain: Lines on the Loss of the Titanic," *The Fortnightly Review* (June 1912).
69. Reverend William D. Moss, "A Tragedy of Speed: Sermon on the Wreck of the *Titanic*, April 21, 1912" (Washington, DC: Washington Heights Presbyterian Church). Courtesy of the New York Historical Society.
70. Ibid.
71. Quoted in Karl Barth, *The Word in This World: Two Sermons by Karl Barth* (Vancouver: Regent College Publishing, 2007), 213.
72. Ibid.
73. Joseph Conrad, "Some Reflections, Seaman-like and Otherwise, on the Loss of the *Titanic*," *English Review* 11 (May 1912), 304–315.
74. Maxtone-Graham, *Only Way to Cross*, 97.
75. Morgan Robertson, *Futility* (New York: M. F. Mansfield, 1898), 2.
76. The poem first appeared in C. R. L. Fletcher, *A History of England* (New York: Doubleday, 1911), 288. This is an unusual book that appears to be a primer for schoolchil-

dren. Fletcher's text is interspersed with Kipling's poems, including a more conventional hymn to the "Big Steamers": "For the bread that you eat and the biscuits you nibble,/ The sweets that you suck and the joints that you carve,/They are brought to you daily by all us Big Steamers,/And if anyone hinders our coming you'll starve!" (pp. 303–305).

77. John Maxtone-Graham goes so far as to change the title from "Secret" to "Song of the Machines," perhaps to deny that any such a secret existed. Maxtone-Graham, *Only Way to Cross*, 10.

78. Fletcher, *History of England*, 303–305.

79. Maxtone-Graham, *Only Way to Cross*, 94.

CHAPTER 5

1. Liz Stanley, ed., *The Diaries of Hannah Cullwick, Victorian Maidservant* (New Brunswick, NJ: Rutgers University Press, 1984), 79.

2. Ibid., 79–80.

3. Ibid., 137 (emphasis added).

4. Ibid., 130.

5. Ibid., 277.

6. Ibid., 277.

7. See Piers Brenton, *Thomas Cook: 150 Years of Popular Tourism* (London: Secker & Warburg, 1991); Lynne Withey, *Grand Tours and Cook's Tours: A History of Leisure Travel, 1750–1915* (London: Aurum Press, 1998).

8. Clarence Day, *Clarence Day Omnibus* (Garden City, NY: Sun Dial Press, 1945), 151.

9. See Susan Barton, *Working Class Organizations and Popular Tourism, 1840–1970* (Manchester, UK: Manchester University Press, 2011).

10. Twain, *Life on the Mississippi*, 383–385.

11. Ibid., 625.

12. This description of Twain's boyhood home would become a central part of his legend. See Ron Powers, *White Town Drowsing* (New York: Anchor Books, 1986).

13. Twain, *Life on the Mississippi*, 378.

14. Ibid., 381.

15. See, generally, Maxtone-Graham, *Only Way to Cross*.

16. Twain, *Life on the Mississippi*, 542.

17. Dickens, *American Notes*, 143.

18. This luxury was not confined to Mississippi boats. Overnight boats between Fall River, Boston, and New York were similarly grand, though constructed along more traditional lines. See McAdam, *Old Fall River Line*.

19. Brinnin, *Sway*, 239.

20. *Cincinnati Gazette* (Cincinnati: January 9, 1851).

21. Petersen, *Steamboating*, 129.

22. Frances Trollope, *Domestic Manners of the Americans* (London: British Library Historical Print Editions, 2011), 9. For more European reaction to American habits, see the following folios, available in the British Library: Tyrone Power, *Impressions of America* (Philadelphia: 1836); Sarah Mytton Maury, *An Englishwoman in America* (Liverpool: 1848); Basil Hall, *Travels in North America* (Edinburgh: 1829).

23. Dickens, *American Notes*, 144.

24. "Progress of the West," in Timothy Flint, *Western Monthly Review* (Cincinnati: E. H. Flint, 1828), vol. I, 26.

25. Twain, *Life on the Mississippi*, 545.

26. John Habermehl, *Life on the Western Rivers* (Pittsburgh: McNary & Simpson, 1901), 83.

27. Johnson, *River of Dark Dreams*, 77–78.

28. Quoted in ibid., 74.

29. See, generally, Francis Prucha, *The Great Father: The United States Government and the American Indians* (Lincoln: University of Nebraska Press, 1984).

30. Quoted in Todd Pruzan, *The Clumsiest People in Europe* (New York: Bloomsbury, 2005), 172.

31. Johnson, *River of Dark Dreams*, 76.

32. Ibid., 81.

33. Susan P. Casteras, "'Too abhorrent to Englishmen to render a representation of it . . . acceptable': Slavery as Seen by British Artists Traveling in America," in Christine DeVine, *Nineteenth-Century British Travelers in the New World* (Burlington, VT: Ashgate Publishing, 2013), 221.

34. Simon Schama, *Landscape and Memory* (New York: Vintage, 1995), 449.

35. Irvin Anthony, *Paddle Wheels and Pistols* (Philadelphia: Macrae Smith, 1929), 234–241.

36. Herman Melville, *The Confidence-Man: His Masquerade* (reprint ed., New York: Hendricks House, 1954), 57.

37. Anthony, *Paddle Wheels and Pistols*, 259.

38. Melville, *Confidence-Man*, 7.

39. Ibid., 1.

40. Ibid., 8. Anacharsis Cloots was a Prussian-born revolutionary in the French Revolution whose ideas for reform were modeled on an all-inclusive world government.

41. Ibid., 43.

42. Agatha Christie, *Five Complete Hercule Poirot Novels* (New York: Avenel Books, 1980), 140.

43. Melville, *Confidence-Man*, 7.

44. McAdam, *Old Fall River Line*, 18–19.

45. Ibid., 33.

46. Lauchlan MacKinnon, *Atlantic and Transatlantic Sketches, Afloat and Ashore* (London: Colburn & Co., 1852), 56.

47. Ibid., 59.

48. See William Leonhard Taylor, *A Productive Monopoly: The Effect of Railroad Control on New England Coastal Steamship Line, 1870–1916* (Providence, RI: Brown University Press, 1970); George H. Foster & Peter C. Weiglin, *Splendor Sailed the Sound* (San Mateo, CA: Potentials Group, 1989); Edwin L. Dunbaugh, *The New England Steamship Company: Long Island Sound Night Boats in the Twentieth Century* (Gainesville: University Press of Florida, 2005).

49. "Fall River Line Programme" (New York: Union Publishing Company, 1876), vol. I, no. 9. Courtesy of the Hay Library.

50. "Evolution of the Fall River Line" (Boston: Fall River Line, 1894), 5. Courtesy of the New York Historical Society.

51. *Fall River Line Journal* (May 19, 1879). Courtesy of the New York Historical Society.
52. MacKinnon, *Sketches*, 57.
53. McAdam, *Old Fall River Line*, 50–54.
54. "Evolution of the Fall River Line," 5.
55. Quoted in Dunbaugh, *New England Steamship Company*, 103–104.
56. Ibid., 35.
57. See, generally, Roger Williams McAdam, *Priscilla of Fall River* (New York: Stephen Daye Press, 1947); Dunbaugh, *New England Steamship Company*, 41–51.
58. Favell Lee Mortimer, *Far Off Part II: Oceania, Africa, and America Described* (originally published 1854; reprint ed., London: Longman's, 1901), 245.
59. "Evolution of the Fall River Line," 14.
60. Johnson, *River of Dark Dreams*, 74.

CHAPTER 6

1. Trumbull White, William Igleheart, George R. Davis, Potter Palmer, & Thomas B. Bryon, *The World's Columbian Exhibition, Chicago 1893* (Philadelphia: Franklin Square Bible House, 1893), 269. For other depictions of ocean liners at the fair, see *The Cunard Line and the World's Fair, Chicago, 1893* (London: Cunard, 1893).
2. White et al., *The World's Columbian Exhibition*, 270–271.
3. Ibid., 271.
4. Ibid., 271.
5. Young, *Titanic*, 48–49.
6. See Sabine Haenni, *The Immigrant Scene: Ethnic Amusements in New York, 1880–1920* (St. Paul: University of Minnesota Press, 2008).
7. Robert Louis Stevenson, *The Amateur Emigrant* (New York: Scribner's, 1905), 14.
8. *Reports from Committees: Colonization from Ireland*, Parliamentary Papers (1847), vol. VI, 86. Courtesy of the National Archives.
9. Edward Laxton, *The Famine Ships: The Irish Exodus to America* (New York: Holt, 1998), 90; see also Kerby A. Miller, *Emigrants and Exiles: Ireland and the Irish Exodus to North America* (Oxford: Oxford University Press, 1988).
10. Fox, *Transatlantic*, 171–172.
11. *Times* (London: April 19, 1850).
12. *New York Herald* (New York: May 4, 1850).
13. *Philadelphia Evening Bulletin* (Philadelphia: April 9, 1852).
14. *Illustrated London News* (London: May 13, 1854). See also *Times* (London: April 22, 1854).
15. William Inman to William S. Lindsay (December 7, 1874), *William S. Lindsay Papers* file 8/1, National Maritime Museum, Greenwich, London.
16. Charles Chapman, *The Ocean Waves: Travels by Land and Sea* (London: George Berridge & Co., 1875), 57.
17. Ibid., 85.
18. Brinnin, *Sway*, 210.
19. Stevenson, *Emigrant*, 4–5.
20. Ibid., 5.

21. Ibid., 7.

22. This continued well into the 20th century. Holland America Line's *Rotterdam* (1959) was equipped with a trick staircase composed of two interlocking spirals modeled after the original in the Chateau Chambord, which allowed King Louis XV to visit his mistress and depart without being caught on the stairs. Even the *Queen Elizabeth 2*, which remained in service until 2008, had legacies of her original configuration as a two-class ship, including elevators that skipped floors and a particularly irritating staircase that ended abruptly on the upper deck, stranding passengers in a windowless, doorless bulkhead until they were obliged to climb back down to a lower floor and escape.

23. Stevenson, *Emigrant*, 89–90.

24. Ibid., 89.

25. Ibid., 17.

26. Ibid., vi.

27. Ibid., 93.

28. Ibid., 37–38.

29. For analysis of the Dahomey exhibition and its impact on the Victorian imagination, see Mandy Treagus, "The South Seas Exhibit at the Chicago World's Fair, 1893," in Richard Fulton & Peter Hoffenberg, eds., *Oceania and the Victorian Imagination: Where All Things Are Possible* (Burlington, VT: Ashgate Publishing, 2013), 45.

30. Clarence Day, *Life with Father* (New York: Alfred Knopf, 1936), 150.

31. White et al., *The World's Columbian Exhibition*, 583.

32. Day, *Life with Father*, 153.

33. Stevenson, *Emigrant*, 14.

34. A detailed analysis of the plight of Third Class appears in Walter Lord, "What Happened to the Goodwins?" in *The Night Lives On* (New York: Avon, 1998).

35. Henry Morford, *Over-Sea: Or, England, France and Scotland as Seen by a Live American* (New York: Hilton & Co., 1867), 38.

36. William Hardman, *A Trip to America* (London: T. Vickers Wood, 1884), 4.

37. Ibid., 4–5.

38. Quoted in Brinnin, *Sway*, 239.

39. Fletcher, *Traveling Palaces*, 164–165.

40. Chapman, *Ocean Waves*, 70.

41. Diary of Mrs. Finlay MacLaren, October 6, 1880. Courtesy of the New York Historical Society.

42. Hardman, *Trip to America*, 8.

43. Chapman, *Ocean Waves*, 1.

44. Ibid., 17.

45. See *Royal Commission on Unseaworthy Ships' Preliminary Report of the Commissioners, Minutes of the Evidence, and Appendix*, Parliamentary Papers (1873), vol. XXXVI.

46. *New York Times* (New York: February 13, 1898).

47. *Magnificent New Steamships*, 17.

48. Stevenson, *Emigrant*, 4.

49. "The Cunard Turbine-Driven, Quadruple Screw Atlantic Liner 'Lusitania,' Constructed and Engined by Messrs. John Brown and Co. Ltd., Sheffield and Clydebank," *Engineering: An Illustrated Weekly Journal* (June 1907), 53.

50. Ibid.
51. *Magnificent New Steamships*, 37.
52. W. Somerset Maugham, *Collected Short Stories* (New York: Penguin Books, 1963), vol. IV, 90–91.
53. Fletcher, *Traveling Palaces*, 254.
54. Ibid., 257.
55. These "wondrous" devices were described in *Scientific American* (February 8, 1896), 84–85; see also Flayhart, *The American Line*, 201.
56. Fletcher, *Traveling Palaces*, 246.
57. Stevenson, *Emigrant*, 14.
58. Ibid., 19.
59. Ibid., 25.

CHAPTER 7

1. Mark Twain to C. M. Crane, October 7, 1868. Courtesy of the Shapell Manuscript Foundation.
2. Albert Bigelow Paine, ed., *Mark Twain's Speeches* (New York: Harper & Bros., 1923), 21–30.
3. Brinnin, *Sway*, 443.
4. See Cushing Strout, *The American Image of the Old World* (New York: Harper & Row, 1963).
5. James Buzard, *The Beaten Track: European Tourism, Literature, and the Ways to "Culture," 1800–1918* (Oxford, UK: Oxford University Press, 1993), 4–15.
6. Babcock, *Spanning the Atlantic*, 167.
7. Judith Adler, "Origins of Sightseeing," *Annals of Tourism Research* 16 (1989), 7–29.
8. *Hamburg–American Gazette* (June 25, 1889). Venice's canals were a perennial source of humor for tourists. Many years later, on his first visit, Robert Benchley telegraphed his friend David Niven: "STREETS FULL OF WATER. PLEASE ADVISE."
9. Paine, *Mark Twain's Speeches*, 30.
10. Herman Melville, "Traveling: A New Lecture," reprint in John Howard Birss, *New England Quarterly* 7 (December 1934), 725–728.
11. See Jeffrey Alan Melton, *Mark Twain, Travel Books, and Tourism: The Tide of a Great Popular Movement* (Tuscaloosa: University of Alabama Press, 2002).
12. Paine, *Mark Twain's Speeches*, 29.
13. Hardman, *Trip to America*, 1.
14. William Makepeace Thackeray, *Notes of a Journey from Cornhill to Grand Cairo* (originally published 1844; reprint ed., Philadelphia: Pennsylvania State University Electronic Classics Series Publication, 2013), 5.
15. W. Outram Tristram, *Coaching Days and Coaching Ways* (New York: Macmillan, 1893), 373.
16. Helga Quadflieg, "Approved Civilities and the Fruits of Peregrination: Elizabethan and Jacobean Travellers and the Making of Englishness," in Berghoff et al., *The Making of Modern Tourism*, 21–46.
17. *General Information for Passengers*, 1.
18. Tristram, *Coaching Days*, 372.

19. See Chloe Chard, *Pleasure and Guilt on the Grand Tour: Travel Writing and Imaginative Geography, 1600–1830* (Manchester, UK: Manchester University Press, 1999).

20. William W. Stowe, *Going Abroad: European Travel in Nineteenth Century American Culture* (Princeton, NJ: Princeton University Press, 1994), 4. Besides those listed, one might also include lesser known authors such as William Cullen Bryant, *Letters of a Traveller* (1850); James Jackson Jarves, *Parisian Sights and French Principles, Seen Through American Spectacles* (1852); Phillips Brooks, *Letters of Travel* (1894); Charles Dudley Warner, *Saunterings* (1872); and Henry Wikoff, *The Reminiscences of an Idler* (1880).

21. Isabella Lucy Bird, *The Englishwoman in America* (originally published 1856; reprint ed., Madison: University of Wisconsin, 1966), 11.

22. Harriet Beecher Stowe, *Sunny Memories of Foreign Lands* (Boston: Phillips Samson, 1854), vol. I, 1.

23. Ibid., 3.

24. Horace Greeley, *Glances at Europe* (New York: Dewitt and Davenport, 1851); Erastus Benedict, *A Run Through Europe* (New York: D. Appleton, 1880); Francis C. Sessions, *On the Wing Through Europe* (New York: Welch, Fracker, 1889); Edward Everett Hale, *Ninety Days' Worth of Europe* (New York: Walker, Wise, 1860).

25. Greeley, *Glances*, 10.

26. Sessions, *On the Wing*, 1–3.

27. Mark Twain, "Some Rambling Notes of an Idle Excursion," *The Atlantic* (December 1877).

28. Quoted in Brinnin, *Sway*, 272. See also Douglas Lobley, *The Cunarders* (London: Peter Barker, 1969).

29. Mark Twain, "About All Kinds of Ships," in Neider, *Sketches*, 543.

30. Julian Street, *Ship-Bored* (New York: Dodd Mead, 1914), 36.

31. John William De Forest, *Oriental Acquaintance: Or, Letters from Syria* (New York: Harper & Bros., 1856), 77.

32. Bird, *Englishwoman in America*, 8–9.

33. See Ahmed Metwalli, "Americans Abroad: The Popular Art of Travel Writing in the Nineteenth Century," in Steven E. Kagle, ed., *America: Exploration and Travel* (Bowling Green, OH: Bowling Green University Popular Press, 1979).

34. Not to be confused with the 20th-century American actor (1914–1958), who was in fact his great-great-grandson.

35. "The Mystery Solved!!, or Narrative of Dr. M. Lorner, One of the Passengers of the Steam Ship *President*, Which Vessel Left New York, Bound for Liverpool, March 11, 1841, Since Which Time, Until Recently, Nothing Has Been Heard Respecting Her Fate" (New York: Knapp & Barclay, 1845).

36. For other examples of 19th-century Anglo-American travel, see Walter Ernest Allen, *Transatlantic Crossing: American Visitors to Britain and British Visitors to America in the Nineteenth Century* (London: Heinemann, 1971).

37. Dickens, *American Notes*, 2.

38. Ibid., 6.

39. Ibid., 2.

40. Ibid., 1.

41. Ibid., 12.

42. Ibid., 16.

43. John McBratney, "The Failure of Dickens's Transatlantic Dream in *American Notes*," in DeVine, *Nineteenth-Century British Travelers*, 69. See also Nathalie Vanfasse, "Intertextuality in Charles Dickens's *American Notes* and Basil Hall's *Travels in North America*," in DeVine, *Nineteenth-Century British Travelers*, 169.

44. Brinnin, *Sway*, 245.

45. E. H. Hoblyn, *Cunard Magazine* (London: July 1919).

46. Thackeray, *Notes of a Journey*, 5.

47. Ibid., 81.

48. Ibid., 11.

49. Christopher Deakes & Tom Stanley, *A Century of Sea Travel: Personal Accounts from the Steamship Era* (London: Seaforth, 2010), 42.

50. Thackeray, *Notes of a Journey*, 130.

51. Ibid., 38.

52. Ibid., 41.

53. Ibid., 74.

54. Ibid., 123.

55. Ibid., 123.

56. Ibid., 25.

57. Deakes & Stanley, *A Century of Sea Travel*, 15.

58. Chloe Chard, "From the Sublime to the Ridiculous: the Anxieties of Sightseeing," in Berghoff et al., *The Making of Modern Tourism*, 60.

59. Deakes & Stanley, *A Century of Sea Travel*, 122.

60. See Robert Cooper, *Around the World with Mark Twain* (New York: Arcade Publishing, 2002).

61. Mark Twain, "About All Kinds of Ships" (1893), in Neider, *Sketches*, 557.

62. See, generally, Gavan Daws, *Shoal of Time: A History of the Hawaiian Islands* (New York: Macmillan, 1968).

63. Quoted in Ward, Duncan, & Burns, *Twain*, 52.

64. Brinnin, *Sway*, 491. For a complete account of the *North Star*'s voyage, see John Overton Choules, *The Cruise of the North Star: To England, Russia . . .* (Boston: Gould & Lincoln, 1854).

65. Mark Twain, *The Innocents Abroad* (originally published 1869; republished New York: Harper, 1911), 1–2.

66. Brinnin, *Sway*, 491.

67. Jeffrey Steinbrink, "Why the Innocents Went Abroad: Mark Twain and American Tourism in the Late Nineteenth Century," *American Literary Realism* 16 (1983), 278–286.

68. Ward, Duncan, & Burns, *Twain*, 61.

69. Twain, *Innocents*, 103.

70. Ibid., 238.

71. Mark Twain, "Back from Yurrup" (1869), in Neider, *Sketches*, 105.

72. Ibid., 105.

73. Ibid., 240.

74. Ibid., 91–92.

75. Ibid., 223.

76. Mark Twain, "Guying the Guides," in Neider, *Sketches*, 109.

77. For a study of Twain as tourist, see Ann M. Ryan & Joseph B. McCullough, eds., *Cosmopolitan Twain* (Columbia: University of Missouri Press, 2008).

78. Quoted in Foster Rhea Dulles, *Americans Abroad: Two Centuries of European Travel* (Ann Arbor: University of Michigan Press, 1964), 111.

79. Maxtone-Graham, *Liners to the Sun*, 98.

80. Charles Dudley Warner, ed., *The Writings of Mark Twain: Innocents Abroad* (New York: G. Wells, 1922), 402.

81. Twain, *Innocents*, 260.

82. See Dugan, *Great Iron Ship*.

83. Twain, *Innocents*, 44.

84. Young, *Titanic*, 43.

85. Thackeray, *Notes of a Journey*, 17.

86. Twain, *Innocents*, 360.

87. Quoted in Brinnin, *Sway*, 500.

88. Forrest G. Robinson, "Patterns of Consciousness in *The Innocents Abroad*," *American Literature* 58 (1986), 46–63. See also Robert Regan, "The Reprobate Elect in *The Innocents Abroad*," *American Literature* 54 (1982), 240–257.

CHAPTER 8

1. *Appleton's European Guide Book* (New York: D. Appleton & Co., 1883), front matter.

2. Stowe, *Going Abroad*, 28.

3. For more examples, see John Shelburne, *The Tourist's Guide* (Philadelphia: G. B. Zieber, 1847); Joachim Siddons, *Norton's Hand Book to Europe* (New York: C. B. Norton, 1860); *The Satchel Guide for the Vacation Tourist in Europe* (New York: Hurd and Houghton, 1872).

4. "Going Abroad," *Putnam's Magazine* I (1868), 530–538.

5. Judith Adler, "Travel as Performed Art," *American Journal of Sociology* 94 (1989), 1366–1391.

6. Stowe, *Going Abroad*, 18–19. See also Nelson Graburn, "Tourism: The Sacred Journey," in Valerie Smith, ed., *Hosts and Guests: The Anthropology of Tourism* (Philadelphia: University of Pennsylvania Press, 1989).

7. *Appleton's Guide*, preface and appendix.

8. Quoted in Dulles, *Americans Abroad*, 43.

9. See Dean MacCannell, *The Tourist: A New Theory of the Leisure Class* (New York: Schocken Books, 1976).

10. *General Information for Passengers*, 12.

11. Maxtone-Graham, *Only Way to Cross*, 190.

12. Kate Reid Ledoux, *Ocean Notes and Foreign Travel for Ladies* (New York: Cook & Jenkins, 1878), 5.

13. Hardman, *Trip to America*, 2.

14. *The Red Star Line, Belgian Royal and U.S. Mail Steamships: Facts for Travelers* (New York: Peter Wright & Sons, 1883). Courtesy of the Independence Seaport Museum, Philadelphia.

15. Ibid.

16. See Lynne Withey, *Grand Tour and Cook's Tours: A History of Leisure Travel, 1750–1915* (New York: William Morrow, 1997).

17. *The New Twin Screw Steamships* City of New York *and* City of Paris (New York: Gilliss Brothers, 1889), 25.

18. See Brian Yothers, *The Romance of the Holy Land in American Travel Writing, 1790–1876* (Aldershot, UK: Ashgate Publishing, 2007).

19. William M. Thomson, *The Land and the Book, or Biblical Illustrations Drawn from the Scenes, Customs and Manners of the Holy Land* (New York: Harper & Bros., 1852), 1.

20. Quoted in Yothers, *Holy Land*, 109.

21. See Withey, *Grand Tours and Cook's Tours*.

22. *North German Lloyd Bulletin*, XXV (April 1908), 17.

23. Ibid., 10.

24. Ibid., 16.

25. Ibid., appendix.

26. Stevenson, *Emigrant*, 104.

27. See Albion, *Rise of New York Port*.

28. Mortimer, *Far Off Part II*, 248.

29. *San Francisco Alta California* (San Francisco: April 5, 1867).

30. Ibid.

31. Day, *Clarence Day Omnibus*, 52.

32. Ibid., 220–221.

33. Ibid., 221.

34. Marcus, *Maiden Voyage*, 118.

35. See Lord, *The Night Lives On*.

36. Day, *Clarence Day Omnibus*, 238–239.

37. Ibid., 122.

38. For example, see Society of Voyages Round the World, *Round the World in Three Hundred and Twenty Days: Completion of Superior Education* (London: Tubner & Co., 1876). Courtesy of the New York Historical Society.

39. See Christopher Mulvey, *Transatlantic Manners: Social Patterns in Nineteenth-Century Anglo-American Travel Literature* (Cambridge, UK: Cambridge University Press, 1983).

40. Elizabeth Wormeley Latimer, *Salvage* (Boston: Roberts Brothers, 1880), 12.

41. Philip Kelland, *Transatlantic Sketches* (Edinburgh: Adam and Charles Black, 1868), 5.

42. Ibid., 340.

43. Marian Lawrence Peabody, *To Be Young Was Very Heaven* (Boston: Houghton Mifflin, 1967), 38.

44. Diary of Mrs. Finlay MacLaren, July 5, 1880. Courtesy of the New York Historical Society.

45. Ibid., October 5, 1880.

46. Ibid., February 18, 1882.

47. David McCullough, *Mornings on Horseback* (New York: Simon & Schuster, 1981), 23.

48. Mortimer, *Far Off Part II*, quoted in Pruzan, *Clumsiest People*, 169.

49. Theodore Roosevelt, *Theodore Roosevelt's Diaries of Boyhood and Youth* (New York: Scribner's, 1928), 156.

50. Ibid., 156.

51. McCullough, *Mornings on Horseback*, 88.
52. Corinne Roosevelt Robinson, *My Brother Theodore Roosevelt* (New York: Scribner's, 1921), 45.
53. See Dennis Porter, *Haunted Journeys: Desire and Transgression in European Travel Writing* (Princeton, NJ: Princeton University Press, 1991).
54. Stowe, *Going Abroad*, 8.
55. William Manchester, *The Arms of Krupp: The Rise and Fall of the Industrial Dynasty That Armed Germany at War* (Boston: Back Bay Books, 2003), 453.
56. Thackeray, *Notes of a Journey*, 15.
57. "On the Way to India," *The Graphic* (November 27, 1875), 524.
58. See Bly, *Around the World*.
59. De Forest, *Oriental Acquaintance*, 60.
60. Maxtone-Graham, *Liners to the Sun*, 118.
61. Deakes & Stanley, *A Century of Sea Travel*, 138.
62. Brinnin, *Sway*, 500.
63. For a contemporary account of this transformation, see John H. Gould, "Ocean Passenger Travel," in French Ensor Chadwick et al., *Ocean Steamships: A Popular Account of Their Construction, Development, Management and Appliances* (New York: Scribner's, 1891).
64. Brinnin, *Sway*, 500.
65. Daniel Shealy, ed., *Little Women Abroad: The Alcott Sisters' Letters from Europe, 1870–1871* (Athens: University of Georgia Press, 2008), 7.
66. *Frank Leslie's Illustrated Newspaper* (New York: June 16, 1883).
67. Mary Crompton, *Journal of a Honeymoon Voyage in SS Great Britain*. Courtesy of the Huntington Library.
68. Ibid.
69. Maxtone-Graham, *Liners to the Sun*, 370.
70. Crompton, *Journal of a Honeymoon Voyage*.
71. Diary of an unidentified young man, July 3–November 11, 1875. Courtesy of the New York Historical Society.
72. Diary of Mrs. Finlay MacLaren, July 5, 1880. Courtesy of the New York Historical Society.
73. Diary of Elizabeth Van Der Peyser, 1874. Courtesy of the New York Historical Society.
74. Ibid.
75. Hardman, *Trip to America*, 5.
76. Kelland, *Transatlantic*, 11.
77. Log of the Steamship *Atlantic*, June 21, 1856. Courtesy of the Huntington Library.
78. Washington Irving, *The Sketch-Book of Geoffrey Crayon* (New York: G. P. Putnam's Sons, 1884), 19.
79. Inman Steamship Company, *The New Inman Twin Screw Steamships* (New York: Inman Steamship, 1889), 32.
80. Pruzan, *Clumsiest People*, 10.
81. Favell Lee Mortimer, *Near Home, or, The Countries of Europe Described* (London: Hatchet & Co, 1866), 190.
82. Deakes & Stanley, *A Century of Sea Travel*, 137.

83. Mortimer, *Near Home,* 394.
84. Ibid., 399.
85. Quoted in Pruzan, *Clumsiest People,* 141.
86. Ibid., 9.
87. Mortimer, *Near Home,* 239.
88. Brinnin, *Sway,* 286.
89. Dulles, *Americans Abroad,* 113.
90. Prickett, "Romantic Versions," in Berghoff et al., The Making of Modern Tourism, 69–70.
91. Thackeray, *Notes of a Journey,* 53.

CHAPTER 9

1. Radhakumud Mookerji, *Indian Shipping: A History of the Sea-Borne Trade and Maritime Activity of the Indians from the Earliest Times* (Bombay: Longmans, Green & Co., 1912), 253.
2. Ibid.
3. See David Cannadine, *Ornamentalism: How the British Saw Their Empire* (Oxford, UK: Oxford University Press, 2001).
4. See David Lambert & Alan Lester, *Colonial Lives Across the British Empire: Imperial Careering in the Long Nineteenth Century* (Cambridge, UK: Cambridge University Press, 2006).
5. Marsden & Smith, *Engineering Empires,* 128.
6. Deakes & Stanley, *A Century of Sea Travel,* 52.
7. Headrick, *Power over Peoples,* 17.
8. See James Belich, *Replenishing the Earth: The Settler Revolution and the Rise of the Anglo-World, 1783–1939* (Oxford, UK: Oxford University Press, 2006). For difficulties in transatlantic political communication, see Jack P. Greene, *Peripheries and Center: Constitutional Development in the Extended Polities of the British Empire and the United States, 1607–1788* (New York: W. W. Norton, 1990).
9. Harcourt, *Flagships of Imperialism,* 41.
10. Headrick, *Power over Peoples,* 186–187.
11. But not forgotten. See *Select Committee on Steam Navigation to India,* Parliamentary Papers 14, 478 (1834); *Select Committee on the Petition of the East India Company,* Parliamentary Papers 7, 343 (1840); *Correspondence Regarding the Establishment of Steam Communication with India,* Parliamentary Papers 53, 693 (1850).
12. Quoted in Headrick, *Power over Peoples,* 189.
13. *Steam Communication with India,* Parliamentary Papers 6, 539 (1837).
14. Headrick, *Power over Peoples,* 189.
15. See, generally, John Nicholson, *Arthur Anderson: A Founder of the P&O Company* (Paisley, Scotland: A. Gardner, 1914).
16. For a description of P&O's early years, see Harcourt, *Flagships of Imperialism.*
17. Ian Marshall, *Passage East* (New York: Howell Press, 1997), 82–84.
18. Philip Dawson & Bruce Peter, *P&O at 175: A World of Ships and Shipping Since 1837* (Ramsay, UK: Lily Publications, 2012), 18.
19. "The *Bentinck*," *Illustrated London News* (August 12, 1843).

20. "A Voyage to China," *Illustrated London News* (November 9, 1872).
21. Dawson & Peter, *P&O at 175*, 24.
22. Deakes & Stanley, *A Century of Sea Travel*, 59.
23. "On the Way to India."
24. For further information on P&O's imperial reach to Chinese ports, see Kwang-Ching Liu, *Anglo-American Steamship Rivalry in China, 1862–1874* (Cambridge, MA: Harvard University Press, 1962).
25. See Steven Rabson & Kevin O'Donoghue, *P&O: A Fleet History* (Kendal, UK: World Ship Society, 1988).
26. Dawson & Peter, *P&O at 175*, 23. See also James Wilson, *Facts Connected with the Origin and Progress of Steam Communication Between India and England* (London: W. S. Johnson, 1850).
27. Dawson & Peter, *P&O at 175*, 17.
28. "Peninsular and Oriental Company's Steam Ship *Mooltan*," *Illustrated London News* (August 3, 1861).
29. Marshall, *Passage East*, 89.
30. Headrick, *Tentacles of Progress*, 41. For more information on individual lines see Andrew Porter, *Victorian Shipping, Business, and Imperial Policy: Donald Currie, the Castle Line, and Southern Africa* (Woodbridge, NY: Boydell Press, 1986); Daniel Thorner, *Investment in Empire: British Railways and Steam Shipping Enterprise in India. 1825–1849* (Philadelphia: University of Pennsylvania Press, 1950).
31. Headrick, *Tentacles of Progress*, 32.
32. Ibid., 43
33. W. J. Loftie, *Orient–Pacific Line Guide: Chapters for Travelers by Sea and by Land, Edited by the Managers of the Line* (London: S. Low, Marston & Co., 1888), 316 (emphasis added). Courtesy of the Huntington Library.
34. See, for example, Charles Hardinge, *My Indian Years, 1910–1916* (London: John Murray, 1948); Harriot Georgina Blackwood, *Our Viceregal Life in India: Selections from My Journal, 1884–1888* (London: John Murray, 1890).
35. David Gilmour, *The Ruling Caste: Imperial Lives in the Victorian Raj* (London: John Murray, 2005), 71.
36. For examples in fiction, see Somerset Maugham, "The Lion's Skin," in *Collected Short Stories* (London: Heinemann, 1955), vol. I; Agatha Christie, *A Caribbean Mystery* (republished New York: William Morrow, 2011).
37. Maugham, "The Lion's Skin," 15.
38. Ibid., 11.
39. Loftie, *Orient–Pacific Line Guide*, 308.
40. Marshall, *Passage East*, 93.
41. Quoted in Marshall, *Passage East*, 93. For more sartorial advice to passengers, see *The P&O Pocket Guide Book* (London: Adam and Charles Black, 1908).
42. Anne C. Wilson, *Hints for the First Years of Residence in India* (London: Clarendon Press, 1904), 5.
43. For a detailed depiction, see Sir Julian Corbett Letterbooks (October 10, 1877–January 7, 1878), National Maritime Museum, Greenwich, London, CBT/18/3/3–4.
44. Quoted in Marshall, *Passage East*, 87.

45. Roald Dahl, *Going Solo* (New York: Farrar, Straus & Giroux, 1986), 5.
46. Gilmour, *Ruling Caste*, 69.
47. Dahl, *Going Solo*, 8.
48. Ibid., 8.
49. Ibid., 8.
50. Loftie, *Orient–Pacific Line Guide*, 256.
51. Maxtone-Graham, *Liners to the Sun*, 197.
52. One such device can still be viewed at Oak Alley, Louisiana.
53. Loftie, *Orient–Pacific Line Guide*, 308.
54. *P&O Valetta, Ship's Newspaper* (March 1887), National Maritime Museum, Greenwich, London, MSS/75/005.
55. Gilmour, *Ruling Caste*, 72.
56. Diary of Samuel Smiles, February 1869, published in *A Boy's Voyage Around the World* (London: John Murray, 1905), 13.
57. *P&O Pocket Guide Book*, 21.
58. Quoted in Marshall, *Passage East*, 103.
59. Ibid., 103.
60. Loftie, *Orient–Pacific Line Guide*, 24.
61. Deakes & Stanley, *A Century of Sea Travel*, 34.
62. For a description, see journals of T. F. Miller, "Voyage to Australia, 1869–70, in the *Walmar Castle*..." National Maritime Museum, Greenwich, London, TRN/61.
63. W. W. Lloyd, *P&O Pencillings* (London: Day & Co., 1891).
64. See Bly, *Around the World*.
65. "On the Way to India."
66. W. Somerset Maugham, "The Outstation," in *Collected Short Stories* (London: Heinemann, 1955), vol. IV, 340.
67. Marshall, *Passage East*, 78–79.
68. Rosa Carnegie-Williams, *A Year in the Andes; or, A Lady's Adventures in Bogota* (London: Literary Society, 1888), 8.
69. Deakes & Stanley, *A Century of Sea Travel*, 61.
70. Loftie, *Orient–Pacific Line Guide*.
71. See Bly, *Around the World*.
72. Deakes & Stanley, *A Century of Sea Travel*, 49.
73. Diary of Samuel Smiles, 216.
74. Deakes & Stanley, *A Century of Sea Travel*, 28.
75. Marshall, *Passage East*, 102.
76. Robinson-Tomsett, *Women, Travel and Identity*, 138.
77. Deakes & Stanley, *A Century of Sea Travel*, 79.
78. See, generally, Brian MacDonald, ed., *Dearest Mother: The Letters of F. R. Kendall* (London: Lloyds of London Press, 1988). Kendall was an officer of the P&O line for many years and kept copious records of his experiences therein and on the ships.
79. Quoted in Robinson-Tomsett, *Women, Travel and Identity*, 134.
80. Deakes & Stanley, *A Century of Sea Travel*, 125.
81. Ibid., 124.
82. Ibid., 114.

83. See Peter Padfield, *Beneath the House Flag of the P&O* (London: Hutchinson Press, 1981).
84. Marshall, *Passage East*, 68.
85. Deakes & Stanley, *A Century of Sea Travel*, 132.
86. See journals of Joseph Fletcher Green (1871–1881), National Maritime Museum, Greenwich, London, MSS/77/126.
87. Marshall, *Passage East*, 111.
88. *P&O Pocket Guide Book*, front matter.
89. Blackwood, *Our Viceregal Life in India*, 4.
90. Gilmour, *Ruling Caste*, 74.
91. See Lambert & Lester, *Colonial Lives Across the British Empire*.
92. Rudyard Kipling, *The Collected Poems of Rudyard Kipling* (Hertfordshire, UK: Wordsworth Editions, 1994), 169.
93. See, generally, Harcourt, *Flagships of Imperialism*.

CHAPTER 10

1. *Rand McNally Handbook of the World's Columbian Exhibition*, 33.
2. *North German Lloyd Bulletin* (April 1908), 16. Courtesy of the New York Historical Society.
3. For images, see Les Streater, Berengaria, *Cunard's "Happy Ship"* (Charleston, SC: Tempus Publishing, 2001), 17; and John Malcolm Brinnin, *Beau Voyage: Life Aboard the Last Great Ships* (New York: Dorset Press, 1981), 160.
4. See Arnold Kludas & Herbert Bischoff, *Die Schiffe der Hamburg–Amerika Linie, 1847–1906* (Berlin: Koehler, 1979); Arnold Kludas, *Die Schiffe der Hamburg–Afrika–Linien, 1880–1945* (Hamburg: Stalling, 1975).
5. Theophile Gautier, quoted in Jean Dethier, *All Stations: A Journey Through 150 Years of Railway History* (London: Science Museum Press, 1981), 6.
6. P. D. Smith, *City: A Guidebook for the Urban Age* (London: Bloomsbury, 2012), 20.
7. For further analysis of this work, see Mark Bills & Vivien Knight, eds., *William Powell Frith: Painting in the Victorian Age* (New Haven, CT: Yale University Press, 2007).
8. Richards & MacKenzie, *The Railway Station*, 3.
9. See Kurt Schlichting, *Grand Central Terminal: Railroads, Engineering and Architecture in New York City* (Baltimore: Johns Hopkins University Press, 2001).
10. Richards & MacKenzie, *The Railway Station*, 68–69.
11. Ibid., 92.
12. Ibid., 70–71. See also Tristram Hunt, *Cities of Empire: The British Colonies and the Creation of the Urban World* (New York: Metropolitan Books, 2014).
13. See, for example, images of the *Fürst Bismarck*, available from the Museum of the City of New York (hereafter MCNY), 93/1/1/12535–12544.
14. *Ocean: Magazine of Travel*, III, 2 (September 1889), 41.
15. MCNY 93/1/1/12737.
16. MCNY 93/1/1/12556.
17. MCNY 93/1/1/12617.
18. "The *Kronprinz Wilhelm* of the North German Lloyd," *Scientific American Supplement*, LIII, 1367, 2901–2902.

19. Brinnin, *Beau Voyage*, 164–165. Bizarrely, Cunard chose almost the same position and pose for their bust of Queen Elizabeth II, which dominated the Queen's Room on board the QE2 from 1969 to 2008.

20. Image courtesy of the New York Public Library, Rare Books Division, Illustrated Collection 273614.

21. For images see *Berliner Cewerbe-Ausstelung*, "Norddeutscher Lloyd, Bremen" (1896). Courtesy of the Gjenvick-Gjønvik Archives.

22. MCNY 93/1/1/12458.

23. MCNY 93/1/1/12454.

24. MCNY 93/1/1/18180; MCNY 93/1/1/13019.

25. William H. Miller, *Picture History of the Italian Line* (Mineola, NY: Dover, 1999), 51.

26. Miller, *Fabulous Interiors*, 10–11.

27. See Flayhart, *The American Line*, 300–312.

28. Brinnin, *Beau Voyage*, 168–169.

29. For examples, see Rabson & O'Donoghue, *P&O: A Fleet History*.

30. See Ross Watton, *The Cunard Liner* Queen Mary: *Anatomy of a Ship* (Annapolis, MD: Naval Institute Press, 1989).

31. See, generally, Peter Newall, *Cunard Line: A Fleet History* (New York: Ships in Focus, 2012).

32. A curious story was told by maritime historian Frank Braynard—that the original name for the *Queen Mary* of 1936 was originally intended to be *Victoria*. Yet when Cunard Line's managing director intimated to King George V that they wished to name the ship after "England's greatest queen," the king purportedly smiled and said, "My wife will be delighted." It is hard to imagine English directors committing a rhubarb of such magnitude, and indeed company records cast some doubt on the tale, yet Braynard claims to have spoken with descendants of the original directors who confirmed the account. Frank O. Braynard & William H. Miller Jr., *Picture History of the Cunard Line, 1840–1990* (New York: Dover, 1991), 72.

33. See Rabson & O'Donoghue, *P&O: A Fleet History*.

34. For a fleet list, see A. G. Course & C. H. Williams, *Ships of the P and O* (London: Adlard Coles, 1954).

35. Dawson & Peter, *P&O at 175*, 33–40.

36. Miller, *The First Great Ocean Liners*, 2–11.

37. See, generally, Arnold Kludas, *Die Seeschiffe des Norddeutscher Lloyd, 1857–1919* (Berlin: Koehler, 1997).

38. One of the few English language histories of the company, which provides an excellent overview of the ships and their careers, is Otto Seiler, *Bridge Across the Atlantic: the Story of Hapag–Lloyd's North Atlantic Service* (Herford: Verlag Mittler, 1991); see also Seiler's *Hapag-Lloyd: One Hundred Years of Liner Shipping: A Century of Far East Service* (Hamburg: Hapag–Lloyd, 1986).

39. Mark Twain, "About All Kinds of Ships," in *The Writings of Mark Twain* (New York: Harper & Bros., 1918), vol. XXII, 288.

40. MCNY X2011/34/1533.

41. Images courtesy of the Cunard Line Archives, University of Liverpool.

42. For examples see Julia Wigg, *Bon Voyage!: Travel Posters of the Edwardian Era* (London: H. M. Stationery Office, 1996).

43. Image courtesy of the P&O Archives at the National Maritime Museum, Greenwich, London.
44. Ibid.
45. Reprinted in Gabrielle Cadringher, *Ocean Liner Posters* (New York: ACC Distribution, 2011), 12.
46. See Ruth E. Iskin, *The Poster: Art, Advertising, Design, and Collecting, 1860s–1900s* (Dartmouth, NH: University Press of New England, 2014).
47. "American Steam Navigation: Speech of Hon. Thomas F. Bayard, of Delaware, for the Collins Steamers . . ." (Washington, DC: Buell & Blanchard, 1852). Courtesy of the New York Historical Society.
48. Flayhart, *The American Line*, 275.
49. Lamar Cecil, Albert *Ballin: Business and Politics in Imperial Germany, 1888–1918* (Princeton, NJ: Princeton University Press, 1967), 156.
50. Ibid., 196.
51. Ibid., 186–198.
52. See, generally, David Ramsay, *Lusitania: Saga and Myth* (New York: W. W. Norton, 2001).
53. Maddocks, *The Great Liners*, 70.
54. Ibid., 70.
55. Brinnin, *Sway*, 451.

CHAPTER 11

1. See, generally, Robert Rotberg & Miles Shore, *The Founder: Cecil Rhodes and the Pursuit of Power* (Oxford, UK: Oxford University Press, 1988).
2. Ibid., 198.
3. Edmund Morris, *Theodore Rex* (New York: Modern Library, 2001), 231.
4. "Civilization (Bongo, Bongo, Bongo)," sung by Danny Kaye and the Andrews Sisters, 1947.
5. Quoted in Lewis Hanke, *Bartolomé de las Casas: An Interpretation of His Life and Writings* (New York: Martinus Nijhoff, 1951), 33.
6. Petersen, *Steamboating*, 100.
7. *American State Papers, Military Affairs*, 25th Congress (1832), vol. II, 68–69.
8. Petersen, *Steamboating*, 201–203.
9. *Reflector* (Huron: August 15, 1837).
10. *Republican Compiler* (Gettysburg: August 1, 1827).
11. Johnson, *River of Dark Dreams*, 6.
12. Headrick, *The Tools of Empire*, 17–41.
13. Headrick, *Power over Peoples*, 184.
14. Ibid., 211.
15. Macgregor Laird & R. A. K. Oldfield, *Narrative of an Expedition into the Interior of Africa, by the River Niger, in the Steam Vessels* Quorra *and* Alburkah, *in 1832, 1833, and 1834* (London: Richard Bentley, 1837), vol. II, 397–398.
16. Kotar & Gessler, *Steamboat Era*, 13.
17. Joseph Conrad, *Heart of Darkness* (reprint ed., New York: Alfred Knopf, 1993), 61.
18. Ibid., 41.

19. Verne, *Around the World*, 66.
20. Verne, *20,000 Leagues*, 162.
21. Jules Verne, *The Steam House* (New York: Scribner's, 1881), 31.
22. Ibid., 28.
23. Ibid., 67.
24. Ibid., 68.
25. Ibid., 72.
26. Verne, *20,000 Leagues Under the Sea*, in *Omnibus*, 165.
27. Verne, *Steam House*, 4.
28. See Jules Verne, *Propeller Island* (New York: W. L. Allison, 1897).
29. Justin Kaplan, *Mr. Clemens and Mark Twain* (New York: Simon & Schuster, 1966), 179.
30. For a complete account of the takeover, see Helena Allen, *The Betrayal of Liliuokalani: Last Queen of Hawaii 1838–1917* (New York: Mutual Publishing, 1991).
31. Mark Twain, *Following the Equator* (1895), in Neider, *Complete Travel Books*, 703.
32. Ibid.
33. Ibid., 720.
34. Ibid., 698.
35. Ibid., 727.
36. Ibid., 864.
37. Ibid., 1041.
38. C. J. Harris, *Mailships of the Union Castle Line* (London: Fernwood Press, 1996), 2–30.
39. William H. Miller, *Picture History of British Ocean Liners, 1900 to the Present* (Mineola, NY: Dover Maritime Books, 2001), 10.
40. Twain, *Equator*, in Neider, *Travel Books*, 859.
41. T. C. McLuhan, *Dream Tracks: The Railroad and the American Indian, 1890–1930* (New York: Abrams, 1985), 34–35.
42. See, generally, Lawrence James, *The Rise and Fall of the British Empire* (New York: St. Martin's Press, 1997).
43. Twain, *Equator*, in Neider, *Travel Books*, 907.
44. Quoted in Ward, Duncan, & Burns, *Twain*, 174.
45. Twain, *Equator*, in Neider, *Travel Books*, 754.
46. Ibid., 705.
47. Ibid., 869.
48. Cooper, *Around the World with Mark Twain*, 256. See also Charles Neider, ed., *Papa: An Intimate Biography of Mark Twain by His Thirteen-Year-Old Daughter Susy* (New York: Doubleday, 1985).
49. Mark Twain, "The United States of Lyncherdom," in *Europe and Elsewhere* (New York: Harper, 1911), 239.
50. Mark Twain, "To the Person Sitting in Darkness," in *Europe and Elsewhere*, 252.
51. Ibid., 264.
52. Ibid., 255. See also Mark Twain, "To My Missionary Critics," *North American Review* 172 (April 1901), 533.
53. Deakes & Stanley, *A Century of Sea Travel*, 133.
54. Quoted in ibid.
55. Mortimer, *Far Off Part II*, 60–61.

56. *Morning Herald* (New York: April 24, 1838).
57. Twain, *Equator*, in Neider, *Travel Books*, 748.

CONCLUSION

1. Kipling, *With the Night Mail*, 47 (emphasis added).
2. Maxtone-Graham, *Only Way to Cross*, 33.
3. Fletcher, *Traveling Palaces*, 93.

BIBLIOGRAPHY

ARCHIVAL COLLECTIONS
British Museum
Cunard Line Archives, University of Liverpool
Gjenvick-Gjønvik Archives, Atlanta, Georgia
Hay Library, Brown University
Huntington Library
Independence Seaport Museum, Philadelphia
Isambard Kingdom Brunel Papers, National Archives at Kew
Library of Congress
Museum of the City of New York (MCNY)
National Maritime Museum, Greenwich, London
New York Historical Society
New York Public Library, Rare Books Division
Shapell Manuscript Foundation

PERIODICALS
Adams Sentinel
The Atlantic
Berliner Gewerbe-Ausstellung
Bristol Times and Mirror
Carrollton Mirror Extra
Cincinnati Gazette
Cork Advertiser
Engineering
The Enquirer
Evening Post
Frank Leslie's Illustrated Newspaper
The Graphic
Hamburg–American Gazette
Illustrated London News
Mechanics Magazine
Morning Herald
New London Morning News
New York Advertiser and Express
New York Albion
New York Express
New York Herald

New York Times
North German Lloyd Bulletin
Ocean: Magazine of Travel
Philadelphia Evening Bulletin
Putnam's Magazine
Reflector
Republican Compiler
San Francisco Alta California
Scientific American
The Sun
Times (London)

PUBLISHED SOURCES

Adler, Judith. "Origins of Sightseeing." *Annals of Tourism Research* 16 (1989), 7–29.

———. "Travel as Performed Art." *American Journal of Sociology* 94 (1989), 1366–1391.

Ainsworth, William F. *All Round the World: An Illustrated Record of Voyages, Travels and Adventures in All Parts of the Globe* (London: William Collins, 1869).

Albion, Robert. *The Rise of New York Port, 1815–1860* (New York: Scribner's, 1939).

All About the Great Eastern (London: W. H. Smith, 1860).

Allen, Helena G. *The Betrayal of Liliuokalani: Last Queen of Hawaii 1838–1917* (New York: Mutual Publishing, 1991).

Allen, Walter Ernest. *Transatlantic Crossing: American Visitors to Britain and British Visitors to America in the Nineteenth Century* (London: Heinemann, 1971).

Allott, Kenneth. *Jules Verne* (reprint ed., Port Washington, NY: Kennikat Press, 1970).

American State Papers, Military Affairs, 25th Congress (1832), vol. II.

"American Steam Navigation: Speech of Hon. Thomas F. Bayard, of Delaware, for the Collins Steamers . . ." (Washington, DC: Buell & Blanchard, 1852).

Anderson, Benedict. *Imagined Communities: Reflection on the Origin and Spread of Nationalism* (revised ed., New York: Verso, 2006).

Anthony, Irvin. *Paddle Wheels and Pistols* (Philadelphia: Macrae Smith, 1929).

Appleton's European Guide Book (New York: D. Appleton & Co., 1883).

Armstrong, Warren. *Atlantic Highway* (London: George Harrap & Co., 1961).

Auerbach, Jeffrey, & Peter Hoffenberg (Eds.). *Britain, the Empire and the World at the Great Exhibition of 1851* (London: Ashgate Publishing, 2008).

———. *The Great Exhibition of 1851: A Nation on Display* (New Haven, CT: Yale University Press, 1999).

Babcock, F. Lawrence. *Spanning the Atlantic* (New York: Alfred Knopf, 1931).

Bailey, Anthony. *Standing in the Sun: A Life of J. M. W. Turner* (New York: HarperCollins, 1997).

Barth, Karl. *The Word in This World: Two Sermons by Karl Barth* (Vancouver: Regent College Publishing, 2007).

Barton, Susan. *Working Class Organizations and Popular Tourism, 1840–1970* (Manchester, UK: Manchester University Press, 2011).

Beasley, Edward. *Mid-Victorian Imperialists: British Gentlemen and the Empire of the Mind* (New York: Routledge, 2005).

Beatty, Charles Robert Longfield. *De Lesseps of Suez: The Man and His Times* (New York: Harper, 1956).

Belich, James. *Replenishing the Earth: The Settler Revolution and the Rise of the Anglo-World, 1783–1939* (Oxford, UK: Oxford University Press, 2006).

Benedict, Erastus. *A Run Through Europe* (New York: D. Appleton, 1880).

Benjamin, Walter, & Rolf Tiedemann. *The Arcades Project* (New York: Belknap Press, 2002).

Berghoff, Harmut, Barbara Korte, Ralf Schneider, & Christopher Harvie (Eds.). *The Making of Modern Tourism: The Cultural History of the British Experience, 1600–2000* (New York: Palgrave, 2002).

Bidwell, W. H. (Ed.). *The Eclectic Magazine: Foreign Literature, Science and Art* (New York: 1850).

Bills, Mark, & Vivien Knight (Eds.). *William Powell Frith: Painting in the Victorian Age* (New Haven, CT: Yale University Press, 2007).

Bird, Isabella Lucy. *The Englishwoman in America* (originally published 1856; reprint ed., Madison: University of Wisconsin, 1966).

Bisland, Elizabeth. *In Seven Stages: A Flying Voyage Around the World* (New York: Harper, 1891).

Blackwood, Harriot Georgina. *Our Viceregal Life in India: Selections from My Journal, 1884–1888* (London: John Murray, 1890).

Bly, Nellie. *Around the World in Seventy-Two Days* (New York: Pictorial Weeklies, 1890).

Boyd, Thomas. *Poor John Fitch: Inventor of the Steamboat* (New York: G. P. Putnam's Sons, 1935).

Braynard, Frank O., & and William H. Miller Jr. *Picture History of the Cunard Line, 1840–1990* (New York: Dover, 1991).

Brenton, Piers. *Thomas Cook: 150 Years of Popular Tourism* (London: Secker & Warburg, 1991).

Briggs, Asa. *Victorian People: A Reassessment of Persons and Themes, 1851–67* (Chicago: University of Chicago Press, 1955).

Brinnin, John Malcolm. *Beau Voyage: Life Aboard the Last Great Ships* (New York: Dorset Press, 1981).

———. *The Sway of the Grand Saloon: A Social History of the North Atlantic* (New York: Delacorte Press, 1974).

Brown, Alexander Crosby. *Women and Children Last: The Loss of the Steamship* Arctic (New York: G. P. Putnam's Sons, 1961).

Brunel, Isambard. *The Life of Isambard Kingdom Brunel, Civil Engineer* (reprint ed., Cambridge, UK: Cambridge University Press, 2011).

Buzard, James. *The Beaten Track: European Tourism, Literature, and the Ways to "Culture," 1800–1918* (Oxford, UK: Oxford University Press, 1993).

Byerly, Alison. *Are We There Yet?: Virtual Travel and Victorian Realism* (Ann Arbor: University of Michigan Press, 2012).

Cadringher, Gabrielle. *Ocean Liner Posters* (New York: ACC Distribution, 2011).

Cannadine, David. *Ornamentalism: How the British Saw Their Empire* (Oxford, UK: Oxford University Press, 2001).

Caple, Jeremy. *The Bristol Riots of 1831 and Social Reform in Britain* (London: Edwin Mellen, 1990).

Carnegie-Williams, Rosa. *A Year in the Andes; or, A Lady's Adventures in Bogota* (London: Literary Society, 1888).

Carrington, Margaret. *Ocean to Ocean: Pacific Railroad and Adjoining Territories* (Philadelphia: J. B. Lippincott, 1869).

Cecil, Lamar. *Albert Ballin: Business and Politics in Imperial Germany, 1888–1918* (Princeton, NJ: Princeton University Press, 1967).

Chadwick, French Ensor, et al. *Ocean Steamships: A Popular Account of Their Construction, Development, Management and Appliances* (New York: Scribner's, 1891).

Chapman, Charles. *The Ocean Waves: Travels by Land and Sea* (London: George Berridge & Co., 1875).

Chard, Chloe. *Pleasure and Guilt on the Grand Tour: Travel Writing and Imaginative Geography, 1600–1830* (Manchester, UK: Manchester University Press, 1999).

Choules, John Overton. *The Cruise of the* North Star*: To England, Russia . . .* (Boston: Gould & Lincoln, 1854).

Christie, Agatha. *Five Complete Hercule Poirot Novels* (New York: Avenel Books, 1980).

Church, William Conant. *The Life of John Ericsson* (New York: Scribner's, 1911).

Claxton, Christopher. *History and Description of the S.S. Great Britain, Built at Bristol, with Remarks on the Comparative Merits of Iron and Wood as Materials for Shipbuilding* (London: J. S. Homans, 1845).

———. *Logs of the First Voyage of the* Great Western (London: British Library, 1838).

Colquhoun, Kate. *The Busiest Man in England: A Life of Joseph Paxton* (Jaffrey, NH: David Godine, 2006).

Conrad, Joseph. *Heart of Darkness* (reprint ed., New York: Alfred Knopf, 1993).

———. "Some Reflections, Seaman-like and Otherwise, on the Loss of the *Titanic*." *English Review* 11 (May 1912), 304–315.

Cooper, Robert. *Around the World with Mark Twain* (New York: Arcade Publishing, 2002).

Course, A. G., & C. H. Williams. *Ships of the P and O* (London: Adlard Coles, 1954).

The Crystal Palace Illustrated Catalogue (originally published London, 1851; republished New York: Dover, 1978).

Cunard Line and the World's Fair, Chicago, 1893 (London: E. P. Hodder for Cunard Line, 1893).

Curtis, Jared (Ed.). *William Wordsworth's Last Poems, 1821–1850* (Ithaca, NY: Cornell University Press, 1999).

Dahl, Roald. *Going Solo* (New York: Farrar, Straus & Giroux, 1986).

Daws, Gavan. *Shoal of Time: A History of the Hawaiian Islands* (New York: Macmillan, 1968).

Dawson, Philip. *The Liner: Retrospective and Renaissance* (New York: W. W. Norton, 2006).

Dawson, Philip, & Bruce Peter. *P&O at 175: A world of Ships and Shipping Since 1837* (Ramsay, UK: Lily Publications, 2012).

Day, Clarence. *Clarence Day Omnibus* (Garden City, NY: Sun Dial Press, 1945).

———. *Life with Father* (New York: Alfred Knopf, 1936).

Deakes, Christopher, & Tom Stanley. *A Century of Sea Travel: Personal Accounts from the Steamship Era* (London: Seaforth, 2010).

De Forest, John William. *Oriental Acquaintance: Or, Letters from Syria* (New York: Harper & Bros., 1856).

DeVine, Christine. *Nineteenth-Century British Travelers in the New World* (Burlington, VT: Ashgate Publishing, 2013).

Dickens, Charles. *American Notes* (New York: St. Martin's Press, 1985).
Dugan, James. *The Great Iron Ship* (New York: Harper & Bros., 1953).
Dunbaugh, Edwin L. *The New England Steamship Company* (Gainesville: University Press of Florida, 2005).
Emmerson, George S. *John Scott Russell: A Great Victorian Engineer and Naval Architect* (New York: Murray Bros., 1977).
Evans, Julian. *Jules Verne and His Work* (New York: Twayne Publishers, 1966).
Everett, Edward (Ed.). *The Writings and Speeches of Daniel Webster* (Boston: Little, Brown, 1903).
"Evolution of the Fall River Line" (Boston: 1894).
Fatout, Paul (Ed.). *Mark Twain Speaking* (Iowa City: University of Iowa Press, 1976).
First Report from the Select Committee on Steam Communications with India, &c. (London: House of Commons, 1851).
Flayhart, William. *The American Line: 1871–1902* (New York: W. W. Norton, 2000).
Fletcher, C. R. L. *A History of England* (New York: Doubleday, 1911).
Fletcher, R. A. *Traveling Palaces: Luxury in Passenger Steamships* (London: Sir Isaac Pitman, 1913).
Flint, Timothy. *Western Monthly Review* (Cincinnati: E. H. Flint, 1828).
Forester, C. S. *Hornblower and the* Atropos (reprint ed., New York: Little, Brown, 1999).
Foster, George H., & Peter C. Weiglin. *Splendor Sailed the Sound* (San Mateo, CA: Potentials Group, 1989).
Foucault, Michel. "Of Other Spaces." *Diacritics* 16, 1 (Spring 1986), 24–27.
Fox, Stephen. *Transatlantic: Samuel Cunard, Isambard Brunel, and the Great Atlantic Steamships* (New York: HarperCollins, 2003).
Freeman, Michael. *Railways and the Victorian Imagination* (New Haven, CT: Yale University Press, 1999).
Fulton, Richard, & Peter Hoffenberg (Eds.). *Oceania and the Victorian Imagination: Where All Things Are Possible* (Burlington, VT: Ashgate Publishing, 2013).
Gannett, Ezra Stiles. *Sermon Delivered in the Federal Street Meeting House, in Boston, July 19, 1840, on the Arrival of the* Britannia (Boston: Joseph Dowe, 1840).
Garrett, Phineas, et al. *One Hundred Choice Selections: A Repository of Readings, Recitations and Plays* (Philadelphia: P. Garrett & Co., 1891).
Gautier, Theophile, quoted in Jean Dethier. *All Stations: A Journey Through 150 Years of Railway History* (London: Science Museum Press, 1981).
General Information for Passengers by the Steamships of the Hamburg–American Packet Company (New York: C. B. Richard and Bros., 1873).
Gilmour, David. *The Ruling Caste: Imperial Lives in the Victorian Raj* (London: John Murray, 2005).
Graham, Gerald S. *A Concise History of the British Empire* (London: Thames and Hudson, 1970).
Great Western Railway Guide (London: James Wyld, 1839).
Greeley, Horace. *Glances at Europe* (New York: Dewitt and Davenport, 1851).
Greene, Jack P. *Negotiated Authorities: Essays in Colonial Political and Constitutional History* (Charlottesville: University of Virginia Press, 1994).

———. *Peripheries and Center: Constitutional Development in the Extended Polities of the British Empire and the United States, 1607–1788* (New York: W. W. Norton, 1990).
Haenni, Sabine. *The Immigrant Scene: Ethnic Amusements in New York, 1880–1920* (St. Paul: University of Minnesota Press, 2008).
Hale, Edward Everett. *Ninety Days' Worth of Europe* (New York: Walker, Wise, 1860).
Haliburton, Thomas. *The Letter Bag of the Great Western* (London: Lee and Blanchard, 1840).
Hall, P. W. "A Minute and Circumstantial Narrative of the Loss of the Steam Packet Pulaski . . ." (Providence, RI: H. H. Hall, 1839).
Hanke, Lewis. *Bartolomé de las Casas: An Interpretation of His Life and Writings* (New York: Martinus Nijhoff, 1951).
Hannavy, John. *The Victorian and Edwardian Tourist* (London: Shire Library, 2012).
Harcourt, Freda. *Flagships of Imperialism: The P&O Company and the Politics of Empire from Its Origins to 1867* (Manchester, UK: Manchester University Press, 2006).
Hardinge, Charles. *My Indian Years, 1910–1916* (London: John Murray, 1948).
Hardman, William. *A Trip to America* (London: T. Vickers Wood, 1884).
Hardy, Thomas. "Convergence of the Twain." *Fortnightly Review* (June 1912).
Harris, C. J. *Mailships of the Union Castle Line* (London: Fernwood Press, 1996).
Hays, Samuel P. *The Response to Industrialism, 1884–1914* (Chicago: University of Chicago Press, 1995).
Headrick, Daniel. *Power over Peoples: Technology, Environments, and Western Imperialism, 1400 to the Present* (Princeton, NJ: Princeton University Press, 2010).
———. *The Tentacles of Progress: Technology Transfer in the Age of Imperialism, 1850–1940* (Oxford, UK: Oxford University Press, 1988).
———. *The Tools of Empire: Technology and Imperialism in the Nineteenth Century* (Oxford, UK: Oxford University Press, 1981).
Hobhouse, Christopher. *1851 and the Crystal Palace* (London: E. P. Dutton, 1937).
Hoblyn, E. H. *Cunard Magazine* (London) (July 1919).
Hugo, Victor. *The Toilers of the Sea* (reprint ed., New York: Modern Library, 2002).
Hunt, Tristram. *Cities of Empire: The British Colonies and the Creation of the Urban World* (New York: Metropolitan Books, 2014).
Irving, Washington. *The Sketch Book of Geoffrey Crayon* (New York: G. P. Putnam's Sons, 1884).
Iskin, Ruth E. *The Poster: Art, Advertising, Design, and Collecting, 1860s–1900s* (Dartmouth, NH: University Press of New England, 2014).
James, Lawrence. *The Rise and Fall of the British Empire* (New York: St. Martin's Press, 1997).
Johnson, Walter. *River of Dark Dreams: Slavery and Empire in the Cotton Kingdom* (New York: Belknap Press, 2013).
Kaplan, Justin. *Mr. Clemens and Mark Twain* (New York: Simon & Schuster, 1966).
Kelland, Philip. *Transatlantic Sketches* (Edinburgh: Adam and Charles Black, 1868).
Kipling, Rudyard. *The Collected Poems of Rudyard Kipling* (Hertfordshire, UK: Wordsworth Editions, 1994).
———. *Selected Works* (New York: Gramercy Books, 1982).
———. *With the Night Mail: A Story of 2000 A.D* (New York: Doubleday, 1905).
Kludas, Arnold. *Die Schiffe der Deutschen Afrika–Linie, 1880–1945* (Hamburg: Stalling, 1975).
———. *Die Seeschiffe des Norddeutscher Lloyd, 1857–1919* (Berlin: Koehler, 1997).

Klusdas, Arnold, & Herbert Bischoff. *Die Schiffe der Hamburg–Amerika Linie, 1847–1906* (Berlin: Koehler, 1979).

Kotar, S. L., & J. E. Gessler. *The Steamboat Era* (New York: McFarland, 2009).

Laird, Macgregor, & R. A. K. Oldfield. *Narrative of an Expedition into the Interior of Africa, by the River Niger, in the Steam Vessels* Quorra *and* Alburkah, *in 1832, 1833, and 1834* (London: Richard Bentley, 1837).

Lambert, David, & Alan Lester. *Colonial Lives Across the British Empire: Imperial Careering in the Long Nineteenth Century* (Cambridge, UK: Cambridge University Press, 2006).

Latimer, Elizabeth Wormeley. *Salvage* (Boston: Roberts Brothers, 1880).

Lavery, Brian. *SS Great Britain, Owner's Workshop Manual: An Insight into the Design, Construction, and Operation of Brunel's Famous Passenger Ship* (London: Haynes Publishing, 2012).

Laxton, Edward. *The Famine Ships: The Irish Exodus to America* (New York: Holt, 1998).

Ledoux, Kate Reid. *Ocean Notes and Foreign Travel for Ladies* (New York: Cook & Jenkins, 1878).

Lindsay, W. S. *History of Merchant Shipping and Ancient Commerce* (London: Samson Low, 1874).

Liu, Kwang-Ching. *Anglo-American Steamship Rivalry in China, 1862–1874* (Cambridge, MA: Harvard University Press, 1962).

Lloyd, W. W. *P&O Pencillings* (London: Day & Co., 1891).

Lobley, Douglas. *The Cunarders* (London: Peter Barker, 1969).

Loftie, W. J., *Orient–Pacific Line Guide: Chapters for Travelers by Sea and by Land, Edited by the Managers of the Line* (London: S. Low, Marston & Co., 1888).

Longfellow, Henry Wadsworth. "The Building of the Ship." In *Evangeline and Other Poems* (New York: Airmont Press, 1965).

Lord, Walter. *The Night Lives On* (New York: Avon, 1998).

———. *A Night to Remember* (New York: Henry Holt, 1955).

Lyman, Samuel P. *Life and Memorials of Daniel Webster*, vol. I (New York: D. Appleton, 1852).

MacCannell, Dean. *The Tourist: A New Theory of the Leisure Class* (New York: Schocken Books, 1976).

MacDonald, Brian (Ed.). *Dearest Mother: The Letters of F. R. Kendall* (London: Lloyds of London Press, 1988).

MacKinnon, Lauchlan. *Atlantic and Transatlantic Sketches, Afloat and Ashore* (London: Colburn & Co., 1852).

Maddocks, Melvin. *The Great Liners* (Alexandria, VA: Time-Life Books, 1978).

The Magnificent New Steamships City of New York *and* City of Paris: *A Pleasant Journey over the Sea* (New York: Gillis Bros., 1889).

Mahan, Alfred Thayer. *The Influence of Sea Power upon History, 1660–1783* (reprint ed., New York: Dover, 1987).

Manchester, William. *The Arms of Krupp: The Rise and Fall of the Industrial Dynasty That Armed Germany at War* (Boston: Back Bay Books, 2003).

Marcus, Geoffrey. *The Maiden Voyage* (New York: Viking Press, 1969).

Marsden, Ben, & Crosbie Smith. *Engineering Empire: A Cultural History of Technology in Nineteenth Century Britain* (New York: Palgrave Macmillan, 2007).

Marshall, Ian. *Passage East* (New York: Howell Press, 1997).

Marx, Leo. *The Machine in the Garden: Technology and the Pastoral Ideal in America* (Oxford, UK: Oxford University Press, 1967).
Maugham, W. Somerset. *Collected Short Stories* (4 vols.) (London: Heinemann, 1955).
Maxtone-Graham, John. *Crossing and Cruising* (New York: Scribner's, 1992).
———. *Liners to the Sun* (New York: Sheridan House, 1990).
———. *The Only Way to Cross* (New York: Barnes & Noble, 1997).
McAdam, Roger. *Old Fall River Line* (Boston: Stephen Daye Press, 1955).
———. *Priscilla of Fall River* (New York: Stephen Daye Press, 1947).
McCluskie, Tom. *Titanic and Her Sisters* Olympic *and* Britannic (New York: PRC Publishing, 1998).
McCullough, David. *Mornings on Horseback* (New York: Simon & Schuster, 1981).
McLuhan, T. C., *Dream Tracks: The Railroad and the American Indian, 1890–1930* (New York: Abrams, 1985).
Melton, Jeffrey Alan. *Mark Twain, Travel Books, and Tourism: The Tide of a Great Popular Movement* (Tuscaloosa: University of Alabama Press, 2002).
Melville, Herman. *The Confidence-Man: His Masquerade* (reprint ed., New York: Hendricks House, 1954).
———. "Traveling: A New Lecture." Reprint in John Howard Birss, *New England Quarterly* 7 (December 1934).
Merrick, George Byron. *Old Times on the Upper Mississippi* (New York: Arthur Clark, 1909).
Metwalli, Ahmed. "Americans Abroad: The Popular Art of Travel Writing in the Nineteenth Century." In *America: Exploration and Travel* (Bowling Green, OH: Bowling Green University Popular Press, 1979).
Miller, Kerby. *Emigrants and Exiles: Ireland and the Irish Exodus to North America* (Oxford, UK: Oxford University Press, 1988).
Miller, William H. *The Fabulous Interiors of the Great Ocean Liners in Historic Photographs* (New York: Dover, 1985).
———. *The First Great Ocean Liners in Photographs* (New York: Dover, 1982).
———. *Picture History of British Ocean Liners, 1900 to the Present* (Mineola, NY: Dover Maritime Books, 2001).
———. *Picture History of the Italian Line* (Mineola, NY: Dover Maritime Books, 1999).
———. *Picture History of the* Queen Mary *and* Queen Elizabeth (Mineola, NY: Dover Maritime Books, 2004).
Mookerji, Radhakumud. *Indian Shipping: A History of the Sea-Borne Trade and Maritime Activity of the Indians from the Earliest Times* (Bombay: Longmans, Green & Co., 1912).
Morford, Henry. *Over-Sea: Or, England, France and Scotland as Seen by a Live American* (New York: Hilton & Co., 1867).
Morgan, Marjorie. *National Identities and Travel in Victorian Britain* (New York: Palgrave, 2009).
Morris, Edmund. *Theodore Rex* (New York: Modern Library, 2001).
Mortimer, Favell Lee. *Far Off Part II: Oceania, Africa and America Described* (originally published 1854; reprint ed., London: Longman's, 1901).
———. *Near Home, or, The Countries of Europe Described* (London: Hatchet & Co, 1866).
Mulvey, Christopher. *Transatlantic Manners: Social Patterns in Nineteenth-Century Anglo-American Travel Literature* (Cambridge, UK: Cambridge University Press, 1983).

"The Mystery Solved!!, or Narrative of Dr. M. Lorner, One of the Passengers of the Steam Ship *President*, Which Vessel Left New York Bound for Liverpool on March 11, 1841, Since Which Time, Until Recently, Nothing Has Been Heard Respecting Her Fate..." (New York: Knapp & Barclay, 1845).

Nanni, Giordano. *The Colonisation of Time: Ritual, Routine, and Resistance in the British Empire* (Manchester, UK: Manchester University Press, 2014).

Neider, Charles (Ed.). *The Complete Humorous Sketches and Tales of Mark Twain* (New York: Doubleday, 1961).

———. *The Complete Travel Books of Mark Twain* (New York: Doubleday, 1967).

———. *Papa: An Intimate Biography of Mark Twain by His Thirteen-Year-Old Daughter Susy* (New York: Doubleday, 1985).

Newall, Peter. *Cunard Line: A Fleet History* (New York: Ships in Focus, 2012).

Newsome, David. *The Victorian World Picture* (New Brunswick, NJ: Rutgers University Press, 1999).

Nicholson, John. *Arthur Anderson: A Founder of the P&O Company* (Paisley, Scotland: A. Gardner, 1914).

Nugent, Walter. *Habits of Empire: A History of American Expansionism* (New York: Random House, 2009).

"On the Beginning of Transatlantic Steamship Service." *Bulletin of the Business Historical Society* 12, 3 (June 1938), 40–43.

Padfield, Peter. *Beneath the House Flag of the P&O* (London: Hutchinson Press, 1981).

Paine, Albert Bigelow (Ed.). *Mark Twain's Speeches* (New York: Harper & Bros., 1923).

Papers Relating to the Loss of the Steam Ship "Atlantic," Parliamentary Papers (1873).

Peabody, Marian Lawrence. *To Be Young Was Very Heaven* (Boston: Houghton Mifflin, 1967).

Petersen, William J. *Steamboating of the Upper Mississippi* (New York: Dover, 1968).

Picard, Liza. *Victorian London: The Life of a City, 1840–1870* (New York: St. Martin's Press, 2005).

The P&O Pocket Guide Book (London: Adam and Charles Black, 1908).

Pond, E. LeRoy. *Junius Smith: Pioneer Promoter of Transatlantic Steam* (New York: Kessinger Publishing, 2007).

Porter, Andrew. *Victorian Shipping, Business, and Imperial Policy: Donald Currie, the Castle Line, and Southern Africa* (Woodbridge, NY: Boydell Press, 1986).

Porter, Dennis. *Haunted Journeys: Desire and Transgression in European Travel Writing* (Princeton, NJ: Princeton University Press, 1991).

Powers, Ron. *White Town Drowsing* (New York: Anchor Books, 1986).

Prager, Frank. "The Steamboat Pioneers Before the Founding Fathers." *Journal of the Patent Office Society* 37 (July 1955), 486–522.

Prager, Frank D. (Ed.). *The Autobiography of John Fitch* (Philadelphia: American Philosophical Society, 1976).

Preble, G. H. *History of Steam Navigation* (Philadelphia: Longworth, 1882).

Prucha, Francis. *The Great Father: The United States Government and the American Indians* (Lincoln: University of Nebraska Press, 1984).

Pruzan, Todd. *The Clumsiest People in Europe* (New York: Bloomsbury, 2005).

Rabson, Steven, & Kevin O'Donoghue. *P&O: A Fleet History* (Kendal, UK: World Ship Society, 1988).

Ramsay, David. Lusitania: *Saga and Myth* (New York: W. W. Norton, 2001).
Rand McNally & Co.'s Handbook of the World's Columbian Exhibition (Chicago: Rand, McNally, 1893).
Rediker, Marcus. "Under the Banner of King Death: The Social World of Anglo-American Pirates, 1716–1726." *William and Mary Quarterly* 38, 2 (April 1981), 203–227.
The Red Star Line, Belgian Royal and U.S. Mail Steamships: Facts for Travelers (New York: Peter Wright & Sons, 1883).
Regan, Robert. "The Reprobate Elect in *The Innocents Abroad*." *American Literature* 54 (1982), 240–257.
Report on the Loss of the "Titanic" (S.S.). Her Majesty's Stationery Office (1912).
Reports from Committees: Colonization from Ireland, Parliamentary Papers (1847).
Richards, Jeffrey, & John M. MacKenzie. *The Railway Station: A Social History* (Oxford, UK: Oxford University Press, 1986).
Robertson, Morgan. *Futility* (New York: M. F. Mansfield, 1898).
Robinson, Corinne Roosevelt. *My Brother Theodore Roosevelt* (New York: Scribner's, 1921).
Robinson, Forrest. "Patterns of Consciousness in *The Innocents Abroad*." *American Literature* 58 (1986), 46–63.
Rolt, L. T. C. *Isambard Kingdom Brunel* (London: Penguin Books, 2006).
Robinson-Tomsett, Emma. *Women, Travel and Identity: Journeys by Rail and Sea, 1870–1940* (Manchester, UK: Manchester University Press, 2011).
Roosevelt, Theodore. *Theodore Roosevelt's Diaries of Boyhood and Youth* (New York: Scribner's, 1928).
Rosen, William. *The Most Powerful Idea in the World* (New York: Random House, 2010).
Rotberg, Robert, & Miles Shore. *The Founder: Cecil Rhodes and the Pursuit of Power* (Oxford, UK: Oxford University Press, 1988).
Royal Commission on Unseaworthy Ships' Preliminary Report of the Commissioners, Minutes of the Evidence, and Appendix, Parliamentary Papers (1873).
Russell, John Scott. *On the Nature, Properties and Application of Steam and on Steam Navigation* (London: 1841).
Russell, William Clark. *North-East Ports and the Bristol Channel* (Newcastle-upon-Tyne: A. Reid, 1883).
Ryan, Ann, & Joseph McCullough (Eds.). *Cosmopolitan Twain* (Columbia: University of Missouri Press, 2008).
Schama, Simon. *Landscape and Memory* (New York: Vintage, 1995).
Schivelbusch, Wolfgang. *The Railway Journey: The Industrialization of Time and Space in the Nineteenth Century* (Los Angeles: University of California Press, 1987).
Schlichting, Kurt. *Grand Central Terminal: Railroads, Engineering and Architecture in New York City* (Baltimore: Johns Hopkins University Press, 2001).
Schwerdtner, Nils. *The New Cunard Queens* (Annapolis, MD: Naval Institute Press, 2008).
Seiler, Otto. *Bridge Across the Atlantic: The Story of Hapag–Lloyd's North Atlantic Service* (Herford: Verlag Mittler, 1991).
———. *Hapag–Lloyd: One Hundred Years of Liner Shipping: A Century of Far East Service* (Hamburg: Hapag–Lloyd, 1986).
Sessions, Francis C. *On the Wing Through Europe* (New York: Welch, Fracker, 1889).

Shealy, Daniel (Ed.). *Little Women Abroad: The Alcott Sisters' Letters from Europe, 1870–1871* (Athens: University of Georgia Press, 2008).

Smiles, Samuel. *A Boy's Voyage Around the World* (London: John Murray, 1905).

———. *Industrial Biography: Iron-Workers and Tool-Workers* (Boston: Ticknor and Fields, 1864).

Smith, Junius. *Letters upon Atlantic Navigation* (London: A. Eccles, 1841).

Smith, P. D. *City: A Guidebook for the Urban Age* (London: Bloomsbury, 2012).

Smith, Valerie (Ed.). *Hosts and Guests: The Anthropology of Tourism* (Philadelphia: University of Pennsylvania Press, 1989).

Society of Voyages Round the World. *Round the World in Three Hundred and Twenty Days: Completion of Superior Education* (London: Tubner & Co., 1876).

Stanley, Liz (Ed.).e *The Diaries of Hannah Cullwick, Victorian Maidservant* (New Brunswick, NJ: Rutgers University Press, 1984).

Steinbrink, Jeffrey. "Why the Innocents Went Abroad." *American Literary Realism* 16 (1983), 278–286.

Stevenson, Robert Louis. *The Amateur Emigrant* (New York: Scribner's, 1905).

Stilgoe, John. *Train Time: Railroads and the Imminent Reshaping of the United States Landscape* (Charlottesville: University of Virginia Press, 2009).

Stowe, Harriet Beecher. *Sunny Memories of Foreign Lands* (vol. I) (Boston: Phillips Samson, 1854).

Stowe, William W. *Going Abroad: European Travel in Nineteenth Century American Culture* (Princeton, NJ: Princeton University Press, 1994).

Streater, Les. Berengaria, *Cunard's "Happy Ship"* (Charleston, SC: Tempus Publishing, 2001).

Street, Julian. *Ship-Bored* (New York: Dodd Mead, 1914).

Strong, George Templeton. *The Diary of George Templeton Strong* (Seattle: University of Washington Press, 1988).

Strout, Cushing. *The American Image of the Old World* (New York: Harper & Row, 1963).

Sutcliffe, Alice Clary. *Robert Fulton and the "Clermont"* (New York: Century Company, 1909).

Sutcliffe, Andrea. *Steam: The Untold Story of America's First Great Invention* (New York: Palgrave Macmillan, 2004).

Swinglehurst, Edward. *Romantic Journey: The Story of Thomas Cook and Victorian Travel* (New York: Pica Editions, 1974).

Taylor, William Leonhard. *A Productive Monopoly: The Effect of Railroad Control on New England Coastal Steamship Line, 1870–1916* (Providence, RI: Brown University Press, 1970).

Thackeray, William Makepeace. *Notes of a Journey from Cornhill to Grand Cairo* (originally published 1844; reprint, Philadelphia: Pennsylvania State University Electronic Classics Series Publication, 2013).

Thompson, E. P. *The Making of the English Working Class* (New York: Random House, 1964).

Thomson, William M. *The Land and the Book, or Biblical Illustrations Drawn from the Scenes, Customs and Manners of the Holy Land* (New York: Harper & Bros., 1852).

Thorner, Daniel. *Investment in Empire: British Railways and Steam Shipping Enterprise in India. 1825–1849* (Philadelphia: University of Pennsylvania Press, 1950).

de Tocqueville, Alexis. *Democracy in America* (New York: Penguin Classics, 2003).

Tristram, W. Outram. *Coaching Days and Coaching Ways* (New York: Macmillan, 1893).

Trollope, Frances. *Domestic Manners of the Americans* (London: British Library Historical Print Editions, 2011).

Tuckerman, Bayard (Ed.). *The Diary of Philip Hone, 1828–1851* (New York: Dodd, Meade & Co., 1889).

Twain, Mark (Samuel Clemens). *Europe and Elsewhere* (New York: Harper, 1911).

———. *The Innocents Abroad* (originally published 1869; republished New York: Harper, 1911).

———. *The Writings of Mark Twain* (Volume XXII) (New York: Harper & Bros., 1918).

———. "To My Missionary Critics." *North American Review* 172, 533 (April 1901), 520–534.

Verne, Jules. *A Floating City* (New York: Scribner's, 1874).

———. *The Steam House* (New York: Scribner's, 1881).

———. *20,000 Leagues Under the Sea*. In *The Omnibus Jules Verne* (New York: Blue Ribbon, 1939).

Visitor's Hand Book, or, How to See the Great Eastern (New York: Baker & Godwin, 1860).

Walters, Samuel. *The* Leviathan *Steam Ship: William Harrison Esqr. Commander; Constructed at the Eastern Steamship Company's Works, Millwall* . . . (London: Lloyd Brothers, 1857).

Ward, Geoffrey, & Dayton Duncan. *Mark Twain* (New York: Alfred Knopf, 2001).

Wardle, Arthur C. *Steam Conquers the Pacific: A Record of Maritime Achievement, 1840–1940* (London: Hodder & Stoughton, 1940).

Watton, Ross. *The Cunard Liner* Queen Mary: *Anatomy of a Ship* (Annapolis, MD: Naval Institute Press, 1989).

Webb, William Henry. *Descriptive Particulars of the* Great Eastern *Steam Ship: With Illustrations and Sectional Plans* (London: Marshall & Sons, 1857).

White, Richard. *Railroaded: The Transcontinentals and the Making of Modern America* (New York: W. W. Norton, 2011).

White, Trumbull, William Igleheart, George R. Davis, Potter Palmer, & Thomas B. Bryon. *The World's Columbian Exhibition, Chicago 1893* (Philadelphia: Franklin Square Bible House, 1893).

Wigg, Julia. *Bon Voyage!: Travel Posters of the Edwardian Era* (London: H. M. Stationery Office, 1996).

Wilkins, William. *Charles Dickens in America* (Toronto: University of Toronto Press, 2011).

Wilson, Anne C. *Hints for the First Years of Residence in India* (London: Clarendon Press, 1904).

Wilson, James. *Facts Connected with the Origin and Progress of Steam Communication Between India and England* (London: W. S. Johnson, 1850).

Withey, Lynne. *Grand Tours and Cook's Tours: A History of Leisure Travel, 1750–1915* (London: Aurum Press, 1998).

Yothers, Brian. *The Romance of the Holy Land in American Travel Writing, 1790–1876* (Aldershot, UK: Ashgate Publishing, 2007).

Young, Filson. *Titanic* (London: Grant Richards, 1912).

Young, Paul. *Globalization and the Great Exhibition: The Victorian New World Order* (New York: Palgrave, 2009).

INDEX

advertising of steamships: 261–265
Albert, Prince of Wales: 3, 5, 54–6, 60, 90, 94
Alcott, May: 212
Arctic (ship): 101–103, 110, 114, 118, 150, 258
Around the World in Eighty Days (Jules Verne): 37, 61–62, 85–89, 214, 225, 275
Astor, John Jacob: 91, 108
Atlantic (ship, 1848): 96–98, 103, 118
Atlantic (ship, 1871): 103–104

Baden-Powell, Robert: 224–225
Ballin, Albert: 260, 266–269
Barnum, P.T.: 215
Beecher, Henry Ward: 109, 171, 184–185
Benjamin, Walter: 4, 24
Bennett, James Gordon: 38–40, 44–45, 61, 99, 168, 171, 285
Bentinck, Lord William: 226–227, 274
Bisland, Elizabeth: 86–87
Bly, Nellie: 86–88, 210, 236, 239, 241
Bombay, port of (Mumbai): 61, 67, 223, 226, 230–231, 243–248, 252–253, 259, 292
Boston, port of: 10, 44, 96, 125, 138, 140, 144, 177, 185, 200, 271
Britannia (ship): 10, 44–45, 59, 81, 83, 175–178, 200, 258–259
Brunel, Isambard: 1, 3–4, 7, 9, 13, 22, 27, 34–37, 40, 42, 45–52, 54–55, 60–70, 72–75, 80–83, 88–89, 91, 94, 102, 104, 224, 229, 251, 289
Burnham, Daniel: 251, 289

Campania (ship): 59–60, 110, 116, 256, 265, 267
Casas, Bartolomeo de las: 272
Centennial Exhibition of 1876 (Philadelphia): 58
Cherokee Nation: 8–9
Churchill, Sir Winston: 71, 267
City of Glasgow (ship): 150–151

City of Paris (ship): 59, 109–110, 158, 265
Civil War, American: 31, 79, 127, 139, 166, 194, 201–204, 277
Claxton, Christopher: 63, 65
coaling of ships: 61–67, 197, 226–231, 243–244
Collins Line: 24, 41, 54, 98–103, 150 258
Columbian Exhibition of 1893 (Chicago): 58–59, 126, 157, 249, 251, 263, 289
Commonwealth (ship): 153
Confidence Man, The (Herman Melville): 134–138
Conrad, Joseph: 115, 274–275, 192
Cook, Thomas: 11, 56, 125, 167, 197, 206, 219
Cooper, James Fenimore: 171
Crompton, Mary: 212–215
cruising, leisure: 15, 92, 111, 179, 183–185, 187–191, 197–200, 210–216, 264, 271, 291
Crystal Palace (Kensington): 55–57, 61, 70, 123, 207
Cullwick, Hannah: 123–127
Cunard, Samuel: 10, 13, 73. 149, 173, 200
Cunard Line: 16, 40, 44–45, 51, 54, 57, 59, 60, 65, 74, 80–81, 94, 98, 101, 109–110, 116, 118, 130. 150, 159, 167, 175–178, 193, 201, 214–215, 249–250, 256, 258, 265, 268–269, 293, 298

Dahl, Roald: 234–235, 242
Day, Clarence: 203–208
Day, Clarence, Jr.: 125, 144, 204–208
Deutschland (ship): 111, 198, 255–256, 260, 269
Devonia (ship): 151–155, 159, 164
Dickens, Charles: 14, 23, 32, 81, 83, 107, 127–131, 133, 175–179, 191, 195, 212
diligences: 169–170, 181
Disraeli, Benjamin: 56

Eliot, Charles: 116–117

Emerson, Ralph Waldo: 171
emigration, transatlantic: 32, 62–65, 149–158, 199–201
engines, design of steamship: 13, 23–27, 31–35, 46, 69, 82, 102–104, 111, 267
Ericsson, John: 27, 46

Fall River Line: 59, 138–146, 208
First World War: 148, 160, 267–269, 287
Fisk, Jim: 141–142
Fitch, John: 25–27
Floating City, A (Jules Verne): 81–85, 189, 277
Following the Equator (Mark Twain): 166, 277–286
Foucault, Michel: 12
Franklin, Benjamin: 25–27, 30
Frith, William: 251, 253
Fulton, Robert: 13, 27–28, 35, 94, 127, 138, 274

"Grand Tour": 166, 184, 192, 196, 207
Great Britain (ship, also known as *Mammoth*): 1–4, 21, 24, 42, 45–53, 58–65, 69, 72–73; career of: 89, 91, 117–119, 212–213, 226–227, 231, 288–289
Great Eastern (ship, also known as *Leviathan*): 1, 14, 22, 118–119, 172, 197, 200, 207, 225, 229, 230, 247, 268, 271, 275–276, 290, 297; design of: 52–53, 60–64, 67–85; career of: 88–91, 95–96, 102–104, 109
Great Exhibition of 1851 (London): 14, 51, 53, 55–62, 64, 66, 69, 78, 89, 104, 123, 127, 136–137, 207
Great Western (ship): 7–10, 27, 35–43, 45–49, 70, 111, 149, 168, 226
Greeley, Horace: 171–172
Greenwood, Rev. T.H.: 97–98, 107, 110
guidebooks, travel: 192–194
Guion Line: 51, 109, 193, 195
gunboat diplomacy: 272–276

Hamburg-America Line: 58, 94, 111, 115, 159, 162, 167, 170, 194, 197, 201, 249, 254, 256, 260, 264–269
Hardy, Thomas: 113–114
Havel (ship): 173, 261
Hindustan (ship): 227–228, 259
Holy Land, travel to: 16, 183, 185, 193, 196–198, 210
Hone, Philip: 39, 41

Honolulu, Hawaii: 183, 278–279, 282
Hope, Henry Thomas: 64, 66, 71
Hosken, James: 7–8, 38, 49
Hugo, Victor: 44

Imperator (ship): 22, 94, 115, 250, 260, 266, 268
imperialism, British: 5, 10–17, 56, 119, 132, 224–247, 270–290, 292, 295
Indian Mutiny of 1857: 61, 64, 71, 229, 252, 276
Indian Removal Act: 9, 133, 272
Inman Line: 59, 109, 112, 150–151, 155, 157–160, 166, 196, 201, 205, 214, 265
Innocents Abroad (Mark Twain): 17, 165, 190, 208
interiors, steamship: 81–82, 108, 118, 132, 139, 161, 199, 235–236. 253–257, 268
Irving, Washington: 171
Ismay, J. Bruce: 92, 195
Ismay, Thomas: 266

James, Henry: 187
Johnson, Walter: 13, 132, 273

Kaiser Wilhelm der Grosse (ship): 254, 260–261, 265, 267
Kipling, Rudyard: 5, 13, 112, 116, 232, 241, 245–246, 250, 277, 281, 287–288

launchings, steamship: 2–5, 13, 21–24, 48–50, 74, 90, 94, 96, 107, 117, 290
Lesseps, Ferdinand de: 85, 105
Life on the Mississippi (Mark Twain): 127, 284
Lightoller, Charles: 113
Lili'oukalani, Queen: 278–279
Lincoln, Abraham: 19
Lindsay, W.S.: 88–89
Longfellow, Henry Wadsworth: 68, 171

MacLaren, Mrs. Finlay: 205–206
Maugham, Somerset: 160, 240
Mauretania (ship): 22, 116, 261, 268, 289
McKay, Donald: 33–34, 170
Melville, Herman: 68, 134–138, 168, 197, 219
Mississippi River: 12, 21, 28, 33, 41, 125, 272, 274, 284; steamboats on: 15, 17, 29, 31, 32, 107, 118, 126–141, 144–146, 173, 246, 273, 291

Mookerji, Radhakumud: 223
Mortimer, Favell Lee: 216–218, 244

naming of steamships, significance of: 257–260
Napoleon III, Emperor of the French: 17, 78, 80
nationalism, steamships and: 5, 13, 22, 38, 48, 51, 117–119, 181, 250, 261, 265, 268, 290– 291
Native American tribes, steamships and: 8–10, 17, 41, 132–136, 146, 272–274
Nautilus (fictional craft): 81–82, 85–86
New York, Port of: 7, 10, 14, 34–38, 41, 46, 49–52, 59–60, 74–80, 86, 95, 99, 108–110, 125, 127, 138–140, 142, 146, 148–158, 175, 183, 185, 194, 197–209, 231–232, 249, 256
North German Lloyd Lines: 198–199, 201, 230, 249, 253, 260, 263–265

Olympic (ship): 47, 115–116, 163, 258, 261, 288
Orient Lines: 119, 197, 224, 231, 235–238, 241, 250, 259

Paxton, Joseph: 55, 57, 70, 207
Peabody, Marian Lawrence: 205
Peninsular & Orient Lines (P&O): 16–17, 51, 62, 64, 95, 160, 169, 178–182, 197, 212, 223–230, 233, 235, 237–250, 252, 257, 259, 262–264, 270, 280–281, 292–293
Pilgrim (ship): 139–140, 142, 146
Pulitzer, Joseph: 86

Quaker City (ship): 165, 173, 183–190, 211, 256
Queen Mary (ship): 65, 71, 116, 177, 257, 288

races, steamship: 3, 5, 13–25, 30–42, 100–101, 110–111, 116, 118, 289
rafting: 28–29
railway stations, architecture and significance of: 10, 16, 25, 69, 95, 250–253, 282, 289, 292–293
railway travel: 45, 52–61, 67–73, 85–86, 125, 129, 170, 192–195, 250–253, 271. 275, 281–283. 290–291, 293
Rhodes, Cecil: 270, 292
Ridge, John: 8
Roosevelt, Theodore Sr.: 17, 206–210, 218

Roosevelt, Theodore Jr.: 208–209, 271
Royal Victoria (ship; completed as *British Queen*): 35–36, 40, 226
Russell, John Scott: 54–55, 60–61, 64, 66, 69–72, 76, 80, 91

St. Paul (ship): 21, 35, 102, 112, 116, 256. 261
Schivelbusch, Wolfgang: 10–11
Scott, Sir Walter: 67
Sirius (ship): 26–40, 226
Smith, E.J.: 109
Smith, Junius: 35–40
Steam House, The (Jules Verne): 276–277
Stephenson, George: 27, 35, 54, 88, 104
Stevenson, Robert Louis: 149, 151–155, 159, 163–164, 199
Stowe, Harriet Beecher: 171–172
Strachey, Lytton: 3
Strong, George Templeton: 77, 99
Suez Canal: 17, 61, 85, 207, 227, 231, 237, 244, 264, 281

Thackeray, William Makepeace: 14, 169, 174, 178–184, 190–191, 196, 209, 220, 227–228, 243, 291
Thompson, E.P.: 5, 53
Titanic (ship): 11, 47, 92, 94–96, 104, 108–118, 148, 151, 155, 163, 203, 251, 258, 287
Tocqueville, Alexis de: 8
tourism, 19th century: 10–12, 17, 56–57, 123, 174–175, 179–190, 196–210, 219, 244, 271, 281–283, 285, 290
Trollope, Frances, 127
Turner, J.M.W.: 43
Twain, Mark (Samuel Clemens): 17, 21, 29, 30–33, 46, 80, 84, 91, 127–132, 165–174, 179, 183–191, 196, 201–202, 208, 212, 219, 225, 250, 261, 277–286, 292
20,000 Leagues Under the Sea (Jules Verne): 84–86

Van der Peyser, Elizabeth: 214
Verne, Jules: 11, 13, 34, 37, 61, 66–68, 80–91, 105, 118, 188, 207–208, 225, 250, 271, 275–277, 287, 292
Victoria, Queen: 7, 22, 35, 40, 56, 69, 175, 224, 247, 259

Waugh, Evelyn: 182

Webster, Daniel: 7–9, 13, 29, 96
White Star Line: 17, 47, 92–96, 103, 109, 111, 155, 159, 163, 166, 194–195, 201, 206, 249–250, 258, 266, 268, 288
Wellesley, Arthur, Duke of Wellington: 53, 56, 61

Wheelwright, William: 105–106
Wilde, Oscar: 8
Wilhelm II, Kaiser: 16, 22, 254, 267, 298
Wordsworth, William: 43–44

Young, Filson: 93, 148, 162